SECOND EDITION

FUNDAMENTALS OF BIOLOGICAL ANTHROPOLOGY

John H. Relethford

State University of New York
College at Oneonta

Mayfield Publishing Company

Mountain View, California
London • Toronto

Library of Congress Cataloging-in-Publication Data
Relethford, John H.
    [Human species]
    Fundamentals of biological anthropology / John H. Relethford. 2nd ed.
    An abridgement of: The human species. 3rd ed. 1997.
        p.   cm.
    Includes bibliographical references and index.
    ISBN 1-55934-667-1
        1. Physical anthropology.   I. Title.
GN60.R392   1996
573—dc20   96-20142
                                                                        CIP

Manufactured in the United States of America
10 9 8 7 6 5 4 3 2 1

Mayfield Publishing Company
1280 Villa Street
Mountain View, California 94041

Sponsoring editor, Janet M. Beatty; production editor, Melissa Kreischer; manuscript
editor, Carol Dondrea; text and cover designer, Anna George; art director, Jeanne M.
Schreiber; art manager, Susan Breitbard; photo researcher, Brian Pecko; illustrators,
John and Judy Waller; manufacturing manager, Amy Folden. Cover photo © Ken
Eward/Science Photo Library/Photo Researchers, Inc. The text was set in 10/12
Goudy Old Style (Monotype) by American Composition and Graphics and printed
on acid-free 50# Somerset Matte by Banta United Graphics.

Preface

This text is an abridged and slightly rewritten version of the third edition of *The Human Species: An Introduction to Biological Anthropology*. Why a brief version of another textbook? No single textbook can accommodate perfectly all the different ways in which an introductory course in biological/physical anthropology is taught. Instructors vary in terms of their interests, use of supplemental materials, and allotted time for their courses. This text will serve several audiences for which the larger version might not be as appropriate. First, a shorter text may be more useful for those teaching on a quarter system. Second, some instructors like to assign supplemental readings, and a shorter text suits this arrangement. Third, some instructors prefer texts with less detail than traditional introductory texts; this text fills that need. Finally, the shorter length of this text makes it suitable as one of several texts for courses such as a basic introduction to anthropology or a combined physical anthropology and archaeology course.

This text introduces the field of biological anthropology (also known as physical anthropology), the science concerned with human biological origins, evolution, and variation. The text addresses the major questions that concern biological anthropologists: "What are humans?", "How are we similar to and different from other animals?", "Where are our origins?", "How did we evolve?", "Are we still evolving?", "How are we different from one another?", and "What does the future hold for the human species?"

Organization

The book is divided into four parts. Part One, "Evolutionary Background," gives readers the grounding they will need in genetics and evolutionary theory to better understand the remainder of the text. Chapter 1 begins with an overview of anthropology and biological anthropology and discusses the scientific method as it relates to evolution. A brief history of evolutionary science and a discussion of the "creation-evolution" debate conclude the chapter.

Chapter 2 reviews molecular and Mendelian genetics as applied to humans in order to provide genetic background for later chapters. It includes a basic review of cell biology. Chapter 3 covers microevolution and macroevolution.

Part Two addresses "Our Place in Nature," specifically the biology, behavior, and evolution of primates. A main focus of this section is the questions "What are humans?" and "How are we related to other living creatures?" Chapter 4 examines issues in classification and looks at the basic biology and behavior of mammals in general, and primates in particular. This chapter also evaluates the different types of primates in terms of classification, biology, and behavior, with particular attention given to our close relatives, the apes. Chapter 5 looks specifically at the human species and includes a comparison of human traits with those of apes. Chapter 6 examines the fossil record for evolution, looking at dating methods and other techniques of fossil analysis and includes a brief summary of the evolution of life prior to the origin of primates. Chapter 6 concludes with an overview of the major events of primate origins and evolution, from the time of the disappearance of the dinosaurs 65 million years ago to the split of ape and human lines 5–7 million years ago.

Part Three devotes three chapters to "Human Evolution." Chapter 7 begins with a brief review of human evolutionary history and follows with a detailed summary of the first hominids, the australopithecines, and the emergence of the genus *Homo* characterized by a larger brain and the advent of stone tool technology. Chapter 8 examines the continued biological and cultural evolution of the genus *Homo*. Chapter 9 looks at the fossil and archaeological evidence for the origin of modern humans and includes a discussion of current controversies (Did modern humans evolve throughout the world, or are our recent ancestors exclusively from Africa?).

Part Four focuses on "Human Variation," with an emphasis on understanding how modern peoples differ from one another and why. This section also looks at the way the human species continues to evolve, both biologically and culturally. Chapter 10 examines different ways we measure human variation and contrasts racial and evolutionary approaches to variation. Chapter 11 provides a number of case studies of microevolution and adaptation in modern and recent human populations. Chapter 12 explores the evolution of patterns of human health and disease in our evolutionary past and in today's world, as well as changes in the demographic structure of human populations.

Not all instructors will use the same sequence of chapters. Some may prefer a different arrangement of topics. I have attempted to write chapters in such a way as to accommodate such changes whenever possible. For example, some instructors may prefer to cover human variation before the sections on primates and human evolution. In that case, a sequence of Parts One, Four, Two, and Three would work well.

Features

Throughout the text, I have attempted to provide new material relevant to the field and fresh treatments of traditional material. Key features include:

- *All areas of contemporary biological anthropology are covered.* In addition to traditional coverage of areas such as genetics, evolutionary theory, primate behavior, and the fossil record, the text includes material often neglected in introductory texts, such as human health and disease and demography. In addition, the study of human growth is incorporated into several chapters.
- *The relationship between biology and culture is a major focus.* The biocultural framework is introduced in the first chapter and integrated throughout the text.
- *Behavior is discussed in an evolutionary context.* The evolutionary nature of primate and human behavior is emphasized in a number of chapters, including those on primate biology and behavior (4–6) and the fossil record of human evolution (7–9).
- *The emphasis is on the human species in its context within the primate order.* Discussions of mammals and nonhuman primates continually refer back to their potential relevance for understanding the human species. In fact, a separate chapter on the biology and behavior of the human species written from a comparative perspective has been added to this edition.
- *Hypothesis testing is emphasized.* From the first chapter, where students are introduced to the scientific method, I emphasize how various hypotheses are tested. Rather than provide a dogmatic approach with all the "right" answers, the text examines evidence in the context of hypothesis testing. With this emphasis, readers can see how new data can lead to changes in basic models and can better understand the "big picture" of biological anthropology.

New to This Edition

Every chapter has been carefully revised in light of new findings in the field and comments from users of the second edition. In fact, a number of chapters have been re-ordered, added, and merged or deleted based on the helpful feedback I received from colleagues. To make the text as clear, accessible, and up-to-date as possible, I've made the following specific changes:

- Each chapter now includes one or more boxes that focuses on a "Special Topic." Some of the topics focus on contemporary issues (for example, "The Coming Plague?"), some on historical issues (for example, "The Piltdown Hoax"), and some on a wide range of other subjects (for example, "Science Fiction and Orthogenesis").

- Chapter 4 is devoted to the variation in the biology and behavior of primates and reviews the entire order, from prosimians to the great apes. Case studies on primate behavior have been added and treatment of the bonobo has been expanded.
- A new chapter (5) has been added that focuses exclusively on the human species. Material on the patterns of human growth and their evolutionary significance has been moved here.
- The chapter on primate evolution (6) has been streamlined and revised to emphasize the major evolutionary trends in primate evolution, underlining the issue of Miocene ape diversity and the way it precludes drawing specific family trees.
- The chapter on the first hominids (7) has been revised to begin with a brief summary of human evolution in order to provide a conceptual framework for the student. Information on new species (*Ardipithecus ramidus* and *Australopithecus anamensis*) has been added, as has new information on dating and anatomy. The section on evolutionary trends has been rewritten to minimize phylogenetic arguments and to emphasize basic questions (for example, "Why did we become bipedal?").
- The chapter on the evolution of the genus *Homo* has been split into two chapters (8 and 9). Chapter 8 now covers *Homo erectus* and "archaic" *Homo sapiens*. New data have been incorporated, including the finding of a possible earlier date for the arrival of *Homo erectus* in Asia. A new Chapter 9 focuses on the origin of modern humans. In addition to a complete revision of the modern human origins debate, this chapter adds new material on modern human archaeology and questions of language origins.
- The chapters on human variation (10–12) have all been placed in a single unit (Part Four). New case studies have been used in Chapter 11 to illustrate human microevolution. The chapter on health and disease and demography (12) has been rewritten to focus on evolutionary issues, and case studies have been revised, added, or deleted to relate to this main point. Material on the secular change in human growth and protein-calorie malnutrition has been moved into Chapter 12.
- The appendix on primate classification has been revised and simplified. Two new appendixes have been added: one on comparative skeletal anatomy and one on metric conversion factors.

Study Helps

To make the text more accessible and interesting, I have included frequent examples and illustrations of basic ideas as well as abundant maps to help orient students. I have kept the technical jargon to a minimum, yet every introductory text contains a number of specialized terms that students must learn. The first mention of these terms in the text appears in **boldface** type and accompanying short definitions appear in the text margins. A glossary is provided at the end of the book, often with more detailed definitions.

Each chapter ends with a summary and a list of supplemental readings. A list of references appears at the end of the book, providing the complete reference for studies cited in the text.

Ancillaries

The *Instructor's Manual* includes a test bank of more than 500 questions, as well as chapter overviews and outlines, topics for class discussion, and sources for laboratory equipment.

A *Computerized Test Bank* is available free of charge to qualifying adopters. Also available to qualifying adopters is a package of 68 color and black-and-white transparency acetates.

Acknowledgments

My thanks go to the dedicated and hardworking people at Mayfield, both those I have dealt with personally and the others behind the scenes. I give special thanks to Jan Beatty, sponsoring editor, for continued encouragement and support. I am also extremely grateful to Melissa Kreischer, production editor, for her excellence, dedication, and patience. Pam Trainer, permissions editor, and Carol Dondrea, manuscript editor, were also very helpful.

I also thank my colleagues who served as reviewers of the third edition of *The Human Species*, from which this text was abridged: Mark N. Cohen, SUNY at Plattsburg; Lynne E. Christenson, San Diego State University; Katherine A. Dettwyler, Texas A & M University; Susan J. Haun, University of Memphis; Janis Faye Hutchinson, University of Houston; Lynnette Leidy, University of Massachusetts at Amherst; Jonathan Marks, Yale University; Jim Mielke, University of Kansas; Deborah Overdorff, University of Texas at Austin; Renee L. Pennington, Pennsylvania State University; and Jane Underwood, University of Arizona. Having been a reviewer myself, I appreciate the extensive time and effort these individuals have taken. I also thank other colleagues who have spent time discussing this edition with me and who have offered many valuable suggestions: Barry Bogin, University of Michigan at Dearborn; Kenneth Kennedy, Cornell University; Lorena Madrigal, University of South Florida; Carol Raemsch, SUNY at Albany; Linda Taylor, University of Miami; and David Tracer, University of Washington.

Last, but not least, I dedicate this to my family: to my wife and best friend, Hollie Jaffe, and to my wonderful sons, David, Benjamin, and Zane. You make it all worthwhile.

Contents

**PART TWO
OUR PLACE IN NATURE** *79*

PART THREE
HUMAN EVOLUTION   *175*

**PART FOUR
HUMAN VARIATION**

PART ONE

Evolutionary Background

The Study of Biological Anthropology

CHAPTER 1

 What is anthropology? To many people, it is the study of the exotic extremes of human nature. To others, it is the study of ancient ruins and lost civilizations. The study of anthropology seems strange to many, and the practitioners of this field, the anthropologists, seem even stranger. The stereotype of an anthropologist is a pith-helmeted, pipe-smoking eccentric, tracking chimpanzees through the forest, digging up the bones of million-year-old ancestors, interviewing lost tribes about their sexual customs, and recording the words of the last speakers of a language. Another popular image presented in the media is Indiana Jones, the intrepid archaeologist of the film *Raiders of the Lost Ark*. Here is a man who is versed in the customs and languages of many societies past and present, feels at home anywhere in the world, and makes a living teaching, finding lost treasures, rescuing beautiful women in distress, and fighting Nazis (Figure 1.1).

Of course, Indiana Jones is a fictional character. Some real-life anthropologists are almost as well known: Jane Goodall, Margaret Mead, Donald Johanson, and the late Dian Fossey. These anthropologists have studied

chimpanzees, Samoan culture, the fossils of human ancestors, and gorillas. Their research conjures up images of anthropology every bit as varied as the imaginary adventures of Indiana Jones. Anthropologists do study all these things, and more. The sheer diversity of topics investigated by anthropologists seems almost to defy any sort of logic. The methods of data collection and analysis are almost as diverse. What pulls these different subjects together?

In one obvious sense, they all share an interest in the same subject—human beings. In fact, the traditional textbook definition of anthropology is the "study of humans." Though this definition is easy to remember, it is not terribly useful. After all, scientists in other fields, such as researchers in anatomy and biochemistry, also study humans. And there are many fields within the social sciences whose sole interest is humans. History, geography, political science, economics, sociology, and psychology are all devoted to the study of human beings, and no one would argue that these fields are merely branches of anthropology.

WHAT IS ANTHROPOLOGY?

What, then, is a suitable definition of anthropology? **Anthropology** could be described as the science of human cultural and biological variation and evolution. The first part of this definition includes both human culture and biology. **Culture** is learned behavior. Culture includes social and economic systems, marriage customs, religion, philosophy, and all other behaviors that are acquired through the process of learning rather than through instinct. The joint emphasis on culture and biology is an important feature of anthropology, and one that sets it apart from many other fields.

Biology and Culture

To the anthropologist, humans must be understood in terms of learned behavior as well as biology. We rely extensively on learned behaviors in virtually all aspects of our life. Even the expression of our sexual drives must be understood in light of human cultural systems. Although the actual basis of our sex drive is biological, the ways in which we express it are shaped by behaviors we have learned. The very inventiveness of humans, with our vast technology, is testimony to the powerful effect of learning. However, we are not purely cultural creatures. We are also biological organisms. We need to eat and breathe, and we are affected by our external environment. In addition, our biology sets certain limits on our potential behaviors. For example, all human cultures have some type of social structure that provides for the care of children until they are old enough to fend for themselves. This is not simply kindness to children; our biological position as mammals requires such attentiveness to children for survival. In contrast with other animal species, whose infants need little or no care, human infants are physically incapable of taking care of themselves.

Anthropology is concerned not only with culture and biology, but also with their interaction. Just as humans are not solely cultural or solely biological, we are not simply the sum of these two, either. Humans are biocultural organisms, which means that our culture and biology influence each other. The **biocultural approach** to studying human beings is a main theme of this book, and you will examine many examples of biocultural interaction.

The biocultural perspective of anthropology points to one of the unique strengths of anthropology as a science: it is **holistic,** meaning that it takes into consideration all aspects of human existence. Population growth again provides an example. Where the sociologist may be concerned with effects of population growth on social structure and the psychologist may be concerned with effects of population growth on psychological stress, the anthropologist is interested potentially in all aspects of population growth. In a given study, this analysis may include the relationship among diet, fertility, religion, disease, social systems, and political systems, to name but a few factors.

Variation

A major characteristic of anthropology is its concern with **variation.** In a general sense, variation refers to differences among individuals or populations. The anthropologist is interested in differences and similarities among human groups, in terms of both biology and culture. Anthropologists use the **comparative approach** to attempt to generalize about those aspects of human behavior and biology that are similar in all populations and those that are unique to specific environments and cultures. How do groups of people differ from one another? *Why* do they differ? These are questions about variation, and they apply equally to cultural and biological traits (Figure 1.2).

■ FIGURE 1.2
Biological variation in a group of children. (© Peter Menzel/ Stock Boston)

anthropology The science that investigates human biological and cultural variation and evolution.

culture Behavior that is learned and socially transmitted.

biocultural approach Studying humans in terms of the interaction between biology and culture in evolutionary adaptation.

holistic Integrating all aspects of existence in understanding human variation and evolution.

variation The differences that exist among individuals or populations.

comparative approach Comparing human populations to determine common and unique behaviors or biological traits.

Evolution

Evolution is change in living organisms over generations. Both cultural and biological evolution interest anthropologists. How and why do human culture and biology change? For example, anthropologists may be interested in the origin of marriage systems. When, how, and why did certain marriage systems evolve? For that matter, when did the custom of marriage first originate, and why? As for skin color, an anthropologist would be interested in what skin color the first humans may have had, and where, when, how, and why other skin colors may have evolved.

Adaptation

In addition to the concepts of variation and evolution, the anthropologist is interested in the process of **adaptation.** At the broadest level, adaptations are advantageous changes. Any aspect of biology or behavior that confers some advantage on an individual or population can be considered an adaptation. Cultural adaptations include technological devices such as clothing, shelter, and methods of food production. Such technologies can improve the well-being of humans. Cultural adaptations also include social systems and rules for behaviors. For example, the belief in certain societies that sexual relations with a woman must be avoided for some time after she gives birth can be adaptive in the sense that these behaviors influence the rate of population growth.

Adaptations can also be biological. Some biological adaptations are physiological in nature and involve metabolic changes. For example, when you are too hot, you will sweat. Sweating is a short-term physiological response that removes excess heat through the process of evaporation. Within limits, it aids in maintaining a constant body temperature. Likewise, shivering is an adaptive response to cold. The act of shivering increases metabolic rate and provides more heat.

Biological adaptations can also be genetic in nature. Here, changes in genes over many generations produce variation in biological traits. The darker skin color of many humans native to regions near the equator is one example of a long-term genetic adaptation. The darker skin provides protection from the harmful effects of ultraviolet radiation.

The Subfields of Anthropology

In a general sense, anthropology is concerned with determining what humans are, how they evolved, and how they differ from one another. Where other disciplines focus on specific issues of humanity, anthropology is unique in dealing simultaneously with questions of origins, evolution, variation, and adaptation.

Even though anthropology has a wide scope and appears to encompass anything and everything pertaining to humans, the study of anthropology in the United States is often characterized by four separate subfields, each with a specific focus. These subfields are cultural anthropology, anthropological archaeology, linguistic anthropology, and biological anthropology. Some anthropologists add a fifth subfield—applied anthropology, which involves the application of anthropological findings to contemporary matters and issues.

CULTURAL ANTHROPOLOGY   **Cultural anthropology** deals primarily with variation in the cultures of populations in the present or recent past. Its subjects include social, political, economic, and ideological aspects of human cultures. Cultural anthropologists look at all aspects of behavior within a society. Even when they are interested in a specific aspect of a culture, such as marriage systems, they look at how these behaviors relate to all other aspects of culture. Marriage systems, for example, may have an effect on the system of inheritance and may also be closely related to religious views. Comparison of cultures is used to determine common and unique features among different cultures.

ANTHROPOLOGICAL ARCHAEOLOGY   Archaeology is the study of cultural behaviors in the historic and prehistoric past. **Anthropological archaeology** uses the methods of archaeology to infer the behaviors of past societies. The archaeologist deals with such remains of past societies as tools, shelters, remains of animals eaten for food, and other objects that have survived. These remains, termed *artifacts*, are used to reconstruct past behavior. To help fill in the gaps, the archaeologist makes use of the findings of cultural anthropologists who have studied similar societies. Archaeological findings are critical in understanding the behavior of early humans and their evolution. Some of these findings for the earliest humans are presented later in this text.

LINGUISTIC ANTHROPOLOGY   **Linguistic anthropology** is the study of language. Spoken language is a behavior that appears to be uniquely human. This subfield of anthropology deals with the analysis of languages usually in nonliterate societies and with general trends in the evolution of languages. A major question raised by linguistic anthropology concerns the extent to which language shapes culture. Is language necessary for the transmission of culture? Does a language provide information about the beliefs and practices of a human culture?

▲▲

evolution Change in populations of organisms from one generation to the next.

adaptation The process of successful interaction between a population and an environment.

cultural anthropology Focuses on variations in cultural behaviors among human populations.

anthropological archaeology Focuses on cultural variation in prehistoric (and some historic) populations by analyzing the culture's remains.

linguistic anthropology Focuses on the nature of human language, the relationship of language to culture, and the languages of nonliterate peoples.

Biological Anthropologists at Work

The research interests of biological anthropologists are quite varied. This photo essay provides some examples.

Dr. Barry Bogin is a professor of anthropology in the Department of Behavioral Sciences at the University of Michigan at Dearborn. His area of specialization is the study of human growth, including studies of seasonal variation in growth rates, the evolution of human growth patterns, and the relationship between social and cultural factors and child growth. Much of his recent research has focused on an analysis of the cultural correlates of differences in growth patterns of Ladinos and Mayans in Guatemala and the United States. He is shown here measuring the height of a Mayan woman who has immigrated to the United States.

Dr. Michael Crawford is a professor of anthropology at the University of Kansas. He specializes in anthropological genetics, the study of the forces affecting genetic variation between and within human populations. Dr. Crawford's research includes studies of genetic markers, DNA, body and cranial measures, fingerprints, and dental

measurements from human populations across the globe. His research has taken him to Mexico, Belize, Ireland, Italy, Alaska, and Siberia, among other places. Currently, he is studying the Evenki reindeer herders of Siberia (shown here), specifically their genetic relationship to the first inhabitants of the New World and their adaptation to extremely cold climates.

Dr. Katherine Dettwyler is an associate professor of anthropology at Texas A&M University. Her research interests include child growth and health and biocultural studies of breast feeding. Her book *Dancing Skeletons* (Waveland Press, 1994) describes her recent research on infant and child growth as it relates to health and nutrition in Mali, West Africa. Dr. Dettwyler is actively involved in a number of organizations to promote improved nutrition in Mali.

Dr. Dean Falk is a professor of anthropology at the State University of New York at Albany. Her primary research interest is the evolution and comparative anatomy of primate brains, including the human brain. Dr. Falk is an expert in the field of paleoneurology, which involves the reconstruction of brain anatomy from fossil evidence. Her recent

Barry Bogin

Michael Crawford

Katherine Dettwyler

Dean Falk

research deals with how the brain cools itself, including implications for human evolution and the origin of an enlarged brain in our early ancestors. Her model of brain evolution is described in *Braindance* (1992).

Dr. Lyle Konigsberg, an associate professor of anthropology at the University of Tennessee, is particularly interested in integrating the study of prehistoric human skeletal remains with genetic and demographic theory. Dr. Konigsberg investigates patterns of prehistoric biological variation across space and time. His current work involves an analysis of prehistoric Native American populations, dating between 500 and 6,000 years ago.

Dr. Henry McHenry is a professor of anthropology at the University of California at Davis. His primary research interest is paleoanthropology, the study of the fossil remains of human ancestors. Dr. McHenry's current research focuses specifically on estimating the body size of early humans from their skeletal remains. He uses these estimates to make inferences regarding a variety of topics, including gender-based differences in body size, variations in relative brain size, and other aspects of ecology and social behavior.

Dr. Lorena Madrigal, an associate professor of anthropology at the University of South Florida, studies the biology and microevolution of human populations in Costa Rica, particularly demography and genetics. Her earlier work focused on the relationship among fertility, genetic change, and the sickle cell gene. Recently, her work has expanded to include aspects of maturation, miscarriage, frequency of twinning, and seasonal variation in demographic rates, among other topics. Most recently, Dr. Madrigal has been involved in the historical demography of Escazú, a small rural population in Costa Rica.

Dr. Barbara Smuts is a professor at the University of Michigan at Ann Arbor. Her work examines the behavior of baboons, particularly the social relationships between mothers and daughters. Her current research focuses on olive baboons in Kenya, Africa, and she also studies mother–infant relationships among bottle-nosed dolphins.

Henry McHenry

Lyle Konigsberg

Barbara Smuts

Lorena Madrigal

Biological anthropology must consider many of the findings of linguistic anthropology in the analysis of human variation and evolution. When comparing humans and apes, we must ask whether language is a unique human characteristic. If it is, then what biological and behavioral differences exist between apes and humans that lead to the fact that one species has language and the other lacks it? Linguistics is also important in considering human evolution. When did language begin? Why?

BIOLOGICAL ANTHROPOLOGY   The subject of this book is the subfield of **biological anthropology,** which is concerned with the biological evolution and variation of the human species, past and present. Biological anthropology is often referred to by another name—*physical anthropology.* The course you are currently enrolled in might be known by either name. Actually, the two names refer to the same field. Early in the twentieth century the field was first known as physical anthropology, reflecting its then primary interest in the *physical* variation of past and present humans and our primate relatives. Much of the research in the field focused on descriptive studies of physical variations, with little theoretical background. Starting in the 1950s, physical anthropologists became more familiar with the rapidly growing fields of genetics and evolutionary science. As a result, the field of physical anthropology became more concerned with biological processes, particularly with genetics. After a while, many in the field began using the term *biological anthropology* to emphasize the new focus on biological processes. In most circles today, the two terms are used more or less interchangeably.

It is useful to consider the field of biological anthropology in terms of four major questions it seeks to answer. First, *What are humans?* That is, How are we related to other living creatures? Who are our closest living relatives? What makes us similar to other living creatures? How are we unique? A second major question concerns our past. *What is the fossil record for human evolution?* Where have we come from? What does the history of our species look like? A third question concerns variation among modern humans. *How are humans around the world like, or unlike, each other?* What causes the patterns of human variation that we see? The fourth question relates back to the biocultural nature of human beings: *How does culture affect biology, and vice versa?* What impact have the rapid and amazing cultural changes in our species' recent past had on our biology? Are our biological and cultural adaptations out of synch?

There are several traditionally defined areas within biological anthropology, such as primate studies, paleoanthropology, and human variation. Primate studies are concerned with defining humans in the natural world, specifically in terms of the primates (a group of mammals that includes prosimians, monkeys, apes, and humans). Primate studies look at the anatomy, behavior, and evolution of the other primates as a standard of comparison with those aspects of humans. In this way, we can learn something about what it is to be human.

Paleoanthropology is the study of the fossil remains of human evolution. Researchers in this field are interested in determining who our ancestors were, and when, how, and why they evolved. Paleoanthropologists work closely with archaeologists to reconstruct the behaviors of our ancestors.

The study of human variation is concerned with how and why humans differ from each other in their biological makeup. This subfield considers the ways in which culture and biology interact in the modern world, including such topics as the genetics of populations, demography (the study of population size and composition), physical growth and development, and human health and disease.

SCIENCE AND EVOLUTION

Biological anthropology is an evolutionary science. All the major questions just presented may be addressed using modern evolutionary theory. Biological evolution simply refers to change in the genetic makeup of populations over time.

Characteristics of Science

Before we consider how evolution works, it is important to understand exactly what a science is.

FACTS   At one time or another, you have probably heard someone make the statement that evolution is a theory, not a fact. Or you might have heard that it is a fact, not a theory. Which is it, theory or fact? The truth of the matter is that someone who makes either of these statements does not understand what a theory or a fact is. Evolution is both fact and theory. A fact is simply a verifiable truth. It is a fact that the earth is round. It is a fact that when you drop something, it falls to the ground (assuming you are in the presence of a gravitational field and you are not dropping something that floats or flies away!). Evolution is a fact. Living organisms have changed in the past and they continue to change today. There are forms of life living today that did not exist millions of years ago. There are also forms of life that did live in the past but are not around today, such as our ancestors (Figure 1.3). Certain organisms have shown definite changes in their biological makeup. Horses, for example, used to have five toes, then three, and today they have one. Human beings have larger brains and smaller teeth today than they did a million years ago. Some changes are even apparent over shorter intervals of time. For example, human teeth are on average smaller today than they were only 10,000 years ago. All of these statements and many others are verifiable truths. They are facts.

▲▲▲▲▲▲▲▲▲▲▲▲▲▲▲▲▲▲▲▲▲▲▲▲▲▲▲▲▲▲

biological anthropology Focuses on the biological evolution of humans and human ancestors, the relationship of humans to other organisms, and patterns of biological variation within and among human populations. Also referred to as physical anthropology.

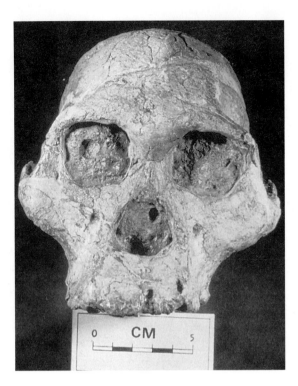

■ **FIGURE 1.3**
A skull of *Australopithecus africanus*, a hominid that lived two to three million years ago. (© K. Cannon-Bonventre/Anthro-Photo)

HYPOTHESES What is a hypothesis? A **hypothesis** is simply an explanation of observed facts. For example, consider gravity. Gravity is a fact. It is observable. Many hypotheses could be generated to explain gravity. You could hypothesize that gravity is caused by a giant living in the core of our planet drawing in air, thus causing a pull on all objects on the earth's surface. Bizarre as it sounds, this is a scientific hypothesis because it can be tested. It is, however, easily shown to be incorrect (air movement can be measured and it does not flow in the postulated direction).

TESTABILITY To be scientific, a hypothesis must be testable. The potential must exist for a hypothesis to be rejected. Just as the presence of the hypothetical giant in the earth can be tested (it doesn't exist!), predictions made about gravitational strength can also be tested. Not all hypotheses can be tested, however, and for this reason they are not scientific hypotheses. That doesn't necessarily mean they are true or false, but only that they cannot be tested. For example, you might come up with a hypothesis that all the fossils we have ever found were put in the ground by God to confuse us. This is not a scientific hypothesis because we have no objective way of testing the statement.

Many evolutionary hypotheses, however, are testable. For example, specific predictions about the fossil record can be made based on our knowledge of evolution. One such prediction is that humans evolved after the extinction of the dinosaurs. The potential exists for this statement to be rejected; all we need is evidence that humans existed before, or at the same time as, the dinosaurs. Because we have found no such evidence, we cannot reject the hypothesis. We can, however, imagine a situation in which the hypothesis could be rejected. If we cannot imagine such a situation, then the hypothesis cannot be tested. For example, imagine that someone tells you that all the people on the earth were created 5 minutes ago, complete with memories! Any evidence you muster against this idea could be explained away. Therefore, this hypothesis is not scientific because there is no possible way to reject it.

THEORIES What is the difference between a theory and a hypothesis? In some disciplines the two terms are sometimes used to mean the same thing. In the natural and physical sciences, however, theory means something different from hypothesis. A **theory** is a set of hypotheses that have been tested repeatedly and that have not been rejected. Evolution falls into this category. Evidence from many sources has confirmed the basic hypotheses making up evolutionary theory (discussed later in the chapter).

The Development of Evolutionary Theory

As with all general theories, modern evolutionary theory is not static. Scientific research is a dynamic process, with new evidence being used to support, clarify, and, most important, reject previous ideas. There will always be continual refinements in specific aspects of the theory and its applications. Because science is a dynamic process, evolutionary theory did not come about overnight. Charles Darwin (1809–1882) is most often credited as the "father of evolutionary thought" (Figure 1.4). It is true that Darwin provided a powerful idea that forms the center of modern evolutionary thought. He did not work in an intellectual vacuum, however, but rather built on the ideas of earlier scholars. Darwin's model was not the first evolutionary theory; it forms, rather, the basis of the one that has stood the test of time.

PRE-DARWINIAN THOUGHT To understand Darwin's contribution and evolution in general, it is necessary to take a look at earlier ideas. For many centuries the concept of change, biological or otherwise, was rather unusual in Western thought. Much of Greek philosophy, for example, posits a static, unchanging view of the world. In later Western thought, the universe, earth, and all living creatures were regarded as having been created by God in their present form, showing little if any change over many generations. Many biologists (then called natural historians) shared this view, and their science consisted mainly of description and categorization. A good example is Carolus Linnaeus (1707–1778), a Swedish naturalist who compiled the first formal classification of all known living creatures. Such a classification is called a **taxonomy,** and

■ **FIGURE 1.4**
Charles Darwin.
(Neg. no. 326697. Courtesy Department of Library Services, American Museum of Natural History)

hypothesis An explanation of observed facts.

theory A set of hypotheses that have been tested repeatedly and that have not been rejected. This term is sometimes used in a different sense in social science literature.

taxonomy A formal classification of organisms.

it serves to help organize information. Linnaeus's taxonomy organized all known living creatures into meaningful groups. For example, humans, dogs, cats, and many other animals are mammals, characterized primarily by the presence of mammary glands to feed offspring. Linnaeus used a variety of traits to place all then-known creatures into various categories. A taxonomy helps clarify relationships between different organisms. For example, bats are classified as mammals because they possess mammary glands—and not as birds simply because they have wings.

Linnaeus also gave organisms a name reflecting their genus and species. A **species** is a group of populations whose members can interbreed and produce fertile offspring. A **genus** is a group of similar species, often sharing certain common forms of adaptation. Modern humans, for example, are known by the name *Homo sapiens*. The first word is the genus and the second word is the species (more detail on genus and species is given in Chapter 3).

The reason for the relationships among organisms, however, was not often addressed by early natural historians. The living world was felt to be the product of God's work, and the task of the natural historian was description and classification. This static view of the world began to change in the eighteenth and nineteenth centuries. One important reason for this change was that excavations began to produce many fossils that did not fit neatly into the classification system. Discovery of the fossil record began to chip away at the view that the world is as it always had been, and the concept of change began to be incorporated into explanations of the origin of life. Not all scholars, however, came up with the same hypotheses.

One French anatomist, Georges Cuvier (1769–1832), analyzed many of the fossil remains found in quarries. He showed that many of these belonged to animals that no longer existed; that is, they had become extinct. Cuvier used a hypothesis called **catastrophism** to explain these extinctions. The hypothesis posited a series of catastrophes in the planet's past, during which many living creatures were destroyed. Following these catastrophes, organisms from unaffected areas moved in. The changes over time observed in the fossil record could therefore be explained as a continual process of catastrophes followed by repopulation from other regions (Mayr 1982).

Another hypothesis was put forth by the French scientist Jean-Baptiste Lamarck (1744–1829). He believed that evolution occurred through a natural process of organisms adjusting to their environment. One of his ideas was that an organism could change during its lifetime and then pass these changes on to its offspring. According to Lamarck's idea of **acquired characteristics,** a jungle cat that developed stronger leg muscles through constant running and jumping would pass along stronger muscles to its offspring. Of course, it is easy now to reject the concept of acquired characteristics. For example, someone who loses a finger in an accident will still have children with the correct number of fingers. Instead of looking back and ridiculing Lamarck for his ideas, however, we must realize that he was actually quite astute in noting the intimate relationship among organisms, their environments, and evolution.

CHARLES DARWIN AND NATURAL SELECTION Cuvier and Lamarck are perhaps the best-known examples of what many have called "pre-Darwinian" theorists. Evolution was well accepted, and various models were being developed to explain this fact, before Darwin. Charles Darwin developed the theory of natural selection that has since been supported by testing. His major contribution was to combine information from a variety of different fields, such as geology and economics, to form his theory.

With this background in mind, let us look at Darwin and his accomplishment. Charles Darwin had been interested in biology and geology since he was a small child. Born to well-to-do parents, Darwin attended college and had planned to enter the ministry, although he was not as enthusiastic about this career as he was about his studies of natural history. Because of his scientific and social connections, Darwin was able to accompany the scientific survey ship *Beagle* as an unpaid naturalist. The *Beagle* conducted a five-year journey around the world collecting plant and animal specimens in South America and the Galapagos Islands (in the Pacific Ocean near Ecuador), among other places (Figure 1.5).

During these travels, Darwin came to several basic conclusions about variation in living organisms. First, he found a tremendous amount of observable variation in most living species. Instead of looking at the world in terms of fixed, rigid categories (as did mainstream biology in his time), Darwin saw that individuals within species varied considerably from place to place.

Darwin also noted that the variations he saw made sense in terms of the environment (Figure 1.6). Creatures in cold climates often have fur for protection. Birds in areas where insects live deep inside tree branches have long beaks to allow them to extract these insects and eat them. In other words, organisms appear well adapted to specific environments. Darwin believed that the environment acted to change organisms over time. But how?

To help answer this question, Darwin turned to the writings of the economist Thomas Malthus (1766–1834), who had noted that more individ-

▲▲

species A group of populations whose members can interbreed naturally and produce fertile offspring.

genus Groups of species with similar adaptations.

catastrophism The hypothesis that explains evolutionary change in terms of repeated natural catastrophes.

acquired characteristics Lamarck's hypothesis that traits change in response to environmental demands and are passed on to offspring.

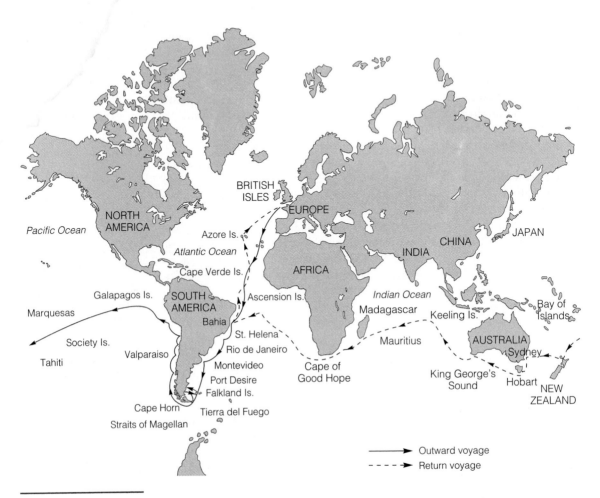

■ FIGURE 1.5
Darwin's observations of variation in the different regions he visited aboard the H.M.S. *Beagle* shaped his theory of natural selection.

uals are born in most species than can possibly survive. In other words, many organisms die before reaching maturity and reproducing. If it were not for this mortality, populations would grow too large for their environments to support them.

To Charles Darwin, the ideas of Malthus provided the needed information to solve the problem of adaptation and evolution. Not all individuals in a species survive and reproduce. Some failure to reproduce may be random, but some is related to specific characteristics of an individual. If there are two birds, one with a short beak and one with a long beak, in an environment that requires reaching inside branches to feed, it stands to reason that the bird with the longer beak is more likely to feed itself, survive, and reproduce. In certain environments, some individuals possess traits that enhance their probability of survival and reproduction. If these traits are due, in part or whole, to inherited characteristics, then they will be passed on to the next generation.

In some ways, Darwin's idea was not new. Animal and plant breeders had used this principle for centuries. Controlled breeding and artificial selection had resulted in many traits in domesticated plants and animals, such as livestock size, milk production in cows, and a variety of other traits. The same principle is used in producing pedigreed dogs and many forms of tropical fish. The difference is that Darwin saw that nature (the environment) could select those individuals that survived and reproduced. Hence, he called his concept **natural selection.**

Although the theory of evolution by natural selection is most often associated with Charles Darwin, another English natural historian, Alfred Russel Wallace (1823–1913), came up with essentially the same idea. In fact, Darwin and Wallace communicated their ideas to each other and first presented the theory of natural selection in a joint paper in 1858. Many scholars feel that Wallace's independent work urged Darwin finally to put forward the ideas he had developed years earlier but had not published. To ensure timely publication, Darwin condensed his many years of work into a 490-page "abstract" entitled *On the Origin of Species by Means of Natural Selection*, published in 1859 (Futuyma 1983).

AN EXAMPLE OF NATURAL SELECTION   One excellent example of how natural selection works is the story of populations of the peppered moth in England over the last few centuries (Figure 1.7). These moths come in two distinct colors, dark and light. Early observations found that most of these moths were light-colored, thus allowing them to camouflage themselves on tree trunks. By blending in, they had a better chance of avoiding the birds that tried to eat them. Roughly 1 percent of the moths, however, were dark-colored and thus at an obvious disadvantage. Naturalists noted that the frequency of dark-colored moths increased to almost 90 percent in the century following the beginning of the Industrial Revolution in England (Grant 1985). The reason for this change was the fact that industrialization brought about massive pollution in the surrounding countryside. The trees became darker in color after being covered with soot. The light moths were at a disadvantage, and the dark moths, now better camouflaged, were better off. Proportionately, more dark moths survived and passed their dark color to the next generation. In evolutionary terminology, the dark moths were *selected for* and the light moths were *selected against*. After antipollution laws were passed and the environment began to recover, the situation reversed: once again light moths survived better, and were selected for, whereas dark moths were selected against.

This well-known study shows us more than just the workings of natural selection. It also illustrates several important principles of evolution. First, we cannot always state with absolute certainty which traits are "good" and which are "bad." It depends on the specific environment. When the trees were light in color, the light-colored moths were at an advantage, but when the situation changed, the dark-colored moths gained the advantage. Second,

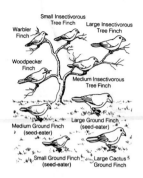

■ FIGURE 1.6
The sizes, beak shapes, and diets of this sample of Darwin's finches show differences in adaptation among closely related species. (From E. Peter Volpe, *Understanding Evolution*, 5th ed. Copyright © 1985 Wm. C. Brown Communication, Inc., Dubuque, Iowa. All Rights Reserved. Reprinted by permission)

▲▲▲▲▲▲▲▲▲▲▲▲▲▲▲▲▲▲▲▲▲▲▲▲▲▲

natural selection
A mechanism for evolutionary change favoring the survival and reproduction of some organisms over others because of their biological characteristics.

■ FIGURE 1.7
Adaptation in the peppered moth. The dark-colored moth is more visible on light-colored tree trunks and therefore at greater risk of being seen and eaten by a bird (*top*). The light-colored moth is at greater risk of being eaten on dark-colored tree trunks (*bottom*). (© Michael Tweedie/Photo Researchers, Inc.)

evolution does not proceed unopposed in one direction. Under certain situations, biological traits can change in a different direction. In the case of the moths, evolution produced a change from light to dark to light again. Third, evolution does not occur in a vacuum. It is affected by changes in the environment and by changes in other species. In this example, changes in the cultural evolution of humans led to a change in the environment, which further affected the evolution of the moths. Finally, the moth study shows us the critical importance of variation to the evolutionary process. If the original population of moths did not possess the dark-colored variation, they might have been wiped out after the trees turned darker in color. Variation must exist for natural selection to operate effectively.

MODERN EVOLUTIONARY THOUGHT   Darwin provided part of the answer of how evolution worked, but he did not have all the answers. Many early critics of Darwin's work focused on certain questions that Darwin could not answer. One important question concerns the origins of variation: Given that natural selection operates on existing variation, then where do those variations come from? Why, at the outset, were some moths light and others dark? Natural selection can act only on preexisting variation; it cannot create new variations. Another question is: How are traits inherited? The theory of natural selection states that certain traits are selected for and passed on to future generations. How are these traits passed on? Darwin knew that traits were inherited, but he did not know the mechanism. Still another question involves how new forms and structures come into being.

Darwin is to be remembered and praised for his work in providing the critical base from which evolutionary science developed. He did not, however, have all the answers, as no scientist does. Even today people tend to equate evolutionary science with Darwin to the exclusion of all work since that time. Some critics of evolutionary theory point to a single aspect of Darwin's work, show it to be in error, and then proceed to claim all of evolutionary thought suspect. In reality, a scientific theory will continue to change as new evidence is gathered and as further tests are constructed.

Modern evolutionary theory relies not only on the work of Darwin and Wallace but also on developments in genetics, zoology, embryology, physiology, and mathematics, to name but a few fields. The basic concept of natural selection as stated by Darwin has been tested and found to be valid. Refinements have been added, and some aspects of the original idea have been changed. We now have answers to many of Darwin's questions. Modern evolutionary theory will be discussed in greater detail in the next two chapters.

Evidence for Evolution

Because this book is concerned with human variation and evolution, you will be provided with numerous examples of how evolution works in human populations, past and present. It is important to understand from the start that biological evolution is a documented fact and that the modern theory of evolution has stood up under many scientific tests.

The fossil record provides evidence of evolution. The story the fossils tell is one of change. Creatures existed in the past that are no longer with us. Sequential changes are found in many fossils showing the change of certain features over time from a common ancestor, as in the case of the horse. Apart from demonstrating that evolution did occur, the fossil record also provides tests of the predictions made from evolutionary theory. For example, the theory predicts that single-celled organisms evolved before multi-celled organisms. The fossil record supports this prediction—multicelled organisms are found in layers of earth millions of years after the first ap-pearance of single-celled organisms. Note that the possibility always remains that the opposite could be found! If multicelled organisms were indeed found to have evolved before single-celled organisms, then the theory of evo-lution would be rejected. A good scientific theory always allows for the pos-sibility that it may be rejected. The fact that we have not found such a case in countless examinations of the fossil record strengthens the case for evolu-tionary theory. Remember, in science you do not prove a theory; rather, you fail to reject it.

The fossil record is not the only evidence we have that evolution has oc-curred. Comparison of living organisms provides further confirmation. For example, the African apes are the closest living relatives of humans. We see this in a number of characteristics. African apes and humans share the same type of dental pattern, have a similar shoulder structure, and have DNA (the genetic code) that is over 98 percent identical. Even though any one of these traits, or others, could be explained as coincidental, why do so many inde-pendent traits show the same pattern? One possibility, of course, is that they were designed that way by an ultimate Creator. The problem with this idea is that it cannot be tested. It is a matter of faith and not of science. Another problem is that we must then ask ourselves why a Creator would use the same basic pattern for so many traits in different creatures. Evolution, on the other hand, offers an explanation. Apes and humans share many charac-teristics because they evolved from a common ancestor (Figure 1.8).

Another example of shared characteristics is the python, a large snake. Like many vertebrates, the python has a pelvis, the skeletal structure that connects the lower legs to the upper body (Futuyma 1983). From a structural standpoint, of what possible use is a pelvis to a creature that has no legs? If the python was created, then what purpose would there have been to give it a pelvis? We can of course argue that no one can understand the motivations of a Creator, but that is hardly a scientific explanation. Evolutionary reason-ing provides an answer: the python has retained the pelvis from an earlier ancestor that did have legs.

Another line of evidence supporting evolution is the laboratory and field studies of living organisms. Ongoing evolutionary change has been documented in many organisms, including humans. Specific predictions of the effect of evolutionary mechanisms have been tested and verified in

■ FIGURE 1.8
The percentage of genetic
distance between humans and
the great apes (chimpanzee,
gorilla, and orangutan).
Combined with other
biological evidence, genetic
data show us how closely
related we are to the apes,
especially the chimpanzee.
(From *Human Evolution: An
Illustrated Introduction* by Roger
Lewin, © 1984 by Blackwell
Scientific Publications. Reprinted
with permission by W. H. Freeman
and Company)

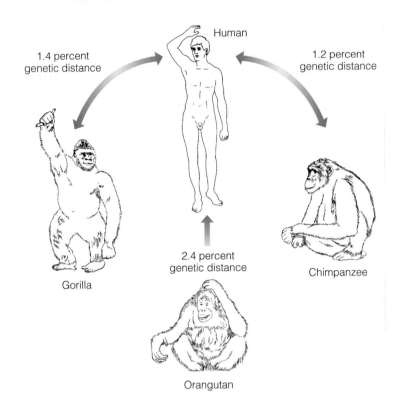

controlled experiments and observational studies. The study of moth color
is but one of many examples of this kind of analysis.

Science and Religion

The subject of evolution has always been controversial, and the implications
of evolution have sometimes frightened people. For example, the fact that
humans and apes evolved from a common ancestor has always upset some
people who feel that their humanity is somehow degraded by having ancestors supposedly less worthy than ourselves. Another conflict lies in the implications evolution has for religious views. In the United States a number of
laws have prohibited the teaching of evolution in public schools. Many of
these laws stayed on the books until the late 1960s.

Numerous legal battles have been fought over these anti-evolution laws.
Perhaps the most famous of these was the "Scopes Monkey Trial" in 1925.
John Scopes, a high school teacher in Dayton, Tennessee, was arrested for
violating the state law prohibiting the teaching of evolution. The town and
trial quickly became the center of national attention, primarily because of
the two celebrities in the case—William Jennings Bryan, a former U.S. Secre-
tary of State, who represented the state of Tennessee, and Clarence Darrow,

one of the most famous American trial lawyers ever, who represented Scopes. The battle between these two eloquent speakers captured the attention of the country (Figure 1.9). In the end, Scopes was found guilty of violating the law, and he was fined $100. The fine was later suspended on a legal technicality. The story of this trial, which has been dramatized in play and movie versions as *Inherit the Wind*, is a powerful story portraying the fight of those who feel strongly about academic freedom and freedom of speech against ignorance and oppression. In reality, the original arrest of Scopes appears to have been planned by several local people, including Scopes, to put the town on the map (Gould 1983).

In retrospect, the Scopes trial may seem amusing. We laugh at early attempts to control subject matter in classrooms and often feel that we have gone beyond such battles. Nothing could be further from the truth, however. For many people, evolution represents a threat to their beliefs in the sudden creation of all life by a creator. Attempts to legislate the teaching of the Biblical view of creation in science classes, however, violate the First Amendment of the Constitution as an establishment of religion. To circumvent this problem, opponents of evolution have devised a new strategy by calling their teachings "creation science," supposedly the scientific study of special creation. The word *God* does not always appear in definitions of creation science, but the word *creator* often does.

In March 1981, the Arkansas state legislature passed a law (Act 590) requiring that creation science be taught in public schools for equal amounts of time as evolution. The American Civil Liberties Union challenged this law, and it was overturned in a federal district court in 1982. A similar law passed in Louisiana in 1981 was later overturned. The Louisiana case has since been appealed and brought to the U.S. Supreme Court, which upheld the ruling of the lower court in 1987. Among other legal problems they raise, both the Arkansas and Louisiana laws have been found to be unconstitutional under the First Amendment.

What is "creation science"? Why shouldn't it be taught in science classes? Shouldn't science be open to new ideas? These questions all center on the issue of whether creation science is a science or not. As typically applied, creation science is not a science; at best, it is a grab bag of ideas spruced up with scientific jargon. One of the original definitions is found in Act 590 of the Arkansas law, which defines creation science as

> the scientific evidence for creation and inferences from these scientific evidences. Creation-science includes the scientific evidences and related inferences that indicate: (1) Sudden creation of the universe, energy, and life from nothing; (2) The insufficiency of mutation and natural selection in bringing about development of all living kinds from a single organism; (3) Changes only within fixed limits of originally created kinds of plants and animals; (4) Separate ancestry for man and apes; (5) Explanation of the earth's geology by catastrophism, including the occurrence of a worldwide flood; and (6) A relatively recent inception of the earth and living kinds. (Montagu 1984:376–377)

■ **FIGURE 1.9**
The Scopes Trial. William Jennings Bryan (*right*) represented the state of Tennessee and Clarence Darrow (*left*) represented John Scopes.
(© AP/Wide World Photos)

None of these statements is supported by scientific evidence, and creationist writers generally use very little actual evidence to support their views. Some have written that the Biblical Flood can be supported by the fossil record. Earth's past is essentially recorded by the order in which different levels of earth and fossils are found. In general, that is, the deeper a fossil is found, the older it is. Creationists explain this order as being caused by the flight of animals from the Flood. As the waters rose, they say, birds flew and small mammals ran up mountains to escape drowning; these creatures were therefore drowned at higher elevations.

According to creationists, then, you will find fish at lower levels and birds and mammals at higher levels. The fossil record does show this phenomenon. Isn't this proof for "creation science"? No. Think about the Flood scenario for a moment and you will see that it just doesn't make sense. Why didn't the winged reptiles fly away like the birds did? Why are single-celled organisms found earlier than multicelled organisms of similar size and overall shape? Why did large, heavy creatures such as giant tortoises and hippopotami survive instead of sinking? Why didn't the small, fast dinosaurs survive? Why did certain fish die before others, when they were just as swift and just as good at swimming? Many challenges can be raised to the idea of a single gigantic flood causing the order found in the fossil record (Kitcher 1982; Futuyma 1983). The fossil record, in short, provides ample evidence to reject the Flood hypothesis.

Another example cited by creationists as "proof" of special creation is the "fact" that dinosaur and human footprints have been found at the same geological level along the Paluxy River in Texas. Closer examination has shown that the footprints were not distinguishable and that a number of tracks had been carved to attract tourists and their money (Kitcher 1982).

The main "scientific" work of the creationists consists of attempting to find fault with evolutionary theory. The reasoning is that if evolution can be rejected, then special creation must be true. This strategy actually uses an important feature of scientific research by attempting to reject a given hypothesis. The problem is that none of the creationists' attacks on evolution has been supported by scientific evidence. Certainly some predictions of evolutionary theory have been proven incorrect, but that is to be expected because science is a dynamic process. The basic finds of evolution, however, have been supported time and time again.

Another problem is that this method works only when the hypothesis and its alternative cover all possible cases. Are evolution and special creation by a single creator the only possible explanations? Perhaps the universe was created by several creators. Perhaps the universe and natural law were created by a creator, but life evolved from natural law. You might try to think up other alternatives. Remember, however, that to be scientific a hypothesis must be testable.

On an emotional level, the doctrines of "creation science" attract many people. Given the concept of free speech, why shouldn't creation science be given equal time? The problem with equal time is that it assumes that both ideas have equal merit. Consider that some people still believe the earth is flat. They are certainly entitled to their opinion, but it would be absurd to mandate "equal time" in geography and geology classes for this idea. Also, the concept of equal time is not really that fairminded after all. The specific story many creationists refer to is the Biblical story of Genesis. Many other cultures have their own creation stories. Shouldn't they receive equal time as well? In one sense, they should, though the proper forum for such discussions is probably a course in comparative religions, not a science class.

Perhaps the biggest problem advocates of "creation science" have introduced is that they appear to place religion and science at odds with each other. Religion and science both represent ways of looking at the world and, though they work on different levels, they are not contradictory. You can be religious and believe in God and still accept the fact of evolution and evolutionary theory. Only if you take the story of Genesis as a literal, historical account does a conflict exist. Most major religions in the world accept the findings of evolution. Many people, including some scientists, look to the evolutionary process as evidence of God's work.

Many creationists fear that science has eroded our faith in God and has therefore led to a decline in morals and values. They imply that science (and evolution in particular) makes statements about human morality. It does not. Science has nothing to say about right and wrong; that is the function of social ethics, philosophies, and religion. Religion and science are important to many people. To put them at odds with each other does both a disservice. It is no surprise that many ministers, priests, and rabbis have joined in the fight against the laws of "creation science."

SUMMARY

Anthropology is the study of human biological and cultural variation and evolution. Anthropology asks questions that focus on what humans are and the origins, evolution, and variation of our biology and behaviors, because humans are both biological and cultural organisms. In the United States, anthropology is characterized by four subfields with specific concerns: cultural anthropology (the study of cultural behavior), anthropological archaeology (the study of past cultures), linguistic anthropology (the study of language as a human characteristic), and biological anthropology (the study of human biological evolution and variation).

As a science, anthropology has certain requirements and characteristics. Hypotheses must be testable and verifiable. The main theoretical base of biological anthropology is the theory of evolution. A major feature of evolutionary theory is Darwin's idea of natural selection. In any environment in which resources are necessarily limited, some organisms are more likely to survive and reproduce than others because of their biological characteristics. Those who survive pass these traits on to the next generation.

A current controversy involves the efforts of certain people to pass laws requiring that "creation science" be taught in public schools. Examination of this field shows that it is not a science at all. Apart from these debates, it should be noted that today there is little conflict between religion and science in the United States. Each perspective addresses different questions in different ways.

SUPPLEMENTAL READINGS

Futuyma, D. J. 1983. *Science on Trial: The Case for Evolution*. New York: Pantheon Books. An excellent review of evolution and a detailed critique of "creation science," particularly strong in its discussion of scientific method and evidence for evolution.

Gould, S. J. 1977. *Ever Since Darwin*. New York: W. W. Norton. The first of several books of essays, most written originally for *Natural History*, on evolutionary biology. Essays deal with evolutionary theory, the history of evolutionary science, and the evolution–creation debate, among other topics. Other books by the same author, also published by W. W. Norton, are *The Panda's Thumb* (1980), *Hen's Teeth and Horse's Toes* (1983), *The Flamingo's Smile* (1985), *Bully for Brontosaurus* (1991), and *Eight Little Piggies* (1993).

For further information on the current status of the scientific, legal, and educational aspects of the evolution–creation debate, contact: National Center for Science Education, P. O. Box 9477, Berkeley, Calif. 94709-0477.

Human Genetics

Is human behavior the result of biology *or* culture? This question has been asked countless times in human history, often with serious cultural and political consequences. To anthropologists, the question is somewhat meaningless; we recognize *both* biological and cultural factors as important and look at the relative potential contributions of both. It is hard to untangle these effects.

To understand human biological variation and evolution, we must consider the science of genetics. The study of genetics actually encompasses a number of different areas, depending on the level of analysis. Genetics can be studied on the molecular level, with the focus on what genes are and how they act to produce biological structures.

Genetics also involves the process of inheritance. To what extent are we a reflection of our parents? How are traits inherited? This branch of the field is called **Mendelian genetics,** after the scientist Gregor Mendel, who first worked out many of the principles of inheritance.

▲▲▲▲▲▲▲▲▲▲▲▲▲▲▲▲▲▲▲▲▲▲▲▲▲▲▲▲▲▲

Mendelian genetics
The branch of genetics concerned with patterns and processes of inheritance. This field was named after Gregor Mendel, the first scientist to work out many of these principles.

Finally, genetics can be studied at the level of a population. Here we are interested in describing the patterns of genetic variation within and among different populations. The changes that take place in the frequency of genes within a population constitute the process of **microevolution.** At the level of the population, we seek the reasons for evolutionary change from one generation to the next. Projection of these findings allows us to understand better the long-term pattern of evolution over thousands and millions of years and the origin of new species (**macroevolution**).

MOLECULAR GENETICS

DNA: The Genetic Code

The study of genetics at the molecular level concerns the amazing properties of a molecule known as deoxyribonucleic acid, or **DNA** for short. The DNA molecule provides the codes for biological structures and the means to translate this code. It is perhaps best to think of DNA as a set of instructions for determining the makeup of biological organisms. Quite simply, DNA provides information for building, operating, and repairing organisms. In this context, the process of genetic inheritance is seen as the transmission of this information, or the passing on of the instructions needed for biological structures. Evolution can be viewed in this context as the transfer of information from one generation to the next, along with the possibility that this information will change.

THE STRUCTURE OF DNA   The physical appearance of the DNA molecule resembles a ladder that has been twisted into the shape of a helix (Figure 2.1). In biochemical terms, the rungs of the ladder are of major importance. These rungs are made up of chemical units called **bases.** There are four possible types of bases, identified by the first letter of their longer chemical names: A (adenine), T (thymine), G (guanine), and C (cytosine). These bases form the "alphabet" used in specifying and carrying out genetic instructions.

All biological structures, from nerve cells to blood cells to bone cells, are made up predominantly of proteins. Proteins in turn are made up of amino acids, whose chemical properties allow them to bond together to form proteins. Each amino acid is coded for by three of the four chemical bases just discussed. There are 64 possible codes that can be specified, using some combination of three bases. This might not seem like a lot, except for the fact that only 20 amino acids need to be specified by the genetic code. The three-base code provides more than enough possibilities to code for these amino acids. A list of the different DNA sequences is shown in Table 2.1.

The ability of the DNA molecule to use the different amino acid codes lies in a simple property of the chemical bases. The base A bonds with the base T, and the base G bonds with the base C. This chemical property allows

■ FIGURE 2.1
The structure of the DNA molecule. DNA consists of two strands arranged in a helix joined together by chemical bases (see text).

■ TABLE 2.1
DNA Base Sequences for Amino Acids

FIRST BASE	SECOND BASE							
	A		T		C		G	
A	AAA	Phenylalanine	ATA	Tyrosine	ACA	Cysteine	AGA	Serine
	AAT	Leucine	ATT	Stop	ACT	Stop	AGT	Serine
	AAC	Leucine	ATC	Stop	ACC	Tryptophan	AGC	Serine
	AAG	Phenylalanine	ATG	Tyrosine	ACG	Cysteine	AGG	Serine
T	TAA	Isoleucine	TTA	Asparagine	TCA	Serine	TGA	Threonine
	TAT	Isoleucine	TTT	Lysine	TCT	Arginine	TGT	Threonine
	TAC	Methionine	TTC	Lysine	TCC	Arginine	TGC	Threonine
	TAG	Isoleucine	TTG	Asparagine	TCG	Serine	TGG	Threonine
C	CAA	Valine	CTA	Aspartic acid	CCA	Glycine	CGA	Alanine
	CAT	Valine	CTT	Glutamic acid	CCT	Glycine	CGT	Alanine
	CAC	Valine	CTC	Glutamic acid	CCC	Glycine	CGC	Alanine
	CAG	Valine	CTG	Aspartic acid	CCG	Glycine	CGG	Alanine
G	GAA	Leucine	GTA	Histidine	GCA	Arginine	GGA	Proline
	GAT	Leucine	GTT	Glutamine	GCT	Arginine	GGT	Proline
	GAC	Leucine	GTC	Glutamine	GCC	Arginine	GGC	Proline
	GAG	Leucine	GTG	Histidine	GCG	Arginine	GGG	Proline

Rows refer to the first of the three bases and columns refer to the second of the three bases. These base sequences are for the DNA molecule. The 64 different combinations code for 20 amino acids and one termination sequence ("Stop"). To convert to messenger RNA, substitute U for A, A for T, G for C, and C for G. To convert to transfer RNA, substitute U for A.

the DNA molecule to carry out a number of functions, including the ability to make copies of itself and to direct the synthesis of proteins.

FUNCTIONS OF DNA   The DNA molecule can make copies of itself. Remember that the DNA molecule is made up of two strands that form the long arms of the ladder. Each rung of the ladder consists of two bases. If one part of the rung contains the base A, then the other part of the rung will contain the base T because A and T bond together.

The DNA molecule can separate into two separate strands. Once separate, each strand attracts free-floating bases. When the new bases have attached themselves to the original strands, the result is two identical DNA

microevolution Short-term evolutionary change.

macroevolution Long-term evolutionary change.

DNA The molecule that provides the genetic code for biological structures and the means to translate this code.

base Chemical unit that makes up part of the DNA molecule whose sequence specifies genetic instructions.

molecules. This process is diagrammed in Figure 2.2. Keep in mind that this description is somewhat oversimplified—in reality, the process is biochemically much more complex.

The ability of the DNA molecule (Figure 2.3) to control protein synthesis also involves the attraction of complementary bases, but with the help of another molecule—ribonucleic acid, or **RNA** for short. In simple terms, RNA serves as the messenger for the information coded by the DNA molecule. One major difference between DNA and RNA is that in RNA the base A attracts a base called U (uracil) instead of T.

■ **FIGURE 2.2**
Replication of the DNA molecule.

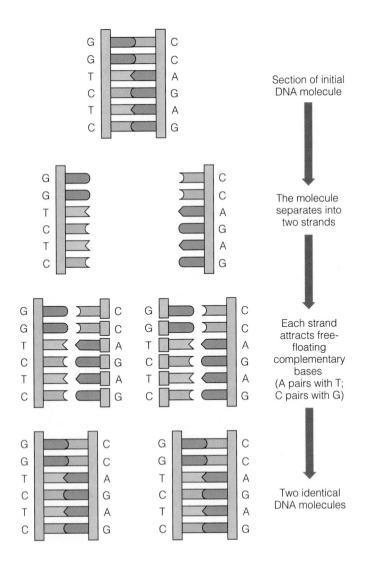

Section of initial DNA molecule

The molecule separates into two strands

Each strand attracts free-floating complementary bases (A pairs with T; C pairs with G)

Two identical DNA molecules

Consider the DNA base sequence GGT. In protein synthesis, the DNA molecule separates into two strands, and one strand (containing CCA) becomes inactive. The active strand, GGT, attracts free-floating bases to form a strand of **messenger RNA.** Because A bonds with T and G bonds with C, this strand consists of the sequence CCA. The strand then travels to the site of protein synthesis. Once there, the strand of messenger RNA transfers its information by attracting **transfer RNA,** which is a free-floating molecule. The sequence of messenger RNA containing the sequence CCA attracts a transfer RNA molecule with a complementary sequence—GGU. The result is that the amino acid proline (specified by the RNA sequence GGU or the DNA sequence GGT) is included in the chain of amino acids making up a particular protein. To summarize, one strand of the DNA molecule produces the complementary strand of messenger RNA, which then travels to the site of protein synthesis and attracts a complementary strand of transfer RNA, which carries the specified amino acid. This process is illustrated for the DNA sequence GGTCTC in Figure 2.4.

This simplified discussion shows the basic nature of the structure and functions of the DNA molecule. More advanced discussion can be found in most genetics textbooks. For our purposes, however, the broad view will suffice. If we consider DNA as a "code," we can then look at the processes of transmission and change of information without actually having to consider the exact biochemical mechanisms.

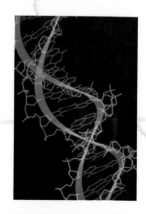

■ **FIGURE 2.3**
Computer representation of the DNA molecule.
(© Will & Demi McIntyre/Photo Researchers, Inc.)

Chromosomes and Genes

DNA is contained within the nucleus of each cell. Another form of DNA, contained in a part of the cell called the mitochondrion, is discussed later in Chapter 9. The DNA sequences are bound together by proteins in long strands called **chromosomes** that are found within the nucleus of each cell. With the exception of those in the sex cells (egg and sperm), chromosomes occur in pairs. Most body cells contain both members of these pairs. Different species have different numbers of chromosomes. For example, humans have 23 pairs, chimpanzees have 24 pairs, fruit flies have 4 pairs, and certain plant species have thousands of pairs. There is no relationship between the

RNA The molecule that functions to carry out the instructions for protein synthesis specified by the DNA molecule.

messenger RNA The form of RNA that transports the genetic instructions from the DNA molecule to the site of protein synthesis.

transfer RNA A free-floating molecule that is attracted to a strand of messenger RNA, resulting in the synthesis of a protein chain.

chromosome A long strand of DNA sequences.

■ FIGURE 2.4
Protein synthesis.

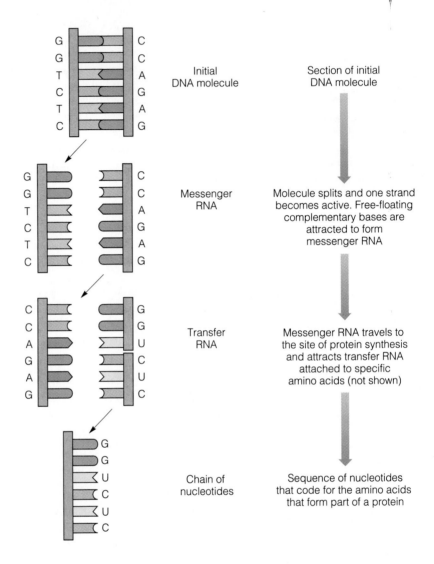

Initial DNA molecule	Section of initial DNA molecule
Messenger RNA	Molecule splits and one strand becomes active. Free-floating complementary bases are attracted to form messenger RNA
Transfer RNA	Messenger RNA travels to the site of protein synthesis and attracts transfer RNA attached to specific amino acids (not shown)
Chain of nucleotides	Sequence of nucleotides that code for the amino acids that form part of a protein

number of chromosome pairs a species has and its intelligence or biological complexity.

With certain exceptions, each cell in the human body contains a complete set of chromosomes and DNA. Nerve cells contain the DNA for bone cells, for example, and vice versa. Some type of regulation takes place within different cells to ensure that only certain genes are expressed in the right places, but the exact nature of this regulation is not known completely at present.

PCR and Ancient DNA

In the summer of 1994, film goers were thrilled by the movie *Jurassic Park*, based on the novel of the same name by Michael Crichton (who studied anthropology as an undergraduate). The plot revolves around the construction of a dinosaur theme park—with live dinosaurs! In *Jurassic Park*, scientists recover amber dating back to the time of the dinosaurs. Trapped in the amber are mosquitoes who, prior to being trapped in the tree sap that becomes amber, had drunk the blood of dinosaurs. Using this blood, the fictional scientists reconstruct the DNA of the original dinosaurs and bring a number of extinct species back to life.

A fascinating story, but how accurate is it? Could we reconstruct sufficient DNA sequences of ancient creatures to bring them back to life? At present, we lack the technology to do so. However, we *can* reconstruct some ancient DNA sequences (although not well enough to recreate a dinosaur). Fragments of ancient DNA *have* been reconstructed, including some from amber many millions of years old. We have also been able to obtain DNA fragments from human populations many thousands of years old (Stone and Stoneking 1993; Hagelberg 1994).

The heart of these achievements is a relatively new technique called the *polymerase chain reaction* (PCR).

This technique involves the laboratory synthesis of millions of copies of DNA fragments from very small initial amounts (Erlich et al. 1991). The process is essentially cyclical—the DNA strands are separated and form the template for new strands, thus resulting in a doubling of the DNA each time through the cycle (see adjoining figure). This method is very efficient in extracting DNA sequences from very small samples. In fact, it is so efficient that one of the technical problems is that it often picks up DNA from people's cells floating around the lab as dust! (Hagelberg 1994). The PCR method is also useful to anthropologists working on living human populations. Samples can be collected and transported easily—such as single plucked hairs!

The PCR method has also proven valuable in the field of forensics. Very small samples can yield sufficient DNA to help identify skeletal remains of murder victims. One notorious case involved the skeletal remains that were attributed to the infamous Nazi doctor Joseph Mengele. Extracts of bone were taken, and the DNA was amplified using PCR and then compared to the known surviving relatives of Mengele. Based on this comparison, the skeletal remains were definitely identified as having been Mengele (Hagelberg 1994).

Simplified diagram of the polymerase chain reaction (PCR) used to amplify small amounts of DNA. Each time through the cycle the amount of DNA doubles.

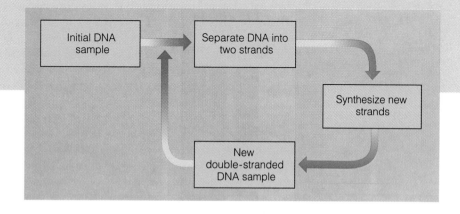

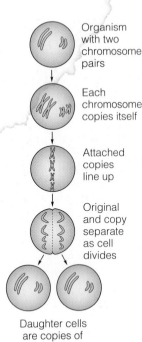

Organism with two chromosome pairs

Each chromosome copies itself

Attached copies line up

Original and copy separate as cell divides

Daughter cells are copies of parent cell

■ **FIGURE 2.5**

The process of mitosis, the formation of body cells. Each chromosome copies itself, the attached copies line up in the cell, and the original and copy split when the cell divides. The result is two identical cells. (From *Human Antiquity: An Introduction to Physical Anthropology and Archaeology,* 2d ed., by Kenneth Feder and Michael Park, Fig 4.2. Copyright © 1993 by Mayfield Publishing Company)

GENES   The term *gene*, although used frequently, actually encompasses a variety of definitions. In the most general sense, a **gene** can be defined as a section of DNA that has an identifiable structure or function (Marks and Lyles 1994). In the past, the gene tended to be defined most often on the basis of its function, such as a gene that controls for a particular blood group. Today, we use a broader definition because we realize that large sections of DNA do not have a specific function. In terms of genes that have a given function, many code for the production of a specific protein.

Aside from manufacture of proteins, another function of genes is the regulation of biological processes. For example, consider the fact that in many humans the enzyme needed to digest milk sugar stops being produced several years after birth. Or consider the fact that sexual maturation in humans occurs during adolescence and not in infancy. Many biological characteristics are subject to regulation in terms of when they take effect or are expressed. Genes that are responsible for this regulation are known as **regulatory genes,** and they act by turning other genes on or off at the appropriate time.

Regulatory genes may have great evolutionary significance. For example, regulatory genes may help explain the great physical differences between chimpanzees and humans even though over 98 percent of their structural genes are identical. The major genetic difference between humans and chimpanzees may be caused by regulatory genes, which act on the timing of growth and development, and could lead to differences in brain size, facial structures, and other physical features.

MITOSIS AND MEIOSIS   The DNA molecule provides for the transmission of genetic information. Production of proteins and regulation are only two aspects of information transfer. Because organisms start life as a single cell that subsequently multiplies, it is essential that the genetic information within the initial cell be transferred to all future cells. The ability of DNA to replicate itself is involved in the process of cell replication, known as **mitosis** (Figure 2.5). When a cell divides, each chromosome duplicates and then splits. Each chromosome has replicated itself, so that when the cell finishes dividing, the result is two cells with the full set of chromosomes.

The process is different when information is passed on from one generation to the next. The genetic code is passed on from parents to offspring through the sex cells—the sperm in males and the egg in females. The sex cells, however, do not contain the full set of chromosomes but only one chromosome from each pair (i.e., only one-half of the set). Whereas your other body cells have a total of 46 chromosomes (2 each for 23 pairs), your sex cells contain only 23 chromosomes (1 from each pair). When you have a child, you contribute 23 chromosomes, and your mate contributes 23 chromosomes. Your child then has the normal complement of 46 chromosomes in 23 pairs.

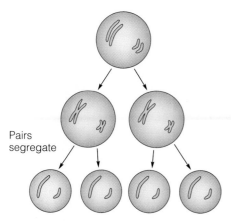

Pairs
segregate

Each sex cell has half the normal
number of chromosomes

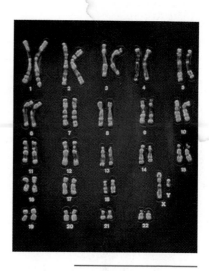

■ FIGURE 2.6
The process of meiosis,
the formation of sex cells.
Meiosis begins in the same
way as mitosis: each chromosome makes a copy of itself.
The pairs of chromosomes
then segregate, forming four
sex cells, each with one
chromosome rather than a
pair of chromosomes.
(Adapted from *Human Antiquity:
An Introduction to Physical
Anthropology and Archaeology*, 2d
ed., by Kenneth Feder and Michael
Park, Fig. 4.2. Copyright © 1993
by Mayfield Publishing Company)

■ FIGURE 2.7
All 23 pairs of chromosomes
typically found in a
human being. This set of
chromosomes came from
a man—note the 23rd pair
has an X chromosome and
a Y chromosome. (© CNRI/
Science Photo Library/Photo
Researchers, Inc.)

Sex cells are created through the process of **meiosis** (Figure 2.6). Basically, this involves the replication of chromosomes followed by cell division, followed by another cell division without an intervening round of
replication. In sperm, the result is that four sex cells are produced from the
initial set of 23 pairs of chromosomes. The process is similar in egg cells
except that only one of the four cells is functional.

The process of meiosis is extremely important in understanding genetic
inheritance. Because only one of each pair of chromosomes is found in a
functional sex cell, this means that a person contributes half of his or her
offspring's genes. The other half comes from the other parent. Usually, each
human child has a full set of 23 chromosome pairs, one of each pair from
each parent (Figure 2.7).

MENDELIAN GENETICS

Many of the facts known about genetic inheritance were discovered over a
century before the structure of DNA was known. Although people knew
where babies came from and noted the close resemblance of parents and

gene A section of DNA
that has an identifiable
structure or function.

regulatory genes
Genes that code for
the regulation of such
biological processes
as growth and
development.

mitosis The process
of replication of
chromosomes in body
cells.

meiosis The creation of
sex cells by replication
of chromosomes
followed by two cell
divisions.

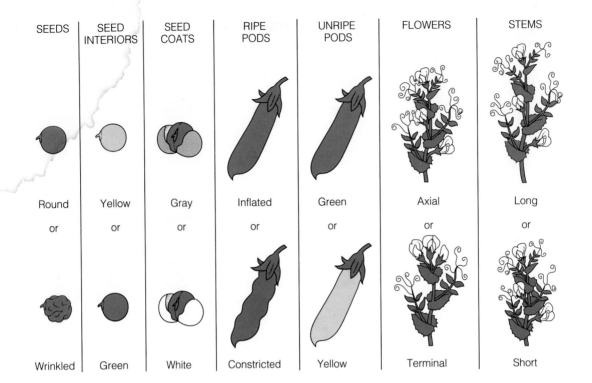

SEEDS	SEED INTERIORS	SEED COATS	RIPE PODS	UNRIPE PODS	FLOWERS	STEMS
Round	Yellow	Gray	Inflated	Green	Axial	Long
or	or	or	or	or	or	or
Wrinkled	Green	White	Constricted	Yellow	Terminal	Short

■ FIGURE 2.8
The seven phenotypic characteristics investigated by Gregor Mendel in his experiments on breeding in pea plants. Each of the seven traits has two distinct phenotypes.

children, the mechanisms of inheritance were unknown until the nineteenth century. An Austrian priest, Gregor Mendel (1822–1884), carried out an extensive series of experiments in plant breeding. His carefully tabulated results provided the basis of what we know about the mechanisms of genetic inheritance.

Before Mendel's research, it was commonly assumed that inheritance involved the blending together of genetic information in the egg and sperm. The genetic material was thought to mix together in the same way that different color paints mix together. Mendel's experiments showed a different pattern of inheritance—the genetic information is inherited in discrete units (genes). These genes do not blend together in an offspring.

In one experiment, Mendel crossed pea plants whose seeds were yellow with pea plants whose seeds were green (Figure 2.8). Under the idea of blending, one might expect all offspring to have mustard-colored seeds—a mixture of the yellow and green. In reality, Mendel found that all the offspring plants had yellow seeds. This discovery suggested that somehow one trait (yellow seed color) dominated in its effects.

When Mendel crossed the plants in this new generation together, he found that some of their offspring had yellow seeds and some had green seeds. Somehow the genetic information for green seeds had been hidden for a generation and then appeared again. Mendel counted how many there were of each color. The ratio of plants with yellow seeds to those with green seeds was very close to a 3:1 ratio. This finding suggested to Mendel that a regular process occurred during inheritance that could be explained in terms of simple mathematical principles. With these and other results, Mendel formulated several principles of inheritance. Though Mendel's work remained virtually unknown during his lifetime, his work was rediscovered in 1900. In recognition of his accomplishments, the science of genetic inheritance is called Mendelian genetics.

Genotypes and Phenotypes

The specific position of a gene on a chromosome is called a **locus** (plural **loci**). The alternative forms of a gene at a locus are called **alleles.** For example, a number of different genetic systems control the types of molecules present on the surface of red blood cells. One of these blood groups, known as the MN system, determines whether or not you have M molecules, N molecules, or both on the surface of your red blood cells. The MN system has two forms, or alleles—M and N. Another blood group system, the ABO system, has three alleles—A, B, and O. Even though three different forms of this gene are found in the human species, each individual only has two genes at the ABO locus. Some genetic loci have only one allele, some have two, and some have three or more.

MENDEL'S LAW OF SEGREGATION   The genetic basis of any trait is determined by an allele from each parent. At any given locus there are two alleles, one on each member of the chromosome pair. One allele came from the mother and one allele came from the father. Alleles occur in pairs, and when sex cells are formed, only one of each pair is passed on (**Mendel's Law of Segregation**).

The two alleles at a locus in an individual specify the **genotype,** the genetic endowment of an individual. The two alleles might be the same form or might be different. If the alleles from both parents are the same, the genotype is **homozygous.** If the alleles from the parents are different, the genotype is **heterozygous.**

The actual observable trait is known as the **phenotype.** The relationship between genotype and phenotype is affected by the relationship between the

---

locus The specific location of a gene on a chromosome.

allele The alternative form of a gene that occurs at a given locus. Some genes have only one allele, some have two, and some have many alternative forms.

Alleles occur in pairs, one on each chromosome.

Mendel's Law of Segregation Sex cells contain one of each pair of alleles.

genotype The genetic endowment of an individual from the two alleles present at a given locus.

homozygous Both alleles at a given locus are identical.

heterozygous The two alleles at a given locus are different.

phenotype The observable appearance of a given genotype in the organism.

two alleles present at any locus. If the genotype is homozygous, both alleles contain the same genetic information. What happens in heterozygotes, where the two alleles are different?

DOMINANT AND RECESSIVE ALLELES   In a heterozygote, an allele is **dominant** when it masks the effect of the other allele at a given locus. The opposite of a dominant allele is a **recessive** allele, whose effect may be masked. A simple example helps make these concepts clearer. One genetic trait in human beings is the ability to taste certain substances, including a chemical known as PTC. The ability to taste PTC appears to be controlled by a single locus and is also affected to some extent by environmental factors such as diet. There are two alleles for the PTC-tasting trait: the allele *T*, which is also called the "taster" allele, and the allele *t*, which is also called the "non-taster" allele. Given these two alleles, three combinations of alleles can be present in an individual. A person could have the *T* allele from both parents, which would give the genotype *TT*. A person could have a *t* allele from both parents, giving the genotype *tt*. Both *TT* and *tt* are homozygous genotypes because both alleles are the same. The third possible genotype occurs when the allele from one parent is *T* and the allele from the other parent is *t*. This gives the heterozygous genotype of *Tt*. It does not matter which parent provided the *T* allele and which provided the *t* allele; the genotype is the same in both cases.

What phenotype is associated with each genotype? The phenotype is affected by both the relationship of the two alleles and by the environment. For the moment, let us ignore possible environmental effects. Consider the *T* allele as providing instructions that allow tasting and the *t* allele as providing instructions for nontasting. If the genotype is *TT*, then both alleles code for tasting and the phenotype is obviously "taster." Likewise, if the genotype is *tt*, then both alleles code for nontasting and the phenotype is "nontaster." What of the heterozygote *Tt*? One allele codes for tasting and one codes for nontasting. Does this mean that both will be expressed and that a person will have the tasting ability but not to as great a degree as a person with genotype *TT*? Or does it mean that only one of the alleles is expressed? If so, which one?

There is no way you can answer this question using only the data provided so far. You must know if either the *T* or *t* allele is dominant, and this can be determined only through experimentation. For this trait, it turns out that the *T* allele is dominant and the *t* allele is recessive. When both alleles are present in a genotype, the *T* allele masks the effect of the *t* allele. Therefore, a person with the genotype *Tt* has the "taster" phenotype (Table 2.2).

The action of dominant and recessive alleles explains why Mendel's second-generation pea plants all had yellow seeds. The allele for yellow seed color is dominant, and the allele for green seed color is recessive.

Dominance and recessiveness refer only to the effect an allele has in producing a phenotype. These terms say nothing about the frequency or value of an allele. Dominant alleles can be common or rare, harmful or helpful.

■ TABLE 2.2
Genotypes and Phenotypes for PTC Tasting

GENOTYPE	PHENOTYPE
TT	Taster
Tt	Taster
tt	Nontaster

Because *T* is dominant, the genotypes *TT* and *Tt* both produce the taster phenotype. This example is oversimplified, because the phenotype can also be affected by diet.

■ TABLE 2.3
Genotypes and Phenotypes of the MN Blood Group System

GENOTYPE	PHENOTYPE
MM	M molecules
MN	M and N molecules
NN	N molecules

The *M* and *N* alleles are codominant, so they are both expressed in the heterozygote.

CODOMINANT ALLELES   Some alleles are **codominant,** meaning that when two different alleles are present in a genotype, then both are expressed. That is, neither allele is dominant or recessive. One example of a codominant genetic system in humans is the MN blood group, mentioned before. There are two alleles—M, which codes for the production of M molecules, and N, which codes for the production of N molecules. Therefore, there are three possible genotypes: MM, MN, and NN.

The phenotypes for the homozygous genotypes are easy to determine. Individuals with genotype MM have two alleles coding for the production of M molecules and will have the M molecule phenotype. Likewise, individuals with the genotype NN will have two N alleles and will have the N molecule phenotype. But what of the heterozygote genotype MN? Again, there is no way to answer this question without knowing the pattern of dominance. Experimentation has shown that the M and N alleles are codominant. When both are present (genotype MN), then both are expressed. Therefore, an individual with genotype MN will produce both M and N molecules. Their phenotype is MN, indicating the presence of both molecules (Table 2.3).

Predicting Offspring Distributions

When parents each contribute a sex cell, they are passing on only one allele at each locus to their offspring. The possible genotypes and phenotypes of the offspring reflect a 50 percent chance of transmittal for any given allele of

dominant allele An allele that masks the effect of the other allele (which is recessive) in a heterozygous genotype.

recessive allele An allele whose effect is masked by the other allele (which is dominant) in a heterozygous genotype.

codominant When both alleles affect the phenotype of a heterozygous genotype and neither is dominant over the other.

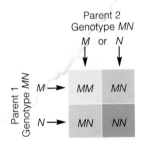

Parent 2
Genotype *MN*

M or N

Parent 1
Genotype *MN*

M → | MM | MN |
N → | MN | NN |

■ FIGURE 2.9
Inheritance of MN blood
group phenotypes for two
parents, both with *MN*
genotype.

a parent. This simple statement of probability allows prediction of the likely distribution of genotypes and phenotypes among the offspring.

Figure 2.9 illustrates this method using the MN blood group system for two hypothetical parents, each with the genotype MN. Each parent has a 50 percent chance of passing on an M allele and a 50 percent chance of passing on an N allele. Given these probabilities, we expect one out of four offspring (25 percent) to have genotype MM, and therefore phenotype M. In two out of four cases (50 percent), we expect the offspring to have genotype MN, and therefore phenotype MN. Finally, in one out of four cases (25 percent), we expect the offspring to have genotype NN, and therefore phenotype N. Of course, different parental genotypes will give a different set of offspring probabilities.

Remember that these distributions give the expected probabilities. The exact distributions will not always occur because each offspring is an independent event. If the hypothetical couple first has a child with the genotype MN, this will not influence the genotype of their next child. The distributions give the proportions expected for a very large number of offspring.

Analysis of possible offspring shows that recessive alleles can produce an interesting effect; it is possible for children to have a different phenotype from either of the parents. For example, consider two parents, both with the genotype *Tt* for the PTC-tasting locus. Both parents have the "taster" phenotype. What genotypes and phenotypes will their children be likely to have? The expected genotype distribution is 25 percent *TT*, 50 percent *Tt*, and 25 percent *tt*.

Given this distribution of genotypes, what is the probable distribution of phenotypes? Genotypes *TT* and *Tt* are both "tasters," and therefore 75 percent of the children are expected to also be "tasters." Twenty-five percent of the children, however, are expected to have the genotype *tt* and will therefore have the "nontaster" phenotype. These children would have a different phenotype from either parent. A recessive trait, then, can remain hidden in one generation.

Chromosomes and Inheritance

Alleles occur in pairs. Mendel showed that when alleles are passed on from parents to offspring, only one of each pair is contributed by each parent. The specific chromosome at any pair that is passed on is random. There is a 50 percent chance of either chromosome being passed on each time a sex cell is created.

MENDEL'S LAW OF INDEPENDENT ASSORTMENT   Mendel's experiments revealed another aspect of probability in inheritance and the creation of sex cells. **Mendel's Law of Independent Assortment** states that the segregation of any pair of chromosomes does not influence the segregation of any other pair of chromosomes. In other words, chromosomes from separate pairs are inherited independently.

Independent assortment provides a powerful mechanism for shuffling different combinations of chromosomes and thus introduces great potential for genetic diversity. In humans, who have 23 chromosome pairs, the number are even more impressive. From any given individual, there are $2^{23} = 8,388,608$ possible combinations of sex cells. This means that two parents could produce a maximum of 70,368,744,177,664 genetically unique offspring!

LINKAGE A major implication of Mendel's Law of Independent Assortment is that genes are inherited independently. This is true only to the extent that genes are on different chromosomes. Remember, it is the pairs of chromosomes that separate during meiosis, not each individual pair of alleles. When alleles are on the same chromosome, they are inherited together. This is called **linkage.** Linked alleles are not inherited independently because they are, by definition, on the same chromosome.

CROSSING OVER An exception to the rule of linkage is **crossing over,** the switching of segments of DNA between the chromosome pairs during meiosis. Suppose, for example, that there are two genetic loci on the same chromosome, the first having alleles A or a and the second having alleles B or b. Suppose that you have the genotypes Aa and Bb, with one chromosome containing the A allele and the B allele, and the other chromosome having the a allele and the b allele. Because these two loci are both on the same chromosome, you would expect linkage to cause the two systems to be inherited together. That is, your possible sex cells would have A and B, or a and b. Any offspring inheriting the A allele would also be expected to inherit the B allele. Likewise, any offspring inheriting the a allele would also inherit the b allele. During meiosis, chromosome pairs sometimes exchange pieces, a process known as crossing over. For example, the segment of DNA containing the a allele could switch with the segment of DNA containing the A allele on the other chromosome. Therefore, you could have a sex cell with a and B, or a sex cell with A and b (Figure 2.10). Crossing over does not change the genetic material. The alleles are still the same, but they can occur in different combinations. Crossing over provides yet another mechanism for increasing genetic variation by providing new combinations of alleles.

SEX CHROMOSOMES AND SEX DETERMINATION One of the 23 pairs of human chromosomes is called the sex chromosome pair because these chromosomes

---

Mendel's Law of Independent Assortment The segregation of any pair of chromosomes does not affect the probability of segregation for other pairs of chromosomes.

linkage When alleles on the same chromosome are inherited together.

crossing over When segments of DNA switch between pairs of chromosomes.

■ FIGURE 2.10
Crossing over in
chromosomes.

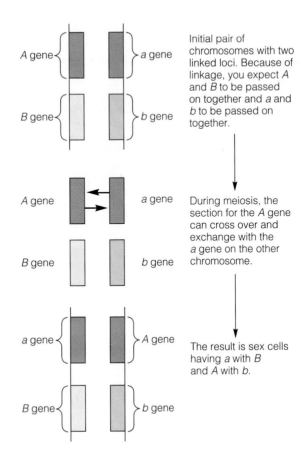

A gene — a gene

B gene — b gene

Initial pair of chromosomes with two linked loci. Because of linkage, you expect A and B to be passed on together and a and b to be passed on together.

A gene — a gene

B gene — b gene

During meiosis, the section for the A gene can cross over and exchange with the a gene on the other chromosome.

a gene — A gene

B gene — b gene

The result is sex cells having a with B and A with b.

contain the genetic information determining the individual's sex. There are two forms of sex chromosomes, X and Y. Females have two X chromosomes (XX), and males have one X and one Y chromosome (XY).

The Y chromosome is much smaller than the X chromosome. Almost all genes found on X are therefore not found on Y. This means that males possess only one allele for certain traits because their Y chromosome lacks the corresponding section of DNA. Therefore, males will manifest a trait given only one allele, whereas females require the same allele from both parents to show the trait.

The Genetics of Complex Physical Traits

The discussion of genetics thus far has focused on simple discrete genetic traits. Traits such as the MN blood group are genetically "simple" because they result from the action of a single locus with a clear-cut mode of inheritance. These traits are also discrete, meaning that they produce a finite number of phenotypes.

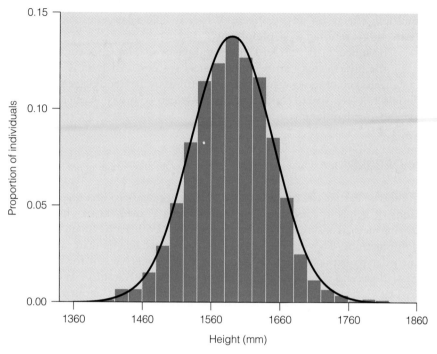

Height (mm)

■ FIGURE 2.11
The distribution of a normally
distributed continuous trait.
This figure is based on the
actual distribution of height
(mm) of 1,986 Irish women
(author's unpublished data).
The height of the curve
represents the proportion of
women with any given height.
Most individuals have a value
close to the average for the
population (the highest
point on the curve, which
corresponds to a height of
1,589 mm). The solid line
is the fit of the normal
distribution.

These simple discrete traits are very useful for demonstrating the basic principles of Mendelian inheritance. It is not wise, however, to think of all biological traits as resulting from a single locus, exhibiting a finite number of phenotypes, or not being affected by the environment. Many of the characteristics of interest in human evolution, such as skin color, body size, brain size, and intelligence, do not fall into this simple category. Such traits have a complex mode of inheritance in that one or more genes may contribute to the phenotype and they may be affected by the environment. The combined action of genetics and environment produces traits with a continuous distribution. An example is human height. People do not come in three different heights (short, medium, and tall), nor five, nor twenty. Height can take on an infinite number of phenotypes. People can be 1,700 mm tall, 1701 mm tall, and any value in between, such as 1,700.3 mm or 1,700.65 mm.

Complex traits tend to produce more individuals with average values than extreme values. It is not uncommon to find human males between 1,676 and 1,981 mm (5.5 and 6.5 feet) tall. It is much rarer to find someone taller than 2,134 mm (7 feet). A typical distribution of a complex trait, human height, is shown in Figure 2.11.

Many complex traits are **polygenic,** the result of two or more loci. When several loci act to control a trait, many different genotypes and phenotypes can result. A number of physical characteristics, such as human skin color and height, may be polygenic. A single allele can also have

polygenic Refers to a genetic trait affected by two or more loci.

multiple effects on an organism. When an allele has effects on multiple traits, this is referred to as **pleiotropy.**

The concepts of polygenic traits and pleiotropy are important in considering the interrelated nature of biological systems. Analysis of simple discrete traits on a gene-by-gene basis is useful in understanding genetics, but it should not lead you to think that any organism is simply a collection of single, independent loci.

MUTATIONS

As shown earlier, the process of genetic inheritance produces new combinations of genes in offspring. The independent assortment of chromosomes during meiosis and the action of crossing over both act to create new genetic combinations. They do not act to create any new genetic material, however. In order to explain past evolution, we need a mechanism for introducing new alleles and variation. The origin of new genetic variation was a problem to Darwin, but we now know new alleles are brought about through the process of mutation.

Evolutionary Significance of Mutations

A **mutation** is a change in the genetic code. Mutations are the ultimate source of all genetic variation. Mutations are caused by a number of environmental factors such as background radiation, which includes radiation from the earth's crust and cosmic rays. Such background radiation is all around us, in the air we breathe and the food we eat. Mutations may also be caused by heat and ingested substances such as caffeine.

Mutations can take place in any cell of the body. To have evolutionary importance, however, the mutation must occur in a sex cell. A mutation in a skin cell on the end of your finger has no evolutionary significance because it will not be passed on to your offspring.

Mutations are random. That is, there is no way of predicting when a specific mutation will take place or what, if any, phenotypic effect it will have. All we can do is estimate the probability of a mutation occurring at a given locus over a given amount of time. The randomness of mutations also means that mutations do not appear when they might be needed. Many mosquitoes have adapted to insecticides because a mutation was present in the population that acted to confer some resistance to the insecticide. If that mutation had not been present, the mosquitoes would have died. The mosquitoes' need for a certain genetic variant had no effect on whether or not the mutation appeared.

Mutations can have different effects depending on the specific type of mutation and the environment. The conventional view of mutations has long been that they are mostly harmful. Some mutations, however, are advantageous. They lead to change that improves the survival and reproduction of organisms. In recent decades, we have also discovered that some mutations are neutral. That is, the genetic change has no detectable effect on survival or reproduction.

Whether or not a mutation is neutral, advantageous, or disadvantageous depends in large part on the environment. Genetic variants that are harmful in certain environments might actually be helpful in other environments.

Types of Mutations

We now recognize that there are a variety of ways in which mutations occur (Marks 1995). Mutations can involve changes in a single DNA base, in larger sections of DNA, and in entire chromosomes. Substitution of one base for another is only one type of mutation. Mutations can also involve the addition or deletion of a base, or of large sections of DNA. In these cases, the genetic message is changed. Also, sections of DNA can be duplicated or moved from one place to another, and sections of DNA can be added or lost when crossing over is not equal.

The genetic information contained in the chromosomes can also be altered by the deletion or duplication of part or all of the chromosome. For example, an entire chromosome from a pair can be lost (**monosomy** = one chromosome) or can occur in duplicate, giving three chromosomes (**trisomy**). One result of the latter is Down syndrome, a condition characterized by certain cranial features (Figure 2.12), poor physical growth, and mental retardation (usually mild). Down syndrome is caused by the duplication of one of the 21st chromosome pair. Affected individuals have a total of 47 chromosomes, one more than the normal 46. Down syndrome can also be caused by mutations of the 21st chromosome. In some individuals the change involves the exchange of parts of the 21st chromosome with other chromosomes.

Rates of Mutations

Specific mutations are relatively rare events, although the *exact* rate of mutations is difficult to determine in many cases. Part of the problem in determining the rate of mutations is the fact that several different base sequences

■ **FIGURE 2.12**
Facial appearance of a child with Down syndrome.
(Courtesy March of Dimes Birth Defects Foundation)

---

pleiotropy When a single allele can have multiple effects on an organism.

mutation A mechanism for evolutionary change resulting from a random change in the genetic code; the ultimate source of all genetic variation.

monosomy When only one chromosome rather than a pair is present in body cells.

trisomy When three chromosomes rather than a pair occur in body cells.

can specify the same amino acid. If there is no observable change, then the mutation will usually go unnoticed. A mutation is also more apparent if it involves a dominant allele.

Another problem in identifying mutations is that harmful mutations may result in spontaneous abortion (miscarriage) before pregnancy has been detected. Some researchers feel that a large number of unrecognized conceptions are expelled spontaneously during the first few weeks after conception. If so, any prediction of mutation rates based on recognized conceptions will be an underestimate.

Despite these problems, research has provided estimates of a range in the rates of mutation. For single-base mutations in humans, this range is from 1 to 100 mutations per million sex cells (Lerner and Libby 1976). This translates to a probability between 0.000001 and 0.0001 of a mutation occurring at a given locus for a given sex cell.

Regardless of the specific mutation rates for a given gene or chromosome, one thing is clear—mutation rates are generally low. Given these low probabilities, it may be tempting to regard mutation as so rare that it has no special evolutionary significance. The problem with this reasoning is that the estimated rates refer to a *single* specific locus. Human chromosomes have many loci. The exact number is not known, but it has been estimated at roughly 100,000 (Woodward 1992). The probability that a specific locus will show a mutation in any individual is low, but the probability of *any* locus showing a mutation is much higher.

SUMMARY

The DNA molecule specifies the genetic code or set of instructions needed to produce biological structures. DNA acts along with a related molecule, RNA, to translate these instructions into proteins. The DNA is contained along structures within the cell called chromosomes. Chromosomes come in pairs. A segment of DNA that codes for a certain product is called a gene. The different forms of genes present at a locus are called alleles. The DNA molecule has the ability to make copies of itself, allowing transmission of genetic information from cell to cell, and from generation to generation.

Meiosis is the process of sex cell formation that results in one of each chromosome pair being transmitted from parent to offspring. Each individual receives half of his or her alleles from each parent. The two alleles together specify the genetic constitution of an individual—the genotype. The physical manifestation of the genotype is known as the phenotype. The relationship between genotype and phenotype depends on whether an allele is dominant, recessive, or codominant. In complex physical traits, the phenotype is the result of the combined effect of genetics and environment.

The ultimate source of all genetic variation is mutation—a random change in the genetic code. Some mutations are neutral in effect; others are helpful or harmful. The effect of any mutation often depends on the specific environmental conditions. Mutations for any given allele are relatively rare events, but given the large number of loci in many organisms, it is highly probable that each individual has at least one mutant allele.

SUPPLEMENTAL READINGS

Marks, J. 1995. *Human Biodiversity: Genes, Race, and History.* New York: Aldine de Gruyter. A historically oriented review of different approaches to human biological variation, with many discussions of the nature of genes and the mechanisms of human genetics.

Woodward, V. 1992. *Human Heredity and Society.* St. Paul, Minn.: West. A well-written introduction to molecular and Mendelian genetics that focuses on humans.

CELL BIOLOGY:
A Review

This section, which focuses on the structure of the cell and on the processes of mitosis and meiosis, can be used as a supplement for students wishing to review the basic biology necessary for an understanding of the fundamental principles of Mendelian genetics.

THE CELL

All living creatures are made up of cells. Humans, like many organisms, are multicelled. Figure 2.13 shows some of the components of a typical cell. Two major structures are the *nucleus* and the *cytoplasm*; the latter contains a number of other structures. The entire body of the cell is enclosed by a *cell membrane*.

Within the cytoplasm, *mitochondria* convert some cellular material into energy that is then used for cellular activity (see Chapter 9 for further discussion). *Ribosomes* are small particles that are frequently attached to a larger structure known as the *endoplasmic reticulum*. Composed of RNA and proteins, ribosomes serve as sites for the manufacture of proteins.

As discussed in Chapter 2, the DNA sequences that make up the genetic code are bound together by proteins in long strands known as *chromosomes*. In body cells, chromosomes come in pairs and humans have 23 pairs of chromosomes. The chromosomes within the nucleus of the cell contain all of the DNA, with the exception of something called mitochondrial DNA (see Chapter 9).

MITOSIS

DNA has the ability to make copies of itself. This ability is vital for transmitting genetic information from cell to cell and for transmitting genetic information from generation to generation. The replication of DNA is part of the process of cell replication. We will examine two basic processes: mitosis, the replication of body cells, and meiosis, the replication of sex cells.

Mitosis produces two identical body cells from one original. Between cell divisions, each chromosome produces an exact copy of itself, resulting in two

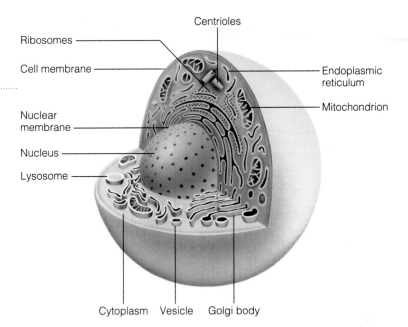

Ribosomes

Cell membrane

Nuclear
membrane

Nucleus

Lysosome

Centrioles

Endoplasmic
reticulum

Mitochondrion

Cytoplasm   Vesicle   Golgi body

the spindle fibers attach to the centromeres. During *anaphase*, the centromere divides and the two strands of chromatids (original and duplicate) split and move toward opposite ends of the cell. During *telophase*, new nuclear membranes form around each of the two clusters of chromosomes. Finally, the cell membrane pinches in the middle, creating two identical cells.

MEIOSIS

Meiosis, the production of sex cells (gametes), differs from mitosis in several ways. The main difference is that sex cells contain only half of an organism's DNA—one chromosome from each pair. Thus, when a new zygote, or fertilized egg, is formed from the joining of egg and sperm, the offspring will have 23 chromosome pairs. One of each pair comes from the mother and one of each pair comes from the father.

Meiosis involves two cycles of cell division (see Figure 2.15). The total sequence of events following the initial duplication of

pairs with two chromosomes each. When a cell divides, each part contains one of each of the pairs of chromosomes. Thus, two identical body cells, each with the full number of chromosome pairs, is produced. As outlined in Figure 2.14, five stages compose the process of mitosis: interphase, prophase, metaphase, anaphase, and telophase. (Some people do not refer to interphase as a stage.)

During *interphase*, the chromosomes that are dispersed throughout the nucleus duplicate. During *prophase*, the chromosomes, each of which

is attached to its copy, become tightly coiled and move toward one another in the nucleus. Each of the two copies is called a *chromatid* and their point of attachment is called the *centromere*. Small structures located outside the nuclear membrane, known as *centrioles* (see Figure 2.13), move toward opposite ends of the cell and *spindle fibers* form between the centrioles. The nuclear membrane then dissolves.

During *metaphase*, the duplicated chromosomes line up along the middle of the cell and

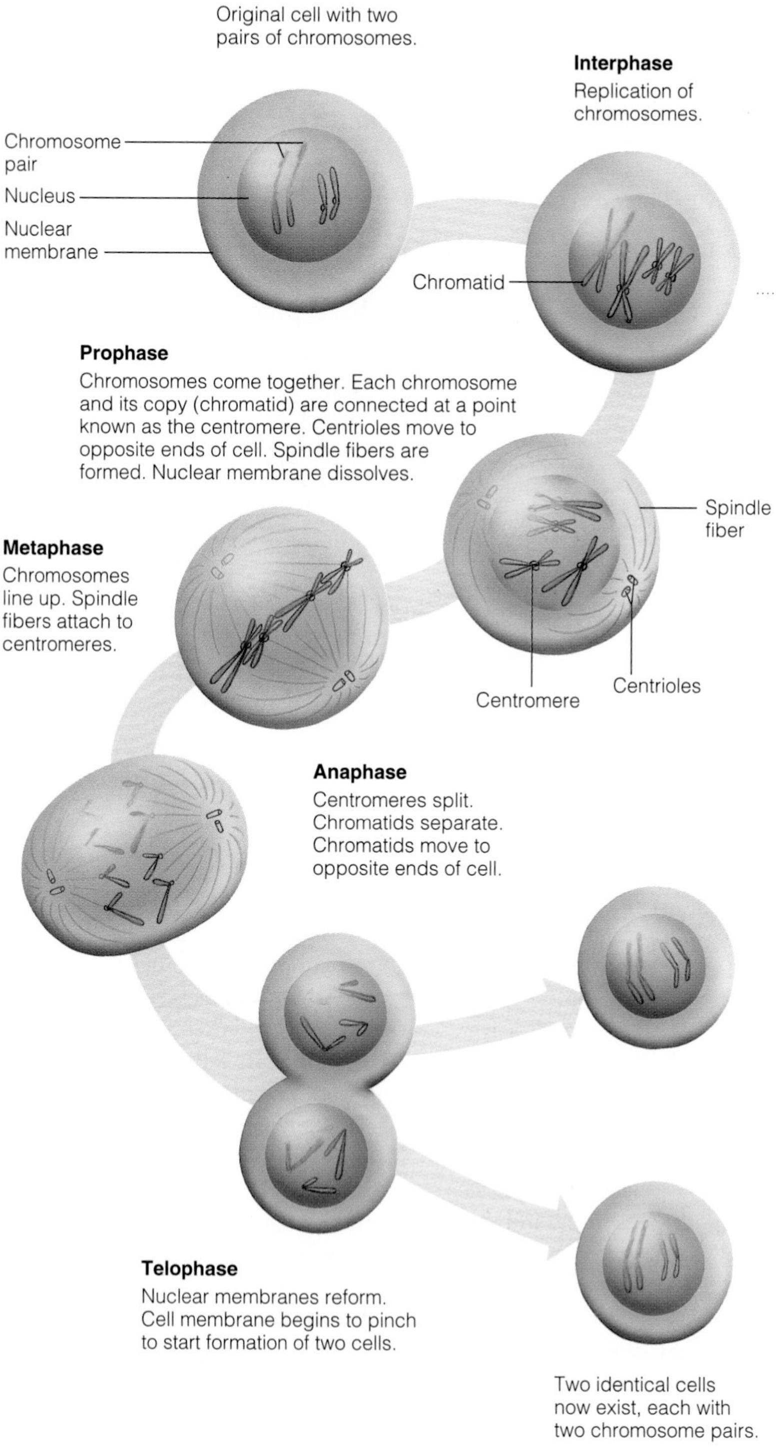

Original cell with two
pairs of chromosomes.

Interphase
Replication of
chromosomes.

Chromosome
pair

Nucleus

Nuclear
membrane

Chromatid

■ **FIGURE 2.14**

■ **FIGURE 2.14**
The five phases of mitosis. In
this example, the original
body cell contains two pairs
of chromosomes. Mitosis
produces two identical body
cells, each containing two
chromosome pairs (a total of
four chromosomes each).

Prophase
Chromosomes come together. Each chromosome
and its copy (chromatid) are connected at a point
known as the centromere. Centrioles move to
opposite ends of cell. Spindle fibers are
formed. Nuclear membrane dissolves.

Metaphase
Chromosomes
line up. Spindle
fibers attach to
centromeres.

Spindle
fiber

Centromere

Centrioles

Anaphase
Centromeres split.
Chromatids separate.
Chromatids move to
opposite ends of cell.

Telophase
Nuclear membranes reform.
Cell membrane begins to pinch
to start formation of two cells.

Two identical cells
now exist, each with
two chromosome pairs.

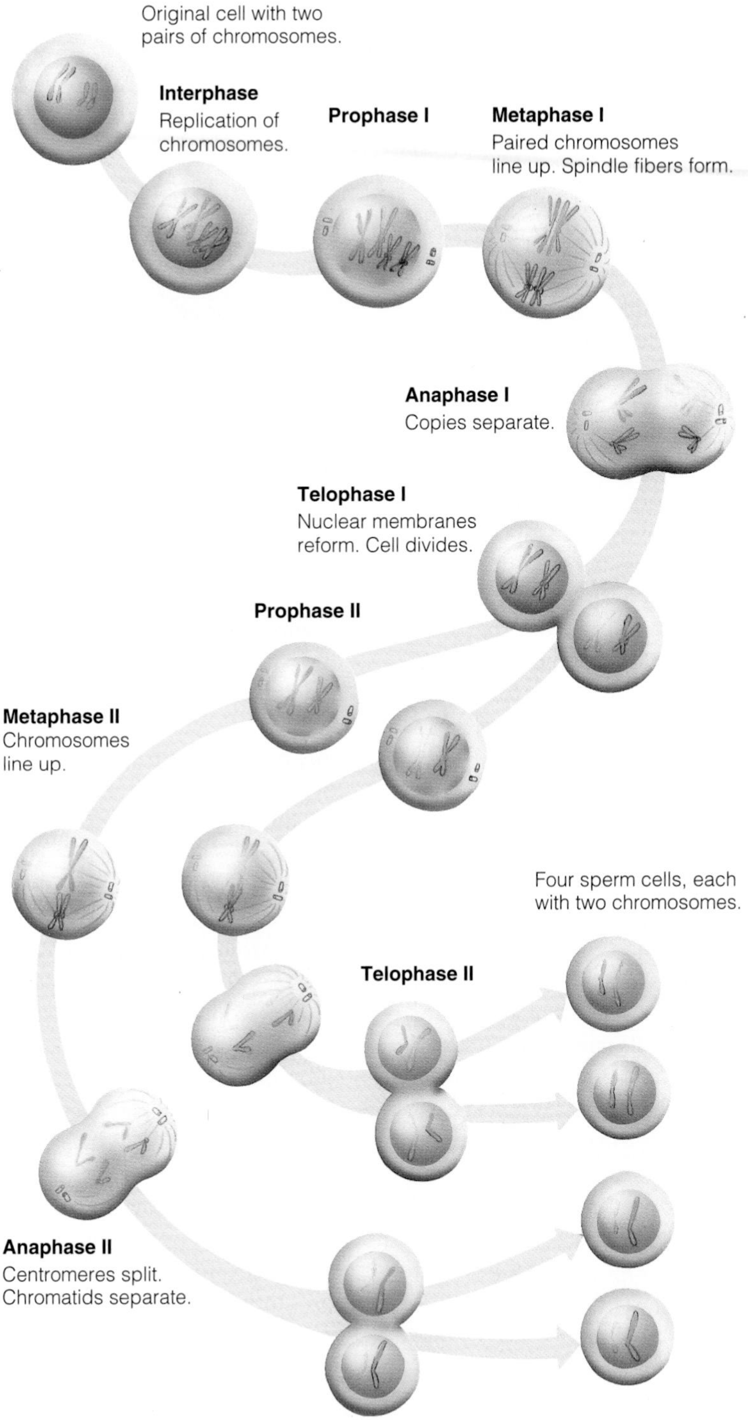

Original cell with two
pairs of chromosomes.

Interphase
Replication of
chromosomes.

Prophase I

Metaphase I
Paired chromosomes
line up. Spindle fibers form.

Anaphase I
Copies separate.

Telophase I
Nuclear membranes
reform. Cell divides.

Prophase II

Metaphase II
Chromosomes
line up.

Four sperm cells, each
with two chromosomes.

Telophase II

Anaphase II
Centromeres split.
Chromatids separate.

■ FIGURE 2.15
The phases of meiosis for a
sperm cell. In this example,
the original cell contained
two chromosome pairs. As a
result of meiosis, four sperm
cells were produced, each
with two chromosomes. The
process is similar for egg
cells, except that one egg cell
and three polar bodies are
produced.

chromosomes (interphase) involves eight stages: prophase I, metaphase I, anaphase I, telophase I, prophase II, metaphase II, anaphase II, and telophase II. Figure 2.15 presents a diagram of this process for the production of sperm cells, for a hypothetical organism with two chromosome pairs. Each of the two pairs of chromosomes has replicated itself by the start of prophase I, leading to eight chromatids: the two chromosomes of each pair duplicate, giving a total of $2 \times 2 \times 2 = 8$ chromatids, each pair of which attaches to one of the centromeres through a process known as *synapsis*. At the end of prophase I the nuclear membrane dissolves. Then, during metaphase I, the paired chromosomes line up and spindle fibers form. The copies separate during anaphase I. During telophase I, the nuclear membranes reform and the cell divides. The realization of two cells, each containing eight chromatids, constitutes prophase II. During metaphase II, the chromosomes line up, after which the centromeres split and the chromatids sepa-

rate, completing anaphase II. The nuclear membranes reform during telophase II, and the cell divides. The net result of this sequence of two cell divisions is four sperm cells, each with two chromosomes—half of the genetic material of the father. The process is similar for the production of egg cells from the female, except that the net result is one egg cell and three structures known as *polar bodies* that do not function as sex cells.

Meiosis thus allows half of a parent's genetic material to be passed on to the next generation. When a sperm cell fertilizes an egg cell, the total number of chromosomes is restored. For humans, the resulting zygote contains $23 + 23 = 46$ chromosomes, or 23 chromosome pairs.

Sex cells may also contain genetic combinations not present in the parent. When synapsis occurs during prophase I, and the chromosomes pair with their copies, becoming attached to one another at several places, the potential exists for genetic material to be exchanged, a process known as *crossing over*.

The resulting genetic combinations allow for variation in each sex cell from its source.

Independent assortment also enhances genetic variability. As discussed in Chapter 2, according to this principle, the segregation of any pair of chromosomes does not affect the probability of segregation of any other pair of chromosomes. If you had two chromosome pairs, A and B, with two chromosomes each (A1 and A2, and B1 and B2), only one of each pair will be found in any sex cell. However, you might have one sex cell with A1 and B1 and another sex cell with A1 and B2. Whichever member of the first pair of chromosomes is found in any given sex cell has no bearing on whichever member of the second pair is also found in that sex cell. Independent assortment results from processes occurring during metaphase I. When the paired chromosomes line up, they do so at random and are not influenced by whether they originally came from the person's mother or father. This process allows for tremendous genetic variability in potential offspring.

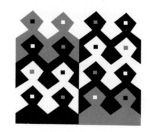

Evolutionary Theory

CHAPTER **3**

Biological evolution is genetic change through time and can be studied at two different levels. Microevolution consists of changes in the frequency of alleles in a population from one generation to the next. Macroevolution comprises long-term patterns of genetic change over thousands and millions of generations as well as the process of species formation.

MICROEVOLUTION

Microevolution takes into account changes in the frequency of alleles from one generation to the next. The focus is generally not on the specific genotypes or phenotypes of individuals, but rather on the total pattern of an entire biological population. We are interested in defining the relative frequencies of different alleles, genotypes, and phenotypes for the entire population being studied. We then seek to determine if any apparent change in these frequencies has occurred over time. If changes have occurred, we try to explain them.

Population Genetics

The term **breeding population** is used frequently in evolutionary theory. In an abstract sense, a breeding population is a group of organisms that tends to choose mates from within the group. This definition is a bit tricky because it is not clear what proportion of mating within a group defines a breeding population.

For example, suppose you travel to a village in a remote mountain region. You find that 99 percent of all the people in the village are married to others who were born in the same village. In this case, the village would appear to fit our ideal definition. But, what if only 80 percent of the people choose their mates from within the village? What if the number were 50 percent? At what point do you stop referring to the population as a "breeding population"? There is no quick and ready answer to this question.

On a practical level, human populations are initially most often defined on the basis of geographic and political boundaries. A small isolated island, for example, easily fits the requirements of a defined population. In most cases, the local geographic unit (such as town or village) is used. Care must be taken, however, to ensure that a local geographic unit, such as a town, is not composed of distinct subpopulations, such as groups belonging to different religious sects.

Once a population has been defined, the next step in microevolutionary analysis is to determine the frequencies of genotypes and alleles within the population.

GENOTYPE AND ALLELE FREQUENCIES The genotype frequency is a measure of the relative proportions of different genotypes within a population. Likewise, an allele frequency is simply a measure of the relative proportion of alleles within a population. Genotype frequencies are obtained by dividing the number of individuals with each genotype by the total number of individuals. For example, consider a hypothetical population of 200 people for the MN blood group system where there are 98 people with genotype MM, 84 people with genotype MN, and 18 people with genotype NN. The genotype frequencies are therefore:

Frequency of MM = 98/200 = 0.49

Frequency of MN = 84/200 = 0.42

Frequency of NN = 18/200 = 0.09

Note that the total frequency of all genotypes adds up to 1 (0.49 + 0.42 + 0.09 = 1).

■ TABLE 3.1
Example of Allele Frequency Computation

Imagine you have just collected information on *MN* blood group genotypes for 250 humans in a given population. Your data are:

Number of *MM* genotype = 40
Number of *MN* genotype = 120
Number of *NN* genotype = 90

The allele frequencies are computed as follows:

GENOTYPE	NUMBER OF PEOPLE	TOTAL NUMBER OF ALLELES	NUMBER OF M ALLELES	NUMBER OF N ALLELES
MM	40	80	80	0
MN	120	240	120	120
NN	90	180	0	180
Total	250	500	200	300

The relative frequency of the *M* allele is computed as the number of *M* alleles divided by the total number of alleles: 200/500 = 0.4.

The relative frequency of the *N* allele is computed as the number of *N* alleles divided by the total number of alleles: 300/500 = 0.6.

As a check, note that the relative frequencies of the alleles must add up to 1.0 (0.4 + 0.6 = 1.0).

Allele frequencies are computed by counting the number of each allele and dividing that number by the total number of alleles. An example of allele frequency computation is given in Table 3.1.

HARDY-WEINBERG EQUILIBRIUM   The mathematical basis of microevolutionary theory rests upon Mendel's principles and the use of a model known as **Hardy-Weinberg equilibrium.** This model provides a method of predicting genotype frequencies in future generations under the assumption that mating is at random and that no evolution takes place.

The Hardy-Weinberg equilibrium model is a mathematical statement using symbols to represent allele frequencies. Many microevolutionary models assume a single locus with two alleles (e.g., A and a). By convention, the symbols p and q are used to represent the frequencies of the A allele and the a allele, respectively. These symbols are a form of shorthand because it is easier to say p than "the frequency of the A allele."

The Hardy-Weinberg equilibrium model states that given allele frequencies of p and q, the expected genotype frequencies are:

Frequency of $AA = p^2$

Frequency of $Aa = 2pq$

Frequency of $aa = q^2$

breeding population A group of organisms that tend to choose mates from within the group.

Hardy-Weinberg equilibrium In the absence of evolutionary forces, allele frequencies remain constant from one generation to the next.

■ FIGURE 3.1

Inbreeding is used with many domesticated animals to produce certain types of characteristics. (Courtesy of Kenneth Feder, Central Connecticut State University)

Assume a population with two alleles (A and a) with allele frequencies of $p = 0.6$ and $q = 0.4$. Using the Hardy-Weinberg equilibrium model, the predicted genotype frequencies are:

$$AA = (0.6)^2 = (0.6)(0.6) = 0.36$$
$$Aa = 2(0.6)(0.4) \qquad = 0.48$$
$$aa = (0.4)^2 = (0.4)(0.4) = 0.16$$

The Hardy-Weinberg equilibrium model can also be used to show that, given certain assumptions, there will be no change in allele frequency from one generation to the next.

The Hardy-Weinberg equilibrium model makes several assumptions. It assumes random mating within the population (with respect to the locus or loci of interest). That is, every individual has an equal chance of mating with any individual of the opposite sex (both sexes are also assumed to have equal allele frequencies). The Hardy-Weinberg equilibrium model also assumes that the population is large enough that there is no variation in allele frequencies caused by sampling (no genetic drift); there is no movement into or out of the population (no gene flow); there are no new alleles (no mutation); and there is no difference in the fertility or mortality of different genotypes (no natural selection). If we compare the expected genotype frequencies with those actually observed and find no difference, then we can conclude that the population is in Hardy-Weinberg equilibrium. If the predicted and observed genotype frequencies are not the same, then the population is not in Hardy-Weinberg equilibrium, and we know that at least one of the assumptions must be incorrect. That is, we know that nonrandom mating, genetic drift, gene flow, mutation, natural selection, or some combination of these factors is present. Further analysis would then be needed to determine which of these assumptions was incorrect.

There are two basic reasons a population might not be in a state of Hardy-Weinberg equilibrium. Observed and predicted genotype frequencies may differ because of the effects of evolutionary forces and/or nonrandom mating. **Evolutionary forces** are those mechanisms that actually lead to a change in allele frequency over time. The evolutionary forces are mutation, natural selection, genetic drift, and gene flow (described in detail in the following section). These four forces are the only mechanisms that can cause the frequency of an allele to change over time.

Random mating is one form of mating system. **Nonrandom mating,** however, refers to the patterns of mate choice within a population and to its genetic consequences. Nonrandom mating includes **inbreeding,** the mating of biologically related individuals (Figure 3.1), and **assortative mating,** mating on the basis of phenotypic similarity or dissimilarity. Mating systems do not change allele frequencies, but they do have an effect on the *rate* of allele frequency change.

Evolutionary Forces

MUTATION Mutation introduces new alleles into a population. Therefore, the frequency of different alleles will change over time. For example, consider a genetic locus with a single allele, A, for a population of 100 people (and therefore 200 alleles, because each person has two alleles). Everyone in the population will have genotype AA, and the frequency of the A allele is 1.0 (100 percent). Now, assume that one of the A alleles being passed on to the next generation changes into a new form, a. Assuming the population stays the same size (to make the mathematics a bit easier), there will be 199 A alleles and 1 a allele in the next generation. The frequency of A will have changed from 1.0 to 0.995 (199/200), and the frequency of a will have changed from 0.0 to 0.005 (1/200).

If there is no further evolutionary change, the allele frequencies will remain the same in future generations. If this mutation continues to recur, the frequency of the a allele will slowly increase, assuming no other evolutionary forces are operating. For typical mutation rates, such a process would take a very long time.

Although mutations are vital to evolution because they provide new variations, mutation rates are low and do not lead, by themselves, to major changes in allele frequency. The other evolutionary forces increase or decrease the frequencies of mutant alleles.

NATURAL SELECTION As discussed in Chapter 1, natural selection filters genetic variation. Individuals with certain biological characteristics that allow them to survive to reproduce, pass on the alleles for such characteristics to the next generation. Natural selection does not create new genetic variation (only mutation can do that), but it does change the relative frequencies of different alleles.

The analysis of natural selection focuses on **fitness,** the probability of survival and reproduction of an organism. For any locus, fitness is measured as the relative genetic contribution of a genotype to the next generation. Imagine a locus with two alleles, A and a, and the genotypes AA, Aa, and aa. If all individuals with genotypes AA and Aa survive and reproduce but only half of those with genotypes aa survive and reproduce, then the fitness

---

evolutionary forces
Four mechanisms that can cause changes in allele frequencies from one generation to the next.

nonrandom mating
Patterns of mate choice that influence the distributions of genotype and phenotype frequencies.

inbreeding Mating between biologically related individuals.

assortative mating
Mating between phenotypically similar or dissimilar individuals.

fitness An organism's probability of survival and reproduction.

■ TABLE 3.2
Example of Natural Selection against a Recessive Homozygote

This example uses an initial population size before selection of 200 people. The locus has two alleles, *A* and *a*. Initially there are 50 people with genotype *AA*, 100 people with genotype *Aa*, and 50 people with genotype *aa*. The allele frequencies before selection are therefore 0.5 for *A* and 0.5 for *a*. The fitness values have been chosen to illustrate total selection against the recessive homozygote.

	GENOTYPE			
	AA	*Aa*	*aa*	TOTAL
Number of people before selection	50	100	50	200
Fitness (percentage that survives)	100%	100%	0%	
Number of people after selection	50	100	0	150

There are 150 people after selection. Using the method of allele frequency computation shown in Table 3.1 and in the text, the allele frequencies after selection are 200/300 = 0.667 for the *A* allele and 100/300 = 0.333 for the *a* allele.

of genotype *aa* is half of that of genotypes *AA* and *Aa*. Fitness refers to the proportion of individuals with a given phenotype who survive and reproduce.

As an example, consider what happens when one allele is dominant and one is recessive. Let A be the dominant allele and a be the recessive allele. Based on what you learned in Chapter 2, the genotypes AA and Aa will both give rise to the same phenotype because A is dominant. Because AA and Aa specify the same phenotype, they have the same fitness. For this hypothetical example, let us assume that the fitness of AA and Aa is 100 percent. That is, all individuals with these genotypes survive and reproduce in equal numbers. Now, let us further assume that the fitness of people with the recessive phenotype (those with the genotype *aa*) have a fitness of 0 percent. That is, no one with this genotype will survive and reproduce. This hypothetical example corresponds to a situation where a recessive allele (*a*) is fatal for those who have two copies (*aa*). Now, assume a population of 200 people before selection with the following distribution of genotypes: AA = 50, Aa = 100, aa = 50. Using the methods discussed earlier, the allele frequencies can be found: the frequency of A is 0.5, and the frequency of *a* is 0.5.

Table 3.2 shows the process of natural selection using these hypothetical numbers. After selection, the number of individuals in each genotype is: AA = 50, Aa = 100, aa = 0. All individuals with genotypes AA and Aa sur-

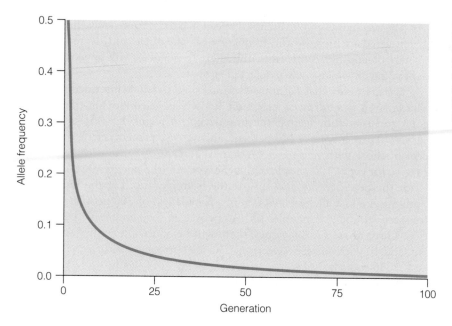

■ FIGURE 3.2
Change over time in the frequency of a recessive allele when there is complete selection against the recessive homozygote, and the initial allele frequency is 0.5.

vive, and none of those with genotype aa survive. After selection, there are 150 individuals, and the allele frequencies are $A = 0.6667$ and $a = 0.3333$.

This example shows the effect of selection against a recessive allele. The frequency of the a allele drops from 0.5 to 0.3333. Because a is a harmful allele, however, you might expect that the a allele would be totally eliminated. This does not occur. Because the heterozygote (Aa) is not eliminated through selection, these individuals continue to pass the a allele on to the next generation. The recessive allele a cannot be eliminated in a single generation. Figure 3.2 shows the continued effects of natural selection for two generations.

A case of selection against recessive homozygotes in humans is Tay-Sachs disease. This affliction is caused by a metabolic disorder that results in blindness, mental retardation, and the destruction of the central nervous system. Children with Tay-Sachs disease generally die within the first few years of life. The disease is caused by a recessive allele and occurs in those individuals who are homozygous. Heterozygotes carry the allele but do not show any major biological impairments.

When deleterious alleles are recessive, such as with Tay-Sachs disease, the frequency is generally not zero, because heterozygotes continue to pass the allele on from generation to generation. Nonetheless, the frequency of a harmful recessive allele will still be very low. This low frequency is maintained by mutation but is kept from increasing by natural selection.

The previous example discussed selection against the recessive homozygote, which acted to increase the frequency of one allele and decrease the frequency of another. With time, the allele frequencies will approach 0 or 1, depending on which allele is selected against.

Is there a way that natural selection could produce intermediate values? The answer is a form of selection known as selection for the heterozygote (and therefore against the homozygotes). Consider fitness values of: AA = 70 percent, Aa = 100 percent, and aa = 20 percent. Here, only 70 percent of those with genotype AA and 20 percent of those with genotype aa survive for every 100 people with genotype Aa (the heterozygote). Selection is for the heterozygote and against the homozygotes. Let the frequency of both the A and a alleles equal 0.5. In a population of 200 people, this means we start with 50 AA people, 100 Aa people, and 50 aa people before selection. Given these fitness values, there will be 35 people with AA, 100 with Aa, and 10 with aa after selection. The allele frequencies after selection are A = 0.586 and a = 0.414.

Why would the frequency of the A allele increase and the frequency of the a allele decrease? In selection for the heterozygote, both alleles are being selected for, because every Aa person can contribute both alleles to the next generation. Also, both alleles are being selected against. When AA people die or fail to reproduce, then two A alleles are lost from the population. When aa people die or fail to reproduce, two a alleles are lost from the population. Selection for the heterozygote involves selection for and against both alleles. Because the fitness of AA is greater in this example than the fitness of aa (70 percent versus 20 percent), proportionately more individuals with genotype AA will survive and reproduce. Hence, proportionately more A alleles will appear in the next generation.

Figure 3.3 shows the pattern of allele frequency change over 20 generations using the initial values and fitness values in this example. Note that the frequency of A continues to increase for the first few generations but soon levels off. There is no change in the allele frequency after approximately eight generations. This is the expected pattern when there is selection for the heterozygote. A balance is reached between selection for and against the two alleles A and a. The exact value of this balancing point will depend on the fitness values of the homozygous genotypes. Selection for the heterozygote is also called **balancing selection.**

GENETIC DRIFT   **Genetic drift** is the random change in allele frequency from one generation to the next. These random changes are the result of the nature of probability. Think for a moment about flipping a coin in the air. What is the probability of its landing with the head facing up? It is 50 percent. Suppose you flip a coin 10 times. How many heads and how many tails do you expect to get? Because the probability of getting a head or a tail is 50 percent, you expect to get five heads and five tails. Try this experiment

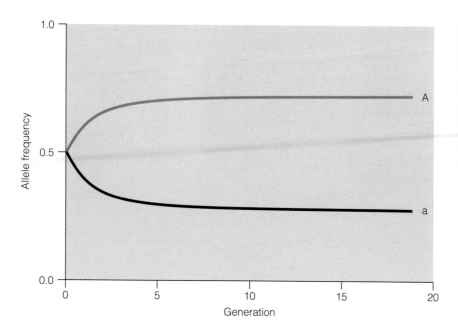

Change over time in allele frequencies when there is selection for the heterozygote (*Aa*). The initial allele frequencies are both 0.5. The fitness of each genotype (the relative frequency of survival) is: *AA* = 70%, *Aa* = 100%, and *aa* = 20%.

several times. Did you always get five tails and five heads? Sometimes you get five heads and five tails, but sometimes you get different numbers.

What does this have to do with genetics? The reproductive process in this way is like a coin toss. During the process of sex cell replication (meiosis), only one allele out of two at a given locus is used. The probability of either allele being passed on is 50 percent, just like a coin toss. Imagine a locus with two alleles, A and a. Now imagine a man and a woman, each with genotype Aa, who have a child. The man can pass on either an A allele or an a allele. Likewise, a woman can pass on either an A allele or an a allele. As we saw in the last chapter, the probable distribution of genotypes among the children is 25 percent AA, 50 percent Aa, and 25 percent aa. If the couple has four children, you would expect one with AA, two with Aa, and one with aa. Thanks to random chance, however, the couple may get a different distribution of genotypes.

When genetic drift occurs in populations, the same principle applies. Allele frequencies can change because of random chance. Sometimes the

balancing selection
Selection for the heterozygote and against the homozygote (the heterozygote is most fit).

genetic drift
A mechanism for evolutionary change resulting from the

random fluctuations of gene frequencies from one generation to the next.

■ **FIGURE 3.4**
Three computer simulations
of 20 generations of genetic
drift for populations of 10
individuals. Each simulation
started with an initial allele
frequency of 0.5.

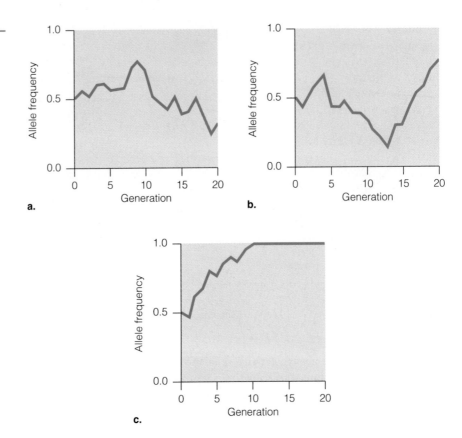

■ **FIGURE 3.4**
Three computer simulations of 20 generations of genetic drift for populations of 10 individuals. Each simulation started with an initial allele frequency of 0.5.

allele frequency will increase, and sometimes it will decrease. The direction of allele frequency change caused by genetic drift is random. The only time drift will not produce a change in allele frequency is when only one allele is present at a given locus. For example, if each parent passed on an A allele to each of the four children, the frequency of the A allele would be 1.0 among the children. The *a* allele would have been lost.

Genetic drift occurs in each generation. Figure 3.4 shows the results of three computer simulations of drift. In each case, the initial allele frequency was 0.5, and the population size was equal to 10 individuals (20 alleles) in each generation. The simulation was allowed to continue in each case for 20 generations. The graphs show the changes in allele frequency over time. Note that each of the three simulations shows a different pattern. This is expected because genetic drift is a random process. Each simulation is an independent event.

The effect of genetic drift depends on the size of the breeding population. The larger the population size, the less change will occur from one generation to the next. Thinking back to the coin toss analogy will show you that this makes sense. If you flip a coin 10 times and get three heads and seven tails, it is not that unusual. If you flip a coin 1 million times, however, it would be much less likely that you would get the same proportions—300,000 heads and 700,000 tails. This is because of a basic principle of probability: the greater the number of events, the fewer deviations from the expected frequencies (50 percent heads and 50 percent tails).

An example of genetic drift in human populations is shown in a case study of a group known as the Dunkers, a religious sect that emigrated from Germany to the United States in the early 1700s. Approximately 50 families composed the initial group. Glass (1953) studied the genetic characteristics of the descendants of the original founding group living in Pennsylvania. These populations have never been greater than several hundred people and thus provide a unique opportunity to study genetic drift in a small human group. Glass found that the Dunker population differed in a number of genetic traits from both the modern German and U.S. populations. Furthermore, the allele frequencies of Germany and the United States were almost identical, suggesting that other factors such as natural selection were unlikely. For example, the allele frequencies for the MN blood group were roughly M = 0.55 and N = 0.45 for both the United States and German samples. In the Dunker population, however, the allele frequencies were M = 0.655 and N = 0.345. Based on these and additional data, Glass concluded that the genetics of the Dunker population were shaped to a large extent by genetic drift over two centuries. Although 200 years seems like a long time to you and me, it is a fraction of an instant in evolutionary time. Genetic drift can clearly produce rapid changes under the proper circumstances.

GENE FLOW   The fourth evolutionary force is **gene flow,** the movement of alleles from one population to another. When gene flow occurs, the two populations mix genetically and tend to become more similar. Under most conditions, the more the two populations mix, the more similar they will become genetically (assuming that the two environments are not different enough to produce different effects of natural selection).

Consider a genetic locus with two alleles, A and *a*. Assume two populations, 1 and 2. Now, assume that all the alleles in population 1 are A and all the alleles in population 2 are *a*. The allele frequencies of these two imaginary populations are:

Population 1	*Population 2*
Frequency of A = 1.0	Frequency of A = 0.0
Frequency of a = 0.0	Frequency of a = 1.0

Now imagine a situation where 10 percent of the people in population 1 move to population 2, and vice versa. This movement constitutes gene flow. What effect will the gene flow have? After gene flow has taken place, population 1 is made up of 90 percent A alleles and 10 percent *a* alleles. Population

gene flow A mechanism for evolutionary change resulting from the movement of genes from one population to another.

■ **FIGURE 3.5**
Effects of gene flow over time. Population 1 started with an allele frequency of 1.0, and population 2 started with an allele frequency of 0.0. The two populations exchange 10 percent of their genes with each generation. Over time, the continued gene flow acts to make the two populations more similar genetically.

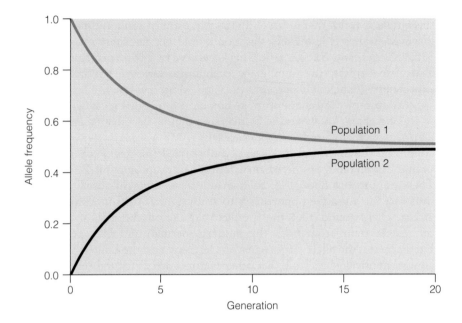

2 is made up of 10 percent *A* alleles and 90 percent *a* alleles. The allele frequencies of the two populations, though still different, have become more similar as the consequence of gene flow. If the same rate of gene flow (10 percent) continues generation after generation, the two populations will become more and more similar genetically. After 20 generations of gene flow, the two populations will be almost identical. The accumulated effects of gene flow over time are shown for this hypothetical example in Figure 3.5.

Apart from making populations more similar, gene flow can also introduce new variation within a population. In the example, a new allele (*a*) was introduced into population 1 as the result of gene flow. A new mutation arising in one population can be spread throughout the rest of a species by gene flow.

Compared to many other organisms, humans are relatively mobile creatures. Human populations show a great deal of variation in degree of migration. Even today, many humans live and work within a small area and choose mates from nearby. Some people are more mobile than others, the extent of their mobility depending on a number of factors such as available technology, occupation, income, and other social factors.

In spite of local and regional differences, humans today all belong to the same species. Even though genetic variation exists among populations, they are in fact characterized more by their similarity. A critical factor in the cohesiveness of the human species, gene flow acts to reduce differences among groups.

The amount of gene flow between human populations depends on a variety of environmental and cultural factors. Geographic distance is a major determinant of migration and gene flow. The farther two populations are apart geographically, the less likely they are to exchange mates. Even in today's modern world, with access to jet airplanes and other devices, you are still more likely to choose a spouse from nearby than from across the country. Exceptions to the rule do occur, of course, but the influence of geographic distance is still very strong.

Geographic distance is a major determinant of human migration and gene flow, but it is not the only one. Ethnic differences also act to limit them. Most large cities have distinct neighborhoods that correspond to different ethnic communities. A large proportion of marriages takes place within these groups because of the common human preference for marrying within one's own social and cultural group. Likewise, religious differences also act as barriers to gene flow because many, though not all, people prefer to marry within the same religion. Further, social class and educational differences can also limit gene flow.

INTERACTION OF THE EVOLUTIONARY FORCES   It is convenient to discuss each of the four evolutionary forces separately, but in reality they act together to produce allele frequency change. Mutation acts to introduce new genetic variants; natural selection, genetic drift, and gene flow act to change the frequency of the mutant allele. Sometimes the evolutionary forces act together, and sometimes they act in opposition. Their exact interaction depends on a wide variety of factors, such as the biochemical and physical effects of different alleles, presence or absence of dominance, population size, population distribution, and the environment, to name but a few. Many biological anthropologists attempt to unravel some of these factors in human population studies.

In general, we look at how natural selection, genetic drift, and gene flow act to increase or decrease genetic variation within and between groups. (Mutation gets less attention because, even though it introduces new genetic variants, the change in allele frequency in one generation is low.) An increase in variation within a population means that individuals within the population will be more genetically different from one another. A decrease in variation within a population means the reverse; individuals will become more similar to one another genetically. An increase in variation among populations means that two or more populations will become more different from one another genetically, and a decrease in variation within populations means the reverse.

Let us first consider the effects of genetic drift, gene flow, and natural selection on allele frequency variation. Genetic drift tends to remove alleles from a population and therefore acts to reduce variation within a population. On the other hand, because genetic drift is a random event and occurs independently in different populations, the pattern of genetic drift will tend to be different on average in different populations. On average, then, genetic drift will act to increase variation among populations. Gene flow acts to introduce new alleles into a population and can have the effect of increasing variation within a population. Gene flow also acts to reduce variation among populations in most cases.

Natural selection can either increase or decrease variation within a population, depending on the specific type of selection and the initial allele frequencies. Selection against recessive homozygotes, for example, will lead to the gradual decrease of one allele and consequently reduce variation. Selection for an advantageous mutation, however, will result in an increase in the frequency of the mutant and act to increase variation within the population. Selection can also either increase or decrease variation among populations, depending on environmental variation. If two populations have similar environments, then natural selection will take place in the same way in both groups and therefore will act to reduce genetic differences between them. On the other hand, if the two populations are in different enough environments that natural selection operates in different ways, then variation between the populations may be increased. Table 3.3 summarizes the effects of different evolutionary forces on variation within and among populations.

Different evolutionary forces can produce the same, or opposite, effects. Different forces can also act in opposition to one another. Genetic drift and gene flow, for example, have opposite effects on variation within and among populations. If both of these forces operate at the same time, they can counteract each other..

MACROEVOLUTION

To many, but not all, evolutionary biologists, macroevolution is merely the net effect of microevolutionary change over long periods of time. Some, however, believe that additional forces must be considered in explaining macroevolution.

Perhaps the single largest task of macroevolutionary theory is to explain the origin of new species. The origin of new species has been observed in historical times and in the present. Some new species have been brought about by human intervention and controlled breeding, as with many species of tropical fish. There are also examples of new species having arisen naturally in the recent past, such as certain types of fruit flies. In addition, we have information on populations in the process of forming new species, such as certain groups of snails. Most of what we observe about new species formation, however, comes from analysis of the fossil record.

How do new species come into being? It is ironic that even though the title of Darwin's book is On the Origin of Species, it did not focus much on this question. Instead, Darwin sought to explain the basic nature of evolutionary change, believing that extension of these principles could explain the formation of new species. Indeed, even though there are different models of species formation, all essentially use the processes of microevolution for explanation.

■ TABLE 3.3
Summary of the Effects of Selection, Drift, and Gene Flow on Variation within and among Populations

EVOLUTIONARY FORCE	VARIATION WITHIN POPULATIONS	VARIATION AMONG POPULATIONS
Selection	Increase or decrease	Increase or decrease
Genetic drift	Decrease	Increase
Gene flow	Increase	Decrease

A decrease in variation within a population makes individuals more similar to one another, whereas an increase in variation within a population makes individuals less similar to one another. A decrease in variation among populations makes the populations more similar to one another, whereas an increase in variation among populations makes the populations less similar to one another. Note that natural selection can either increase or decrease variation; the exact effect depends on the type of selection and differences in environment (see text).

Taxonomy and Evolution

An understanding of the origin of species begins with consideration of the definition of the term *species*. There is considerable controversy regarding its definition and how it relates to models of evolutionary change (Ereshefsky 1992). Therefore, a discussion of macroevolution and the origin of species must begin with an understanding of certain principles of biological classification.

If you think for a moment, you will realize that a great deal of your daily life revolves around your use and understanding of different systems of classification. In biology, a taxonomy is a system of classification that shows relationships between different groups of organisms. This may sound simple enough but can actually be rather difficult. For example, consider the following list of organisms: flounder, bat, shark, canary, lizard, horse, and whale. How would you classify these creatures? One way might be to put certain animals together according to size: the flounder, bat, canary, and lizard in a "small" category; the shark and horse in a "medium" category, and the whale in a "large" category. Another method would be to put the animals in groups according to where they live: the flounder, shark, and whale in the water; the bat and canary in the air; and the lizard and horse on the land. Still another method would be to put the shark in a separate category from all the others because the shark's skeleton is made of cartilage instead of bone.

The problem with this example is that none of these three ways of classification agrees with the other two. There is no consistency. Biologists actually classify these animals into the following groups: fish (flounder and shark), reptiles (lizard), birds (canary), and mammals (bat, horse, whale). These groups reflect certain common characteristics, such as mammary glands for the mammals. But what makes this system of classification any better than those based on size or habitat? For our purposes, we require tax-onomies that reflect evolutionary patterns. As we will see, organisms can have similar traits because they inherited these traits from a common ances-tor. Thus, the presence of mammary glands in the bat, horse, and whale rep-resents a trait that has been inherited from a common ancestral species.

Taxonomies are useful in trying to understand evolutionary relation-ships. In order to reflect the evolutionary process, the taxonomy must reflect evolutionary changes.

TAXONOMIC CATEGORIES   A taxonomy is a hierarchical classification. That is, each category contains a number of subcategories, which contain further sub-categories, and so on. Biological classification uses a number of categories. The more commonly used categories are: kingdom, phylum (plural *phyla*), class, order, family, genus (plural *genera*), and species. In addition, prefixes are often added to distinguish further breakdowns within a particular category, such as subphylum or infraorder. The scientific name given to an organism consists of the genus and species names in Latin. The scientific name for the common house mouse is *Mus musculus*. Modern human beings are known as *Homo sapiens*, translated roughly as "wise humans."

Any given genus may contain a number of different species. The genus *Homo*, for example, contains modern humans (*Homo sapiens*) as well as ex-tinct human species (*Home erectus* and *Homo habilis*). These three species are placed in the same genus because of certain common characteristics, such as large brain size.

The categories of classification are often vaguely defined. Genus, for ex-ample, refers to a group of species that shares similar environments, patterns of adaptation, and physical structures. An example is the horse and the zebra, different species that are placed in the genus *Equus* (there are several species of zebra). These species are four-legged, hoofed grazers. The basis for assigning a given species to one genus or another is often unclear. This uncer-tainty is even more problematic when fossil remains are assigned to different categories. The only category with a precise meaning is the species, and even that has certain problems in application.

THE BIOLOGICAL SPECIES CONCEPT   Species may be defined on the basis of repro-duction. If organisms from two populations are capable of breeding naturally and can produce fertile offspring, then they belong to the same species. Note that this definition has several parts. First, organisms from two populations must be capable of interbreeding. Second, these matings must occur in nature. Recent advances in biology have allowed individuals usually considered to be separate species to produce offspring under lab-oratory conditions. In understanding who we are and how we evolved, we are interested in breeding that takes place naturally. Third and finally, the offspring must be *fertile*—that is, capable of producing further offspring.

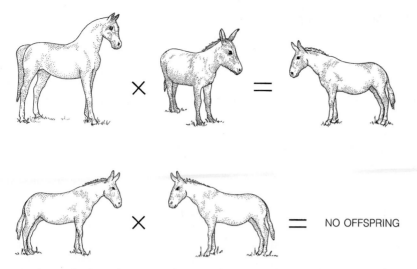

NO OFFSPRING

Perhaps the best known example of an application of the species concept is the mule. Mules are farm animals produced as the offspring of a horse bred with a donkey. The horse and the donkey interbreed naturally, which satisfies the first and second parts of the species definition. The offspring (mules) are sterile, however, and cannot produce further offspring. The only way to get a mule is to mate a horse and a donkey. Because the offspring are not fertile, the horse and the donkey are considered separate species (see Figure 3.6). On the other hand, all human populations around the world belong to the same species because members can interbreed and produce fertile offspring.

The concept of biological species appears to provide a useful test for the purposes of classification. One of its problems, however, is that it only provides a simple yes or no answer to the question of similarity. It does not reflect any degree of similarity among organisms that belong to different species. For example, horses and donkeys are obviously more similar to each other than either is to an ant. The different species names show only that all are different species, but not which species are more similar to each other. The fact that horses and donkeys can interbreed shows us that they are closely related species.

MODES OF SPECIES CHANGE The biological species concept is useful when comparing two or more populations living at a single point in time. In theory, reproductive isolation can be tested to determine if these populations belong to the same species. How can the biological species concept be applied when comparing groups of organisms over a period of time? This question requires looking at two different modes of the evolutionary change of species.

First, a species can change over time. According to this mode of evolutionary change, a single species exists at any given point in time but evolves over a period of time. An example is the evolution of humans. The most likely scenario of human evolution over the past two million years (see Chapters 7–9) is a change from a species known as *Homo habilis* into a species

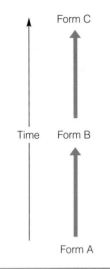

Form C

Time   Form B

Form A

■ FIGURE 3.7
Anagenesis, the linear
evolution of a species over
time. Form A changes over
time into form B and then
further changes into form C.

known as *Homo erectus* into our own species *Homo sapiens*. Although a single species exists within the genus *Homo* at any point in time, there is continued evolutionary change such that the most recent forms (ourselves) are quite different from the earliest forms. For example, our brains are roughly twice as large. The suggestion here is of a single species evolving over time.

This mode of species change is known as **anagenesis,** or straight-line evolution. It is illustrated as a straight line, as shown in Figure 3.7 where form A evolves into form B and then into form C. Although this mode of evolutionary change is fairly straightforward, complications arise when considering the naming of species. Should form A be called a different species from form B? In the case of human evolution, should *Homo erectus* actually be given a different species name from *Homo sapiens*? The problem is that the traditional biological species concept doesn't really apply. Form A and form B are by necessity isolated from each other reproductively because they lived at different times.

Anagenesis is not the only mode of species change. If you think about it, anagenesis is not completely sufficient as an explanation of macroevolution. Where do new species come from? The other mode of species change is **cladogenesis,** or branching evolution. Cladogenesis involves the formation of new species (speciation) whereby one or more new species branch off from an original species. In Figure 3.8, a portion of species A first branches off to produce species B (living at the same time), then a portion of species B branches to produce species C. This example starts with one species and ends up with three.

Patterns of Macroevolution

Evolutionary forces interact to change populations over time (anagenesis) and lead to the formation of new species (cladogenesis). In addition to these processes, the study of macroevolution is concerned with the rate of evolutionary change and the failure of species to adapt over time.

SPECIATION   The fossil record shows many examples of new species arising. How? You know that genetic differences between populations come about as a result of evolutionary forces. For a population to become a new species, these generic differences must be great enough to prevent successful interbreeding with the original parent species. For this to occur, the population must become reproductively isolated from the original parent species. **Reproductive isolation** is genetic change that can lead to an inability to produce fertile offspring. How does this happen? Evolutionary forces can produce such a situation. The first step in **speciation** (the formation of a new species from a parent species) is the elimination or reduction of gene flow between populations. Because gene flow acts to reduce differences between populations, its continued action tends to

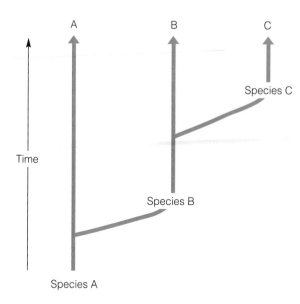

A   B   C

Species C

Time

Species B

Species A

■ FIGURE 3.8
Cladogenesis, the origin of
new species. Species A splits
and forms a new species B,
which later splits to form
species C. The process begins
with a single species (A)
and ends with three species
(A, B, C).

keep all populations in the same species. Gene flow does not need to be eliminated altogether, but it must be reduced sufficiently to allow the other evolutionary forces to make the populations genetically different. Populations must become genetically isolated from one another for speciation to occur.

The most common form of isolation in animal species is geographic isolation. When two populations are separated by a physical barrier, such as a river or mountain range, or by great distances, gene flow is cut off between the populations. As long as the populations remain isolated, genetic changes occurring in one group will not spread to other groups.

Isolation is the first step in the speciation process. By itself, this isolation does not guarantee speciation. Elimination of gene flow provides the opportunity for speciation. Other evolutionary forces must then act upon this isolation to produce a situation in which the isolated groups have changed sufficiently to make fertile interbreeding no longer possible. Isolation, however, does not always lead to speciation.

How can the evolutionary forces lead to speciation? Mutation might act to increase variation among populations because it occurs independently in the genetic composition of separate groups. Without gene flow to spread

anagenesis The transformation of a single species over time.

cladogenesis The formation of one or more species from another over time.

reproduction isolation The genetic isolation of population that may render them incapable of producing offspring.

speciation The origin of a new species.

them, individual mutations will accumulate in each group, making isolated populations genetically divergent. Genetic drift also contributes to differences in allele frequencies among small populations. In addition, if the two populations are in separate environments, then natural selection will lead to genetic differences. Once gene flow has been eliminated, the other evolutionary forces will act to make the populations genetically divergent. When this process continues to the point where the two populations can no longer interbreed and produce fertile offspring, they have become separate species.

There is continued debate over the role of the various evolutionary forces in producing genetic divergence. For many years, speciation was felt to be solely the by-product of natural selection. In recent years, however, more attention has been given to the contributions to speciation of mutation and genetic drift in small populations.

ADAPTIVE RADIATION   The process of speciation minimally results in two species: the original parent species and the new offspring species. Under certain circumstances, many new species can come into being in a short period of time. This rapid diversification of species is associated with changing environmental conditions. When new environments open up, or when new adaptations to a specific environment develop, many new species can form— a process known as **adaptive radiation.**

New environments often open up following the demise of other species. One example, discussed in greater detail in Chapter 6 is the rise of mammals following the extinction of the dinosaurs. Once the dinosaurs were gone, there were vacant environments for mammals to adapt to. The result was an adaptive radiation of mammalian species.

THE TEMPO AND MODE OF MACROEVOLUTION   During the past 25 years, considerable attention has been given to the tempo (how fast?) and mode (the mechanism) of macroevolutionary change.

Charles Darwin saw speciation as a slow and gradual process, taking thousands or millions of years. To Darwin, natural selection acted on populations ultimately to produce new species. The view that macroevolution is a slow and gradual process is called **gradualism.** According to this view, small changes in each generation over time result in major biological changes.

Gradualism, then, regards speciation as a slow process that takes a long time to occur. New species form from large portions of an original species. In such large populations, genetic drift and mutation have little impact in each generation. Natural selection, slowly operating on some initial mutation(s), is primarily responsible for speciation.

The gradualistic model predicts that, given a suitable fossil record, we will see a smooth and gradual transition from one species into another. Although there are examples of such change in the fossil record, it is not always apparent. An alternative theory has been suggested by Niles Eldredge and Stephen Jay Gould in the form of a model known as **punctuated equi-**

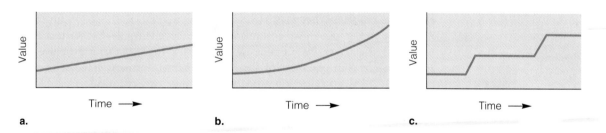

a.   b.   c.

librium (Eldredge and Gould 1972; Gould and Eldredge 1977). This theory suggests that the pattern of macroevolution consists of long periods of time when little evolutionary change occurs (**stasis**) and short periods of time when rapid evolutionary change occurs. To Eldredge and Gould, the tempo of macroevolution is not gradual; rather, it is static at times and rapid at other times. Long periods of stasis are punctuated by short periods of rapid evolutionary change. Examples of gradualism and punctuated equilibrium are given in Figure 3.9.

Eldredge and Gould also view speciation as a rapid event occurring within small, isolated populations on the periphery of a species range. Mutations can spread quickly in small populations as a consequence of inbreeding and genetic drift. If such genetic changes are adaptive and if the newly formed species gains access to the parental species' range it may then spread throughout an area, replacing the original parent species. According to this model, most biological change occurs during speciation. Once a species has been established, it changes little throughout time. Eldredge and Gould argue that selection and other factors act to keep a species the same over time. This view contrasts with the gradualistic model, which sees biological change occurring at a slow rate, ultimately leading to separate species.

There is little doubt among evolutionary biologists that stasis and rapid speciation have occurred in some organisms in the fossil record. It is also clear that the fossil record shows many examples of gradualism. Neither model is entirely correct in all cases, however, nor was it meant to be. Both represent different extremes of thinking about the tempo and mode of evolution. Though there is some debate over the genetic mechanisms of punctuated equilibrium, there is less debate on the facts of stasis and rapid speciation (Futuyma 1988).

■ **FIGURE 3.9**
The tempo of macroevolution: gradualism and punctuated equilibrium. Each portion of this figure has a line showing the change in value of a physical trait over time. (a) Gradualism: the change over time is linear and constant. (b) A geometric, gradual pattern. The rate of change increases with time, but the curve is still smooth; there are no discontinuities. (c) Punctuated equilibrium: there are periods of no change (stasis) punctuated by periods of rapid change; the net result is a "staircase" pattern.

---

adaptive radiation The formation of many new species following the availability of new environments or the development of a new adaptation.

gradualism A model of macroevolutionary change whereby evolutionary changes occur at a slow, steady rate over time.

punctuated equilibrium A model of macroevolutionary change in which long periods of little evolutionary change (stasis) are followed by relatively

short periods of rapid evolutionary change.

stasis Little or no evolutionary change occuring over a long period of time.

EXTINCTIONS AND MASS EXTINCTIONS   In considering macroevolutionary trends, we must not forget the most common pattern of them all—extinction. It is estimated that over 99 percent of all species that ever existed have become extinct (Futuyma 1986). In historic times, humans have witnessed (and helped cause) the extinction of a number of organisms, such as the passenger pigeon.

What causes extinction? When a species is no longer adapted to a changed environment, it may die. The exact causes of a species' death vary from situation to situation. Rapid ecological change may render an environment hostile to a species. For example, temperatures may change and a species may not be able to adapt. Food resources may be affected by environmental changes, which will then cause problems for a species requiring these resources. Other species may become better adapted to an environment, resulting in competition and ultimately the death of a species.

Extinction seems, in fact, to be the ultimate fate of all species. Natural selection is a remarkable mechanism for providing a species with the ability to adapt to change, but it does not always work. When the environment changes too rapidly or when the appropriate genetic variations do not exist, a species can become extinct.

The fossil record shows that extinction has occurred throughout the history of the planet. Recent analyses have also revealed that on some occasions a large number of species became extinct at the same time—a **mass extinction.** One of the best-known examples of mass extinction occurred 65 million years ago with the demise of dinosaurs and many other forms of life. Perhaps the largest mass extinction was the one that occurred roughly 225 million years ago, when approximately 95 percent of all species were wiped out (Gould 1991).

MISCONCEPTIONS ABOUT EVOLUTION

Evolution is a frequently misunderstood subject. Many of our basic ideas regarding evolution are misconceptions that have become part of the general culture. The often used phrase "survival of the fittest" conjures up images that are sometimes at odds with the actual findings of evolutionary science. It is common for such misconceptions to continue even after initial exposure to evolutionary theory.

The Nature of Selection

Many people have a basic understanding of the general principles of natural selection. The problem lies in our misinterpretation of the nature of natural selection.

MISCONCEPTION: BIGGER IS BETTER A common misconception is that natural selection will *always* lead to larger structures. According to this idea, the bigger the brain, the better, and the bigger the body, the better. At first, this idea seems reasonable. After all, larger individuals may be more likely to survive because they can compete more successfully for food and sexual partners. Therefore, larger individuals are more likely to survive and pass their genes on to the next generation. Natural selection is expected to lead to an increase in the size of the body, brain, and other structures. However, this isn't always true. There are numerous examples of species in which *smaller* body size or structures were more adaptive and selected for. Keep in mind that in evolution nothing is free! A larger body may be more adaptive because of sheer size, but a larger body also has greater energy needs. Any advantage gained by a larger body may be offset by the disadvantage of needing more food. What we have to focus on is a *balance* between the adaptive and nonadaptive aspects of any biological characteristic. By walking upright, humans have their hands free, which is rather advantageous. However, we pay the price with varicose veins, back pain, fallen arches, and other nonadaptive consequences of walking on two legs. Again, we need to focus on the relative costs and benefits of any evolutionary change. Of course, this balance will obviously vary in different environments.

MISCONCEPTION: NEWER IS BETTER There is a tendency to believe that traits more recent in origin are superior because they are newer. Humans walk on two legs, a trait that appeared more than four million years ago. We also have five digits (fingers and toes) that date back many hundreds of millions of years. Is upright walking better because it is newer? Of course not. Both features are essential to our tool-making way of life. The age of a structure has no bearing on its usefulness.

MISCONCEPTION: NATURAL SELECTION ALWAYS WORKS The idea that natural selection will always provide an opportunity for some members of a species to survive is not accurate. Occasionally this author has heard statements such as "we will evolve to tolerate air pollution." Such statements are absurdities. Natural selection only operates on variations that are present. If no genetic variation occurs to aid in breathing polluted air, natural selection will not help us. Even in cases where genetic variation is present, the environment may change too quickly for us to respond through natural selection. All we have to do is to examine the fossil record to see how inaccurate this

▲▲

mass extinction Many species becoming extinct at roughly the same time.

Science Fiction and Orthogenesis

Evolution, especially human evolution, is a common theme in science fiction. Although a good many science fiction stories have a strong scientific base, others—most likely due to plot needs—do not. Even these stories, though, are valuable in terms of what they tell us about misconceptions about evolution, one of the themes of this chapter.

A personal favorite of mine is an episode of the 1960s science fiction television show, *The Outer Limits*. The episode entitled "The Sixth Finger" is an entertaining treatment of a popular science fiction question: What will humans evolve into? The story, aired in 1963, begins with a young coal miner, Gwyllm Griffiths, who yearns for something more than a life of manual labor. Through his girlfriend Cathy, he meets a local scientist, Professor Mathers, who had once worked on an atomic bomb project. Because of guilt, the scientist is seeking an end to violence and war—through evolution. Reasoning that humans will someday evolve beyond the need for violence, and tormented by the "slow pace of evolution," Mathers invents a machine that will move an organism into its own predestined evolutionary future.

Gwyllm volunteers as a human subject, and the results are predictable. With each exposure to the machine, his head and brain increase in size, as does his intelligence. Additionally, he "evolves" a sixth finger (for "increased dexterity") and assorted mental powers (the sixth finger is particularly interesting because some people today are born with a sixth finger, and there does not appear to be any evolutionary advantage). Gwyllm also develops a dislike for the people around him and eventually decides to destroy them. On his way to demolish the town with his mental powers, he suddenly "evolves beyond the need for violence." He returns to the professor's laboratory and enlists the help of Cathy to operate the machinery while he evolves into "the man of the future." Once Gwyllm is in the machine's chamber, Cathy cannot bear to lose him forever, and pushes the machine's lever to "Backward" rather than "Forward." For a brief moment she pushes too much and the viewer sees Gwyllm evolve back to some sort of subhuman ape, but she quickly corrects the lever and they live happily ever after (in one alternate ending, the script called for Gwyllm to continue evolving back to protoplasm) (Schow and Frentzen 1986).

This episode is quite entertaining, and also provides some good examples of evolutionary misconceptions. For example, the doctrine of orthogenesis, the notion that evolution follows a particular path, is central to the entire plot. This message is not subtle—at one point, Gwyllm speaks about "the goal of evolution." The professor's machine embodies the idea of orthogenesis, with its lever marked "Forward" and "Backward," implying that all of life evolves along a fixed path from past to present. Orthogenesis is also apparent in the continued expansion of the brain and mental powers as Gwyllm evolves "forward," enabling him to read massive volumes at a glance and become a concert pianist overnight.

Despite the scientific inaccuracies, "The Sixth Finger" remains a captivating story. It was also somewhat controversial in that it dealt, on television, with evolution, a theme that had drawn criticism from the network's censor.

---

misconception is—that 99 percent of all past species are extinct shows us that natural selection obviously doesn't always work!

MISCONCEPTION: THERE IS AN INEVITABLE DIRECTION IN EVOLUTION An idea popular in the nineteenth century was **orthogenesis,** the notion that evolution would continue in a given direction because of a vaguely defined nonphysical "force" (Mayr 1982). As an alternative to the theory of natural selection, orthogenesis suggested that evolutionary change would continue in the same direction either until a perfect structure was attained or a species became extinct. Apart from the problems of dealing with metaphysical

■ FIGURE 3.10
The theory of orthogenesis predicts continued change in a given direction. Illustrated here is the popular but incorrect notion that humans in the future will have progressively larger brains.

"forces," orthogenesis has long been rejected by analysis of the fossil record and the triumph of natural selection as an explanatory mechanism for evolutionary change. Some of its basic notions, however, are still perpetuated. A common belief is that humans will evolve larger and larger brains, as a continuation of earlier trends (Figure 3.10). The view of orthogenesis is tied in with notions of "progress" and with the misconception that bigger is better. There are many examples from the fossil record of nonlinear change, and many examples of reversals in sizes of structures. In the case of human evolution, brains actually stopped getting larger 50,000 years ago. In fact, the average brain size of humans since that time has decreased slightly as a consequence of a general decrease in skeletal size and ruggedness (Henneberg 1988).

Is it possible for a trend to continue to change in a given direction under the right circumstances? Of course, but change comes through the action of natural selection, not some mysterious internal force. Continuation of any trend depends on the environment, present genetic variation, and basic biological limits. (A 50-foot spider can't exist because it wouldn't be able to absorb enough oxygen for its volume.) Such change also depends on the relative cost and benefits of change. Suppose that an increase in human

▲▲▲▲▲▲▲▲▲▲▲▲▲▲▲▲▲▲▲▲▲▲▲▲▲▲▲▲▲▲

orthogenesis A discredited idea that evolution would continue in a given direction because of some vaguely defined "force."

brain size was combined somehow with an increase in pelvic size (assuming genetic variation was present for both features). A larger pelvis would make walking difficult or even impossible. Evolution works on the entire organism and not one trait at a time. Any change can have both positive and negative effects, but it is the net balance that is critical to the operation of natural selection.

Structure, Function, and Evolution

A number of misconceptions about evolution focus on the relationship between biological structures and their adaptive (or nonadaptive) functions.

MISCONCEPTION: *NATURAL SELECTION ALWAYS PRODUCES PERFECT STRUCTURES*   There is a tendency to view nature as the product of perfect natural engineering. Granted, there are many marvelous and wondrous phenomena in the natural world, but a closer examination shows that biological structures are often far from perfect. Consider human beings. Is the human body perfect? Hardly. Just to note one aspect, consider your skeleton when you stand upright. What is holding in your internal organs? Skin and muscles. Your rib cage provides little support for lower internal organs because it reflects ancestry from a four-legged form. When humans stood up (adaptive), the rib cage offered less support. The result—a variety of complaints and complications, such as hernias. The human skeleton is not perfect, but rather the result of natural selection operating on the variation that was present.

MISCONCEPTION: *ALL STRUCTURES ARE ADAPTIVE*   Natural selection is such a powerful model that it is tempting to apply it to all biological structures. Indeed, many anthropologists and biologists have done so. They examine a structure and explain its function in terms of natural selection. Are all structures adaptive? Many structures simply reflect a by-product of other biological changes and have no adaptive value of their own (Gould and Lewontin 1979). Other structures, such as the human appendix, may have served a function in the past but appear to have no present function.

MISCONCEPTION: *CURRENT STRUCTURES ALWAYS REFLECT INITIAL ADAPTATIONS*   The idea here is that any given structure, with an associated function, originally evolved specifically for that function. Human beings, for example, walk on two legs; this allows them to hold tools and other objects that are constructed with the aid of an enlarged brain. Although it is tempting to say that both upright walking and a larger brain evolved at the same time because of the adaptive value of having both structures, this is not what happened. Upright walking evolved at least 1.5 million years before the use of stone tools and the expansion of the brain (Chapter 10).

As another example, consider your fingers. You have five of these digits on each hand, which allow you to perform a variety of manipulative tasks. Humans use their hands to manipulate both natural and human-made objects. Manipulative digits are essential to our nature as tool-using creatures. We might therefore suggest that our grasping hands *first* evolved to meet this need; this is not the case. Grasping hands *first* developed in early primate ancestors to meet the needs of living in the trees (Chapter 7). Even though we don't live in trees, we have retained this trait and use it *for a different purpose*. Natural selection operates on the variation that is present. Structures are frequently modified for different uses.

SUMMARY

Evolution is understood in terms of microevolution and macroevolution. Microevolution looks at changes in allele frequencies from one generation to the next. There are four evolutionary forces that alter allele frequencies in the short term and provide us with inferences about long-term patterns of evolution: mutation, natural selection, genetic drift, and gene flow.

Mutation is the ultimate source of all genetic variation but occurs at low enough rates that additional factors are needed to explain large changes in allele frequency. The other three evolutionary forces act to increase or decrease the frequency of a mutant allele. Natural selection changes allele frequencies through the process of differential survival and reproduction of individuals with different genotypes. Genetic drift is the random change in allele frequencies from one generation to the next and has the greatest effect on small populations. Gene flow, the movement of alleles between populations, acts to reduce genetic differences between different populations.

Macroevolution, the process of long-term evolution, can occur in two ways: anagenesis, the evolution of a single species over time, or cladogenesis, the splitting off of one or more species from the original parent species. In cladogenesis, new species form through the process of reproductive isolation followed by genetic divergence. Both steps are understood in terms of the evolutionary forces. Reduction or elimination of gene flow provides for the beginning of reproductive isolation. Mutation, genetic drift, and natural selection can then act on this isolation to produce a new species. Two models of macroevolutionary change can be applied to the fossil record. Gradualism predicts that most evolutionary change is the result of slow and gradual change over many generations. Punctuated equilibrium predicts that there are long periods of time with little evolutionary change (stasis), punctuated by rapid evolutionary events.

There are many misconceptions regarding natural selection and evolution. Some of the more common of these are: that bigger is better, that newer is better, that natural selection always works, and that there is an inevitable direction to evolution. There are also misconceptions regarding the relationship of biological structures, their functions, and their evolutionary origin.

SUPPLEMENTAL READINGS

Bodmer, W. F. and L. L. Cavalli-Sforza. 1976. *Genetics, Evolution, and Man.* San Francisco: W. H. Freeman. This text provides a basic, essentially nonmathematical discussion of evolutionary forces.

Futuyma, D. J. 1986. *Evolutionary Biology.* 2d ed. Sunderland, Mass: Sinauer. An excellent text on the evolutionary process focusing on macroevolution.

In addition, the books by Gould listed at the end of Chapter 1 provide many interesting and relevant essays on macroevolution.

PART TWO

Our Place in Nature

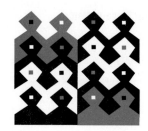

The Primates

In order to understand the place of humans in nature, it is first necessary to understand the group of mammals to which humans belong—the **primates.** Humans are primates, as are other creatures such as the apes, the monkeys, and the primitive primates known as prosimians. The basic nature of primate biology and behavior is discussed in this chapter. However, because primates belong to a group known as mammals, who in turn belong to a larger group known as vertebrates, it is first necessary to understand the basic characteristics of these larger taxonomic groups. We begin, therefore, by first discussing vertebrates and then mammals, and then go on to discuss the special characteristics of primates.

TAXONOMY

Taxonomy was discussed briefly in Chapters 1 and 3. Here, we turn to a more detailed examination of the philosophies and methods used in constructing biological classifications.

▲▲▲▲▲▲▲▲▲▲▲▲▲▲▲▲▲▲▲▲▲▲▲▲▲▲▲▲▲

primates The order of mammals that has a complex of characteristics related to an initial adaptation to life in the trees.

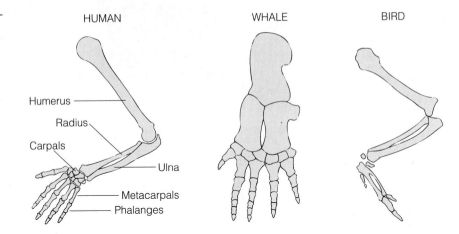

■ **FIGURE 4.1**
Homologous structures: the forelimbs of a human, whale, and bird. Note that the same bones are found in all three vertebrates. Even though the limbs are used differently by all three organisms, the bones show a structural correspondence, reflecting common ancestry.
(Adapted with permission from T. Dobzhansky, F. J. Ayala, G. L. Stebbins, and U. W. Valentine, *Evolution,* 1977, page 264, publisher W. H. Freeman)

HUMAN   WHALE   BIRD

Humerus
Radius
Carpals
Ulna
Metacarpals
Phalanges

Methods of Classification

Two species may have the same characteristic for several reasons. First, they both may have inherited the trait from a common ancestor. Humans and monkeys, for example, both have five digits on each limb because they both inherited this trait from a distant common ancestor. Second, the two species may have developed the same trait independently in their evolution. The canary and bat are both small animals capable of flight. The shared characteristic of flight, however, is not due to a common ancestor; rather, both species evolved flight independently.

HOMOLOGOUS AND ANALOGOUS TRAITS   One of our first steps is to look at a biological trait and determine its structure (how it is put together) and its function (how it is used). **Homologous traits** are traits that show similar structure but may or may not show the same function. For example, each of your arms or legs is composed of a single upper bone and two lower bones. These bones are found in many other organisms, including creatures that use their limbs in quite different ways. Figure 4.1 illustrates the arm bones of a human, a bird, and a whale. Note that each of these has an upper arm bone (humerus) and two lower arm bones (radius and ulna). Furthermore, note that the "hand" of each has five digits made up of carpal and metacarpal bones. These three animals use their limbs for different purposes, but the basic structure is the same; they are the same bones, but they differ in size, shape, and function. The correspondence of the arm and hand bones of the animals in Figure 4.1 indicates these bones are homologous structures. The reason for this correspondence is that these traits have been inherited from a common ancestor.

Traits that have the same function but not the same structure are called **analogous traits.** Figure 4.2 illustrates the wings of a bird and a flying insect.

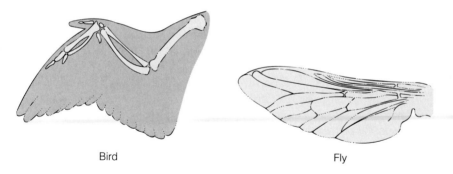

Bird   Fly

■ FIGURE 4.2
Analogous structures: the
wings of a bird and a fly. Even
though both structures
provide the same function
(flight), they are structurally
different, reflecting
independent evolutionary
origin. (Adapted with permission
from T. Dobzhansky, F. J. Ayala,
G. L. Stebbins, and U. W.
Valentine, *Evolution*, 1977, page
264, publisher W. H. Freeman)

The two structures are quite different, but they serve the same function—flight. In this case, evolution has led to the same function from two different starting points.

PRIMITIVE AND DERIVED TRAITS   Biological traits can also be characterized as primitive or derived. When a trait has been inherited from an earlier form, we refer to that trait as **primitive.** Traits that have changed from an ancestral state are referred to as **derived.** As an example, consider the number of digits in humans and horses. Both humans and horses are mammals. From fossil evidence we know that the first mammals had five digits on each hand and foot (as did other early land vertebrates). Humans have retained this condition, and we refer to the five digits of the human hand and foot as primitive traits. The horse's single digit (a toe), however, is a derived trait relative to the first mammals.

The Vertebrates

As with all living creatures, human beings can be classified according to the different levels of Linnaean taxonomy—kingdom, phylum, class, and so on. The complete taxonomic description of modern humans is given in Table 4.1.

■ TABLE 4.1
Taxonomic Classification of Human Beings

TAXONOMIC CATEGORY	PLACEMENT OF HUMANS
Kingdom	Animals
Phylum	Chordates
Subphylum	Vertebrates
Class	Mammals
Subclass	Placental mammals
Order	Primates
Suborder	Anthropoids
Superfamily	Hominoids
Family	Hominids
Genus/Species	*Homo sapiens*

homologous trait
Physical trait in two
species that has a similar
structure but may or
may not show a similar
function.

analogous trait Physical
trait that has a similar
function in two species
but a different structure.

primitive trait A trait
that has not changed
from an ancestral state.
The five digits of the
human hand and foot
are primitive traits
inherited from earlier
vertebrate ancestors.

derived trait A trait
that has changed from
an ancestral state.

THE ANIMAL KINGDOM   Kingdom is the most inclusive taxonomic category. All living organisms can be placed into one of five kingdoms: plants, animals, fungi, nucleated single-celled organisms, and bacteria. Major differences among these kingdoms are their source of food and their mobility. Whereas plants produce their own food through photosynthesis, animals must ingest food. Humans belong to the animal kingdom.

VERTEBRATE CHARACTERISTICS   Humans belong to the phylum **Chordata** (the chordates, animals with a spinal cord). Humans belong to the subphylum **Vertebrata** (the vertebrates, animals with backbones). One characteristic of vertebrates is that they have **bilateral symmetry,** which means that the left and right sides of their bodies are approximately mirror images. This pattern contrasts with other phyla of animals such as starfish. Another characteristic of vertebrates is an internal spinal cord covered by a series of bones known as vertebrae. The nerve tissue is surrounded by these bones and has an enlarged area of nerve tissue at the front end of the cord—the brain.

The general biological structure of human beings can be found in many other vertebrates. Figure 4.1 showed the limb bones of three vertebrates— human, bird, and whale. It is important to note the similarity among these three different organisms. Like most vertebrates, all have the same basic skeletal pattern: a single upper bone and two lower bones in each limb, and five digits. Some vertebrates have changed considerably from this basic pattern. For example, a modern horse has one digit (a toe) on the end of each limb. Humans may seem to be rather specialized and sophisticated creatures, but actually they have retained much of the earliest basic vertebrate skeletal structure.

The subphylum of vertebrates also includes several classes of fish along with the amphibians, reptiles, birds, and mammals. Humans belong to the class of mammals, and much of our biology and behavior can be understood in terms of what it is to be a mammal.

THE MAMMALS

The first primitive mammals evolved from early reptiles approximately 200 million years B.P. The distinctive features of modern mammals and modern reptiles are the result of that long period of separate evolution in the two classes. It is important to realize that the further back in time we look, the more difficult it is to tell one form from another.

Because mammals and reptiles are related through evolution, it is logical and useful to compare these two classes to determine the unique features of each. Modern mammals differ from modern reptiles in reproduction, temperature regulation, diet, skeletal structure, and behavior.

Reproduction

Some mammals, such as the platypus, lay eggs. Others, such as kangaroos, give birth to an extremely immature fetus that completes development inside a pouch in the mother. The most common mammal found today belongs to the subclass of placental mammals, characterized by the development of the fetus inside of the mother's body. Humans are placental mammals.

PLACENTAL MAMMALS   The **placenta** is an organ that develops inside the female during pregnancy. It functions as a link between the circulatory systems of the mother and child, acting to transport food, oxygen, and antibodies as well as to filter out waste products. The efficiency of the placenta means that the developing offspring of placental mammals have a much greater chance of survival than does a reptile developing in an egg or in a nonplacental mammal.

A main feature of mammals is the female mammary glands, which provide food for the newborn infant. Important immunities are also provided in mother's milk. The ready availability of food increases the child's chance of survival. Although advantageous, nursing also has a price; energy is expended by the mother during this process, and only a limited number of offspring can be taken care of at one time.

PARENTAL CARE   The **prenatal** (before birth) and **postnatal** (after birth) patterns of parental care in mammals contrast with those of reptiles, which expend less energy during reproduction and care of offspring. Pregnancy and raising offspring take energy; the more offspring an organism has, the less care a parent can give each of them. Consequently, some animals have many offspring but provide little care to them while other animals have few offspring and provide much more care to each. Compared to other animals, mammals have relatively few offspring but provide much more parental care. The development of the placenta and the mammary glands are biological

▲▲

Chordata A vertebrate phylum consisting of organisms that possess a notochord at some period during their life.

Vertebrata A subphylum of the phylum Chordata, defined by the presence of an internal, segmented spinal column and bilateral symmetry.

bilateral symmetry Symmetry in which the right and left sides of the body are approximately mirror images.

placenta An organ that develops inside a pregnant placental mammal that provides the fetus with oxygen and food and helps filter out harmful substances.

prenatal The period of life from conception until birth.

postnatal The period of life from birth until death.

features that maximize the amount of care given to an offspring. As mammals, humans beings have few offspring and provide a great deal of care to each. However, we also differ from the general pattern in that we have more offspring than our closest relatives, the apes, and still provide a great deal of parental care. Our pattern of reproduction is different from that of apes in that we do not wait until a child is fully mature before having another.

From an evolutionary viewpoint, which strategy is better: Having many offspring but providing little care, or having fewer offspring and providing greater care? Each strategy has its advantages and disadvantages. In general, those species that have many offspring tend to be at an advantage in rapidly changing environments, whereas those that provide greater care are at an advantage in more stable environments (Pianka 1983).

Temperature Regulation

Modern mammals are **homoiotherms;** they are able to maintain a constant body temperature under most circumstances. Modern reptiles are cold-blooded and cannot keep their body temperature constant; they need to use the heat of the sun's rays to keep them warm and their metabolism active.

Mammals can maintain a constant body temperature by ingesting large quantities of food and converting the food to energy in the form of heat. The ability to convert food energy to heat allows mammals to live comfortably in many environments where reptiles would slow down or even die.

Mammals are thus able to exploit a large number of environments. Heat production and temperature regulation, however, though obviously useful adaptations in certain environments, are not without a price. To obtain energy, mammals need to consume far greater quantities of food than reptiles. In environments where food resources are limited, mammals may be worse off than reptiles. Again, the evolutionary benefit of any trait must be looked at in terms of its cost.

Teeth

The saying, "You are what you eat," is not usually made literally, but in fact it embodies an important truth of ecology and evolution. The nutritional requirements of organisms dictate, in part, their environmental needs. Also, diet is reflected in the physical structure of organisms, particularly the teeth and jaws. Because mammals maintain a constant body temperature by converting food energy to heat, they require a considerable amount of food. The physical features of mammalian teeth reflect this need.

The teeth of modern reptiles are all the same; they all have sharp sides and continue to grow throughout life. The function of reptilian teeth is to hold and kill prey. The food is then most often eaten whole. Mammals, on

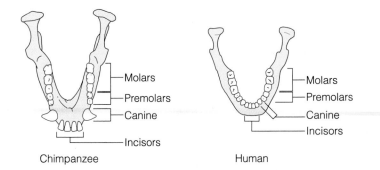

■ FIGURE 4.3
The lower jaws and teeth of
a chimpanzee and a modern
human.

Chimpanzee   Human

the other hand, have different types of teeth in their jaws. Mammals only have two sets of teeth during their lives: a set of deciduous ("baby") teeth and a set of permanent teeth. As a mammal grows and matures, the baby teeth fall out and are replaced with the adult teeth. In modern humans this replacement normally starts around age 6 and takes the first 18 or 20 years of life to complete.

Mammals have four types of teeth: **incisors, canines, premolars,** and **molars.** These teeth are shown for a chimpanzee and a human in Figure 4.3. The incisor teeth are flat and located in the front of the jaw. Both the human and the chimpanzee (and other higher primates) have a total of four incisors in each jaw. These teeth are used for cutting and slicing of food. Behind the incisors are the canine teeth, which are often long and sharp, resembling fangs or tusks. Apes and humans have two canine teeth in each jaw. In many mammals the canine teeth are used as weapons or to kill prey. Although the canine teeth of most mammals are rather large and project beyond the level of the rest of the teeth, human canines are usually small and nonprojecting.

The premolar and molar teeth are also known collectively as the back teeth. Both of these types of teeth are often large in surface area and are used for grinding and chewing food. When you chew food between your back teeth, you do not simply move your lower jaw up and down. Instead, your upper and lower back teeth grind together in a circular motion as your jaw moves up and down and sideways as well. The structure of the premolar

homoioterm
Organism capable of maintaining a constant body temperature under most circumstances.

incisor The flat front teeth used for cutting, slicing, and gnawing food.

canine The teeth located in front of the jaw behind the incisors that are normally used by mammals for puncturing and defense.

premolar One of the types of back teeth used for crushing and grinding food.

molar The teeth furthest back in the jaw used for crushing and grinding food.

■ FIGURE 4.4
The orientation of the limbs
to the body in reptiles and in
mammals.

Reptile   Mammal

and molar teeth are different, and in some mammals they have different functions as well.

The nature of mammalian diet and teeth relates to their warm-bloodedness. Mammals need more food than reptiles, and their teeth allow them to utilize a wider range of food and to process it more productively. The benefits of differentiated teeth lie in these abilities. The cost is the fact that the teeth tend to wear out over time.

Skeletal Structure

Both mammals and reptiles share the basic skeletal structure of all verte-brates, but there are some differences, especially in movement. In reptiles, the four limbs come out from the side of the body for support and move-ment (Figure 4.4). In four-legged mammals, the limbs slope downward from the shoulders and hips. Having the limbs tucked in under the body allows more efficient and quicker movement. The weight of the body is supported better.

Behavior

The brains of all vertebrates have similar structures but differ in size, relative proportions, and functions. All vertebrates have a hindbrain, a midbrain, and a forebrain. In most vertebrates, the hindbrain is associated with hearing, balance, reflexive behaviors, and control of the autonomic functions of the body, such as breathing. The midbrain is associated with vision, and the forebrain is associated with chemical sensing such as smelling ability. Compared to fish, reptiles have a relatively larger midbrain and hindbrain because they rely more extensively on vision and hearing. The midbrain of a reptile is particularly enlarged because it functions to coordinate sensory information and body movements.

The brain of a mammal reveals several important shifts in structure and function. The mammalian brain has a greatly enlarged forebrain that is responsible for the processing of sensory information and coordination. In particular, the forebrain contains the **cerebrum,** the outermost layer of brain cells, which is associated with learning, memory, and intelligence. The cerebrum becomes increasingly convoluted, which allows huge numbers of interconnections between brain cells. It accounts for the largest proportion of the mammalian brain.

The overall functions of a brain include basic body maintenance as well as the ability to process information and respond accordingly. Mammals rely more on learning and flexible responses than do reptiles. Behaviors are less instinctual and rigid. Previous experiences (learning) become more important in responding to stimuli. As a consequence, mammals are more capable of developing new responses to different situations and are capable of learning from past mistakes. New behaviors are more likely to develop and can be passed on to offspring through the process of learning.

The behavioral flexibility of mammals ties in with their pattern of reproduction. In general, the more a species relies on parental care, the more intelligent it is and the more it relies on learning rather than instinct. Extensive parental care requires increased intelligence and the ability to learn new behaviors in order to provide maximum care for infants. The increased emphasis on learning requires, in turn, an extended period of childhood during which to absorb the information needed for the adult life. Furthermore, the extension of childhood requires more extensive child care, so that offspring are protected during the time they need to complete their growth and learning.

The major characteristics of mammals are all interrelated. Reproductive behaviors are associated with learning, intelligence, and social behaviors. The ability to maintain body temperature is related to diet and teeth; warm-bloodedness requires vast amounts of energy that in turn is made available from differentiated teeth and a wide dietary base. Also, the reproductive pattern of placental mammals requires great amounts of energy, which in turn

cerebrum The area of the forebrain that consists of the outermost layer of brain cells, associated with memory, learning, and intelligence.

relates to diet. In fact, the major characteristics of any group of animals are not merely a list of independent traits; they represent an integrated complex of traits.

PRIMATE CHARACTERISTICS

There are many different forms of mammals—they are as diverse as mice, whales, giraffes, cats, dogs, and apes. The mammalian class is broken down into a number of orders. Humans, as noted, are primates, as are the apes, such as the chimpanzee and gorilla, which are our closest living relatives. Monkeys are also primates, as are more biologically primitive forms known as prosimians.

No single characteristic identifies primates; rather, they share a set of features. Many of these features relate to living in the trees. Though it is clear that humans, as well as other modern primates, do not live in the trees, they still retain certain features inherited from ancestors who did.

An **arboreal** (tree-living) environment presents different challenges than a **terrestrial** (ground-living) environment. Living in the trees requires an orientation to a three-dimensional environment. Animals that live on the ground generally contend with only two dimensions: length and width. Arboreal animals must also deal with the third dimension, height. Perception of distance and depth is vital to a tree-living form, which moves quickly from one branch to the next, and from one level of the forest to another. Agility is also important, as is the ability to anchor oneself in space.

Primates are capable of extensive rapid movement through the trees and are able to move to all areas of a tree, including small terminal branches. The two major characteristics of primates that account for their success in the trees are the ability to use hands and feet to grasp branches (rather than digging in with claws), and the ability to perceive distance and depth.

The Skeleton

First let us consider some general characteristics in the primate skeletal structure.

GRASPING HANDS   A characteristic of the earliest known mammals (and reptiles) is five digits on each hand or foot. Certain mammals, such as the horse, have changed from this ancestral condition and only have a single toe on each limb. Other mammals, such as the primates, have kept the ancestral condition.

Primates, including humans, are primitive in the number of digits on the hands and feet. In the case of primates, the retention of the primitive characteristics of five digits on the hands and feet turned out to be an important adaptation. The hands and feet of primates are **prehensile,** meaning that they are capable of being used to grasp objects. The ability to grasp involves the movement of the fingers to the palm, thus allowing the fingers to wrap around an object. This grasping ability is a remarkable adaptation to living in the trees. Primates can grab onto branches to move about, to provide support while eating, and in general to allow for a high degree of flexibility in moving about their environment.

Another feature of primate hands and feet is their expanded tactile pads (such as the ball of your thumb) and nails instead of claws. Nails serve to protect the sensitive skin at the ends of the fingers and the toes. The numerous nerve endings in the tips of fingers and toes of primates provide an enhanced sense of touch that is useful in manipulating objects.

GENERALIZED STRUCTURE   Biological structures are often classified as specialized or generalized. **Specialized structures** are used in a highly specific way, whereas **generalized structures** can be used in a variety of ways. The hooves of a horse, for example, are a specialization that allows rapid running over land surfaces. The basic skeletal structure of primates is generalized because it allows movement flexibility in a wide variety of circumstances.

The arm and leg bones of primates follow the basic pattern of many vertebrates: each limb consists of an upper bone and two lower bones (refer back to Figure 4.1). This structure allows limbs to bend at the elbows or knees. That the lower part of the limb is made up of two bones provides even greater flexibility. This flexibility is obtained by the retention of a generalized skeletal structure.

Vision

The three-dimensional nature of arboreal life requires keen eyesight, particularly depth perception. This feature has evolved from the need to judge distances successfully. (Jumping through the air from branch to branch demands the ability to judge distances. After all, it is not very adaptive to fall short of your target and plunge to the ground!)

Depth perception involves **binocular stereoscopic vision.** *Binocular* refers to overlapping fields of vision. The eyes of many animals are located

arboreal Living in trees.

terrestrial Living on the ground.

prehensile Capable of grasping.

specialized structure A biological structure adapted to a narrow range of conditions and used in very specific ways.

generalized structure A biological structure adapted to a wide range of conditions and used in very general ways.

binocular stereoscopic vision Overlapping fields of vision with both sides of the brain receiving images from both eyes, thereby providing depth perception.

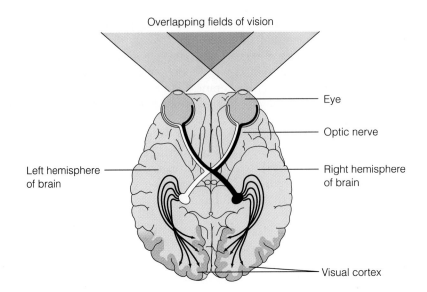

■ FIGURE 4.5
Binocular stereoscopic vision in primates. The fields of vision for each eye overlap, and the optic nerve from each eye is connected to both hemispheres of the brain. (From *Human Antiquity: An Introduction to Physical Anthropology and Archaeology,* 2d ed., by Kenneth Feder and Michael Park. Fig. 5.1. Copyright © 1993 by Mayfield Publishing Company)

at the sides of the skull so that each eye receives a different image with no overlap (Figure 4.5). The eyes of primates are located in the front of the skull so that the fields of vision overlap. Primates see objects in front of them with both eyes. The *stereoscopic* nature of primate vision refers to the way in which the brain processes visual signals. In nonstereoscopic animals, the information from one eye is received in only one hemisphere of the brain. In primates, the visual signals from both eyes are received in both hemispheres of the brain. The result is an image that has depth. Moving quickly and safely in three dimensions makes use of depth perception.

Primates are vision-oriented. On average, their sense of smell is less keen. As a result, the areas of the face devoted to smelling are reduced in primates. Compared to other mammals, primates have short snouts.

The Brain and Behavior

Primates have expanded on the basic pattern of mammalian brains. Their brains are even larger relative to body size. Primate brains have larger visual areas and smaller areas for smelling, corresponding to their increased emphasis of vision over smell as the main sense. Also, primate brains are even more complex than those of most other mammals. Primates have larger proportions of the brain associated with learning and intelligence. Areas of the brain associated with body control and coordination are also proportionately larger, as expected from the demands of arboreal life. Hand–eye coordination, for example, is crucial for moving about in the trees.

Primates rely even more extensively than other mammals on learned behaviors. As a result, it is often difficult to assign specific behaviors to a given species of primate because the increased emphasis on learning allows a great deal of flexibility in behavior patterns.

The increased emphasis on learning means that primates spend a greater proportion of their lives growing up, both biologically and socially, than other animals. The more an animal needs to learn, the longer the period of time needed for learning. An increase in the amount of time spent as an infant or child further means that greater amounts of attention and care are required from parents.

Reproduction and Care of Offspring

As with all mammals, primates are characterized by a small number of offspring and a great deal of parental care.

THE MOTHER–INFANT BOND   Primates have a strong and long-lasting bond between mother and infant. Unlike some mammals, infant primates are entirely helpless. They depend on their mothers for food, warmth, protection, affection, and knowledge, and they remain dependent for a long time. Of all the different types of social bonds in primate societies, the mother–infant bond is the strongest. In many primate species this bond continues well past childhood.

PATERNAL CARE   Paternal care is highly variable among primate species. In general, primates that are **monogamous** (characterized by a more or less permanent bond forming between a single male and female) are most likely to show high levels of paternal care. By contrast, species that are polygamous tend, on average, to show less paternal involvement with offspring. This difference may relate to the fact that in monogamous species it is easy for the male to tell he is the father! In a **polygamous** species, paternal behaviors may be less appropriate from a genetic perspective because a male can never be sure if he is the father.

GROWING UP   The importance of the extended period of infant and child growth in primates cannot be overstated. The long period of growth is necessary for learning motor skills and social behaviors. The close bond between mother and infant provides the first important means by which an infant primate learns. It is not the only important social contact for a growing

---

monogamy An exclusive sexual bond between an adult male and an adult female for a long period of time.

polygamy A sexual bond between an adult male and an adult female in which either individual may have more than one mate at the same time.

Social Structure and Testes Size in Primates

Bizarre as it might sound at first, scientists have collected information on the size of the testes, the male reproductive organ that produces sperm, in different primate species, and have made some interesting observations. For example, the size of the testes ranges from roughly 1.2 grams (0.04 oz) in one New World monkey species to 119 grams (over 4 oz, or 1/4 lb) in chimpanzees. However, not all hominoids have such large testes. The average testes size is roughly 30 grams (1 oz) in gorillas, 35 grams (1.25 oz) in orangutans, and 41 grams (1.4 oz) in humans.

A quick look at the testes size of all primate species for which we have data shows that part of the reason for so much variation is differences in body size. In general, the larger the body, the larger the testes. The graph shows the overall relationship between average body size and average testes size for 33 primate species, including prosimians, monkeys, apes, and humans. For technical reasons, we plot the logarithms of both body weight and testes weight. The straight line shows the best fit between the logarithm of body weight and the logarithm of testes weight and clearly shows that the larger the body, the larger the testes. (The relationship is actually curved somewhat,

---

Source of data: Harcourt et al. (1981).

which is why we use logarithms. This means that the increase is not linear.)

Nevertheless, when we look at the actual data points on the curve, we can see that, although there is an average relationship between body weight and testes weight, it is not perfect. Some species are above the line, meaning they have larger testes than expected, and some species are below the line, meaning they have smaller testes than expected. For example, humans have testes that are about two-thirds the size expected on the basis of our body weight. Chimpanzees, however, have testes that are 2.5 times that expected! Both orangutans and gorillas have smaller testes than expected on the basis of body weight.

Are these deviations random, or do they reflect that some factor other than body weight might be responsible for testes size? Harcourt and colleagues (1981) investigated this question and came to the conclusion that an important factor was the type of social structure associated with each primate species. The graph shows their results. Species that have a single male (either family structure or uni-male structure) are indicated by the filled-in squares. There is a definite tendency for those species to fall below the predicted line—that is, to have smaller testes than

primate, however. The process of socialization in most primates depends to a large extent on close contact with peers. Interaction with other individuals of the same age provides the opportunity to learn specific types of social behaviors as well as how to interact socially in general.

Social Structure

Primates are essentially social creatures. The close bond between mother and infant, the importance of learning, and the great flexibility in behaviors all point to this fact. Apart from this general need, primates show an amazing amount of variation in the ways in which their societies are structured. The main social group of primates can range in size from two individuals up to several hundred and can have different proportions of males, females, young, and old.

A social group is generally defined as a group within which there is frequent communication or interaction among members. **Social structure** con-

expected. Species with a multimale social structure, indicated by filled-in circles, tend to fall above the predicted line, showing that they have larger testes than expected. The bottom line is that once we control for body size, males in multimale societies have larger testes.

What is the reason for differences according to social structure? Harcourt and colleagues suggest that larger testes are needed in primate societies where mating is frequent and where many males mate with a female during estrus. Chimpanzees are a good example of this. They suggest that natural selection favored males with larger testes, and hence a greater amount of sperm, so they could compete genetically with other males. In primate societies with less frequent mating, and where females generally mate with only one male, larger testes would not be selected for. Examples here include orangutans and gorillas.

Of course, testes size is not only a function of body size and social structure. Harcourt and colleagues note other potential influences, such as seasonality of mating. However, the strong relationship observed in their study suggests that there is often a link between biology and behavior that is best interpreted in an evolutionary context.

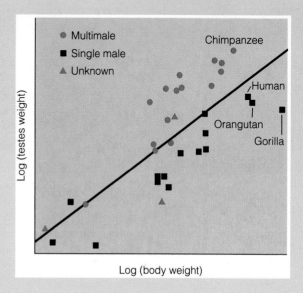

Relationship between body weight (logarithm) and testes weight (logarithm) in 33 primate species. The solid line is the predicted relationship between body weight and testes weight. Individual points correspond to the different species. Species with a uni-male society in breeding are indicated by a filled-in square. Species with a multi-male society are indicated by a filled-in circle. Species with an unknown social structure are indicated by a filled-in diamond.

sists of the composition of the social group and the way in which it is organized. There are five basic types of primate social structure, with variations on most of these.

SOCIAL GROUPS   The smallest social group is the **solitary group,** which consists of the mother and dependent offspring. Adult males and adult females have infrequent contact, generally for mating. A slightly larger social group is the **monogamous family group,** consisting of an adult male, an adult female,

▲▲

social structure The composition of a social group and the way it is organized, including size, age structure, and number of each sex in the group.

solitary group The smallest primate social group, consisting of the mother and her dependent offspring.

monogamous family group Social structure in which the primary social group consists of an adult male, an adult female, and their immature offspring.

■ FIGURE 4.6
Two adult male baboons engaged in a dominance dispute. Though physical violence does occur in such encounters, much of the display is bluff. (Irven Devore/Anthro-Photo)

and their immature offspring. The adult male and female form a long-term pair bond, and are sexually active only with each other. Although this corresponds to a typical Western notion of "family," it is not that common among primates. The social unit of a few primate species is the **polyandrous group,** a small group of adult males and one or more adult females and their offspring. Although there may be more than one adult female in the group, only one is reproductively active. A **uni-male group** consists of one adult male, several adult females, and their offspring. The most common social structure in nonhuman primate societies is the **multimale/multifemale group,** which consists of more than one adult of each sex and the offspring. Given multiple adult males and adult females, these are complex social groups that are often quite large. Given multiple adults, mating tends to be promiscuous. There is considerable variation in this type of social structure, in terms of size, composition, and distribution (Wolfe 1995).

SOCIAL ORGANIZATION AND DOMINANCE Nonhuman primate societies show a ranking of individuals in terms of their relative dominance in the group. A **dominance hierarchy** is the ranking system within the society and reflects which individuals are most and least dominant (Figure 4.6). Dominance hierarchies are found in most nonhuman primate societies, but they vary widely in their overall importance in everyday life. The dominance hierarchy provides stability in social life. All individuals know their place within the society, eliminating to some extent uncertainty about what to do or whom to follow. An individual's place in the dominance hierarchy is influenced by many factors, including size, strength, age, the ability to cooperate, and even the dominance rank of the mother.

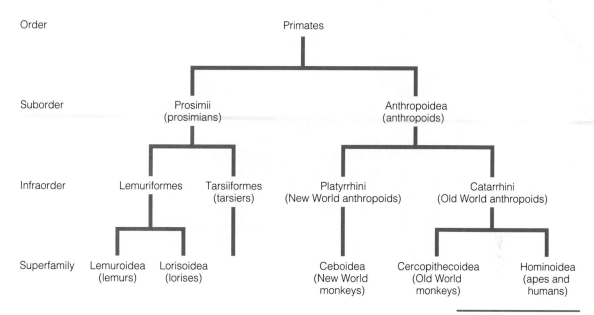

Order	Primates

Suborder — Prosimii (prosimians) / Anthropoidea (anthropoids)

Infraorder — Lemuriformes / Tarsiiformes (tarsiers) / Platyrrhini (New World anthropoids) / Catarrhini (Old World anthropoids)

Superfamily — Lemuroidea (lemurs) / Lorisoidea (lorises) / Ceboidea (New World monkeys) / Cercopithecoidea (Old World monkeys) / Hominoidea (apes and humans)

■ FIGURE 4.7
Summary of traditional primate taxonomy. Names within parentheses are common names. A more detailed taxonomy is provided in Appendix 1.

TYPES OF PRIMATES

The two major subgroups of the living primates are the suborder **Prosimii** and the suborder **Anthropoidea.** These are the official scientific names (in Latin) for the two suborders, although here we will use the more common terms prosimians and anthropoids. Each of these suborders is broken down into smaller taxonomic units, such as infraorders, superfamilies, families, and so on. Figure 4.7 shows the traditional primate taxonomy used throughout most of this chapter.

polyandrous group A rare type of primate social structure, consisting of a small number of adult males, one reproductively active adult female, and their offspring. Other adult females may belong to the group but are not reproductively active.

uni-male group Social structure in which the primary social group consists of a single adult male, several adult females, and their offspring.

multimale/multifemale group A type of social structure in which the primary social group is made up of several adult males, several adult females, and their offspring.

dominance hierarchy The ranking system within a society that indicates which individuals are dominant in social behaviors.

Prosimii (prosimians) The suborder of

primates that are biologically primitive compared to anthropoids.

Anthropoidea (anthropoids) The suborder of primates consisting of monkeys, apes, and humans.

■ FIGURE 4.8
A loris, a prosimian from Southeast Asia. (© Stouffer Enterprises/Animals Animals)

■ FIGURE 4.9
A tarsier, a prosimian from Southeast Asia. Unlike other prosimians, the tarsier does not have a moist nose.
(© Zoological Society of San Diego)

Prosimians

The word *prosimian* means literally "before simians" (monkeys and apes). In biological terms, prosimians are more primitive, or more like early primate ancestors, than are monkeys and apes. The prosimians often lack one or more of the general characteristics of primates. For example, some prosimians lack color vision, and some have a single claw on each hand or foot.

Another primitive characteristic of prosimians is that they rely to a much greater extent on the sense of smell than do the anthropoids. Prosimian brains are also generally smaller relative to body size than are the brains of anthropoids. Prosimians are usually small in size, tend to be solitary, and many are **nocturnal** (active at night). Prosimians themselves show considerable variation. Some prosimians have larger body sizes, some have larger social groups, and some are **diurnal** (active in daylight).

There are three different groups of prosimians in the world today, each with a number of different species. One group, the **lorises,** are small, solitary, nocturnal prosimians found in Asia and Africa (Figure 4.8). Another group, the **tarsiers,** also small, solitary, and nocturnal, are found in Indonesia. The nocturnal nature of tarsiers is evidenced by their large eyes, the size of which serves to gather available light (Figure 4.9).

The most biologically diverse group of prosimians is the **lemurs,** which are found only on the island of Madagascar off the southeast coast of Africa (Figure 4.10). Some species of lemurs are nocturnal and some are diurnal. Social structure is highly variable among the lemurs: some have the family group structure, some have the uni-male group structure, and some have the multimale/multifemale group structure. Other characteristics, such as body size, diet, and group size, are also variable among lemur species.

Anthropoids

The anthropoids are the higher primates and consist of monkeys and hominoids (apes and humans). Anthropoids are generally larger in overall body size, have larger and more complex brains, rely more on visual abilities, and show more complex social structures than other primates. Except for one monkey species, all anthropoids are diurnal. The anthropoids include both arboreal and terrestrial species.

All living prosimians are found in the Old World, but anthropoids are found in both the New World and the Old World. (The Old World consists

nocturnal Active during the night.

diurnal Active during the day.

loris Nocturnal prosimian found today in Asia and Africa.

tarsier Nocturnal prosimian found today in Indonesia.

lemur A prosimian found today on the island of Madagascar.

of the continents of Africa, Asia, and Europe; the New World is the Americas.) New World anthropoids are found today in Central and South America. Old World anthropoids are found today in Africa and Asia (and one monkey species in Europe). The only New World anthropoids are monkeys, whereas Old World anthropoids include monkeys, apes, and humans.

THE MONKEYS

Anthropoids include monkeys and hominoids (apes and humans). Monkeys and apes are often confused in the popular imagination. In reality, they are easy to tell apart. Monkeys have tails, apes and humans do not. Monkeys also have smaller brains relative to body size than apes or humans. The typical pattern of monkey movement is on all fours (**quadrupedal**), and their arms and legs are generally of similar length so that their spines are parallel to the ground. By contrast, apes have longer arms than legs and humans have longer legs than arms.

New World Monkeys

The only form of anthropoids found native to the New World are the New World monkeys (there are no New World apes). Although they share many similarities with Old World monkeys, several important differences reflect separate lines of evolution over the past 30 million years or so.

Some of the differences between the New World and Old World monkeys are useful in reconstructing evolutionary relationships. For example,

■ **FIGURE 4.11**
A spider monkey, capable of using its tail as a "fifth limb." (© Zoological Society of San Diego)

New World monkeys have four more premolar teeth than Old World monkeys. Other differences relate to the way in which the monkeys live; for example, many New World monkeys have prehensile tails.

Because the tail of many New World monkeys is capable of grasping, it is highly useful in moving about and feeding in the trees (Figure 4.11). Typically, the monkey uses this "fifth limb" to anchor itself while feeding on the ends of small branches. Old World monkeys have tails, but none of them have prehensile tails. Those New World monkeys with prehensile tails are thus more proficient in terms of acrobatic agility.

Old World Monkeys

Old World monkeys are biochemically and physically more similar to humans than are New World monkeys. For example, Old World monkeys have the same number of teeth as apes and humans. Old World monkeys inhabit a wide range of environments. Many species live in tropical rain forests, but other species have adapted to the **savanna** (open grasslands). One species has even learned to survive in the snowy environment of the Japanese mountains (Figure 4.12).

quadrupedal A form of movement in which all four limbs are of equal size and make contact with the ground, and the spine is roughly parallel to the ground.

savanna An environment consisting of open grasslands in which food resources tend to be spread out over large areas.

The Old World monkeys, like the New World monkeys, are quadrupedal, running on the ground and branches on all fours. Though Old-World monkeys are agile in the trees, many species have adapted to spending more time on the ground in search of food. Most Old World species eat a mixed diet of fruits and leaves (Figure 4.13), although some show dental and digestive specializations for leaf eating. Some Old World species occasionally supplement their primarily vegetarian diet with insects or small animals that they hunt.

Social structure is highly variable among Old World monkeys. Most known species have been characterized as having either multimale/multifemale or uni-male social groups. However, a large proportion of Old World monkey species has been observed with more than one social structure, depending on the specific group, once again showing behavioral variation. For example, the baboon, a widely studied Old World monkey, lives in large, multimale/multifemale groups on the African savanna (Figure 4.14).

■ FIGURE 4.12
Japanese macaques, adapted to living in the snow. (© Steven Kaufman/Peter Arnold, Inc.)

■ FIGURE 4.13
A mandrill, an Old World monkey. (© Zoological Society of San Diego)

■ FIGURE 4.14
Baboons on the savanna. (Shirley C. Strum, © 1987 National Geographic Society)

■ **FIGURE 4.15**
Top view of the shoulder complex of a monkey (*top*) and a human (*bottom*) drawn to the same scale top to bottom. In hominoids (apes and humans), the clavicle is larger and the scapula is located more toward the rear of the body.

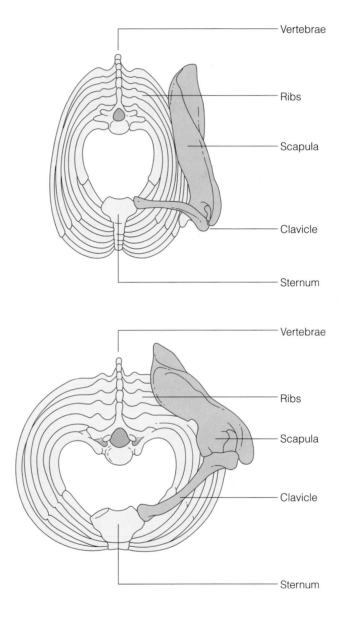

The Hominoids

In addition to the monkeys, the other major group of living anthropoids are the **hominoids,** which is a group composed of apes and humans.

Unlike monkeys, hominoids do not have tails. Another hominoid characteristic is size: in general, apes and humans are larger than monkeys. Hominoid brains as a rule are larger than monkey brains, both in terms of absolute size and in relationship to body size. Their brains are also more complex, which correlates with the hominoid characteristics of greater intelligence and learning abilities. Hominoids invest the most time and effort in raising their young.

Perhaps one of the most important characteristics of hominoids is their upper body and shoulder anatomy. Hominoids can raise their arms above their heads with little trouble, whereas a monkey would find this difficult. This ability of hominoids to raise their arms above their heads is based on three basic anatomical features. First, hominoids have a larger and stronger collarbone than monkeys. Second, the hominoid shoulder joint is very flexible and capable of a wide angle of movement. Third, hominoid shoulder blades are located more toward the back. By contrast, monkeys' shoulder blades are located more toward the sides of the chest (Figure 4.15). Hominoid shoulder joints face outward, compared to the shoulder joints of monkeys, which are downward-facing.

Hominoid anatomy allows them a different type of movement from that of monkeys. Hominoids are adept at climbing and hanging from branches. They are **suspensory climbers.** As hominoids, humans have retained this ability, although we seldom use it in our daily lives. One exception is children playing on so-called "monkey bars" at playgrounds (which should more properly be called "hominoid bars"). The ability to suspend by the arms and then swing from one rung of the bars to the next is a basic hominoid trait.

Living hominoids all share this basic ability but vary quite a bit in terms of their normal patterns of movement. Some apes, for example, are proficient arm swingers, whereas others are expert climbers. Humans have evolved a totally different pattern in which the arms are not used for movement; this allows us to carry things while walking on two legs.

Living hominoids are divided into three categories: the lesser apes, the great apes, and humans. The lesser apes are the gibbon (six species) and the siamang (one species), and are the least related to humans. The great apes are the Asian orangutan and the African ape, the gorilla, chimpanzee, and bonobo. A list of the scientific and common names of all living hominoids is given in Table 4.2.

That all of these species have certain shared characteristics allows us to classify them as hominoids and to infer that they are related through evolution. The specific evolutionary relationship of the different hominoids is more difficult to establish. To uncover our own origins, we are interested in determining which ape species is the most similar to us. In this way we are able to compare the anatomy of living and fossil hominoids to determine what changed in our line, what changed in the ape line, and what stayed the same.

The *exact* nature of the relationship among the great apes and humans has long been debated. The oldest of these ideas places all the great apes in a group separate from humans (humans were classified as hominids and all great apes were classified as pongids), implying that all great apes are equally similar to one another and that humans are quite distinct. This model,

▲▲▲▲▲▲▲▲▲▲▲▲▲▲▲▲▲▲▲▲▲▲▲▲▲▲▲▲▲▲▲

hominoid A superfamily of anthropoids consisting of apes and humans.

suspensory climbing The ability to raise the arms above the head and hang on branches and to climb in this position.

■ TABLE 4.2
Traditional Taxonomy of Living Hominoids

FAMILY	GENUS	SPECIES	COMMON NAME
Hylobatidae (lesser apes)	*Hylobates*	*agilis*	Agile gibbon
	Hylobates	*concolor*	Crested gibbon
	Hylobates	*hoolock*	Hoolock gibbon
	Hylobates	*klossi*	Kloss's gibbon
	Hylobates	*lar*	White-handed gibbon
	Hylobates	*moloch*	Silver gibbon
	Symphalangus	*syndactylus*	Siamang
Pongidae (great apes)	*Gorilla*	*gorilla*	Gorilla
	Pan	*paniscus*	Bonobo (pygmy chimpanzee)
	Pan	*troglodytes*	Chimpanzee (common chimpanzee)
	Pongo	*pygmaeus*	Orangutan
Hominidae (humans)	*Homo*	*sapiens*	Human

Source: Bramblett (1994)

which had its roots in the then-prevailing concept of human uniqueness, is now rejected. Anatomical and genetic data show that humans and the African apes are more similar to one another than any are to the Asian great ape, the orangutan.

Biochemical and genetic comparisons clearly demonstrate that the African apes and humans are most similar to one another. In a classic study of protein differences and DNA sequences between chimpanzees and humans, King and Wilson (1975) found that the two species are over 98 percent identical. Subsequent research confirmed this finding and extended it to the bonobo and the gorilla. The finding implies that humans and African apes all split from a common ancestor at roughly the same time.

The traditional view of humans as separate from all apes is shown in Figure 4.16, which illustrates the traditional taxonomy of hominoids. This perspective is still widespread, in part because it necessitates a separate family (hominids) for human beings and their immediate ancestors. Although many question humans' uniqueness, it is still useful to separate us from the great apes for certain discussions of anatomy, behavior, and evolution. Figure 4.16 represents a phenetic view, emphasizing overall physical (and behavioral) similarity but does not, however, reflect what we know about overall evolutionary similarity.

A different view, shown in Figure 4.17, correctly shows the finding of many genetic and anatomical studies that African apes and humans form a group separate from that of the Asian apes.

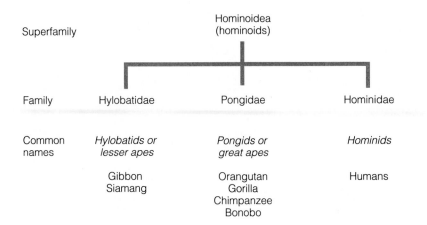

■ FIGURE 4.16
Traditional taxonomic classification of hominoids. Names within parentheses refer to common names. To emphasize certain aspects of behavior and physical characteristics, the orangutan, gorilla, chimpanzee, and bonobo are all placed in a separate category from humans. Although useful for some purposes (such as classifying by behaviors), this classification does not reflect the fact that humans and the African apes are more genetically similar to each other than any are to the orangutan. Compare this classification with Figure 4.17.

Part of the confusion (especially for introductory students) lies in the different uses of the same names. The term *hominid*, for example, is used to refer only to humans in Figure 4.16, whereas it refers to both humans *and* African apes in Figure 4.17. In order to make things somewhat less confusing in later chapters, we use the traditional classification given in Figure 4.16. Keep in mind, however, that such a classification does not reflect the evolutionary relationships in terms of common ancestors.

THE LIVING APES

Although the living hominoids all share a number of features, they also show a great deal of biological and behavioral variation.

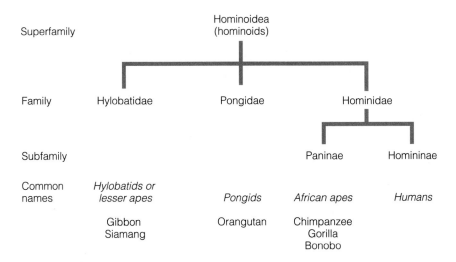

■ FIGURE 4.17
Revised taxonomic classification of hominoids to emphasize genetic and evolutionary relationships. The African apes and humans form a group separate from the Asian apes. This classification does not fit our usual informal notion of "ape" versus "human." Although useful, the classification does not reflect common aspects of behavior or physical appearance. Compare this classification with Figure 4.16.

FIGURE 4.18
A gibbon brachiating. Gibbons and siamangs are the most acrobatic of the apes and can swing by their arms easily.
(Kenneth Feder)

Gibbons and Siamangs

The gibbon and closely related siamang are the smallest of the living apes. There are six recognized species of gibbon and one species of siamang. For the purpose of this discussion, the term *gibbon* applies to all these forms.

The physical characteristics of gibbons reflect adaptation to life in the trees. The climbing and hanging adaptations of hominoids have evolved in the gibbon to allow highly agile movement through trees. The gibbon's usual form of movement, known as **brachiation,** consists of hand-over-hand swinging from branch to branch. Many primates are often portrayed as arm swingers, but only the gibbon can perform this movement quickly and efficiently (Figure 4.18).

Gibbons and siamangs are found in the tropical rain forests of Southeast Asia, specifically Thailand, Vietnam, Burma, and the Malay Peninsula. The rain forest environment is characterized by heavy rainfall that is relatively constant throughout the year. Rain forests have incredibly rich and diverse vegetation. The gibbons' diet consists primarily of fruits supplemented by leaves.

The social group of gibbons is a monogamous family structure: an adult male, an adult female, and their offspring. The male and female form a mating pair for their entire lives. For the most part, neither males nor females are dominant over the other. Both exhibit equal levels of aggression.

■ **FIGURE 4.19**
Mother and baby orangutans. (© Zoological Society of San Diego)

■ **FIGURE 4.20**
An orangutan foraging. (Animals Animals © Mickey Gibson)

Orangutans

The orangutan is a large ape found only in certain areas of Southeast Asia. The word *orangutan* translates from Malay as "man of the forest" (Figure 4.19).

Males are roughly twice the size of females; an average adult male weighs between 80 and 90 kg (roughly 175 to 200 lb), and an average adult female weighs between 33 and 45 kg (roughly 73 to 99 lb) (Markham and Groves 1990).

Orangutans are agile climbers and hangers. In the trees, they use both arms and legs to climb in a slow, cautious manner. They will use one or more limbs to anchor themselves to branches while using the other limbs to feed (Figure 4.20). Younger orangutans occasionally brachiate, but the larger adults generally move through the trees in a different manner. A large orangutan will not swing from one tree to the next; rather, it will rock the tree it is on slowly in the direction of the next tree and then move over when the two trees are close together. The orangutan's great agility in climbing is due, in part, to its basic hominoid shoulder structure.

brachiation A method of movement that uses the arms to swing from branch to branch.

■ FIGURE 4.21
An adult male gorilla knuckle walking. Note the angle of the spine relative to the ground because of the longer front limbs. (© Zoological Society of San Diego)

Orangutans are largely arboreal. Males, however, frequently come to the ground and travel along the forest floor for long distances. On the ground, orangutans walk on all fours but with their fists partially closed. Unlike monkeys, who rest their weight on their palms, orangutans rest on their fists: a form of movement often called fist walking.

The orangutan is found today only in Sumatra and Borneo in Southeast Asia. Orangutans are vegetarians, with over 60 percent of their diet consisting of fruit (Jolly 1985). As does the gibbon, the orangutan lives in tropical rain forests.

Orangutans have the solitary social group structure, consisting of a mother and infant. Males are not needed for protection because there is little danger from predators (Horr 1972). Adult males generally live by themselves, interacting only during times of mating. Orangutans are polygamous; they do not form long-term bonds with any one partner.

Gorillas

Gorillas, the largest living primates, are found only in equatorial Africa. An adult male gorilla weighs 160 kg (roughly 350 lb) on average. Adult females weigh less but are still very large for primates (70 kg/155 lb) (Leutenegger

■ **FIGURE 4.22**
A gorilla social group.
(© Michael K. Nichols/Magnum Photos Inc.)

1982). Besides a much larger body size, the adult males also have larger canine teeth and often large crests of bone on top of their skulls for anchoring their large jaw muscles. Gorillas usually have blackish hair; fully mature adult males have silvery gray hair on their backs. These adult males are called "silverbacks."

Their large size makes gorillas predominantly terrestrial. Their typical means of movement is called **knuckle walking:** they move about on all fours, resting their weight on the knuckles of their front limbs. Because their arms are longer than their legs, gorilla spines are at an angle to the ground (Figure 4.21).

Gorillas are found only in certain forested areas in Africa. Their range is disappearing rapidly, primarily as the result of the replacement of forests by human farming land and human poaching (Fossey 1983). Gorillas live in humid rain forests in both the lowlands and in the mountain regions. Compared to the rain forests of the orangutans, the gorilla's environment is characterized by greater clumping of food resources (Denham 1971).

Gorillas live in small social groups of about a dozen individuals. The social group consists of an adult male (the silverback), several adult females, and their immature offspring (Figure 4.22). Occasionally, one or more younger adult males are part of the group, but they tend not to mate with the females. Though dominance rank varies among the females and subadult

▲▲▲▲▲▲▲▲▲▲▲▲▲▲▲▲▲▲▲▲▲▲▲▲▲▲▲▲▲

knuckle walking A form of movement used by chimpanzees and gorillas that is characterized by all four limbs touching the ground, with the weight of the arms resting on the knuckles of the hands.

■ FIGURE 4.23
Variation in chimpanzee faces.
(© Wrangham/Anthro-Photo)

males, the adult silverback male is the most dominant individual in the group and is the leader. The silverback sets the pace for the rest of the group, determining when and how far to move in search of food.

Chimpanzees

Chimpanzees are found in Africa. They are smaller than gorillas and show only slight sexual dimorphism. Adult males weigh about 45 kg (99 lb) on average and adult females weigh about 37 kg (82 lb) on average (Leutenegger 1982). Chimpanzees have extremely powerful shoulders and arms. Like humans, chimpanzees show great variation in facial features and overall physical appearance (Figure 4.23).

Chimpanzees, like gorillas, are knuckle walkers, with longer arms than legs. Chimpanzees, however, are more active and agile than gorillas. Chimpanzees are both terrestrial and arboreal. They spend considerable time in the trees, either sleeping or looking for food.

Most chimpanzees are found in the African rain forests, although some groups are also found in the mixed forest–savanna environments on the fringe of the rain forests. The chimpanzee diet consists mainly of fruit (almost 70 percent), although they also eat leaves, seeds, nuts, insects, and meat. Chimpanzees have been observed hunting small animals, such as monkeys, and sharing the meat. Though some of the hunting occurs spontaneously when chimpanzees encounter small animals, other hunting behavior appears to be planned and coordinated.

Chimpanzees live in large communities of 50 or more individuals. Their social structure constantly changes, with individuals and groups fragmenting and later rejoining the main group. All chimpanzees recognize and interact with others in the group. Chimpanzee groups are less rigid than other multimale primate societies such as baboons. Although all members of the group do interact to some extent, it is common for smaller subgroups to form much of the time. The actual composition of these subgroups also changes frequently.

Bonobos

The **bonobo** is the third and least well known of the African apes. The bonobo is closely related to the chimpanzee and is commonly considered a separate species of chimpanzee known as the "pygmy chimpanzee" (compared to what is often termed the "common chimpanzee"). Although the bonobo is somewhat smaller than the chimpanzee (about 85 percent of the weight), the term "pygmy chimpanzee" is not really accurate; hence, we use the name "bonobo" here. The close similarity of chimpanzees and bonobos is reflected in their assignment to the same genus—*Pan* (the scientific names are *Pan troglodytes* for the chimpanzee and *Pan paniscus* for the bonobo).

At first glance, bonobos seem quite similar to chimpanzees (Figure 4.24). On closer examination, however, we see that the bonobo has relatively longer legs, a higher center of gravity, and a narrower chest. It tends to have a higher forehead and differently shaped face (Savage-Rumbaugh and Lewin 1994). Like gorillas and chimpanzees, bonobos are frequent knuckle walkers. Of particular interest is the fact that bonobos can walk upright more easily than other apes (Figure 4.25). This observation, combined with other evidence, suggests that the first hominids may have been quite similar in many ways to bonobos.

Bonobos are found only in a restricted rain forest region in Zaire in central Africa. It is estimated that there are fewer than 10,000 bonobos alive today. Their diet consists primarily of fruit, supplemented with plants. Unlike chimpanzees, bonobos consume little animal protein, and do not hunt monkeys (de Waal 1995).

As with chimpanzees, bonobos live in multimale/multifemale groups. However, there are important differences in the social organization of these two species. In chimpanzee society, males are dominant over females, and some of the strongest bonds in the social order are between adult males. In

■ FIGURE 4.25
A bonobo. (© Frans
Lanting/Minden Pictures)

bonobo society, things are quite different. Here, the strongest social bonds are between adult females, and even though they are physically smaller, it is the females who are most dominant. In addition, the dominance status of a male depends in large part on the dominance of his mother (de Waal 1995).

Some of the most interesting observations of bonobo behavior have to do with the function of sexual activity in their social interactions. In addition to sexual intercourse, bonobos also engage in a variety of sex play, including rubbing of genitals and oral sex. Continued observation of bonobo groups has revealed that such sex play is frequently used to reduce tension and avoid conflict. Researchers have shown repeatedly that bonobos will engage in a brief period of sex play in a tense social situation. In bonobo society, sexual play is a method of peacemaking (de Waal 1995).

SUMMARY

The biological and behavioral nature of human beings is found in similarities to other living creatures. Humans are animals, chordates, and vertebrates. We share certain characteristics, such as a more developed nervous system, with other creatures in these categories. Humans are also mammals, which means that we rely a great deal on a reproductive strategy of few births and extensive parental care. This reproductive pattern is associated with high intelligence and a great capacity for learning behaviors.

Humans belong to a specific order of mammals known as primates. The primates have certain characteristics, such as grasping hands and depth perception, that evolved in order to meet the demands of living in the trees. Primates show a great deal of variation in the size and structure of their social groups, ranging from solitary groups consisting of a female and her offspring to large communities with many adults and offspring.

The order Primates is composed of the more biologically primitive prosimians and the anthropoids, which consist of monkeys (New World and Old World) and the hominoids (apes and humans). Monkeys are quadrupedal (four-footed) and have a tail. Although New World monkeys are exclusively arboreal, some Old World monkeys are arboreal and some are terrestrial. The hominoids are a group of anthropoids that share certain characteristics, such as the lack of a tail and a shoulder complex suitable for climbing and hanging.

The living apes are found in Asia and Africa. The asian apes consist of the gibbon (and siamang) and the orangutan. The African apes, our closest living relatives, consist of the gorilla, the chimpazee, and the bonobo. The living apes show a great deal of environmental, anatomical, and behavioral variation. The gibbon and saimang live in family groups, the orangutan is solitary, the gorilla lives in uni-male groups, and the chimpanzee and bonobo live in large, complex multimale/multifemale groups.

SUPPLEMENTAL READINGS

Fossey, D. 1983. *Gorillas in the Mist*. Boston: Houghton-Miffin. A popular and well-written account of the late Dian Fossey's researches on the behavior of the mountain gorilla. Deals specifically with the problem of human intervention and the likely extinction of the mountain gorilla.

Goodall, J. 1986. *The Chimpanzees of Gombe: Patterns of Behavior*. Cambridge, Mass.: Harvard University Press. A comprehensive review of Jane Goodall's research since the early 1960s, this is a well-written and superbly illustrated description of chimpanzee behavior.

Jolly, A. 1985. *The Evolution of Primate Behavior*. 2d ed. New York: MacMillan. An introduction to primate biology and behavior with particular emphasis on studies of social structure and primate psychology.

Richards, A. F. 1985. *Primates in Nature*. New York: W. H. Freeman. An introduction to primate biology and behavior that emphasizes primate ecology.

CHAPTER 5

The Human Species

What are humans? This question has been a focus of science, art, and literature. Many different fields, from theology to psychology, have addressed its ultimate significance. Our perspective on ourselves is not abstract; the way we define what we are affects the way we treat others and the rest of the world.

One of the earliest written definitions of humanity is found in Psalm 8:4–6 of the Bible, where the question is put to God:

> What is man, that thou art mindful of him? and the son of man, that thou visitest him? For thou hath made him a little lower than the angels, and hast crowned him with glory and honor. Thou hast madest him to have dominion over the works of thy hands; thou hast put all things under his feet.

This brief statement reflects a long-standing belief of Western civilization that humans are inherently superior to all other life forms on the planet, ranking far above animals yet "lower than the angels." The view that humans are the supreme creatures in the natural world is also apparent in the works of many Greek philosophers. Aristotle, for example, constructed an arrangement of all things with inanimate matter at the "bottom" and humans at the "top" (Kennedy 1976).

This chapter examines modern humans from the same perspective as the last chapter, focusing on the biologic and behavioral uniqueness assigned to human beings. The final part of this chapter examines the question of how unique we are by comparing certain human behaviors (tool use, language) with similar behaviors seen in some living apes.

CHARACTERISTICS OF LIVING HUMANS

This section focuses on certain key features of modern humans, particularly our brains, upright walking, teeth, reproductive patterns, physical growth, and social structure. Some of these characteristics are also used to identify humanlike ancestors that lie along our evolutionary line since the split of apes and humans some 5 to 7 million years ago (discussed in Chapter 6). Humans and humanlike ancestors are also known by the term **hominid.**

Distribution and Environment

Humans are the most widely distributed living primate species. As later chapters will outline, humans originally evolved in a tropical environment. In fact, much of our present-day biology reflects the fact that we are tropical mammals. During the course of human evolution, however, we have expanded into many different environments. Biological adaptations have aided humans in new environments, such as cold weather and high altitude. The cultural adaptations of humans have allowed even greater expansion. Today there is no place on the planet where we cannot live, given the appropriate technology. Humans can live in the frozen wastes of Antarctica, deep beneath the sea, and in the vacuum of outer space. Our cultural adaptations have allowed us to range far beyond our biological limitations. These adaptations have also permitted incredible population growth. In the past, the planet supported no more than roughly 1 to 6 million people at a hunting-and-gathering level of existence (Weiss 1984). Today the population of the world is over five billion and continuing to grow. It is easily argued that the quality of life is still low for much of the world's human population, but there is no doubting that our ability to learn and develop technology has led to immense potential for population expansion.

Brain Size and Structure

One very obvious biological characteristic of the human species is the large brain. Our bulging and rounded skulls and flat faces contrast with these features in other animals, including the rest of the hominoids. Whereas an

hominid Humans and humanlike ancestors.

TABLE 5.1
Brain Volume of Selected Living Primates (in Cubic Centimeters)

PRIMATE SPECIES	RANGE	AVERAGE
Macaque monkey		100
Baboon		200
White-handed gibbon	82–125	102
Siamang	100–152	124
Orangutan	276–540	404
Gorilla	340–752	495
Common chimpanzee	282–500	385
Modern human	900–2000	1345

Averages for macaque and baboon from Campbell (1985:233). Hominoid data from Tobias (1971:34–40), where the averages were taken as the means of males and females.

ape's skull is characterized by a relatively small brain and large face, modern humans have relatively large brains and small faces.

Table 5.1 lists the brain size (in cubic centimeters) for a number of primate species. There is a clear relationship between taxonomic status and brain size: monkeys have the smallest brains, followed by the lesser apes, great apes, and humans. Absolute brain size is not as useful a measure of intellectual ability because larger animals tend to have larger brains. Elephants and whales, for example, have brains that are four to five times the size of the average human brain.

An alternative way of looking at brain size is to express the weight of the brain as a ratio of body weight. The larger this ratio, the larger the brain is relative to body size. For humans, this ratio is 1/49 = 0.020. However, this ratio is not very useful: many other primates have larger ratios, but we tend not to think of them as more intelligent (for example, the ratio for the squirrel monkey is 1/31 = 0.032) (Passingham 1982).

Among mammals, however, the relationship of brain and body weight is not linear. That is, as the body size increases, the brain size increases—but not at the same rate. Differences in size because of disparate growth rates among various parts of the body (known as **allometry**) are common. Parts of the body grow at different rates. Brain size increases at a nonlinear rate with body size. Because of this relationship, larger species appear to have smaller brain/body size ratios.

This allometric relationship between brain size and body size is quite regular among almost all primates. The most notable exception is humans. We have brains that are three times the size we would expect for a primate of our body size (Figure 5.1). In addition, our brains have proportionately more cerebral cortex than other primate brains. The cerebral cortex is the part of the brain involved in forming complex associations.

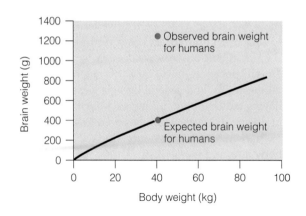

■ FIGURE 5.1
Relationship between body weight and brain weight in primates. The solid line indicates the average relationship obtained from various primate species excluding humans. The two dots show the expected and observed brain weight for humans. Our brains are three times the weight expected if we followed the typical primate curve. (*Source:* Harvey et al. 1987)

What exactly is the relationship between brain size, relative to body size, and intelligence? This question has been long debated, but with little resolution. Most texts state there is no relationship between relative brain size and intelligence within the human species, although only a few studies were without methodological flaws. It is problematic, however, whether the fossil record of human evolution shows an increase in absolute and relative brain size that corresponds to an increase in mental abilities. Could there be a relationship between relative brain size and intelligence between species, but not within species? A recent study by Willerman and colleagues (1991) helps resolve some of the conflict. They measured the brain size of 40 adults using magnetic resonance imaging and compared these values, adjusted for body size, with IQ test scores. Adjusting their results to the general population, they found a correlation of 0.35 between relative brain size and IQ scores (a positive correlation can take on a value from 0 to 1; the higher the value, the closer the correspondence). Several other studies have shown similar results, with an average correlation between relative brain size and IQ of roughly 0.4. In statistical terms, this means that roughly 16 percent of the observed variation in IQ is related to variation in relative brain size (without getting into the technical details, this number is derived by squaring the correlation coefficient and multiplying by 100—consult most any introductory statistics book for an explanation).

If 16 percent of the observed variation in IQ is related to brain size, then 84 percent of the observed variation is *not* related to such variation. Overall, the results show that relative brain size is a contributing factor, but not the only one. In terms of evolution, the correlation is sufficient to show that natural selection has had an impact. However, the correlation is also low enough that one could not predict accurately a person's IQ from his or her relative brain size. Even the observed correlation might be an overestimate of

▲▲▲▲▲▲▲▲▲▲▲▲▲▲▲▲▲▲▲▲▲▲▲▲▲▲▲▲▲

allometry The change in proportion of various body parts as a consequence of different growth rates.

the relationship between relative brain size and IQ scores. The correlation, for example, may reflect other factors known to affect both growth and IQ, such as nutrition. Also, although we are interested in the general issue of "intelligence," IQ tests measure much more specific aptitudes, such as test-taking ability, and general knowledge, and are also generally acknowledged as having cultural bias. Taking such problems into account, the relatively small brain size–IQ correlation has even less significance.

Recent studies have also looked at the relationship among brain size, body size, and metabolism. Larger mammals have larger brain sizes and produce greater amounts of metabolic energy. Mammals show a great deal of variation, however, in the amount of energy used by the brain. The brains of many mammals, such as dogs and cats, use 4 to 6 percent of their body metabolism. Primate brains use a considerably greater proportion of energy; the Old World macaque uses 9 percent and modern humans use 20 percent (Armstrong 1983).

What does all this mean? The human brain is not merely large; it also has a different structure than other primates, with the cortex being disproportionately larger. This difference in structure is also probably related to the higher proportion of metabolic energy used by the human brain. The bottom line is that brain size does not tell the whole story. Thus, the human brain is not only larger than the brain of a chimpanzee; it is also structurally different. The increased convolution of the human cerebral cortex (the folding of brain tissue) means that the brain of a human child with the same volume of that of a chimpanzee has more cerebral cortex.

Bipedalism

Another striking difference between humans and apes is the fact that humans walk on two legs. We are **bipedal** (meaning "two legs"). This does not mean that apes cannot walk on two legs. They can, but not as well and not as often. The physical structure of human beings shows adaptations for upright walking as the normal mode of movement.

Humans are not the only animal that is routinely bipedal. The kangaroo also moves about on two legs, but in a totally different manner than humans. The human form of bipedal movement is best characterized as a "striding gait." Consider walking in slow motion. What happens? First, you stand balanced on two legs. Then you move one leg forward. You shift your body weight so that your weight is transferred to the moving leg. As that leg touches the ground on its heel, all your body weight has been shifted. Your other leg is then free to swing forward. As it does so, you push off with your other foot.

Human walking is more graceful than a slow-motion description sounds. The act of walking consists of alternating legs from swinging free to standing still. We balance on one leg while the other leg moves forward to

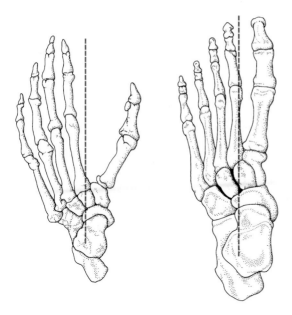

■ FIGURE 5.2
The skeletal structure of the feet of a chimpanzee (*left*) and a modern human (*right*). Note how the big toe of the human lies parallel to the other toes.

continue our striding motion. We tend to take these acts for granted, but they are actually quite complicated, requiring both balance and coordination. For example, when you pick one leg up to move it forward, what keeps your body from falling over?

Human bipedalism is made possible by anatomical changes involving the toes, legs, spine, pelvis, and muscles. In terms of actual anatomy, these changes are not major: after all, no bones are added or deleted; the same bones can be found in humans and in apes. The changes involve shape, positioning, and function. The net effect of these changes, however, is dramatic. Humans can move about effectively on two legs, allowing the other limbs to be free for other activities.

The feet of human beings reflect adaptation to bipedalism. The feet of a human and a chimp are shown in Figure 5.2. The big toe of the chimp sticks out in the same way that the thumb of all hominoids sticks out from the other fingers. The divergent big toe allows chimps to grasp with their feet. The big toe of the human is tucked in next to the other toes. When we walk, we use the nondivergent big toe to push off during our strides.

Our balance while we stand and walk is partly the result of changes in our legs. Figure 5.3 shows a human skeleton from the frontal view. Note that the width of the body at the knees is less than the width of the body at the hips. Humans are literally "knock-kneed." Our upper leg bones (the femurs) slope inward from the hips. When we stand on one leg, the angle of the femur transmits our weight directly underneath us. The result is that we continue to be balanced while one leg is moving. In contrast, the angle of an ape femur is very slight. The legs of an ape are almost parallel from hips to feet. When an ape stands on two legs and moves one of them, the ape is off balance and tends to fall toward one side. When an ape walks on two legs, it must shift its whole body weight over the supporting leg to stay on

▲▲▲▲▲▲▲▲▲▲▲▲▲▲▲▲▲▲▲▲▲▲▲▲▲▲▲▲▲▲▲

bipedal Moving about on two legs. Unlike the movement of other bipedal animals such as kangaroos, human bipedalism is further characterized by a striding motion.

■ FIGURE 5.3
The modern human skeleton from a frontal view.

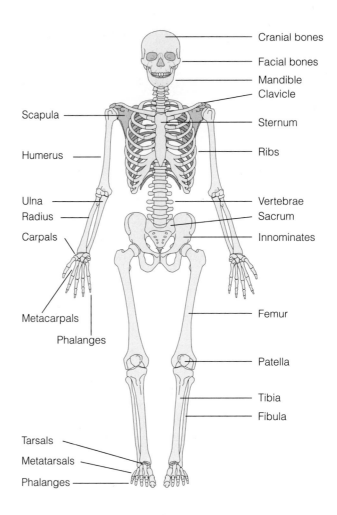

Cranial bones

Facial bones

Mandible

Clavicle

Scapula

Sternum

Humerus

Ribs

Ulna

Vertebrae

Radius

Sacrum

Carpals

Innominates

Metacarpals

Phalanges

Femur

Patella

Tibia

Fibula

Tarsals

Metatarsals

Phalanges

■ FIGURE 5.4
Side view of the skeletons of a chimpanzee (*left*) and a modern human (*right*) illustrating the shape and orientation of the spine. (Adapted with permission from: Bernard Campbell, *Human Evolution,* Third Edition [New York: Aldine de Gruyter]. Copyright © 1985 Bernard Campbell)

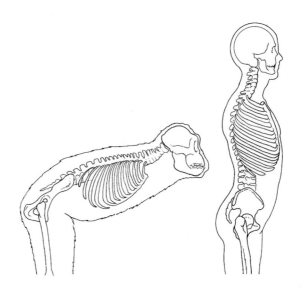

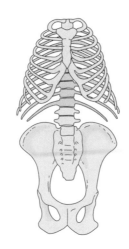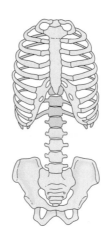

balance. This shifting explains the characteristic waddling when apes walk on two legs.

The human spine also allows balance when we walk upright (Figure 5.4). The spinal column of humans is vertical, allowing weight to be transmitted down through the center of the body. In knuckle-walking apes, the spine is bent in an arc so that when the apes stand on two legs, the center of gravity is shifted in front of the body. The ape is off balance and must compensate greatly to stay upright. What is difficult for apes is easy for humans. The human spine is vertical but not straight. It curves in several places, allowing it to absorb the shocks occurring while we walk.

The human pelvis is shaped differently than an ape pelvis (Figure 5.5). It is shorter top to bottom, and wider side to side. The sides of the pelvis are broader and flair out more to the sides, providing changes in muscle attachment that permit striding bipedalism. The shortness of the human pelvis allows greater stability when we stand upright.

The changes in the human pelvis also involve changes in the positioning of various muscles. For example, certain leg muscles attach more on the sides of the pelvis. This change allows humans to maintain their balance while standing without having to bend their knees. Other muscles, such as the gluteus maximus (the large buttock muscle), are larger in humans than in apes. This muscle helps in standing up and in climbing over uneven terrain. The gluteus minimus and gluteus medius muscles have also shifted position relative to apes, allowing the pelvis to remain stable when one leg is lifted during walking.

Canine Teeth

Human canine teeth are different from canine teeth in many other mammals. Human canines are small and do not project beyond the level of the other teeth. Human canine teeth serve much the same function as the incisor teeth.

That we have small nonprojecting canines has led to much speculation concerning causes and effects of human evolution. Given that canine teeth serve as weapons in many primate species, the lack of large canine teeth in humans seems to imply that we do not need them for weapons anymore. One scenario is that when human ancestors began using tools, they no longer required large canines. As you will see in later chapters, the uniqueness of human canine teeth is more complex a topic than we once thought.

Sex and Reproduction

We humans consider ourselves the sexiest primates. That is, we are more concerned with sex than is any other primate. The fact that humans do not have the estrus cycle has often been cited as a unique aspect of human sexuality. For the most part, temperate-zone domestic animals breed only during certain seasons and mate around the time of ovulation. Human females, in contrast, cycle throughout the year and often mate at any time during the cycle. This may be a primitive characteristic, however. Some mice and rats cycle continuously. It now appears that orangutans also lack the estrus cycle. In addition, field studies on other primates suggest that many individuals, such as bonobos, mate outside the usual cycle to some extent (Jolly 1985).

The human pattern of reproduction is basically the same as that of most primates: single births. Unlike apes, humans have additional children before the previous children have grown up socially or physically. Because of cultural adaptations, humans have increased reproduction without sacrificing parental care. Compared to apes, a greater proportion of the human life cycle is taken up by physical and social growth prior to maturity. Consider, for example, that a chimpanzee is sexually mature at about 10 years and lives roughly 40 years (Jolly 1985). This means that roughly 25 percent of the chimp's life is spent growing up. Further consider that a human matures at roughly 15 years and that throughout most of history and prehistory, we estimate that humans had an average length of life of roughly 30 years. Compared to other primates, we mature more slowly and require a greater amount of our life for growing and learning. This logic may seem strange since the average length of life today in the United States is roughly 75 years, not 30. However, keep in mind that our relatively long life is neither universal nor very old. Most of the increase in our average length of life has come only in the past century or so (see Chapter 12).

Human Growth

The human life cycle includes changes in physical growth. The major stages of growth are prenatal (before birth) and postnatal (after birth). The general nature of these two stages is reviewed briefly, followed by consideration of what is unique about human growth.

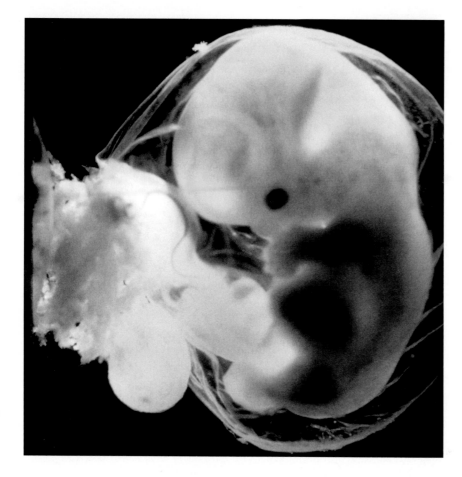

PRENATAL GROWTH   Prenatal life is the period from fertilization through childbirth. After fertilization, the fertilized egg (**zygote**) develops into a cluster of identical cells deriving from the initial fertilized egg. During the first week, the fertilized egg multiplies as it travels into the uterus. By this time, there are roughly 150 cells arranged in a hollow ball that implants itself into the wall of the uterus. Cell differentiation begins. During the second week, the outer layer of this ball forms the beginning of the placenta. Some early differentiation of cells can be seen in the remainder of the ball.

The embryonic stage stretches from roughly two to eight weeks after conception. The **embryo** is very small during this time, reaching an average length of 25 mm (1 in.) by the eighth week. During this time the basic body structure is completed and many of the different organ systems have developed; the embryo has a recognizably human appearance although it is still not complete (Figure 5.6). The fetal stage lasts from this point until birth.

zygote A fertilized egg.

embryo The stage of human prenatal life lasting from roughly two to eight weeks following conception; characterized by structural development.

■ FIGURE 5.7
Typical distance curve for
human height. (From *Growth
and Development* by Robert M.
Malina © 1975, publisher Burgess
Publishing Company, Minneapolis,
MN; modified as per Bogin 1995)

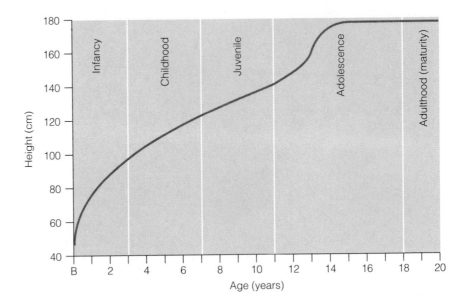

Development of body parts and organ systems continues, along with a tremendous amount of body growth and changes in proportions. During the second trimester of pregnancy, the **fetus** shows rapid growth in overall length. During the third trimester, the fetus shows rapid growth in body weight, head size, and brain growth.

THE PATTERN OF HUMAN POSTNATAL GROWTH   We can identify five basic stages in the growth from birth until adulthood (Bogin 1995). The first stage, *infancy*, refers to the time from birth until weaning (typically up to three years in nonindustrialized societies), and is characterized by rapid growth. The second stage, *childhood*, refers to the time from weaning until the end of growth in brain weight, which takes place at about seven years (Cabana et al. 1993). The *juvenile* stage is from this point until the beginning of the fourth stage, *adolescence*, which is the time of sexual maturation and a spurt in body growth. Adolescence begins at about age 10 in females and 12 in males, although there is considerable variation across people and populations. The fifth stage is labeled *adulthood*.

Human growth is usually studied by looking at growth curves. One type of growth curve, the **distance curve,** is a measure of size over time—it shows how big someone is at any given age. Figure 5.7 is a typical distance curve for human height. As we all know, until you reach adulthood, the older you get, the taller you get. However, note that this is not a straight line—you do not grow the same amount each year. This shows that the rate of body growth is not the same from year to year. Changes in the rate of growth are best illustrated by a **velocity curve,** which plots the rate of

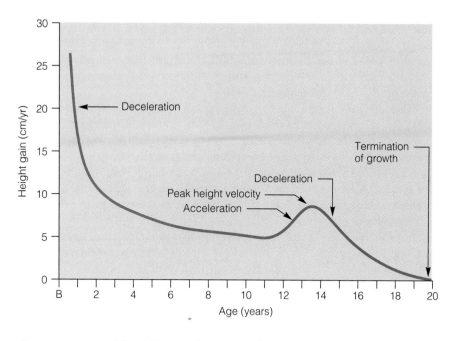

■ FIGURE 5.8
Typical velocity curve for
human height.
(From *Growth and Development*
by Robert M. Malina © 1975,
publisher Burgess Publishing
Company, Minneapolis, MN)

change over time. The difference between a distance curve and velocity curve
can be illustrated by a simple analogy—driving a car. Imagine driving a car
on a highway between two cities. How far you have come is your distance,
and how fast you are going is your velocity.

A typical velocity curve for human height is shown in Figure 5.8. The
rate of growth is greatest immediately after birth, followed by a rapid decel-
eration during infancy. Even though the rate of growth decreases, we still
continue to grow. Referring again to the car analogy, if you decelerate from
50 miles per hour to 30 miles per hour, you are still going forward, although
not as fast. During childhood and the juvenile stage, height velocity
decreases slightly, but then increases rapidly for a short time during adolescence. At adulthood, the rate of growth again decreases until there is no further significant growth.

Comparing distance and velocity curves for human body size with other
organisms has revealed two basic differences: humans have an extended

fetus The stage of prenatal growth from
roughly 8 weeks follow-
ing conception until
birth; characterized by
further development and
rapid growth.

distance curve A mea-
sure of size over time.
For example, a distance
curve would show how
tall someone is at different ages.

velocity curve A mea-
sure of the rates of
change in growth over
time.

childhood and an adolescent period (Bogin 1988, 1995). In most mammals, the rate of growth decreases from childbirth, and adulthood occurs without any intervening stages. In other mammals, there is a stage of juvenile growth. Only in humans, however, do we see childhood, adolescence, and a long post-reproductive period (Bogin 1995).

This discussion thus far has centered on body size. In order to understand the unique aspects of the human growth pattern, it is also necessary to look at changes in growth for other parts of the body, such as the head and brain tissue. Quite simply, not everything grows at the same rate. Figure 5.9 compares human distance curves for body size, brain size, and the reproductive system. All three are drawn to illustrate the percentage of total adult size attained at any given age. Note the differences in these curves—our brains and reproductive systems obviously do not grow at the same rate as our bodies. In particular, our brain grows most rapidly at first, reaching adult weight by roughly seven years of age (Cabana et al. 1993). The reproductive system grows most slowly, showing hardly any growth until adolescence.

Social Structure

Human social structure is a topic of almost infinite complexity that is thoroughly explored in cultural anthropology textbooks. One observation is obvious—there is extensive variation. Because variation in social structure is great even among the apes, it should come as no surprise that humans, with an even greater emphasis on learned behavior, show greater variation.

A common Western assumption is that the "normal" social structure of human beings is the nuclear monogamous family group: mother, father, and children. Actually, the majority (almost 90 percent) of human societies studied have a stated preference for **polygyny**—a pattern in which one husband has several wives (Harris 1987). A few cultures also practice **polyandry,** in which one woman has several husbands. Because of this, anthropologists have often argued that the basic human pattern is polygyny. However, it must be noted that although many societies state a *preference* for polygyny, it is still much more common for men to have a single wife. In many cases, only the most wealthy or powerful have multiple wives. Fisher (1992) has reviewed the evidence and concludes that for all practical purposes, monogamy is the predominant marriage pattern for humans. This is not to deny the exceptions, but rather it points to our need to contrast stated cultural preferences with actual cultural practices.

Humans show a great deal of variation as well in other aspects of their culture, such as economic systems, political systems, and legal systems. There are also some biological limitations on human cultural behavior, however. Humans are social animals and do not survive well when isolated. Apart from the occasional hermit, humans thrive best in groups. Humans have biological needs, such as food and sex, that structure our behaviors.

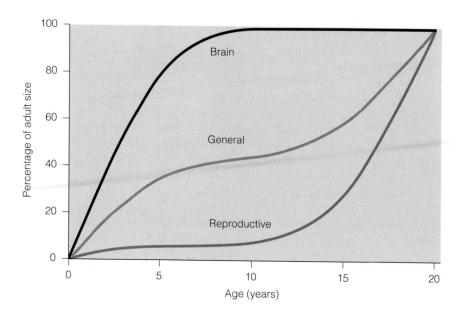

■ **FIGURE 5.9**
Distance curves for different body tissues, showing the percentage of total adult size reached at different ages. The general curve represents overall body size (height or weight). The brain curve represents brain weight. The reproductive curve represents the weight of sex organs and tissues. From Bogin (1995), based on Scammon (1930) and updated to include new data on brain growth (Cabana et al. 1993). (Barry Bogin)

ARE HUMANS UNIQUE?

Humans and apes show a great many similarities as well as a great many differences. When we ask whether humans are unique, we do not suggest that we cannot tell an ape and a human apart. Rather, we ask what the extent of these differences is. Are the behaviors of apes and human completely different, or are differences present only in the expression of specific behaviors? Can we say, for example, that humans make tools and apes do not? Or should we say instead that there are differences in the way in which these two groups make and use tools?

According to the view that apes and humans show distinct and major differences, humans possess culture and apes do not. Any cultural behaviors found in apes are labeled as fundamentally different from human cultural behaviors. According to the view that ape–human differences are variations on something that is fundamentally similar, both humans and apes possess culture—the only difference being that humans rely more on culture or that humans have a more developed culture. This debate is semantic to a large extent. A more worthwhile approach is to examine some of the suggested differences between apes and humans in an effort to determine what is truly different.

polygyny A form of marriage in which a husband has several wives.

polyandry A form of marriage in which a wife has several husbands.

Tool Use and Manufacture

Tool use has often been cited as a unique human behavior. As defined here, a tool is an object that is not part of the animal. Human tools include pencils, clothes, eating utensils, books, and houses. All of these are objects that are not part of the biological organism (humans) but are used for a specific purpose. Tool use, however, does not seem to be even a unique primate characteristic. Birds use sticks for nests and beavers use dirt in their dams. Both sticks and dirt can be considered tools by this definition.

A more common definition of modern humans focuses on humans as toolmakers (this definition is complicated by the fact that the earliest hominids may not have made tools—see Chapter 7). The key element of this definition is that some object is taken from the environment and modified to meet a new function. Humans take trees to make lumber to build houses. It can be argued that birds modify sticks and beavers modify dirt, but tool manufacture implies something different. Birds, for example, use sticks for building nests but they do not use these sticks for defensive or offensive weapons. Humans, however, can take sticks and use them to make shelters, defend themselves, hunt, dig up roots, and draw pictures in the sand. When we discuss tool manufacture, we mean the new and different ways to modify an object for a task. Humans can apply the same raw materials to a variety of tasks.

In this sense, tool manufacture has long been considered a unique human activity. But research on apes, particularly Goodall's work on chimpanzees, has since shown that this is not true. Apes make and use tools. Though their tools are extremely simple by modern human standards, it is clear that the difference between apes and humans cannot be reduced to humans making tools and apes not making tools. Differences exist in the method and use of manufactured tools, but not the presence or absence of toolmaking.

CHIMPANZEE TERMITE FISHING   In the early 1960s, Jane Goodall reported a remarkable finding—chimpanzees were making and using tools! Though chimpanzees are predominantly fruit eaters, they also enjoy a variety of other foods, including termites. One group of chimpanzees demonstrated a method for capturing termites. They took a grass stem or a stick, went up to a termite mound, and uncovered one of the entrance holes left by the termites. They inserted the stick into the hole, twirled the stick a bit to attract termites down in the mound, and then withdrew the stick. Termites had attached themselves to the stick, and the chimpanzees ate them directly off the stick.

Close analysis of this "termite fishing" behavior shows it to be true tool manufacture along with rather complex tool use. Chimpanzees often spent a great deal of time selecting the appropriate stick. When a suitable stick was not available, they pulled a branch out of the ground or off a bush and

■ **FIGURE 5.10**
The chimpanzees have
fashioned simple tools to
fish for ants. The infant
chimpanzee watches and
learns this process.
(James Moore/Anthro-Photo)

stripped away the leaves. This is deliberate manipulation of an object in the environment—toolmaking. The act also reflects a conscious decision-making process.

Termite fishing is not an innate chimpanzee behavior. It is passed on to others in the group by means of learning. Young chimpanzees watch their elders and imitate them, thus learning the methods and also developing practice. As Goodall has documented, termite fishing has become part of the local group's culture.

OTHER EXAMPLES OF TOOLMAKING　　Termite fishing is only one of many types of tool manufacture reported among chimpanzees. Sticks are also used to hunt for ants (Figure 5.10). A chimpanzee will dig up an underground nest with its hands and then insert a long stick into the nest. The ants begin swarming up the stick and the chimpanzee withdraws it to eat the ants. Sticks have also been used to probe holes in dead wood and to break into bee nests (Goodall 1986).

In addition, chimpanzees have been observed making sponges out of leaves. After a rainfall, a chimpanzee often drinks out of pools of water that collect in the holes of tree branches. Often the holes are too small for the chimp to fit its head into, so the chimp creates a tool to soak up the water: he takes a leaf, puts it into his mouth, and chews it slightly. (Chewing increases the ability of the leaf to absorb water.) The chimp inserts this "sponge" into the hole in the branch to soak up the water.

Other examples of chimpanzee toolmaking and tool use include using leaves as napkins and toilet paper, using sticks as weapons, and using rocks to break open nuts and hard fruits (Goodall 1986).

Can Apes Make Stone Tools?

Toolmaking had long been one of the cited unique characteristics of humans, a behavior that set them apart from other animals. The pioneering work of Jane Goodall in the 1960s totally revised how anthropologists defined humankind. Her observations of toolmaking, including the use of fashioned sticks to "fish" for termites and ants, led to the realization that "toolmaking" in and of itself could not be claimed as a unique human trait. Instead, the definition of toolmaking had to be modified, focusing on how *human* toolmaking differed from *ape* toolmaking.

One such qualification dealt with the raw material and type of tool. The archaeological record shows that hominids have been fashioning stone tools for at least 2.5 million years (see Chapter 7). Living apes, however, do not fashion stone tools. (They *do* use stones to crack nuts, but we are talking here about striking one stone against another to fashion a cutting edge or sharp flake.) This seems to be a reasonable distinction. The problem, however, is figuring out exactly what this distinction means. Does the fact that apes do not make stone tools mean that they *can't* make stone tools? Not necessarily.

Sue Savage-Rumbaugh, an ape language researcher, and Nick Toth, an archaeologist, joined forces to look at these questions (Savage-Rumbaugh and Lewin 1994). Their basic question was, Could an ape be motivated to learn how to make stone tools? For their research, they worked with the bonobo Kanzi (discussed in this chapter as part of the ape language experiments). Rather than condition Kanzi to make tools, they chose a strategy where Kanzi could learn through observation. They placed a reward in a box with a transparent lid and secured the box with string. Nick then showed Kanzi how to hit stones together to produce a sharp flake which could be used to open the box.

In recent years, researchers have observed that toolmaking and tool use are not specieswide characteristics among chimpanzees. Not all groups have shown the same behaviors. Some use sticks for ant or termite fishing or sponges for drinking; others do not (McGrew 1992). This variation may reflect the importance of individual discoveries. It might also relate to environmental differences, with tool use being more frequent in areas with less immediately available food.

HUMAN AND CHIMPANZEE TOOLMAKING   It is obvious that chimpanzees make and use tools in a systematic manner. It is also clear that they use genuine problem-solving abilities in their toolmaking. They see a problem (e.g., termites in the mounds) and create a tool to solve the problem. The implication of these studies is that we can no longer define humans as the only toolmakers. Our definition must be modified, and we must focus on differences in toolmaking between apes and humans.

There are several important differences between chimpanzee and human toolmaking and tool use. First, humans depend on tools; chimpanzees do not. Termite fishing provides a tasty treat for the chimpanzees, but it is not essential for their survival. Chimpanzees survive without tools in many places. Humans, on the other hand, depend on tools for survival. Toolmaking and tool use are not an option for humans; they are an imperative.

A second difference is that humans save their tools. Chimpanzees start over each time they make a tool (one exception is saving the rocks used to

Through observation, Kanzi eventually began attempting to make his own flakes. At first, he was very tentative about striking the stones together with sufficient force, but ultimately developed the appropriate level of force. Kanzi's flaking was still somewhat crude when he invented a different technique: throwing the stones against the hard tile floor. Because Savage-Rumbaugh and Toth were interested in Kanzi's flaking ability, they carpeted the floor to keep him from making flakes with his newly invented, and easier, method. Kanzi was not easily deterred; he pulled up a corner of the carpet to expose part of the hard floor. Even when taken outside, Kanzi would attempt to make flakes by throwing one stone against another.

When prevented from using his own method, Kanzi became increasingly better at flaking stone tools. His blows became harder and more precise. Eventually, Savage-Rumbaugh and Toth were able to conclude that apes *can* make stone tools. The next question is, How do these tools compare with those found with our early ancestors? Although Kanzi had progressed considerably, his tools were still not as sophisticated as the earliest known stone tools. There may be some basic difference here between the toolmaking capabilities of humans and apes—a finding that implies that the abilities of the earliest hominid toolmakers had already progressed beyond those of the apes.

There is still a question as to the significance of the difference between Kanzi's tools and those of our early ancestors. Are the differences a reflection of mental ability? Of manipulative ability? Or experience? Although much remains to be answered by such research, we again see the gap between human and ape to be less than once thought.

crack open nuts). Chimpanzees who fish termites do not save the sticks they have made. Humans save their tools, presumably because of the greater importance tools have for human survival.

Third, humans use tools to make other tools. This allows for the construction of a complex technological system. Thus far, no one has seen chimpanzees do this. A further key distinction of modern humans is that we accumulate our knowledge of toolmaking, building on it generation after generation.

In any case, it is clear that we cannot define modern humans solely in terms of having the ability to make tools. The observations made by Goodall and others regarding chimpanzee tool manufacture have caused us to redefine human behavior and to reconsider our relationship with the apes. We now acknowledge much closer similarities than we did several decades ago. The methods, goals, and complexities of human toolmaking are clearly quite different from those of apes. However, we must acknowledge that we are not as dissimilar as was once thought.

Language Capabilities

Language has long been considered a unique human property. Language is not merely communication but rather a symbolic form of communication. The nonhuman primates communicate basic emotions in a variety of ways.

■ **FIGURE 5.11**
A chimpanzee hooting.
(© Marine World Africa USA,
Vallejo, CA)

Chimpanzees, for example, have a large number of vocalizations that they use to convey emotional states such as anger, fear, or stress (Figure 5.11).

WHAT IS LANGUAGE?   Primate communication through vocalizations, grooming, or other methods does not constitute language. Language, as a symbolic form of communication, has certain characteristics that distinguish it from simple communication. Language is an *open system;* that is, new ideas can be expressed that have never been expressed before. Chimpanzee vocalizations, on the other hand, form a closed system capable of conveying only a few basic concepts or emotions. Human language can use a finite number of sounds and create an infinite number of words, sentences, and ideas from these sounds.

Another important characteristic of language is *displacement.* Language allows discussion of objects and events that are displaced—that is, not present—in time and/or space. For example, you can say, "Tomorrow I am going to another country." This sentence conveys an idea that is displaced in both time ("tomorrow") and space ("another country"). We can discuss the past, the future, and faraway places. Displacement is very important for our ability to plan future events—imagine the difficulty in planning a hunt several days from now without the ability to speak of future events!

Language is also arbitrary. The actual sounds we use in our languages need not bear any relationship to reality. Our word for "book" could just as easily be "gurmf" or some other sound. The important point is that we understand the relationship of sounds to objects and ideas. This in turn shows yet another important feature of language—it is learned.

APES AND AMERICAN SIGN LANGUAGE   Early efforts to teach English to apes were failures. One classic experiment was conducted on a young female chimpanzee named Vicki. After years of extensive work Vicki could speak only four words: "Mama," "Papa," "up," and "cup." Later researchers noted that the failure of this experiment might mean only that apes cannot speak English; it said nothing about their ability to understand. Looking back at this study, it is no surprise that Vicki could not speak very well, because the vocal anatomy of chimpanzees makes speaking a human language next to impossible.

In the 1960s, two scientists, Allen and Beatrice Garner, began teaching the American Sign Language to a young female chimpanzee named Washoe. Devised for the deaf, American Sign Language (ASL) is a true symbolic language that does not require vocalization but instead uses hand and finger gestures. Because chimpanzees are capable of making such signs, ASL was considered the most suitable medium to determine whether or not they were capable of using language (Figure 5.12). Washoe quickly learned many signs and soon developed an extensive vocabulary.

■ FIGURE 5.12
A chimpanzee is using the American Sign Language to convey the message "more eat." (H. S. Terrace/Anthro-Photo)

Washoe also demonstrated the ability to generalize: to take a concept learned in one context and apply it to another. For example, she would use the sign meaning *open* to refer to boxes as well as doors. This suggests that Washoe truly understood the general concept of *open* and not just the use of the sign in one specific context. Washoe also invented new signs and "talked" to herself while playing alone, an act human children perform when learning language. Washoe was even observed to swear!

One of the most intriguing findings of the Gardners' research was that Washoe would form simple two- and three-word sentences (for example, "You tickle me"). Early observations suggested that Washoe was not only capable of symbolism but also of grammar and sentence construction.

Washoe was the first ape taught American Sign Language. Since then there have been many experiments into the nature of the language capabilities of apes. Gorillas, as well as chimpanzees, have been taught ASL. Other languages were also invented, including one based on plastic tiles and another using a computer keyboard. Experiments were devised that required two chimpanzees to interact with each other using language. These experiments confirmed the ability to generalize signs and to create new ones. For example, one chimpanzee named Lucy combined the signs *drink* and *fruit* to refer to a watermelon for which she had not been taught a sign. She also invented the phrase "cry hurt food" to refer to radishes, which presumably she found bitter.

HUMAN AND APE LANGUAGE ABILITIES   The purpose of the original research with Washoe was to determine what was unique about the way in which a human child learns language. It was suggested that a comparison of human and chimpanzee language acquisition would reveal at what point human abilities surpassed those of the ape. Washoe's abilities exceeded early expectations, and soon the research focus shifted to the language capabilities of the apes themselves. The ability of Washoe and other apes to learn a symbolic language suggested that language acquisition could no longer be regarded as a unique human feature.

There is considerable debate about the meaning of these studies. Some claim that many of the positive results are the result of unconscious cues given to the apes by humans. Also, there is the problem of interpreting the data and seeing what one wants to see. For example, Washoe signed "water bird" the first time she saw a swan. Some researchers interpreted this as a true invention. Others suggested that Washoe simply saw the water and then the bird, and responded with the two signs in sequence. Obviously, much of this research is fraught with the danger of speculation and excessive interpretations for the simple reason that we cannot get inside the chimpanzee's mind.

In spite of the debates, however, there is little doubt that apes can learn and understand the meaning of many signs. Chimpanzees, gorillas, and orangutans have all mastered a certain number. Some chimps have learned over 150 signs by the time they were 7 years old (Snowden 1990). Carefully controlled experiments have shown that the basic vocabulary of apes is not a reflection of unconscious cues given by the scientists. The behavior of signing correctly while playing alone strongly suggests that the apes actually do understand, *in some manner*, the meaning of signs.

Much of the controversy over language acquisition in apes revolves around two different training approaches. Many studies, including the Washoe project, attempted to teach language in an environment similar to that in which human children develop linguistic skills, one offering continued exposure in an unstructured environment with many opportunities for creativity and expression. Other ape studies used controlled, less flexible environments. The controlled experiments were of course designed to minimize cues from humans and to provide more definitive measurements. The problem is that this type of sterile approach is not the most conducive to learning language.

One of the most interesting observations came about by accident during a study conducted by Savage-Rumbaugh, in which researchers were attempting to teach a female bonobo a keyboard-based language. At the time, the bonobo was caring for an infant, Kanzi, who frequently interrupted his mother. Later, when the mother was returned to the breeding colony, Kanzi began to use the keyboard to make requests. Over time, he performed well on a variety of measures (Savage-Rumbaugh and Lewin 1994). Significantly, he learned language by observation, and not through direct training. (After all, the experiment was not designed to teach him; he was simply there to be nursed.) In other words, Kanzi learned elements of language in the same way that human children do.

The suggested ability of apes to understand grammar and to construct sentences is also controversial. Though apes do create correct two- and three-word sentences, the few longer sentences they create are often grammatically incorrect. There has also been evidence that the apes respond to unconscious cues in constructing sentences (as opposed to simple vocabulary identification). Though some see definite evidence of grammar (e.g., Linden 1981), others see little evidence (e.g., Terrace 1979). The debate continues.

Regardless of the outcome, it is clear that the difference between human and ape is not as great as we once thought. We can no longer define modern humans in terms of the capability to learn certain aspects of symbolic language. Apes are certainly capable of symbolic behavior, even if we can debate over exactly how much. Both humans and apes can learn symbols, though humans are clearly better at it. Perhaps one of the major differences is the fact that humans rely on language and apes do not. In their natural habitat, apes do not use sign language. The fact that they are capable of learning language to a certain extent should not detract from the point that they do not use language in their natural environment. As with tool manufacture, we see evidence of capabilities in the apes for behaviors that are optional for them but mandatory for modern humans.

The question of human uniqueness becomes more complicated when we consider possible behaviors of our fossil ancestors. Given a common ancestry with the African apes, at what point did our own patterns of tool-making and language acquisition begin? Studies of modern apes help answer such questions because we can see the *potential* for such behaviors in the modern apes. Using these potentials as a guide to the behavior of the common ancestor of African apes and humans, we can attempt to determine what changes were necessary to arrive at the modern human condition.

SUMMARY

Humans share many features with the other hominoids but also show a number of differences. The main biological characteristics of humans are a large and complex brain, three times its expected value; bipedalism; and small canine teeth. In addition, humans have a growth pattern that is different from other primates in its extended childhood and adolescent growth spurt. Behaviorally, humans are quite variable.

Past behavioral definitions of humans have often focused on humans as toolmakers. However, studies of apes in their native habitat show that they also make and use simple tools. Another oft-cited human characteristic is the use of symbolic language. Although apes are unable physically to speak a human language, studies of American Sign Language and other symbolic, visually-oriented languages show that apes have some language acquisition capabilities. Studies of toolmaking and language acquisition show that the difference between apes and humans may be more a matter of degree than kind. Modern humans remain unique in the specific ways they use tools and language and in their reliance on these behaviors for survival. What is mandatory for humans is optional for apes. Still, the capabilities shown by apes provide us with possible clues regarding human origins.

SUPPLEMENTAL READINGS

Fisher, H. 1992. *Anatomy of Love: A Natural History of Mating, Marriage, and Why We Stray.* New York: Ballantine. A well-written and fascinating account of evolutionary explanations of human marriage and mating.

Linden, E. 1986. *Silent Partners: The Legacy of the Ape Language Experiments.* New York: Ballantine.

Patterson, F. and Linden, E. 1981. *The Education of Koko.* New York: Holt, Rinehart and Winston.

Savage-Rumbaugh, S., and Lewin, R. 1994. *Kanzi: The Ape at the Brink of the Human Mind.* New York: John Wiley & Sons.

These last three books are excellent popular accounts of the studies of ape language acquisition.

Primate Origins and Evolution

This chapter reviews the fossil evidence for the origin and evolution of the primates, emphasizing the major events in primate evolution between 65 and 5 million years ago. Since the past 65 million years are but a fraction of the 4.6-billion-year history of our planet, and since the origin of primates has its roots in previous patterns of vertebrate and mammalian evolution, it is necessary to review some major events in evolution *before* the primates.

THE FOSSIL RECORD

Before proceeding to a review of evolution before the primates, it is necessary to look briefly at some of the methods used in paleontological research. The two major questions are: How can we assign dates to the fossil record? and How can we reconstruct past environments?

Dating Methods

Two basic classes of methods are used to date fossil remains. **Relative dating** determines which fossils are older but not their exact date. **Chronometric dating** determines an "exact" age (subject to some measurement of possible error and statistical fluctuation).

When we refer to exact dates in the fossil record, we conventionally use the term B.P., which means "Before Present." "Present" has been set arbitrarily as the year 1950. Some people use the term B.C., meaning "Before Christ," but because not all peoples share the belief in Christ, the term B.P. is preferable and has been agreed on internationally. A date of 800,000 years B.P. would mean 800,000 years before the year 1950.

RELATIVE DATING METHODS   If we have two sites containing fossil material, relative dating methods can tell us which is older, but not by how much. It is preferable to have exact dates, but this is not possible for all sites. Relative dating methods can tell us the basic time sequence of fossil sites. **Stratigraphy** makes use of the geological process of superposition, which refers to the cumulative buildup over time of the earth's surface. When an organism dies or a tool is discarded on the ground, it will ultimately be buried by dirt, sand, mud, and other materials. Winds move sand over the site, and water can deposit mud over the site. In most cases, the older a site is, the deeper it is. If you stand on the ground and dig down through the earth, the lower layers are older.

A number of other methods provide relative dates for fossils. One such method is **faunal correlation,** which involves comparison of animal remains found at different sites to determine any similarity in time levels. Imagine that you have discovered a site that contains a certain species of fossil pig. Suppose that you know from previous studies that this species of pig has always been found between 2.0 and 1.5 million years B.P. Logically, this suggests that your newly discovered site is also between 2.0 and 1.5 million years old. The only other possibility would be that patterns of evolution occurred in the same way, but at different rates in different areas—an unlikely proposition. Plant pollens sometimes can be used in a similar manner.

Chemical methods also provide relative dates. Fluorine dating, for example, is a method that looks at the accumulation of fluorine in bones. When an organism dies, its bones lose nitrogen and gain fluorine. The rate at which this process occurs varies, so we cannot tell exactly how old a bone is by using the method. The method does, however, allow us to determine if two bones found at the same site are the same age.

CHRONOMETRIC DATING METHODS   Chronometric dating methods provide an "exact" date, subject to statistical variation. Chronometric dating relies on constant physical and chemical processes in the universe. Many of these methods utilize the fact that the average rate of radioactive decay is constant for a given radioactive atom no matter what chemical reaction it might be involved in. If we know that a certain element decays into another at a constant rate, and if we can measure the relative proportions of the original and new elements in some object, then we can mathematically determine the age of the object. Radioactive decay is a probabilistic phenomenon, meaning that we know the average time for decay over many atoms. Such processes allow us to specify an average date within the limits of statistical certainty.

Carbon-14 dating is one such method. Living organisms take in the element carbon throughout their lives. Ordinary carbon, carbon-12 (^{12}C), is absorbed by plants, which take in the gas carbon dioxide from the air, and by animals, which eat the plants (or animals that eat the animals that ate the plants). Because of cosmic radiation, some of the carbon in the atmosphere is a radioactive isotope known as carbon-14 (^{14}C). An organism takes in both ^{14}C and ^{12}C, and the proportion of ^{12}C to ^{14}C is constant during the organism's life because the proportion is constant in the atmosphere. When an organism dies, no additional ^{14}C is ingested, and the accumulated ^{14}C begins to decay. The rate at which ^{14}C decays is constant; it takes 5,730 years for one-half of the ^{14}C to decay into ^{14}N (nitrogen-14). Carbon-14 is therefore said to have a **half-life** of 5,730 years. The half-life is the time it takes for half of a radioactive substance to decay.

Carbon-14 dating uses this constant rate of decay to determine the age of materials containing carbon. The process of the radioactive decay of ^{14}C results in the emission of radioactive particles that can be measured, which allows us to estimate a date. In theory, any sample containing carbon can be used. In practice, however, bone tends not to be reliable in all cases because of the chemical changes during fossilization, in which carbon is replaced. In most circumstances, charcoal is the best material to use.

Carbon-14 dating is only useful for sites dating back over the past 50,000 years at most. Any older samples would contain too little ^{14}C to be detected. Though carbon-14 dating is extremely valuable in studies of recent hominid evolution, it is not useful for dating most of earth's geological history.

▲▲▲

relative dating The method of estimating the older of two or more fossils or sites but not a specific date.

chronometric dating The method of estimating the specific date of fossils or sites.

B.P. Before Present (1950), the internationally accepted form of designating past dates.

stratigraphy A relative dating method based on the fact that older remains are found deeper in the earth because of cumulative buildup of the earth's surface over time.

faunal correlation Assigning an approximate age to sites based on the similarity of animal remains with other dated sites.

half-life The average length of time it takes for half of a radioactive substance to decay into another form.

carbon-14 dating A chronometric dating method based on the half-life of carbon-14 that can be applied to organic remains, such as charcoal, dating back over the past 50,000 years.

■ **FIGURE 6.1**
Hypothetical example of the use of potassium-argon dating. Homonid remains are found between two layers of volcanic ash, one dating to 3.8 million years B.P. and the other dating 3.2 million years B.P. The hominid can therefore be dated at between 3.8 and 3.2 million years B.P. (From *Human Antiquity: An Introduction to Physical Anthropology and Archeology*, 2d ed., by Kenneth Feder and Michael Park, Fig. 7.7. Copyright © 1993 by Mayfield Publishing Company)

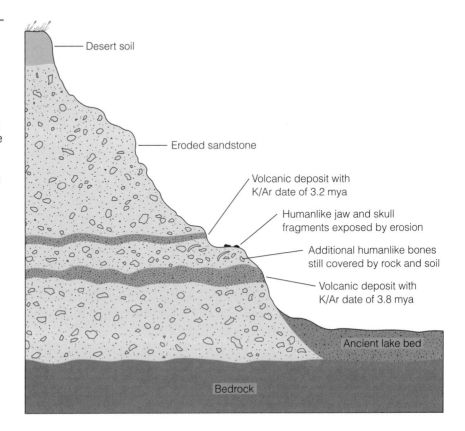

Another chronometric dating method that utilizes the process of radioactive decay is **potassium-argon dating.** Here, an isotope of potassium (^{40}K) decays into argon gas (^{40}Ar) with a half-life of approximately 1.31 billion years. This rate of radioactive decay means that this method is best used on samples older than 100,000 years (Figure 6.1).

Potassium-argon dating requires rocks that did not possess any argon gas to begin with. The best material for this method is volcanic rock, for the heat generated by volcanic eruptions removes any initial argon gas. Thus, we are sure that any argon gas we find in a sample of volcanic rock is the result of radioactive decay. By looking at the proportions of ^{40}K and ^{40}Ar, we can determine the number of elapsed half-lives and therefore the age of the volcanic rock.

A newer and related method, **argon-argon dating,** involves looking at the decay of an argon isotope (^{39}Ar) into argon gas (^{40}Ar). Laser technology allows this method to be applied to very small samples—as small as a single crystal.

Another method of dating involves paleomagnetism. When we use a compass to find direction, we rely on the fact that the needle points north.

During many times in the past, this was not the case. The magnetic pole has at times shifted to the southern end of the planet. These **paleomagnetic reversals** provide a means by which to date certain rocks. When rocks initially form, they retain the magnetic orientation at the time they came into being—either "normal" (north) or "reversed" (south). By using other dating methods, such as potassium-argon, a chart of the reversals over the last eight million years has been developed. Because these reversals last for different amounts of time, they form a varying pattern. A section of rock can then be compared to the chart to determine the age.

Many other types of chronometric dating methods can be used in certain circumstances. Some utilize radioactive decay and some use other constant effects for determining age. Archaeologists working on the relatively recent past (within the last 10,000 years) often use a method known as **dendrochronology,** or tree ring counting. We know that a tree will accumulate a new ring for every period of growth. The width of each ring depends on available moisture and other factors during that specific period. In dry areas there is usually only one growth period in a year. By looking at the width of tree rings, archaeologists have constructed a master chart of tree ring changes. Any new sample, such as a log from a prehistoric dwelling, can be compared to this chart to determine its age.

In addition to radioactive decay, other physical constants allow an estimate of age to be assigned to a sample. **Fission-track dating** relies on the fact that when uranium decays into lead in volcanic glass (obsidian), it leaves small "tracks" across the surface of the glass. We can count the number of tracks and determine the age of the obsidian from the fact that these tracks occur at a constant rate.

Thermoluminescence is a dating method that relies on the fact that certain heated objects accumulate trapped electrons over time, thus allowing us to determine, in some cases, when the object was initially heated. This

---

potassium-argon dating
A chronometric dating method based on the half-life of radioactive potassium that can be used to date volcanic rock older than 100,000 years.

argon-argon dating
A chronometric dating method based on the half-life of radioactive argon that can be used with very small samples.

paleomagnetic reversal
A method of dating sites based on the fact that the earth's magnetic pole has shifted back and forth from the north to the south in the past at irregular intervals.

dendrochronology
A chronometric dating method based on the fact that trees in dry climates tend to accumulate one growth ring per year.

fission-track dating
A chronometric dating method based on the number of tracks made across volcanic rock as uranium decays into lead.

thermoluminescence
A chronometric dating method based on the capacity of certain heated objects to accumulate trapped electrons over time, which allows the date when the object was initially heated to be determined.

method has been applied to pottery, bronze, and burned flints. Thermoluminescence can be used to date objects as far back as one million years.

Electron spin resonance is a fairly new method that provides an estimate of dating from observation of radioactive atoms trapped in the calcite crystals present in a number of materials, such as bones and shells. Although this method can be used for sites over a million years old, it works best for dates less than 300,000 years (Grün 1993).

Reconstructing the Past

In addition to dating fossil and archaeological sites, we also need to consider other sources of evidence when putting together a sequence of evolutionary events, and for interpreting them.

TAPHONOMY   When describing the behavior of early hominids, or other organisms, we rely on a wide variety of data to reconstruct their environment and to provide information on population size, diet, presence or absence of predators, and other ecological aspects. Some of these questions can be answered by methods developed within the field of **taphonomy,** the study of what happens to plants and animals after they die. This field provides us with valuable information about which bones are more likely to fossilize, which bones are more likely to wash away, the distribution of bones left over by a predator, the likely route of pollen dispersal in the air, and many other similar topics. Taphonomic studies also provide us with ways of finding out whether objects or fossils have been disturbed or whether they have stayed where they were first deposited. Such studies can also help us distinguish between human and natural actions.

PALEOECOLOGY   When reconstructing the past, we need to know more than just what early organisms looked like. We also need to know about the environment in which they lived. What did they eat? Were they predators, or prey? What types of vegetation were available? Where were water sources? These questions, and many others, involve **paleoecology,** the study of ancient environments.

One example of the many methods used in reconstructing ancient environments is **palynology,** the study of fossil pollen. By looking at the types of pollen found at a given site, experts can identify the specific types of plants that existed at that time. They can then make inferences about yearly and seasonal changes in temperature and rainfall based on the relative proportion of plant species. Further information on vegetation can be extracted from analysis of fossil teeth. Microscopic analysis of scratch patterns on teeth can tell us whether an organism relied more heavily on leaves, fruits, or meat. Chemical analysis of teeth can also tell us something about diet.

EVOLUTION BEFORE THE PRIMATES

Looking at the early beginnings of life also helps us realize the short length of time humans have been in existence. The genus *Homo* is over 2 million years old. Hominids are over 4 million years old. Astronomers estimate the age of our universe to be roughly 15 billion years old. Geological evidence shows the earth to be roughly 4.6 billion years old. Compared to these numbers, 4 million years is a short time.

The Origin of Life

Geologists and paleontologists divide the history of the earth into two **eons,** each of which is broken into **eras,** which are further broken into **periods.** The **Precambrian eon** dates from the beginning of the planet 4.6 billion years B.P. until 545 million years B.P. (thus covering almost 90 percent of earth's history). Major events of the Precambrian eon are the origin of life (obviously a major event!), the development of single-celled organisms, and the first appearance of multicelled organisms. Although the fossil record preserves some of the earliest life, we lack direct fossil evidence for the first signs of life. We must rely instead on a knowledge of the early conditions of the planet and combine these observations with laboratory evidence suggesting possible origins of life.

   Our evidence to date suggests that life first began through a process of chemical evolution. Laboratory experiments in the 1950s demonstrated that amino acids could be produced under conditions thought similar to those of the early earth. Some scientists suggest that a process of chemical selection took place in which certain chemical forms and reactions may have been favored. These models rely on chemical analogies to variation and natural selection in what we might term a "prebiotic" world (Stebbins 1982). The different hypotheses for the initial origin of life are too detailed to cover here, but are reviewed by Cowen (1995).

---

electronic spin resonance A chronometric dating method that estimates dates from observation of radioactive atoms trapped in the calcite crystals present in a number of materials, such as bones and shells.

taphonomy The study of what happens to plants and animals after they die.

paleoecology The study of ancient environments.

palynology They study of fossil pollen.

eon The major subdivision of geological time.

era Subdivision of a geological eon.

period Subdivision of a geologic era.

Precambrian eon The eon from the earth's beginning (4.6 million years B.P.) until 545 million years B.P. During this eon, single-celled and simple multicelled organisms first evolved.

Killer From the Sky?

A large asteroid traveling through space hits our planet. The energy released is astounding. The asteroid collides with rock containing large amounts of sulfur. As a consequence, highly acidic rain falls, killing many animals and plants, and further altering the balance of oxygen and carbon dioxide in the atmosphere. In addition, dust and smoke caused by the impact cut down on the available sunlight for perhaps several months. Photosynthesis is affected, and many plants and algae die. Animals dependent on the plants and algae starve, as do animals that prey on the plant eaters. And as if this weren't bad enough, the lack of sunlight also leads to freezing temperatures around the planet.

The above sounds very much like a science fiction plot. Indeed, the ecological and social implications of asteroid impact are a favorite science fiction theme, such as in *Lucifer's Hammer* by Larry Niven and Jerry Pournelle. In this case, however, the scenario is one of several hypotheses regarding the evolutionary effect of asteroid impact (Cowen 1995). Why is so much attention given to the possible effects of an asteroid hitting the earth? To many (but not all) paleontologists, the extinction of the dinosaurs (and other life forms) 65 million years ago was due to such an event. Many characterize events like these as "bad luck" for the species affected. After all, there is no way to evolve to protect against an asteroid impact!

The extinction of the dinosaurs is a well-documented fact. In addition to dinosaurs, other large vertebrates, marine invertebrates, and much of the world's plankton also became extinct. This mass extinction occurred at 65 million years B.P., the agreed-upon boundary between the Cretaceous period of the Mesozoic era and the Tertiary period of the Cenozoic era (the Cretaceous-Tertiary boundary is abbreviated as the K-T boundary).

The idea of an asteroid impact being responsible is fairly new. In 1980, Alvarez and colleagues introduced evidence that such an impact had taken place. Their key finding was large amounts of the metal iridium at the K-T boundary. Normally scarce on earth, iridium is found in higher quantities in meteorites and asteroids. According to Alvarez et al. (1980), the high amount of iridium at the K-T boundary worldwide is best explained by an asteroid hitting the earth at this time. Since initial publication, more and more evidence has accumulated to support the asteroid impact hypothesis (although it is not accepted by all). For example, the finding of quartz crystals altered by sudden pressure at the K-T boundary supports the hypothesis, as does evidence of the crater left by an asteroid (estimated to have been 6 miles in diameter) off the Yucatán Peninsula of Mexico.

What does this all mean for the study of human evolution? As shown in this chapter, mammals had been restricted to a relatively narrow range of environments during the time of the dinosaurs. The expansion of mammals during the past 65 million years has in part been due to the elimination of competition. When the dinosaurs became extinct, new environments became available to mammals. Viewed in this way, all of mammalian evolution (including human evolution) can be seen as contingent upon the extinction of the dinosaurs. What was bad luck for the dinosaurs was good luck for the mammals.

In terms of the fossil record, fossilized microscopic cells have been found dating back 3.5 billion years B.P., and suggest considerable biological diversity, including the origin of photosynthesis (Schopf 1993). Fossils that indicate cell division have been found in deposits dating back to 850 million years B.P., and evidence for multicelled organisms goes back to at least 750 million years B.P. (Reader 1986). The past 545 million years of earth's history lies in the **Phanerozoic eon,** which is broken down into three geological eras: Paleozoic, Mesozoic, and Cenozoic. Table 6.1 lists the eras and periods of the Phanerozoic eon and the major evolutionary events that occurred during each.

■ TABLE 6.1
Geological Eras and Periods of the Phanerozoic Eon

ERA	PERIOD	MILLIONS OF YEARS B.P.	SOME MAJOR EVOLUTIONARY EVENTS
Cenozoic	Quaternary	1.8–today	Evolution of the genus *Homo*
	Tertiary	65–1.8	Origin and evolution of the primates; origin of hominids
Mesozoic	Cretaceous	145–65	Extinction of the dinosaurs; first birds and placental mammals
	Jurassic	210–145	Dinosaurs dominate; first birdlike reptiles
	Triassic	245–210	First dinosaurs; egg-laying mammals
Paleozoic	Permian	290–245	Radiation of reptiles; mammallike reptiles
	Carboniferous	360–290	Radiation of amphibians; first reptiles and insects
	Devonian	410–360	Many fish; first amphibians; first forests
	Silurian	440–410	First fish with jaws; land plants
	Ordovician	505–440	Early vertebrates, including jawless fish; trilobites and many other invertebrates
	Cambrian	545–505	"Explosion" of life; marine invertebrates

Sources: Cowen (1995), Schopf (1993)

The Paleozoic Era

The **Paleozoic era** lasted from 545 million to 245 million years B.P. The first geological period of the Paleozoic era is the Cambrian, which was a time of rapid evolution of many life forms. In fact, the term *Cambrian explosion* is often used to describe the beginning of this period. Creationists like to suggest that the rapid appearance of life forms is proof of an instantaneous creation. As you read earlier, this is not correct. Life forms existed before the Cambrian period and we have fossil evidence of them. The "explosion" actually took place over millions of years.

Early life forms included organisms similar to modern sponges and jellyfish, as well as a wide variety of marine invertebrates that have no living

Phanerozoic eon The past 545 million years.

Paleozoic era The first geologic era of the Phanerozoic eon, dating roughly between 545 and 245 million years B.P. when the first vertebrates appeared.

counterpart. Such diversity shows us that many species have become extinct, and only a few have living descendants.

Of particular interest to us are some of the early vertebrates, which first appear at the beginning of the Paleozoic, especially the jawless fish. These creatures possessed the internal segmented vertebral column common to all vertebrates but lacked jaws and teeth. The jawless fish came in many forms and were quite successful several hundred million years ago. Today, only two specialized descendants of this once successful group survive: the hagfish and the lamprey.

Some of these jawless fish developed armor plating around their heads from a hard material known as dentin. The first teeth were nothing more than spikes of dentin folded inward. This new feature may have been a powerful adaptation, allowing them to eat a greater variety of food. Later, the teeth developed further and jaws evolved.

We are used to thinking that fish have gills that allow oxygen to be absorbed from water, and land animals have lungs that allow oxygen to be absorbed from the air. Actually, many fish, such as the lungfish, have lunglike structures. If you observe tropical fish, you will soon learn that some must periodically swim to the surface of the water to get air. Examples are the gourami and the Siamese fighting fish.

Looking at tropical fish in a store also can give you clues about the origin of movement on land, another important feature of land colonization. Many fish, such as catfish, are bottom dwellers. They rest on the bottom of the fish tank on strongly developed fins. In the Paleozoic era a group of fish called lobe-fins evolved this ability. Some of these adaptations survive in a fish commonly called the "walking catfish," which often moves on land to get from one stream to another, obtaining oxygen from the air as well.

Recent evidence suggests a different, and very interesting, possibility for the origin of legs. A creature that has been named *Acanthostega* lived 360 million years ago, and appears to be a fish with legs! Current thinking suggests that legs evolved in some early fish well before movement onto the land, perhaps as an adaptation for moving through underwater thickets (Zimmer 1995). If so, then some species of early fish had an adaptation that was well suited for further development into structures capable of movement on land. As with the evolution of lungs, the evolution of legs may represent the modification of preexisting adaptations (developed in the water) to meet a new challenge—living on land.

The fossil evidence suggests that such creatures next spent at least some time on land, perhaps for laying eggs. Amphibians represent a transitional form of vertebrate that lives both in water and on land. The early amphibians were successful and many of these forms evolved into modern amphibians. Some early amphibians became highly successful on the land and evolved into early reptiles during the Carboniferous period. Reptiles were the dominant form of animal life on the land surface of the planet for more than the next 200 million years.

Mammals and birds eventually evolved from the reptiles. The evolution of mammals from reptiles suggests that an intermediate form of animal intervened. To many, an intermediate form implies some sort of strange-looking creature with a mixture of *modern* reptilian and mammalian features. This is an incorrect view of evolution. Modern reptiles and mammals represent millions of years of evolution from a common ancestor. The first reptiles did not look exactly like modern-day reptiles. In fact, some of the earliest primitive reptiles included a group referred to as the **therapsids,** or mammallike reptiles.

The therapsids are classified as reptiles because they have more features that we would call reptilian. However, they also possessed certain mammalian features, such as different types of teeth (see Chapter 4). We therefore call them, for lack of a better term, mammallike reptiles. Therapsids underwent an adaptive radiation during the Permian period of the Paleozoic era, with a wide variety of shapes and sizes.

The dental adaptations of the therapsids were well suited to life on land, allowing them to forage plants effectively. Although this group was highly successful, it ultimately declined following an adaptive radiation of what we might term "true reptiles" during the Mesozoic.

The Mesozoic Era

The **Mesozoic era,** lasting from 245 million to 65 million years B.P., is often called the "Age of Reptiles" because it was the time when reptiles became the dominant form of life on the earth's surface. One of the most successful groups of reptiles were the dinosaurs (Figure 6.2). The major characteristic of the dinosaurs was the modification of the leg and pelvic structures. Many dinosaurs were bipedal, and some appear to have been extremely quick movers and efficient walkers and runners (Wilford 1985).

Ultimately, the dinosaurs emerged as the dominant form of animal life on land and the therapsids declined in number. Eventually the therapsids became extinct, but before this happened some of the therapsids evolved into what we call "true mammals."

During the Triassic period the monotremes, or egg-laying mammals, evolved. Some, such as the platypus, have survived until the present day. The first placental mammals evolved during the Jurassic period, which was the heyday of the dinosaurs. Birdlike reptiles also evolved during this time

▲▲▲

therapsid An early group of reptiles also known as the mammallike reptiles.

Therapsids were the ancestors of later mammals.

Mesozoic era The second geologic era of the Phanerozoic eon, dating roughly between

245 and 65 million years B.P., when the first mammals and birds appeared.

■ FIGURE 6.2

Two well known dinosaurs: *Triceratops* (*top*) and *Tyrannosaurus* (*bottom*).

period. At the end of the Cretaceous period the dinosaurs became extinct, and mammals became the dominant animal life.

Why did the dinosaurs (and many other organisms) become extinct? Recent explanations of dinosaur extinction have relied on the idea that an asteroid or comet hit the earth with tremendous force, kicking up clouds of dust and blocking the sun. Temperatures dropped and many plant forms be-

■ TABLE 6.2
Epochs of the Cenozoic

Epoch	Millions of years b.p.	Major events in primate evolution
Holocene	0.01–Present	Humans develop agriculture and industry, explore outer space
Pleistocene	1.8–0.01	Evolution of the genus *Homo* (*Homo erectus* and *Homo sapiens*)
Pliocene	5–1.8	First hominids and origin of the genus *Homo*
Miocene	22–5	Radiation of early apes, divergence of apes and hominids
Oligocene	38–22	Radiation of anthropoids
Eocene	55–38	First primates (primitive prosimians); first anthropoids?
Paleocene	65–55	Primatelike mammals

came extinct. As plants died, so did the plant eaters and those who ate the plant eaters. In other words, the entire ecology of the planet was altered. There is growing geologic evidence for such a catastrophic event (e.g., Sheehan et al. 1991), although many researchers suggest other factors may have also played a part.

In any case, the fossil record shows clearly that dinosaurs died out and mammals took their place during the last of the Cretaceous period. New opportunities opened up for the mammals, and they began an adaptive radiation, filling vacant environmental niches. The last 65 million years of the earth's history is the **Cenozoic era,** often called the "Age of Mammals." Some mammals ultimately evolved to exploit the grasslands. Others developed adaptations that allowed them to become sea creatures, such as the whale and dolphin. The important event for our purposes was the continued adaptation to life in the trees by certain mammals—the primates.

EARLY PRIMATE EVOLUTION

Primates evolved during the Cenozoic era, which is the past 65 million years. (The **epochs** of this era are listed in Table 6.2). Primate evolution should not be thought of as a simple evolutionary "tree" with a few branches. A better analogy would be a series of "bushes" with many different branches at each stage of primate evolution. One or more adaptive radiations of primate forms occurred during each epoch. Many of the new forms became extinct, some evolved to become present-day representatives, and some evolved into the next phase of primate evolution.

▲▲▲▲▲▲▲▲▲▲▲▲▲▲▲▲▲▲▲▲▲▲▲▲▲▲▲▲▲▲
Cenozoic era The third, and most recent geologic era of the Phanerozoic eon, dating roughly to the last 65 million years. The first primates appeared during the Cenozoic era.

epoch Subdivision of a geologic period.

Overview of Early Primate Evolution

Before getting into the details of primate origins and evolution, it is useful to summarize some of the major events that took place. An adaptive radiation of primatelike mammals led to the origin of what we would call "true primates." The primatelike mammals showed evidence of an initial adaptation to life in the trees. Most of these species died out, but some evolved into primitive prosimians, which were fully adapted to living in the trees. These early prosimians then underwent another adaptive radiation. Although many of these early promisian species became extinct, some species survived to ultimately evolve into the different lines of modern prosimians. Some of the early prosimians evolved into early anthropoids. A subsequent adaptive radiation led to separate groups of New World monkeys, Old World monkeys, and the first primitive apes.

■ FIGURE 6.3
A tree shrew, an insectivore similar in certain respects to primates. (© Zoological Society of San Diego)

Primate Origins

At the end of the Mesozoic era there existed a number of mammals called **insectivores** that were arboreal, nocturnal, and ate insects. A modern-day representative of this group is the tree shrew (Figure 6.3), which illustrates the probable morphology of the ancestor of primates. Of all living mammals, the insectivores are most similar to the primates, suggesting that they are ancestral to primates. Paleoanthropologists look at the variation in this early group to try to identify forms that show the transition to the order Primates.

CONTINENTAL DRIFT AND PRIMATE EVOLUTION   Most of the fossil evidence on primate origins comes from deposits over 55 million years ago in North America and Europe of a group of insectivores known as the primatelike mammals. This widespread distribution may seem strange, given the fact that North America and Europe are now separated by the Atlantic Ocean. This was not, however, the configuration at that time. The continents continually move about on large crusted plates on top of a partially molten layer of the earth's mantle—a process known as **continental drift.** This process continues today: North America is slowly drifting away from Europe, toward Asia. The expansion of the South Atlantic has even been measured from satellites. The placement of the different continents at various times in the past is shown in Figure 6.4.

An understanding of past continental drift is crucial in interpreting the fossil evidence for primate evolution. As continents move, their environments change. When continents separate, populations become isolated; when continents join, there is an opportunity for large-scale migrations of populations. By the time of the primatelike mammals, South America had split off from Africa, but North America and Europe were still joined.

■ **FIGURE 6.4**
Continental drift. Over 200
million years B.P., all of the
continents formed a single
land mass (called Pangea).
By 180 million years B.P.,
two major land masses
had formed (Laurasia and
Gondowana). By 65 million
years B.P. (the beginning of
primate evolution), South
America had split from Africa,
but North America and Europe
were still joined. (From *Human
Antiquity: An Introduction to
Physical Anthropology and
Archaeology,* 2d ed., by Kenneth
Feder and Michael Park. Copyright
1993 by Mayfield Publishing
Company)

More than 200 million years ago

180 million years ago

65 million years ago

Present

▲▲

insectivore An order of
mammals adapted to
insect eating.

continental drift
The movement of
continental land masses
on top of partially
molten layer of the

earth's mantle that bas
altered the relative
location of the
continents over time.

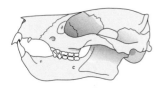

■ FIGURE 6.5
Side view of a skull of a
Paleocene primatelike
mammal. (Redrawn from
Fleagle, *Primate Adaptation and
Evolution*, 1988, with permission,
Academic Press, Inc.)

Thus, it is no surprise to find fossils of primatelike mammals on both continents—they represent part of the group's range on a single land mass.

THE PRIMATELIKE MAMMALS   During the **Paleocene epoch** (65–55 million years
B.P.), we find evidence of what are referred to as "primatelike mammals,"
which were small creatures, usually no larger than a cat and often smaller.
They were quadrupedal (four-footed) mammals whose arms and legs were
well adapted for climbing. Within this general group there was considerable
diversity. Most of this extensive variation was in body size and dental specializations. These small insectivores had some ability to climb and thus
were able to exploit many different types of food.

In spite of their arboreal adaptations, these creatures are not considered
true primates. A picture of the skull of one of these creatures (Figure 6.5)
shows why. The front teeth are far apart from the rest of the teeth, a feature
not found in primates. The eyes are located more toward the sides of the
skull, unlike the forward-facing eyes of primates. In addition, the primatelike mammals lack a **postorbital bar,** a bony ring separating the orbit of the
eye from the back of the skull. Primates have a postorbital bar. Also, the
hands and feet of these animals did not have the grasping ability of primates,
and they had claws instead of nails.

If these forms are not primates, then how can we say they are related to
primates? You should not expect to examine the fossil record and see some
point at which modern-day primate structure immediately appears. Evolution is **mosaic,** meaning that not all new structures appear at the same time.
Examination of the primatelike mammals shows a number of primate features, such as changes in the teeth and development of climbing abilities. In
particular, the molar teeth are primatelike, as are the base of the skull and
the structure of the ankle (Gingerich 1986). Not enough changes have occurred
that we would call them primates, but enough have taken place that we call
them primatelike mammals. They are another example of transitional forms
in the fossil record.

MODELS OF PRIMATE ORIGINS   The first true primates evolved from a population
of primatelike mammals. The general scenario for this change involves continuing adaptation to life in the trees. The primatelike mammals had the
beginnings of arboreal adaptations, and many also possessed the more generalized teeth capable of exploiting different types of foods and environments. In an arboreal environment, natural selection would favor those
individuals better able to cope with the demands of life in the trees. As discussed in Chapter 4, living in the trees is quite a different experience from
living on the ground. First, a three-dimensional orientation is needed. Leap-
ing from branch to branch requires depth perception, which involves forward rotation of the eyes so that the visual fields overlap. Vision, particularly
depth perception, becomes a more important sense than smell. The sense of
smell is less important in the trees, where constant breezes and winds act to
dissipate any smells.

Second, living in the trees also requires an agile body capable of bending and twisting in midair. The early insectivores retained the early generalized vertebrate skeletal structure, and the first primates made use of this flexibility in the trees. The retention of the primitive trait of five digits was also important because having five digits on hands and feet allows the grasping of limbs and branches. Finally, good hand-eye coordination and a brain capable of rapidly processing a large volume of visual information are essential to arboreal survival.

The early primatelike mammals already had traits on which natural selection could act. They had a generalized skeletal structure and five digits. Individuals possessing certain variations such as more forward-facing eyes and grasping abilities would be selected for. Over time, the primatelike mammals adapted to life in the trees and became the first true primates.

Another scenario is the **visual predation model,** developed by Matthew Cartmill (1974), who sees the initial changes in grasping ability and vision as adaptations for hunting insects. Other animals besides primates have stereoscopic vision; it is also found in cats, owls, and hawks, among others. These animals are all active hunters, an activity for which the ability to gauge distance is invaluable. Could insect hunting be the reason for the initial origin of several primate characteristics? Cartmill suggests that the early insectivores hunted out their prey on the ground and on low-lying slender branches in the forest. The development of grasping hands allowed more successful hunting of prey along small branches. The development of stereoscopic vision made it easier for the insectivores to locate prey. In particular, stereoscopic vision allowed them to judge the distance to potential prey without moving their head (which could alert the prey). Cartmill notes that a similar development of stereoscopic vision occurred in cats. According to Cartmill's model, primate adaptations first arose as adaptations to more successful insect predation. Once these traits were established, these adaptations later allowed further exploitation of the trees. As is often the case in evolution, preexisting structures can be used for different purposes. The fossil record is not complete enough to test fully Cartmill's model, but the dental evidence does show that many of the early primatelike mammals were insect eaters. This observation is consistent with the insect predation idea, but it is not conclusive.

▲▲

Paleocene epoch
The first epoch of the Cenozoic era, dating roughly between 65 and 55 million years B.P., when the primatelike mammals appeared.

postorbital bar The bony ring that separates the eye orbit from the back of the skull in primates.

mosaic evolution The concept that major evolutionary changes tend to take place in stages, not all at once.

visual predation model The view of primate origins that hypothesizes that stereoscopic vision and grasping hands first evolved as adaptations for hunting insects along branches.

■ FIGURE 6.6
Side view of the skull of an
Eocene primate.(Redrawn from
Fleagle, *Primate Adaptation and
Evolution,* 1988, with permission,
Academic Press, Inc.)

THE FIRST PRIMATES   The first "true" primates appeared roughly 50 to 55 million years ago at the beginning of the **Eocene epoch** (55–38 million years B.P.). The climate during this time was warm and humid, and the predominant land environment was tropical and subtropical. Initially, the continents of Europe and North America were still joined, resulting in migration and similarity among the fossils we find in this region. Many orders of modern-day mammals first appeared during this time, including aquatic mammals (whales, porpoises, and dolphins), rodents, and horses.

Fossil primates from the Eocene epoch have been found both in North America and in Europe. During the Eocene, there was an adaptive radiation of the first true primates—the early prosimians. This adaptive radiation was part of the general increase in the diversity of mammals associated with the warming of the climate and related environmental changes.

The Eocene forms possessed stereoscopic vision, grasping hands, and other anatomical features characteristic of primates. A picture of the skull of an Eocene primate (Figure 6.6) shows many of these changes. Compared to the Paleocene primatelike mammals, the snout is reduced and the teeth are closer together. These forms possessed a postorbital bar and had larger brain cases and features of cerebral blood supply similar to that of modern primates (Fleagle 1988). The large size of the eyes of some of the Eocene primates suggests they were still nocturnal.

These early primitive primates were similar, in a *general* sense, to living prosimians. In a rough sense, there are two basic groups of early Eocene primates. One group, primarily diurnal leaf and fruit eaters, is broadly similar to modern lemurs and lorises. The other group, primarily smaller, nocturnal fruit and insect eaters, is broadly similar to modern tarsiers.

What became of these early primates? Many different species ultimately became extinct, leaving no descendants. Others evolved into the present-day prosimians. We lack sufficient data, however, to identify individual species as the ancestors of present-day prosimians. Only in a general sense can we link these two groups of early primates to living prosimians.

Anthropoid Origins

What of the anthropoids? Although living anthropoids are more similar to tarsiers than to lemurs or lorises, identification of the first anthropoids and their relationship to other fossil primates is not as clear. Recent fossil discoveries have suggested that anthropoids first evolved fairly early in primate evolution, perhaps as much as 50 million years ago (Godinot and Mahboubi 1992; Simons and Rasmussen 1994). It is possible that anthropoids developed not from the lemur-loris group or the tarsier group, but from a third, independent line in early primate evolution. It is too soon to determine which of these ideas (if any) is correct. The major lesson we have learned from recent fossil discoveries is that past diversity was much greater than we

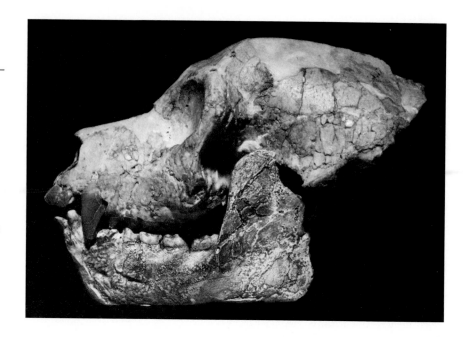

■ FIGURE 6.7
Side view of the Oligocene anthropoid *Aegyptopithecus*, which lived about 33 million years B.P. The smaller eye orbit, relative to the size of the skull, shows that this form was diurnal (nocturnal creatures have bigger eyes). *Aegyptopithecus* was once considered a possible early ape, but is now recognized as an anthropoid that lived prior to the split of the Old World monkey and ape lines.
(Peabody Museum of Natural History, Yale University)

once thought, and even given our recent accumulation of data, we are unlikely to have sampled more than a fraction of early primate diversity.

OLD WORLD ANTHROPOIDS We have evidence of anthropoid fossils from the start of the **Oligocene epoch** (38–22 million years B.P.) at several locations in the Old World and the New World. The climate cooled during this time, and there was an expansion of grasslands and a reduction in forests. This change in climate seems to have resulted in the southward movement of primate populations, and we find little evidence of further evolution in North America or Europe. Most of the fossil evidence for anthropoid evolution is found in southern climates in Africa and South America, and parts of eastern Asia (Fleagle 1995).

The Oligocene primates show the continued radiation of anthropoid forms in both the Old World and the New World. The Oligocene anthropoids show continued reduction of the snout and nasal area, indicating greater reliance on vision than on smell. In addition to the postorbital bar shared with all primates, the Oligocene anthropoids have a fully enclosed eye socket, characteristic of modern anthropoids. All of the Oligocene anthropoids were small and arboreal and were generalized quadrupeds; none show signs of specialized locomotion. Their diet appears to have consisted primarily of fruit supplemented with insects and leaves. The smaller eye orbits of many early anthropoids suggests that these forms were diurnal (Figure 6.7).

Eocene epoch The second epoch of the Cenozoic era, dating roughly between 55 and 38 million years B.P., when the first true primates, early prosimians, appeared

Oligocene epoch The third epoch of the Cenozoic era, dating roughly between 38 and 22 million years B.P., when there was an adaptive radiation of anthropoids.

The Giant Ape

One of the most interesting Miocene apes found so far is *Gigantopithecus*, which literally means "giant ape." The remains of *Gigantopithecus* have been found in Asia—China, India, and Vietnam—dating back as far as 9 million years B.P. (Ciochon et al. 1990). The Chinese specimens may be as recent as 500,000 years B.P., meaning that this ape lived at the same time as our ancestral species *Homo erectus* (discussed in Chapter 11).

Although it sounds strange, *Gigantopithecus* was first found in a drugstore! Throughout much of Asia, fossil teeth and bones are ground into powder and used in various potions that are said to have healing properties. The teeth are often called "dragon's teeth" and are sold in apothecary shops. In 1935, the anthropologist Ralph von Koenigswald discovered huge teeth in one such store, and later named it *Gigantopithecus*. Since then, additional teeth and jaws have been recovered from fossil sites.

The major characteristic of *Gigantopithecus* is that it had huge molar and premolar teeth set in a massive jaw. Another interesting feature is that while the canine teeth are large, they are not that large relative to the rest of the teeth. The *relatively* smaller canines, and

the thick enamel on the molar teeth, suggested to some that *Gigantopithecus* might be related to humans, who have the same characteristics. We now realize that Miocene ape evolution is a lot more complicated than we once thought. *Gigantopithecus* is in some ways similar to *Sivapithecus*, and probably represents a side branch in Asian ape evolution.

The large teeth and jaws have always captured people's imaginations. Based on the size of the teeth, some have suggested that *Gigantopithecus* might have stood over 9 feet tall! However, there are wide differences among species in the relationship between tooth size and body size, and it is more likely that *Gigantopithecus* was around 6 feet tall (which is still pretty big!). Until we find more of the body, we will not know for sure.

The large molars, thick molar enamel, small canines, and large jaws all suggest an ape that was well adapted for a diet consisting of items that were very hard to chew. In fact, the tips of the canines are worn down in a manner consistent with heavy chewing.

Some have suggested that *Gigantopithecus* is somehow related to the mythical "Abominable Snowman," presumably because of its geographic location and possible size. There is no support for this idea (nor for the existence of the Snowman). What *Gigantopithecus* really shows us is yet another example of the diversity of Miocene apes.

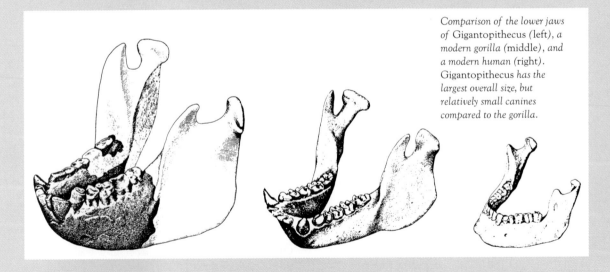

Comparison of the lower jaws of Gigantopithecus *(left), a modern gorilla (middle), and a modern human (right).* Gigantopithecus *has the largest overall size, but relatively small canines compared to the gorilla.*

EVOLUTION OF THE NEW WORLD MONKEYS What about the New World monkeys? The earliest fossil record of New World monkeys dates back roughly 30 million years. Where did the New World monkeys come from? Decades ago, it was thought that New World and Old World monkeys represented a good example of parallel evolution from prosimians. However, current evidence points to enough similarities between the two groups of monkeys to make it more reasonable to assume a single origin for anthropoids somewhere in the Old World. How did the New World monkeys get to the New World? By this time, continental drift had resulted in the separation of the Old and New Worlds.

One explanation is that anthropoids reached South America by "rafting." No, this does not mean that these early primates built rafts and sailed to South America! Ocean storms often rip up clumps of land and trees near the shore, which are then pulled out into the ocean. Sometimes these trees contain helpless animals. Often they drown, but occasionally they will be washed up on an island or continent.

Present geological evidence supports this rafting hypothesis, most likely from Africa to South America. At present, the evidence supports an African origin for three reasons. First, no suitable early anthropoid ancestors have been discovered in North America. Second, there is evidence of other animals (rats) rafting from Africa (Fleagle 1995). Third, New World fossil evidence points to a close similarity with African anthropoids (Flynn et al. 1995).

EVOLUTION OF THE MIOCENE APES

Continued evolution of the Old World anthropoids led to two major branches, one line leading to the modern Old World monkeys and the other line leading to the modern hominoids (apes and humans). The oldest evidence for fossil apes is based primarily on dental evidence and comes from Old World sites dating to the **Miocene epoch** (22 to 5 million years B.P.). Most Miocene mammals are fairly modern in form, and roughly half of all modern mammals were present during this time. South America and Australia were isolated due to continental drift. The land mass of **Eurasia** (a term given to the combined land masses of Europe and Asia) and Africa joined during part of the Miocene, roughly 16–17 million years ago.

The early and middle Miocene (before 16 million years B.P.) was a time of heavy tropical forests, particularly in Africa. Subsequently, the climate

▲▲

Miocene epoch The fourth epoch of the Cenozoic era, dating between 22 and 5 million years B.P., when there was great diversity in apes.

Eurasia The combined land mass of Europe and Asia.

■ TABLE 6.3
Genera of Miocene Apes

	DATE			
REGION	EARLY MIOCENE		MIDDLE MIOCENE		LATE MIOCENE
Africa	*Dendropithecus* *Limnopithecus* *Micropithecus* *Proconsul* *Rangwapithecus* *Simiolus* *Turkanapithecus*	*Afropithecus* *Nyanzapithecus*	*Otavapithecus*	*Kenyapithecus*	
Asia	*Dionysopithecus* *Platydontopithecus*				*Gigantopithecus* *Laccopithecus* *Lufengpithecus* *Sivapithecus*
Europe			*Crouzelia*	*Dryopithecus* *Pliopithecus*	*Ouranopithecus* *Oreopithecus* *Sivapithecus*

Note that *Sivapithecus* is represented in both Asia and Europe. *Gigantopithecus* is also found in Asia in more recent times, perhaps as little as 500,000 years ago. *Ouranopithecus* is sometimes referred to as *Graecopithecus*.

Sources: Fleagle (1988), Conroy et al. (1992), de Bonis and Koufos (1993)

became cooler and drier, and there was an increase in open grasslands and mixed environments consisting of open woodlands, bushlands, and savannas.

The Diversity of Miocene Apes

Looking at modern primates, it is apparent that there are more genera and species of monkeys than there are of apes. Monkeys are more diverse than apes. During the Miocene epoch, however, just the reverse was true—apes were incredibly diverse until the past 5 to 10 million years. Since that time, the number of ape species has been declining. This decline is evident when we consider the diversity of fossil Miocene apes now known. Table 6.3 lists the known genera of Miocene apes, which have been found on three continents. There were 23 different genera, many with more than one species. Compare that to the few apes alive today (see Chapter 4).

Why have apes declined and monkeys flourished since the Miocene? One possibility is the slow reproduction rate of modern apes. If Miocene apes had been as nurturing of their offspring as modern apes are, then they may have reproduced too slowly and died out. This problem would have been exacerbated by environmental changes over time.

For the purpose of reconstructing the evolution of the apes, this past diversity creates a problem. Given that there were more species in the past than are alive today, this means that many fossil species have no living descendants. Decades ago, when the fossil record was less complete, it was tempting to identify any newly discovered fossil ape as the Miocene ancestor of one of the living apes, such as the chimpanzee or gorilla (Fleagle 1995). Today, we have evidence of greater diversity in the past, but we now realize that evolution often produces initial diversity followed by later extinction of many branches. It therefore becomes more difficult to find the ancestors of modern apes. We can certainly recognize fossil apes in a general sense, and see general evolutionary trends, but it is much more difficult to arrange the known fossils into a definitive evolutionary tree.

The Fossil Evidence

In general, the identification of the Miocene forms listed in Table 6.3 as *ape* is based on dental and cranial features. In most cases, much less is known about the **postcranial** skeleton (the skeleton below the skull), and such evidence as does exist shows characteristics different from those of modern apes. Overall, it appears that the postcranial structure of Miocene apes was often more generalized than that of modern apes, whose particular adaptations (e.g., knuckle walking) may be more recent. In light of the great diversity of Miocene apes, only a few selected forms are discussed here. Keep in mind that many other forms existed.

PROCONSUL   One form of early Miocene ape that appears to have evolutionary significance is the genus ***Proconsul,*** which lived in Africa between 23 and 17 million years B.P. The skeletal structure of *Proconsul* shows a mixture of monkey and ape features (Figure 6.8). Like modern apes, *Proconsul* did not have a tail (Ward et al. 1991). The limb proportions, however, are more like that of a monkey than an ape, with limbs of roughly the same size. In a modern ape, the front limbs are generally longer than the rear limbs, reflecting knuckle walking. The arms and hands of *Proconsul* are monkeylike, but the shoulders and elbows are more like those of apes. The most recent analyses of the limb structure suggest that *Proconsul* was an unspecialized quadruped that lived in the trees and ate fruit (Pilbeam 1984; Walker and Teaford 1989).

▲▲

postcranial Referring to that part of the skeleton below the skull.

Proconsul A genus of fossil apes that lived in Africa between 23 and

17 million years B.P. and that shows a number of monkey characteristics.

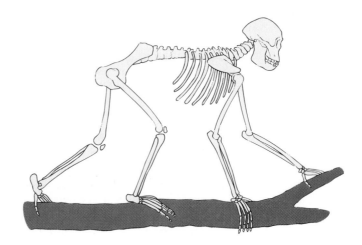

The skull of a typical *Proconsul* specimen (Figure 6.9) is more like that of an ape in that it is large relative to overall body size. The teeth also demonstrate that these forms were hominoid. They possessed hominoid molars and had large protruding canines (Figure 6.10). *Proconsul* also had a thin layer of enamel on the molar teeth, similar to that found on the teeth of modern African apes. By contrast, humans and orangutans have thick molar enamel.

Overall, the teeth and jaws of *Proconsul* are similar enough to those of modern African apes that they were once thought to be direct ancestors of the chimpanzee and gorilla. Today we realize that the situation is more complex than this. Environmental reconstructions show that *Proconsul* lived in

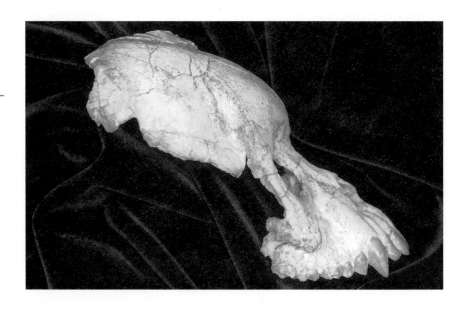

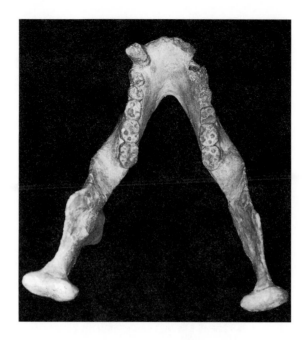

■ FIGURE 6.10
The lower jaw of a specimen of *Proconsul nyanzae,* a medium-sized species of *Proconsul.* Note in particular the large canine tooth.
(Courtesy of Milford Wolpoff, University of Michigan)

the Miocene forests and primarily ate fruits. The mixture of monkey and ape traits points to them as typical of a transition form from early generalized anthropoid to what we think of as an ape. Though definitely not identical to a modern ape, their overall structure is more like that of an ape than a monkey; hence we refer to them as an early form of hominoid.

Proconsul was adapted to forest living and was a successful group for millions of years. As the climate cooled and became drier in certain regions during the Miocene, their habitat shrank. As competition for dwindling resources increased, other apes developed that were more successful in dealing with the new environments.

SIVAPITHECUS The genus **Sivapithecus** lived in Asia and Europe between 14 and 7 million years B.P. The genus name means "Siva's ape," after the Indian deity Siva (pronounced "SHE-va"). Like *Proconsul,* *Sivapithecus* was a diverse genus ranging in size and geographic distribution.

A major distinguishing feature of *Sivapithecus* lies in the jaws and teeth. First, the molars are relatively large and low-cusped and have thick enamel. Second, the jaws are relatively massive but do not protrude forward as much as in other apes. Third, in many forms the canines are relatively smaller than those in other apes and do not protrude as much. These features are all probably related to a change in diet from soft fruits to foods that are harder to chew, such as nuts, seeds, and hard fruits. This change in diet seems to be associated with the fact that the climate was on average cooler and drier, leading to a change in available foods. The upper and lower jaws of a *Sivapithecus* specimen are shown in Figure 6.11.

Thicker enamel represents an adaptation to a diet that is difficult to chew. Given the wear on teeth, harder enamel is more adaptive for heavy

▲▲▲▲▲▲▲▲▲▲▲▲▲▲▲▲▲▲▲▲▲▲▲▲▲▲▲▲▲▲

Sivapithecus A genus of fossil ape found in Asia and Europe dating between 14 and 7 million years B.P., probably an ancestor of the modern-day orangutan.

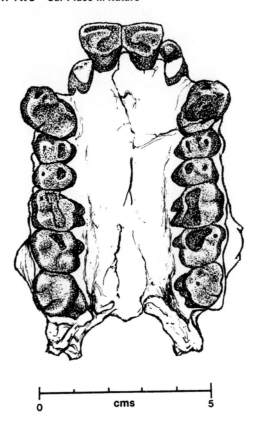

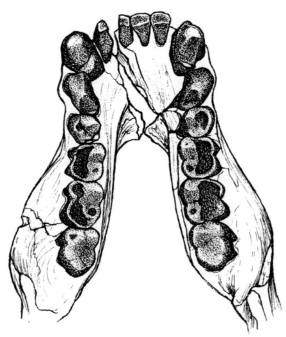

■ FIGURE 6.11
Upper and lower jaws of a
Sivapithecus specimen from
Pakistan. (From Clark Spencer
Larsen, Robert M. Matter, and
Daniel L. Gebo, *Human Origins:
The Fossil Record,* Second
Edition, p. 37. Copyright © 1991,
1985 by Waveland Press, Inc.,
Prospect Heights, Illinois.
Reprinted with permission from
the publisher)

■ **FIGURE 6.12**
Side view of *Sivapithecus*
specimen from Pakistan.
(From Clark Spencer Larsen,
Robert M. Matter, and Daniel L.
Gebo, *Human Origins: The Fossil
Record,* Second Edition, p. 36.
Copyright © 1991, 1985 by
Waveland Press, Inc., Prospect
Heights, Illinois. Reprinted with
permission from the publisher)

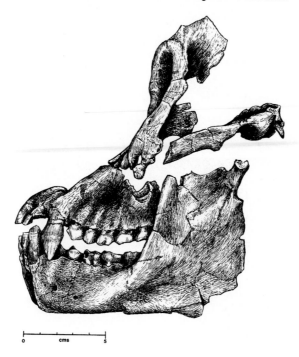

chewing and grinding between the back teeth. Larger molars would also be adaptive for heavier chewing. The shorter and more massive jaw relates to diet as well because more power can be applied between the back teeth when the jaw is tucked further under the face. Smaller canines have also been thought to relate to such a diet. Large canines would make the circular motion more difficult. Therefore, smaller canines are seen as an adaptation to a hard diet because they allow more successful rotary chewing. According to another hypothesis, because larger molars take up more room in the jaw, leaving less room for the canines, the crowding of the teeth leads to dental problems and is therefore selected against.

In what type of environment did *Sivapithecus* live? Environmental data suggest a mosaic of mixed woodland, grassland, and forest regions. Our reconstructions of *Sivapithecus* are hampered by the fact that we know very little about their form of locomotion. The few postcranial bones found suggest a generalized skeleton and locomotion (Pilbeam et al. 1977; Rose 1986).

In the 1970s and early 1980s, a number of *Sivapithecus* specimens were found with rather complete skulls, offering us for the first time a glimpse at something other than jaws and teeth. One of these specimens (Figure 6.12) was discovered by David Pilbeam in 1980 during excavations in Miocene deposits in Pakistan (Pilbeam 1982). Its general appearance is extremely similar to a modern orangutan, as shown in Figure 6.13.

The overall shape and orientation of the two skulls is very similar and quite unlike that of either the chimpanzee or gorilla. The eye orbit of the *Sivapithecus* skull is oval in shape and the two eyes are close together, both

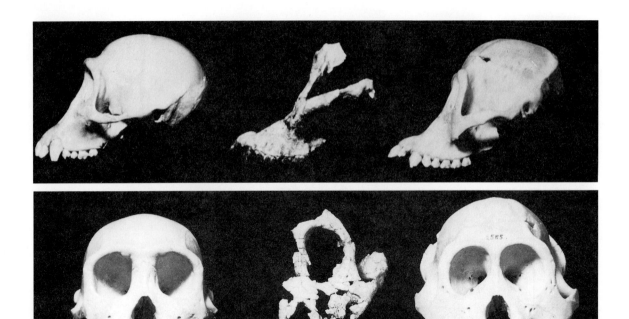

■ **FIGURE 6.13**
Side views (*top*) and frontal views (*bottom*) comparing the *Sivapithecus* specimen GSP 15000 (*center*) with a modern chimpanzee (*left*) and a modern orangutan (*right*). (Peabody Museum, Harvard University)

features found in the orangutan. The unique triangular appearance of an orangutan's nasal region is also found in *Sivapithecus*. Other similarities include the shape and size of the incisor teeth. Note the difference in size between the middle two incisor teeth and the outer two in both specimens. Since Pilbeam's discovery, additional *Sivapithecus* skulls showing the same features have been found in various sites in Asia.

Not every species of *Sivapithecus* exhibits all of these features. This variation suggests that there were a number of Asian species of *Sivapithecus*, one of which appears ancestral to the modern-day orangutan.

Genetic Evidence

In addition to fossil evidence, our interpretations of Miocene ape evolution must also take genetic evidence from the living apes into account. Since the 1960s, a comparison of the genetics of living organisms using a set of methods known as **molecular dating** has shed new light on hominoid evolution.

Molecular information is routinely used to judge the relative relationship between living hominoids. These methods provide some idea of which primates are most closely related. If certain assumptions are made, these methods can be used to provide an estimate of the date at which two species split from a common ancestor. When two species separate, mutations occur

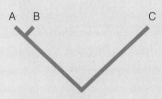

The diagram shows the genetic relationship between three hypothetical species (A, B, and C). Let us assume that the genetic distances between these species have been measured and are:

Distance between species A and species B = 2
Distance between species A and species C = 20
Distance between species B and species C = 20

Based on these data:

The distance between A and B is one-tenth the distance between A and C (2/20 = 1/10)

The distance between A and B is one-tenth the distance between B and C (2/20 = 1/10)

Therefore, the date that species A and B diverged is one-tenth the date that species C diverged from the common ancestor of A and B. If we know from fossil evidence that species C diverged at 40 million years B.P., then species A and B diverged at 4 million years B.P. (40 × 1/10 = 4).

and neutral mutations accumulate in each line independently. If the rate of accumulation is constant in both lines, then a comparison of molecular differences in living forms will provide us with a relative idea of how long the two species have been separated (Figure 6.14).

The first use of molecular dating was by Sarich and Wilson (1967), who looked at differences in albumin protein and found that the difference between humans and the African apes was one-sixth that found between either and the Old World monkeys. Using the then-established estimate of 30 million years for the separation of Old World monkeys, they computed that humans and the African apes had shared a common ancestor 5 million years ago. At that time most paleoanthropologists thought a date of 15 to 20 million years was more likely and disagreed strongly with Sarich and Wilson's estimate.

Since that time, a great deal of research has been done on molecular dating and its assumptions. Some researchers disputed the idea of constancy in mutation fixation rates and proposed nonlinear models in their place. Other proteins have been analyzed. Additional fossil material was found, and new interpretations of older data were made. Most paleoanthropologists now accept a much more recent split of humans and apes than was the consensus several decades ago.

Different methods of analysis give different estimates from molecular dating. For example, Cronin (1983) computed a split of human and

▲▲▲▲▲▲▲▲▲▲▲▲▲▲▲▲▲▲▲▲▲▲▲▲▲▲▲▲▲▲▲

molecular dating
Estimating the sequence and timing of divergent evolutionary lines by applying methods of genetic analysis.

■ FIGURE 6.15
Jaw fragments of *Kenya-pithecus*. Note the small canine teeth. (Courtesy of Dr. Alan Walker, The Johns Hopkins University School of Medicine)

chimpanzee at roughly 5 million years ago, with the orangutan splitting off at roughly 10 million years ago. Arguing that the data should be interpreted using nonlinear rates of change, Gingerich (1985) computed an average date of 9 million years for the chimpanzee and 16 million years for the orangutan. The controversy still continues, but the predominant view from molecular dating is that humans and the African apes split sometime between 7 and 5 million years B.P.

Conclusions

By the early 1960s, anthropologists felt that they had reconstructed the general evolutionary tree of the living hominoids and had suitable fossil species identified as the ancestors of modern species. The preliminary dental evidence suggested a number of fossil apes dating back 20 to 15 million years B.P., some big and some smaller. Given the ape features of the teeth, the fossils were thought to represent the ancestors of gorillas (big) and chimpanzees (small). In addition, some apes showed small canines (Figure 6.15), a characteristic felt to be uniquely human, and therefore evidence of the first hominids.

We now realize that these initial conclusions were premature. The Miocene apes were much more diverse than we once thought. The postcranial remains of these early forms (e.g., *Proconsul*) showed us that the earliest Miocene apes were quite primitive in many features. This evidence, combined with insights from molecular dating, led to our current observation of a much later divergence of modern hominoids. Instead of an ape–human split some 20 to 15 million years B.P., we now suggest an earlier date of 7 to 5 million years B.P.

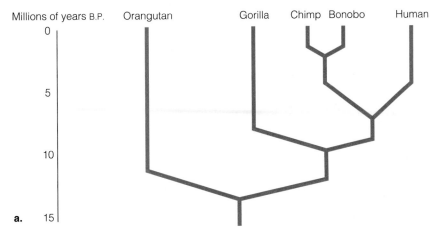

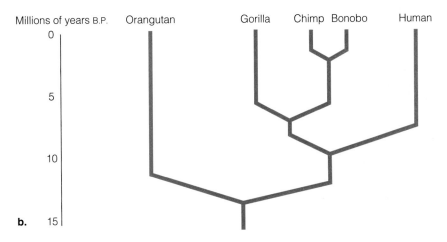

■ FIGURE 6.16
Alternate models of hominoid evolution showing the evolutionary relationships between the great apes and humans. These two models are similar, differing only in the exact relationship between the African apes and humans. (a) The gorilla splits off first and the chimpanzee-bonobo and human lines have a more recent common ancestor. (b) The common ancestor of the African apes and humans splits off first, and the gorilla and chimpanzee-bonobo lines have a more recent common ancestor. Anatomical and genetic data have been used to support both of these positions, but at present we lack a definitive answer.

The genetic evidence, combined with anatomical studies of living hominoids, allows us to reconstruct a general evolutionary "tree" of the great apes and humans. Orangutans split off from a common ancestor first, followed by a later split between the African apes and humans. The specific pattern of the African ape–human split is still being debated, as shown in Figure 6.16. Some favor the gorilla splitting off first, followed by a split between the chimpanzee-bonobo line and the human line (Figure 6.16a). Others favor an initial split of an African ape line and a human line, followed by subsequent splits of the gorilla and chimpanzee-bonobo lines (Figure 6.16b). At present, neither genetic nor anatomical evidence is able to definitively choose between these hypotheses.

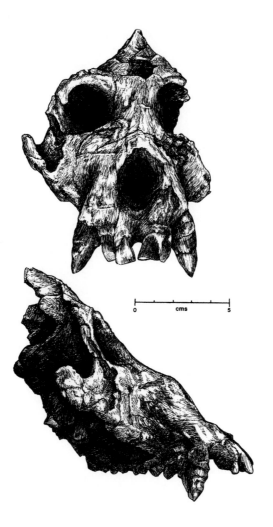

0   cms   5

■ FIGURE 6.17
Another example of the
diversity of Miocene apes—
the genus *Afropithecus.* This
specimen dates to roughly 17
million years B.P. In some
respects, it is similar to both
Proconsul and to later apes
such as *Sivapithecus,* but in
other details (such as facial
profile) it is quite different. It
may represent a common
ancestor of African and Asian
apes or may be a side branch
in ape evolution. (From Clark
Spencer Larsen, Robert M. Matter,
and Daniel L. Gebo, *Human
Origins: The Fossil Record,*
Second Edition, p. 27. Copyright
© 1991, 1985 by Waveland Press,
Inc., Prospect Heights, Illinois.
Reprinted with permission from
the publisher)

Regardless of the fine details of the tree, the basics provide us with a
framework for assessing the evolutionary significance of the Miocene fossil
apes. Estimates from molecular dating add the needed time element to Figure 6.16. Once we know the pattern (the "tree"), we can then determine
where on the tree we should place a given fossil species. This would be
straightforward enough if the actual evolutionary tree were as simple as
shown in Figure 6.16. As we have seen, however, there were more ape species
living during the Miocene than are alive today (Figure 6.17). This means that
any given fossil species might *not* lie on the tree of Figure 6.16, but rather be
a member of a now-extinct side branch of ape evolution. In fact, given the
large number of ape species in the past, the odds are that any given species
will probably represent an extinct branch, and *not* a direct ancestor of a
modern hominoid.

We can be more definite for some parts of the tree than for others. Based on primitive morphology, the mix of monkey and ape features, and the date, it seems reasonable to suggest that *Proconsul* (or something similar to it) was the common ancestor of the great apes and humans. This position would place *Proconsul* at the base of Figure 6.16—a common ancestor of the orangutan, African ape, and human lines.

The part of the tree for which there is the most evidence is the line leading to the orangutan. Because of its close dental and cranial similarity with modern orangutans, a species of *Sivapithecus* seems to be a reasonable ancestor. The dates for *Sivapithecus* also agree with estimates of the divergence of the orangutan line based on molecular dating. As noted, the best candidate for an orangutan ancestor is the Pakistan species of *Sivapithecus* because it is most similar to modern orangutans.

What of the African ape–human line? Here, we cannot be as definitive. A number of potential candidates for the common ancestor of the African apes and humans have been suggested. These include *Kenyapithecus* (Figure 6.15), *Ouranopithecus* (de Bonis and Koufos 1993), and *Dryopithecus* (Begun 1994). We lack sufficient evidence, however, to determine which of these (if any) is the most reasonable common ancestor of African apes and humans. This does not mean we have no evidence; instead, it means we cannot choose between the alternatives at present. In addition, we must keep in mind that the Miocene fossil record continues to unfold as each year brings new discoveries.

SUMMARY

Life on earth began following a period of chemical evolution. The earliest life forms evolved in ancient oceans. The first vertebrates were the jawless fish, which evolved into fish with jaws. One group of jawed fish, the lobe-fins, were the ancestors of all later land vertebrates. After the amphibians conquered the land, an adaptive radiation of reptiles fully adapted to land conditions began. One of the first sort of reptiles were the therapsids, or mammallike reptiles. The later adaptive radiation of dinosaurs ultimately led to the extinction of the therapsids. Before they disappeared, however, some therapsids evolved into the first true mammals. The extinction of the dinosaurs allowed an adaptive radiation of mammals, starting 65 million years ago.

Some early insectivores began to adapt more and more to life in the trees, developing grasping hands and binocular stereoscopic vision. These changes may have begun in response to the needs of insect hunting and were later used to exploit additional food resources in a three-dimensional environment. The origin of primates began with the primatelike mammals of the Paleocene epoch and the ancient promisians of the Eocene. Primitive anthropoids evolved from a group of Eocene primates. The early Oligocene anthropoids ultimately gave rise to separate lines of monkeys and hominoids.

The Miocene epoch is characterized by two major adaptive radiations. In the early Miocene, primitive hominoid forms appeared in Africa. These species (in the genus *Proconsul*), were similar in some ways to later apes, but were also monkeylike in a number of features. They had jaws and teeth similar to later apes and also lacked tails. Their postcranial skeleton was generalized and primitive in a number of features.

During the middle Miocene, several new genera of apes evolved. They had relatively large molars and thick molar enamel. These dental changes correspond to changing climatic conditions and available food resources, specifically the need to process food that was harder to chew. These thick-enameled apes appear to be the ancestors of present-day apes and humans, although the specific evolutionary relationships between Miocene species and modern species are not clear at present. One species of the genus *Sivapithecus* appears to be the ancestor of modern-day orangutans.

We are not able at present to identify precisely the common ancestor of the African apes and humans. Evidence from molecular dating supports a fairly recent split, roughly 7 to 5 million years B.P. Although several genera of fossil apes could be a common ancestor, we cannot be definite about which one makes the most likely common ancestor. What is clear, however, is that there was extensive diversity in apes during the Miocene; more so than exists today.

SUPPLEMENTAL READINGS

Conroy, G. C. 1990. *Primate Evolution.* New York: W. W. Norton. A thorough review of the fossil record of primate origins and evolution.

Cowen, R. 1995. *History of Life.* 2d ed. Boston: Blackwell Scientific Publications. An up-to-date and very thorough review of the fossil record from the origins of life to the present.

Fleagle, J. G. 1988. *Primate Adaptation and Evolution.* San Diego: Academic Press. An excellent and thorough review of primate biology, ecology, and evolution.

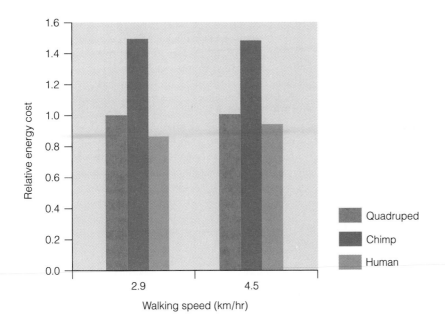

■ FIGURE 7.21
The relative energy cost of movement for chimpanzees and humans compared with a quadruped of similar size (set equal to 1.0 in this graph). The knuckle-walking chimpanzee uses more energy for movement (values > 1) and the bipedal human uses less (< 1). These comparisons have been made at two speeds: 2.9 km per hour (the normal speed of a chimpanzee) and 4.5 km per hour (the normal speed of a human). These results show that bipedalism is more energy-efficient at normal walking speeds. (*Source of data:* Rodman and McHenry 1980)

of heat dissipation and effective evaporation of sweat. According to Wheeler, bipedalism might have been extremely adaptive for early hominoids venturing into the savanna in search of food.

Of course, it is possible (and perhaps likely) that more than one of the factors listed above played a role in the origin of bipedalism. Many of these are interrelated in an organism's survival. For example, the ability to walk long distances efficiently would enhance food gathering and infant care. As another example, improved temperature regulation would allow a hominid to forage at higher temperatures and to go further distances without having to consume as much water or food (Wheeler 1991a). This increased food-gathering ability would also benefit infants.

Given what we know about prehominid locomotion, the shift to bipedalism is reasonable because it involves relatively minor genetic and anatomical changes. Bipedalism is an adaptation that occurred in a changing environment to provide increased survival and reproduction. This change was the first step in human evolution (pun intended).

The Increase in Brain Size

H. habilis shows the beginnings of both large brains and stone tool technology. Although it is reasonable to link larger brains with intelligence and cultural adaptations, the origin of larger brains is more difficult to explain. Any model requires explanation of a genetic mechanism for larger brains as well as the selective advantages of such larger brains.

The Piltdown Hoax

One of the main points made in this chapter is that characteristics of modern humans did not all appear at the same time. In particular, we know from the fossil record that bipedalism started at least 1.5 to 2 million years before we see any significant increase in brain size or the origin of stone tools. This finding is based on the fossil and archaeological records.

Early ideas about human origins suggested just the reverse—that brain size evolved first. Because there were few fossils to show otherwise at that time, this hypothesis could not then be rejected and was quite popular. The model predicted that the fossil record would ultimately show that, of all modern human characteristics, large brain size would be the oldest. Of course, today we have sufficient information to reject this hypothesis altogether. At the beginning of the twentieth century, however, we did not.

In fact, fossil evidence *was* found to support the antiquity of the large human brain. Between 1911 and 1915, hominid fossils were discovered at Piltdown, England, alongside stone tools and the fossils of prehistoric animals such as mastodons. A primary specimen ("Piltdown Man") consisted of a large skull and an apelike jaw. The teeth, however, were worn flat, more closely resembling the condition of human teeth. The specimen showed a mixture of ape and human traits and had a modern human brain size. It offered clear proof that large brains came first in human origins.

Because of Piltdown, any fossil that had human characteristics but did not have the large brain were rejected, for a time, as possible human ancestors. Indeed, this was part of the reluctance of scientists to accept *Australopithecus* as a hominid. The first australopithecine specimen was discovered by Raymond Dart in 1924. The specimen consisted of the face, teeth, and cranial fragments (including a cast of the brain case) of a young child. Dart named the specimen *Australopithecus africanus*. Based on cranial evidence relating to the angle at which the spinal cord enters the skull, he claimed it was an upright walker. The brain size was apelike, as was the protruding face. The teeth, however, were more like those of humans, particularly in having small canines. Here was another specimen that had a mixture of ape and human traits,

but that suggested the large brain evolved *after* bipedalism and humanlike teeth. At the time, more people tended to support Piltdown (in fairness, some of their criticisms of *Australopithecus*, including the difficulty in interpreting remains of children, were valid).

Some scientists, however, were more skeptical about Piltdown Man. And, eventually, continuing investigation showed that the find was a fake. In 1953, a fluorine analysis (see Chapter 5) confirmed that the jaw bones and skull bones did not come from the same time period. Closer inspection showed that the skull was that of a modern human and the jaw that of an orangutan. The teeth had been filed down, and all of the bones had been chemically treated to simulate age. To this day, no one knows exactly who was responsible for the hoax, although a number of suspects had both motive and opportunity.

The story of Piltdown Man is often offered up as evidence that anthropologists (and other scientists) often do not know what they are talking about. After all, look how easily they were fooled. This criticism misses the point altogether. Science and scientists make mistakes, and sometimes commit outright fraud. It is ridiculous to expect otherwise. Science does not represent truth per se, but rather a means of arriving at the truth. When Piltdown was discovered, scientific investigation did not stop. Instead, scientists kept looking at the evidence, questioning it and various assumptions, and devising new ways of testing. As a result, the hoax was uncovered. This is how science is supposed to work.

Side view of Piltdown Man. The dark-colored areas and the back part of the lower jaw were found; the rest was reconstructed. This find, which confirmed the then-popular notion that early humans had large brains and apelike jaws, was a hoax; the remains of a modern human and an orangutan were placed together at the Piltdown site.

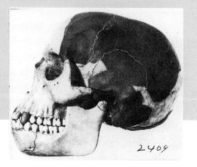

The genetic basis for larger brains in *H. habilis* and later hominid species most likely lies in the regulation of prenatal and postnatal brain growth. Primates in general show rapid rates of prenatal brain growth. Because primates require larger brains early in life, such rapid rates are necessary. Following birth, the usual primate pattern is for the size of the brain to double during the growth process. Modern humans are different in having more rapid rates of postnatal brain growth, so that our adult brain size is roughly four times that at birth.

NEOTENY Our large brains can be explained by the process of **neoteny,** which is the retention of juvenile characteristics into adulthood (Gould 1977). This process is best explained by looking at the differences between an infant chimpanzee and an adult chimpanzee, then comparing these differences to those found between infant and adult humans. Figure 7.22 shows an infant and an adult chimpanzee. With its large rounded skull and relatively small face, the infant looks very similar to an infant human. The adult chimpanzee is different, with a relatively small brain and a large, protruding face. An adult human, however, looks very similar to an infant human. In other words, the shape and relative proportions of brain and face do not change much in humans. Infant apes have relatively large brains because of rapid rates of prenatal brain growth. After birth, however, the rate of brain growth slows down and the face continues to grow. The end result is an adult ape with a relatively small brain. In humans the rapid rate of prenatal brain growth is extended into infancy. Our brains continue to enlarge as our bodies grow. We retain the infant characteristic of a large, well-rounded skull.

Changes in the timing and rates of brain and facial growth can explain the major physical differences between ourselves and apes. Such changes could be the result of a small number of regulatory genes. The increase in cranial capacity of *H. habilis* could be a consequence of selection for some initial mutations leading to neoteny. This idea assumes that larger brains and greater intelligence are adaptive. Are they?

ADVANTAGES AND DISADVANTAGES OF LARGER BRAINS The benefits of larger brains and greater mental abilities are obvious. They allow greater behavioral flexibility in adaptation through cultural transmission from one generation to the next. Large brains also have a cost, however. The extension of fetal growth rates into infancy means that offspring will be born extremely helpless and require greater parental care, which in turn requires greater reliability of food, more protection, and social structures capable of assisting others. Also, rapid fetal brain growth requires greater maternal energy, which in turn also requires adequate food and environmental stability. Martin (1981) has shown that a lack of adequate maternal energy limits fetal brain growth.

Selection for larger brains requires that the advantages of larger brains outweigh the disadvantages. In a population that does not have adequate maternal energy or postnatal parental care, such genes would be selected against. On the other hand, if conditions existed in which adequate mater-

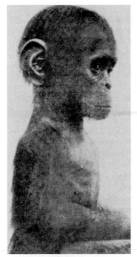

■ FIGURE 7.22
An infant and adult chimpanzee. (From *Human Antiquity: An Introduction to Physical Anthropology and Archeology*, 2d ed., by Kenneth Feder and Michael Park, Fig. 8.8. Copyright © 1993 by Mayfield Publishing Company)

▲▲▲▲▲▲▲▲▲▲▲▲▲▲▲▲▲▲▲▲▲▲▲▲▲▲▲▲▲

neoteny The retention of juvenile characteristics in adulthood.

nal energy and postnatal care were available, then more helpless infants with greater rates of brain growth would be selected for. The increase in brain size, intelligence, and cultural adaptations would then provide the basis for additional selection for larger brains.

THE RADIATOR THEORY   If larger brains have an overall advantage, then why didn't they develop among the robust australopithecines? Dean Falk (1990, 1992) has proposed a model of brain evolution in hominids that focuses on heat stress as a constraint on the development of larger brains. Quite simply, large brains in large heads must shed quite a bit of heat. This is particularly a problem if a large-brained hominid is spending a great deal of its time in hot climates such as equatorial Africa. How does the brain cool itself? During heat stress, blood that is cooled by evaporation flows from the skin into the brain case. In modern humans, blood circulates through a network of veins that also allows blood to drain from the brain into the rest of the body. One of Falk's interesting findings was that although some early hominids had this type of drainage system, others had a different one, whereby blood circulated through enlarged sinuses in the occipital and mastoid regions of the skull. Falk suggests that this other drainage system is not as effective in cooling the brain.

It turns out that the robust australopithecines (and the A. afarensis fossils from Hadar) had the less efficient system. Skulls of A. africanus and H. habilis showed a higher frequency of specific foramina (openings in the skull) characteristic of the more effective system. Therefore, it seems that the robust australopithecines did not have a system that would allow a larger brain—they would not have been able to handle the heat stress.

Why didn't the robust australopithecines evolve such a system? Again, evolution works on what variation already exists. For whatever reason (it may have been random, such as genetic drift), the robust australopithecines had a biological constraint that would have limited any increase in brain size. Their drainage system could only handle the heat stress of a smaller brain. Other hominids, such as A. africanus, had a system that allowed them to evolve larger brains. Once again, any evolutionary change must be viewed in terms of both costs and benefits. For the robust australopithecines, the costs outweighed the benefits, so they did not evolve larger brains.

SUMMARY

The first hominids belong to the genera *Ardipithecus* and *Australopithecus*, all of which lived in Africa, dating back as far as 4.4 million years B.P. Early hominids were bipedal, with small brains, large faces, and large teeth. Early species had many primitive characteristics in terms of both teeth and the skeleton. By 2.5 million years B.P., there were at least two major lines of hominids. One line, the robust australopithecines, had large back teeth, large jaws, and large chewing muscles. The robust species were well adapted for chewing hard foods, such as seeds, nuts, and hard-skinned fruits. Although successful for some time, they ultimately became extinct roughly 1 million years B.P.

The other line of hominid evolution shows an increase in brain size (although still roughly only half the size of a modern human) and the development of a stone tool technology. These hominids, generally referred to as *Homo habilis* (although there might be more than one species), lived in Africa from roughly 2.5 to 1.5 million years B.P. The archaeological evidence suggests that *H. habilis* was a scavenger. The ability to make and use stone tools, along with increased brain size, marks the beginnings of the genus *Homo*. The genus's continued evolution is discussed in the next two chapters.

SUPPLEMENTAL READINGS

Falk, D. 1992. *Braindance*. New York: Henry Holt. This well-written and lively book provides an interesting discussion of ideas regarding the evolution of hominid brains, including a review of the "radiator theory."

Johanson, D., and Edey, M. 1981. *Lucy: The Beginning of Humankind*. New York: Simon & Schuster. The story of the senior author's discovery and interpretation of "Lucy" and other specimens of *Australopithecus afarensis*. Somewhat out of date but still interesting.

Lewin, R. 1987. *Bones of Contention: Controversies in the Search for Human Origins*. New York: Simon & Schuster. An excellent account of several controversial subjects in human origins. Chapters 3, 4, and 7–12 focus on Plio-Pleistocene evolution.

Morell, V. 1995. *Ancestral Passions: The Leakey Family and the Quest for Humankind's Beginnings*. New York: Simon & Schuster. A detailed and fascinating history of the lives and discoveries of Louis, Mary, and Richard Leakey, and their impact on the field of human origins.

Schick, K. D., and Toth, N. 1993. *Making Silent Stones Speak: Human Evolution and the Dawn of Technology*. New York: Simon & Schuster. A review of stone tool technology and its relationship to human origins and evolution, including excellent descriptions of how stone tools are made and used.

CHAPTER **8**

The Evolution of the Genus Homo

Three species are generally recognized in the genus *Homo*: *Homo habilis*, *Homo erectus*, and *Homo sapiens*. The evolution of the genus *Homo* involved an increase in brain size, a reduction in the size of the face and teeth, and increased sophistication of stone tool technologies and other cultural adaptations. This chapter looks at the major biological and cultural changes associated with the evolution of *Homo erectus* and early *Homo sapiens*.

HOMO ERECTUS

The species name **Homo erectus** literally means "upright walking human." This may sound odd, given the fact that earlier species also walked upright. When the first specimens of *H. erectus* were found in the late nineteenth century, they were thought to represent the oldest evidence of bipedalism.

This section of the chapter reviews the currently known biological and behavioral evidence for *Homo erectus*. We will also look at evolutionary

■ FIGURE 8.1
Location of major *Homo erectus* sites in Africa and Asia.

trends within *Homo erectus* and its relationship with earlier (*Homo habilis*) and later (*Homo sapiens*) hominids.

Distribution in Time and Space

The distribution of *H. erectus* sites is shown in Figure 8.1 and a list of the major fossil sites is given in Table 8.1. The most important feature of the spatial distribution of *H. erectus* is the species' move out of Africa; it is the first hominid species to do so. Current evidence points to an African origin for *H. erectus*, followed by movement of some populations into Asia (Indonesia and China). As discussed below, it is still not clear to what extent *H. erectus* lived in Europe, if it did so at all.

H. erectus fossils have been dated to be as old as 1.8 million years B.P. and as recent as 0.2 million years (200,000 years) B.P., and possibly younger.

▲▲▲▲▲▲▲▲▲▲▲▲▲▲▲▲▲▲▲▲▲▲▲▲▲▲▲▲▲▲

Homo erectus A species of genus *Homo* that lived between 1.8 and 0.2 million years B.P., first appearing in Africa and later spreading to Asia (and possibly Europe).

■ TABLE 8.1

List of Some Major Fossil Sites for *Homo erectus* in Africa and Asia

GEOGRAPHIC REGION	COUNTRY	SITE/SPECIMEN	AGE (MILLIONS OF YEARS B.P.)	FIGURE NUMBER(S) IN TEXT
East Africa	Kenya	East Turkana	1.8–1.3	8.4
		West Turkana	1.6	8.9
	Tanzania	Olduvai Gorge	1.2–0.7	
South Africa	Republic of South Africa	Swartkrans	1.7–0.9	
North Africa	Algeria	Ternifine	0.7	
	Morocco	Salé	0.2	
Southeast Asia	Indonesia	Sangiran	1.75*	8.6
		Trinil	0.9?	
		Sambungmachan	0.4	
		Ngandong	0.25	
East Asia	China	Lantian	0.8	
		Zhoukoudian	0.5–0.2	8.5
		Hexian	0.25	

The range of dates for Olduvai Gorge indicates a series of different levels, the youngest dating 0.7 million and the oldest dating 1.2 million years B.P.

*See text.

Source: Klein (1989); Larsen et al. (1991); Swisher et al. (1994)

There appears to be some overlap in time with later *H. habilis*. This type of overlap may reflect uncertainties about dating or species identification, or it may simply reflect a common form of evolutionary change—"parent" species frequently survive for some time after the appearance of a new "daughter" species. In this case, we suggest that *some* population(s) of *H. habilis* evolved into *H. erectus*, but not all of them. That is, some *H. habilis* populations may have persisted for a short time after the initial origin of *H. erectus*.

For many years, researchers believed that Asian *H. erectus* was much younger than African *H. erectus*. Until recently, they dated the African populations back to 1.8 million years B.P. and the oldest Asian populations (in Indonesia) at roughly 1 million years B.P. Given these dates, it appeared that *H. erectus* had remained in Africa for 800,000 years before some groups moved out to Asia. However, recent evidence, based on argon-argon dating, has caused a reassessment of this scenario. The new evidence dates *H. erectus* to 1.7 million years B.P. in Indonesia (Swisher et al. 1994). This new date suggests that some *H. erectus* populations moved out of Africa into Asia soon after the initial species origin.

The evidence for possible European settlement by *H. erectus* is less clear. Most of the possible European sites are archaeological; they provide tools

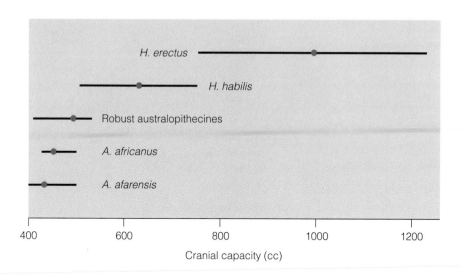

■ FIGURE 8.2
Comparison of the cranial
capacities of *Australo-
pithecus, Homo habilis,*
and *Homo erectus.* The
dots indicate the average
cranial capacity (in cubic
centimeters) for each group.
The lines indicate the range of
cranial capacity from
minimum to maximum.
(*Source of data:* Aiello and Dunbar
1993)

but few fossils. Although the tools at these sites are typical of H. *erectus*, similar tools have been found with early *Homo sapiens* as well. Thus, the tools alone do not tell us whether the sites were occupied by H. *erectus* or early H. *sapiens*.

The few European fossils that have been found are mostly dental remains whose origins are not altogether clear. Some recent evidence, however, suggests that the *fringes* of Europe may have been occupied by H. *erectus*. A lower jaw in the Georgian region of the former Soviet Union has been assigned to H. *erectus*, and has been tentatively dated between 1.8 and 1.6 million years B.P. (Gabunia and Vekja 1995).

H. *erectus* was around for 1.6 million years. This is a long time for a hominid species. Such longevity suggests that H. *erectus* was a well-adapted species. Even though it is in many ways intermediate in appearance between H. *habilis* and H. *sapiens*, we should not regard it as a transitional form. H. *erectus* was not simply a species in the process of becoming us; rather, it was a long-lived, highly successful life form. We need to examine the biological and cultural adaptations of H. *erectus* to understand its evolutionary success.

General Physical Characteristics

The following section focuses on the physical characteristics of *Homo erectus*, specifically those of the skull, teeth, and postcranial skeleton.

BRAIN SIZE   The most obvious characteristic of H. *erectus*, compared to earlier forms such as H. *habilis*, is its larger brain size (Figures 8.2 and 8.3). The average cranial capacity of H. *erectus* is roughly 1,000 cc, which is approximately 75 percent that of a modern human. On average, the brain size of H. *erectus*

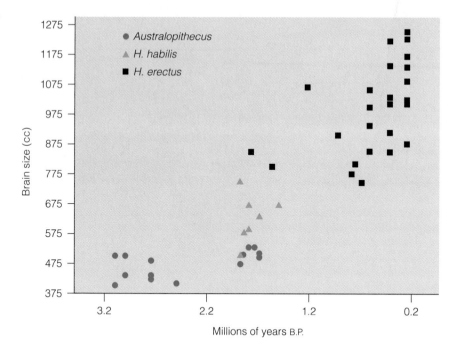

■ **FIGURE 8.3**
Plot of cranial capacities of
fossil specimens over time for
*Australopithecus, Homo
habilis,* and *Homo erectus.*
(*Source of data:* Aiello and Dunbar
1993)

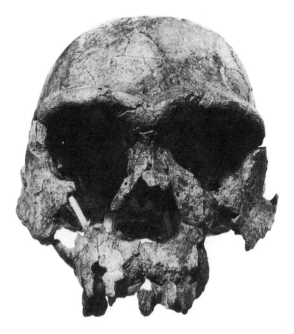

■ **FIGURE 8.4**
Homo erectus skull, specimen
KNM-ER 3733, Lake Turkana,
Kenya. Dated at 1.8 million
years B.P., this is one of the
oldest known specimens of
Homo erectus. (© The National
Museums of Kenya)

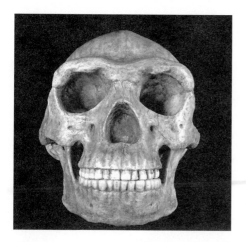
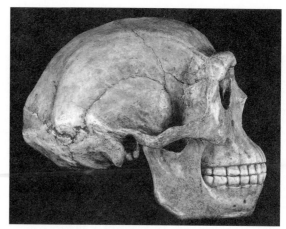

■ **FIGURE 8.5**
Frontal and side views of
Homo erectus from the site
of Zhoukoudian, China. The
specimens from this site
are sometimes referred to
as "Peking Man" in older
literature. (Neg. No. 315446,
315447. Courtesy Department
of Library Services, American
Museum of Natural History)

is almost 60 percent larger than that of *H. habilis*. Figure 8.3 shows that the brain size of *H. erectus* increased somewhat over time, particularly after 700,000 years B.P. (Leigh 1992).

CRANIAL AND DENTAL CHARACTERISTICS   One of the earliest *H. erectus* skulls, from Lake Turkana, Africa, is shown in Figure 8.4. Examples of Asian *H. erectus* are shown in Figure 8.5 (China) and Figure 8.6 (Indonesia). Overall, the brain case of *H. erectus* is larger than that of *H. habilis*, but it is still smaller than that of modern *H. sapiens*. The skull is lower and the face still protrudes more than in modern humans. Neck muscles attach to a ridge of bone along the back side of the skull. The development of this bony ridge shows that *H. erectus* had powerful neck muscles.

Figure 8.7 shows a *H. erectus* skull and a *H. sapiens* skull from a top view. The frontal region of the skull is still rather narrow (**postorbital constriction**), suggesting lesser development in the frontal and temporal lobes of the brain relative to modern humans. This implies that the intellectual abilities of *H. erectus* were not as great as in modern humans. The best evidence for the mental aptitude of *H. erectus*, however, comes from the archaeological record, discussed later. Figure 8.8 shows a *H. erectus* skull and a *H. sapiens* skull from the rear view. Note that the brain case of *H. erectus* is much broader toward the bottom of the skull. The jaws and teeth of *H. erectus* are still large compared to those of modern humans but smaller than those of earlier hominids. Electron-scanning-microscopic analysis shows that the wear patterns on *H. erectus* teeth are characteristic of extensive meat eating.

The face of *H. erectus* protrudes, but not as much as in earlier hominids. One noticeable characteristic of the *H. erectus* face is the development of large ridges of bone above the eye orbits (**brow ridges**). These brow ridges

▲▲▲

postorbital constriction
The narrowness of the
skull behind the eye

orbits, a characteristic of
early hominids.

brow ridges The large
ridges of bone above
the eye orbits, most

noticeable in *Homo
erectus* and archaic *Homo
sapiens.*

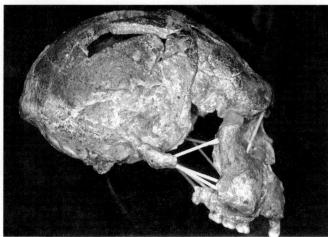

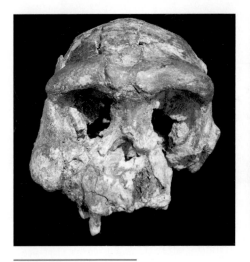

■ FIGURE 8.6
Front and side views of *Homo
erectus* skull, specimen
Sangiran 17, from Sangiran,
Indonesia. (Courtesy of Milford
Wolpoff, University of Michigan)

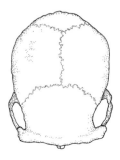

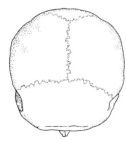

■ FIGURE 8.7
Top views of the skulls of
Homo erectus (*left*) and
modern *Homo sapiens* (*right*).
Note the greater constriction
behind the eyes in *Homo
erectus.*

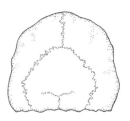

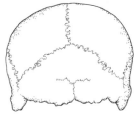

■ FIGURE 8.8
Rear views of the skulls of
Homo erectus (*left*) and
modern *Homo sapiens* (*right*).
Note the broader brain case of
Homo sapiens.

are not apparent in *H. habilis* and are much smaller in archaic and modern
H. sapiens. On the face, the various forces exerted by chewing and neck muscles meet above the eyes. The brow ridges of *H. erectus* are a structural adaptation to strengthen the face at this critical juncture (Wolpoff 1980).

THE POSTCRANIAL SKELETON   For many years, the postcranial evidence for *H. erectus* was limited to portions of individuals—a femur here or a pelvic bone
there. In 1984, this situation changed with the discovery of a nearly com-

plete *H. erectus* skeleton at Lake Turkana dating back to 1.6 million years B.P. (Brown et al. 1985). This skeleton (Figure 8.9) is that of a young male. The pattern of dental eruption suggests he was about 12 years old when he died. One of the most striking features of this extremely complete skeleton is that he was tall; had he lived to adulthood, he might have been 6 feet tall, well above the height of many modern human populations! Also, note that the body proportions are very similar to those of modern humans, and different from those of earlier hominids, which had slightly longer arms.

Cultural Behavior

Given the change in brain size from *H. habilis* to *H. erectus*, it is no surprise that corresponding changes took place in cultural adaptations. The stone tool technology of *H. erectus* was more sophisticated and specialized than that of *H. habilis*. Although not all agree, most anthropologists suggest that *H. erectus* was a skilled cooperative hunter. Some populations of *H. erectus* used caves for shelter and others, perhaps, made their own temporary shelters when caves were not available. *H. erectus* also used fire for cooking and warmth, although it is not clear whether they made fire or relied instead on natural fire.

STONE TOOL TECHNOLOGY   In general, the stone tool technology of *H. erectus* was more diverse and sophisticated than the simple Oldowan tool technology used by *H. habilis*. This cultural change did not, however, take place immediately with the origin of *H. erectus*. That is, these biological and cultural changes did not occur simultaneously. Initially, early *H. erectus* in Africa made tools similar to but somewhat more sophisticated than Oldowan tools. Starting 1.4 million years B.P., however, *H. erectus* developed a new type of stone tool technology referred to as the **Acheulian tradition**. Acheulian tools are found in Africa and Europe.

Acheulian tools are **bifaces;** the stone is worked on both sides. These tools are flatter and have straighter, sharper sides than Oldowan tools. The change in manufacture produced a more efficient tool. To produce a biface tool, smaller flakes must be removed than is necessary to produce an Oldowan chopping tool, a process that requires greater skill. One method of flake removal involves the use of some softer material, such as wood or antler, instead of another stone. Softer materials absorb much of the shock in flake removal, allowing more precise control over flaking.

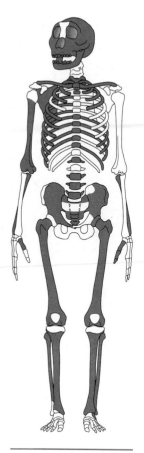

■ FIGURE 8.9
Homo erectus skeleton, specimen KNM-WT 15000, Lake Turkana, Kenya. This skeleton of a 12-year-old boy, dated to 1.6 million years B.P., is the most complete specimen of *Homo erectus* yet found. The shaded ares are the bones that were found.

▲▲

Acheulian tradition The stone tool technology associated with some groups of *Homo erectus*.

biface Stone tool with both sides worked, producing greater symmetry and efficiency.

■ FIGURE 8.10
Making an Acheulian tool. Nicholas Toth uses a piece of antler to remove small flakes from both sides of the flint, producing a symmetric hand axe. Shown are flint hand axes and a cleaver.
(Courtesy of Nicholas Toth, Indiana University)

■ FIGURE 8.11
Examples of tools made by *Homo erectus:* (a) hand axe, (b) side scraper, (c) small chopping tool, (d) chopper, (e) cleaverlike tool. (From *The Old Stone Age* by F. Bordes, 1968. Reprinted with permission of the publisher, Wiedenfeld and Nicolson, Ltd.)

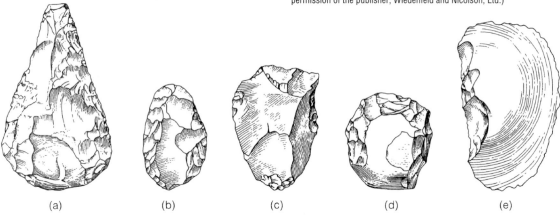

(a)   (b)   (c)   (d)   (e)

The basic Acheulian tool is the hand axe (Figure 8.10), which could be used for a variety of purposes, including meat preparation. Other tools were made for different purposes. Scrapers were used for cleaning animal flesh, and cleavers were used for breaking animal bones during butchery (Figure 8.11).

The use of individual tools for different purposes marks an important step in the cultural evolution of hominids. Increased specialization allows more efficient tool use and also requires greater mental sophistication in tool design and manufacture.

Not all *H. erectus* populations made Acheulian tools. At sites in China, the tools used by *H. erectus* are somewhat different. The Chinese sites contain many of the smaller tools characteristic of the Acheulian, but not hand axes. Instead, there are large chopping tools that were manufactured differently (see Figure 8.11d and 8.11e). Geographically, the Acheulian and chopping tool cultures are distinct.

This cultural difference has always puzzled anthropologists. How could two populations so biologically similar give rise to distinct cultures? One possibility has to do with natural resources. Pope (1989) has suggested bamboo was frequently used as a raw material in Asia. Bamboo is a convenient natural and renewable resource from which a variety of tools can be made, including knives, spear points, and containers. If tools like these were made from bamboo, then stone tools would have been used only for tasks such as cutting wood. Pope's hypothesis is supportable if the distribution of bamboo in the past reflects his theory; unfortunately, however, the hypothesis cannot be tested directly because bamboo tools are not preserved over time.

Another possible reason for these cultural differences relates to the revised dates for the Indonesian sites at 1.7 million years B.P., which is earlier than the initial invention of Acheulian tools (at 1.4 million years B.P.). If *H. erectus* had arrived in Indonesia by this date, it means that some *H. erectus* had left Africa *before* Acheulian tools were invented.

HUNTING AND GATHERING Recent evidence suggests that *H. habilis* was a scavenger instead of a hunter, but the fossil and archaeological records show that *H. erectus* was definitely a hunter of small and large game. The earliest evidence of hunting dates from Olduvai Gorge 1.5 million years B.P. The bones of animals found at these sites differ in several ways from those at earlier *H. habilis* sites. All of the bones from larger animals are found, suggesting a single butchering site, rather than fragmentary scavenging. The bones are also more fragmented, showing greater use of the animal carcass (Wolpoff 1980). The complete use of animal carcasses matches the pattern found with modern hunting-and-gathering groups and is different from that expected from scavenging. The increased variety of stone tools for butchering also supports the idea that *H. erectus* was a hunter, as does dental evidence, which shows a significant amount of meat in the diet.

One of the best known *H. erectus* sites with evidence of hunting is Zhoukoudian, China. Here *H. erectus* populations lived intermittently in caves between roughly 460,000 and 230,000 years B.P. The caves were used as living sites and are littered with animal bones, remnants of fire, tools and tool scraps, and fossilized hominid feces. In addition, parts of the remains of over 40 *H. erectus* individuals have been found at the Zhoukoudian caves. This site has long been known as the place of "Peking Man," named after the nearby city of Beijing (Peking), China.

The Zhoukoudian caves show evidence of two major cultural adaptations of *H. erectus*: fire and hunting. There are large hearths in the caves, some with ash as deep as 7 ft. Fire was important in the northern environments for warmth, light, and chasing off predators. Fire was also used by *H. erectus* to cook animal flesh. Charred bones found in the cave represent a number of animal species, including wild pigs and water buffalo. Deer bones are the most numerous and represent the major prey for *H. erectus* in this region.

The bones and stones at different sites show that hunting was an important source of food. Was it the only source? Gathering of vegetables, fruits, nuts, and other foods was surely just as important to the survival of *H. erectus* as hunting was. In modern hunting-gathering societies, up to 75 percent of the total caloric intake of a group comes from gathering. In the past, anthropologists have tended to focus more on hunting than on gathering. This focus was in part a consequence of the nature of the archaeological record (bones and stones preserve more easily than do vegetables or wooden containers).

Another factor was male bias, unfortunately common in many scientific fields. Modern hunting-gathering societies show a clear division of labor by sex—men are generally the hunters and women the gatherers. The early interpretation of (mostly male) anthropologists focused on what was considered the more "important" and "difficult" task of male hunting. This interpretation influenced other hypotheses on prehistoric human behavior. Males were assumed to be the hunters because they had the necessary strength. However, although males are generally stronger than females, this slight difference would not have mattered in hunting. Not even the strongest male today can knock down an elephant by himself! Hunting requires skill and stealth more than strength. The important distinction between hunting and gathering is that the former activity requires greater mobility, and moving around may not be conducive to successful human pregnancy or nursing. Gathering can be performed in a local area, whereas hunting requires traveling long distances over many days.

Because gathering accounts for the majority of calories, we could also argue for a female-centered view: instead of "man the hunter" we could have "woman the gatherer." Both of these ideas, however, miss the main feature of hunting-and-gathering society—food sharing. Hunting and gathering were equally important activities, and the survival and geographic expansion of *H. erectus* depended on both. The division of labor and food sharing of hunter-gatherers show close and cooperative social structures.

FIRE   The movement of *H. erectus* into East Asia shows the importance of cultural adaptations. Hominids are tropical primates, and expansion into colder climates required an appropriate level of technology. Fire was an important source of warmth, light, and cooking. In addition, fire can be used for tool manufacture. The tip of a wooden spear can be placed in a fire for a short period to harden the point. We can also speculate that fire allowed social interactions and teaching after dark.

Evidence for controlled fire comes from the cave hearths at Zhoukoudian and other *H. erectus* sites. The earliest known use of controlled fire dates to almost 1 million years B.P. (Pfeiffer 1985), although recent evidence from South Africa suggests a possible earlier date of up to 1.5 million years B.P.

The use of fire marks an important step in human cultural evolution. Making and using fire represent the controlled exploitation of an energy source. Because we rely on many other sources of controlled energy today, we tend to overlook the vital importance of fire as an energy source.

ARCHAIC *HOMO SAPIENS*

At the simplest level, the fossil record shows the evolution of *H. erectus* into *H. sapiens*. Closer examination, however, shows this statement to be a bit too simplistic, masking variation across time and space. As we have seen, some populations of *H. erectus* survived until roughly 200,000 years ago. Elsewhere in the Old World, however, we see fossils that are different from *H. erectus* appear roughly 400,000 years ago. Many anthropologists classify these non-*erectus* fossils as early *H. sapiens*, in large part because they are clearly not *H. erectus* and they had larger brains. However, they are not the same as modern *H. sapiens*, thus creating a problem in naming and classification. What do we call them?

There are several solutions to this problem, each reflecting a different view of hominid macroevolution. Some anthropologists suggest that we are simply seeing a transition in morphology over time, and that it is not useful to break up this continuous evolutionary line into distinct species. According to this view, the change from what we call *H. erectus* into *H. sapiens* is a good example of anagenesis, the transformation of a single species over time. Here, species names are to a large extent arbitrary. Another school of thought sees the change from *H. erectus* to modern *H. sapiens* as an example of cladogenesis, the formation of one or more new species from a previous species. In this school of thought, the fossils are not viewed as transitional, but as a separate species (or several species) lying in time between *H. erectus* and ourselves.

Most anthropologists prefer to label these hominids as *H. sapiens*, in large part because their brain size is roughly the same as that of modern *H.*

■ FIGURE 8.12
Map of some archaic *Homo sapiens* sites.

sapiens. To reflect the differences that exist between *H. erectus* and *H. sapiens*, these anthropologists add the label "archaic." Thus, they contrast **archaic Homo sapiens** with **anatomically modern Homo sapiens.** The adjectives "archaic" and "modern" are not proper taxonomic labels, but they serve a crude purpose in showing that the two groups are similar yet different.

Distribution in Time and Space

Archaic *H. sapiens* has been found at a number of sites in Africa, Europe, and Asia (Figure 8.12) dating, for the most part, between roughly 400,000 and 35,000 years B.P. This time range is conservative—recent discoveries from the Atapuerca site in Spain suggest that members of the genus *Homo* might date back as far as 780,000 years B.P. (Carbonell et al. 1995; Parés and Pérez-González 1995). Although these remains are not those of *H. erectus*, it is not clear whether they are an early group of archaic *H. sapiens* or a different species altogether.

■ TABLE 8.2
List of Some Major Fossil Sites for Archaic *Homo sapiens*

GEOGRAPHIC REGION	COUNTRY	SITE/SPECIMEN	AGE (THOUSANDS OF YEARS B.P.)	FIGURE NUMBER(S) IN TEXT
Africa	Tanzania	Lake Ndutu	350	
	Ethiopia	Bodo	500–200	
	Zambia	Kabwe	150–125	8.16
North Africa	Morocco	Jebel Irhoud	127–87	
Asia	India	Narmada	730–150	
	China	Yinkou	263	
		Dali	200–150	8.17
		Maba	140–119	
Europe	France	Arago	400–200	
		La Chapelle (N)	56–47	8.19
		La Quina (N)	55–40	
		La Ferrassie (N)	50–40	8.18
		Le Moustier (N)	40	
		St. Césaire (N)	36	
	Greece	Petralona	300–200	8.15
	England	Swanscombe	250–200	
	Germany	Steinheim	250–200	
		Neandertal (N)	70–35	
	Croatia	Krapina (N)	70	
	Gibraltar	Forbe's Quarry (N)	70–45	
	Italy	Saccapastore (N)	60	
		Mt. Circeo (N)	60–40	
	Hungary	Vértesszölös	225–185	
Middle East	Israel	Kebara (N)	64–60	
		Tabun (N)	120	8.20
		Amud (N)	50–42	
	Iraq	Shanidar (N)	51–47	8.21

N = Neandertal

This table is not meant to be complete; many other specimens of archaic *Homo sapiens* have been found.

Source: Klein (1989); Kennedy et al. (1991); Larsen et al. (1991); Stringer and Gamble (1993)

Given the large number of sites and specimens, it is useful to look more closely at patterns of regional variation. Some of the better-known regions include sub-Saharan Africa, North Asia, South Asia, and Southeast Asia and Australia (often lumped together as "Australasia"). Table 8.2 lists a number of the major sites of archaic *H. sapiens*.

▲▲▲

archaic *Homo sapiens*
An earlier variant of *Homo sapiens*, found at dates ranging from over 400,000 to 35,000 years B.P.

anatomically modern *Homo sapiens* Modern *Homo sapiens* dating to roughly the last 100,000 years.

■ FIGURE 8.13
Comparison of the cranial
capacities of *Australo-
pithecus, Homo habilis, Homo
erectus,* and archaic *Homo
sapiens.* The dots indicate the
average cranial capacity (in
cubic centimeters) for each
group. The lines indicate the
range of cranial capacity from
minimum to maximum.
(*Source of data:* Aiello and Dunbar
1993)

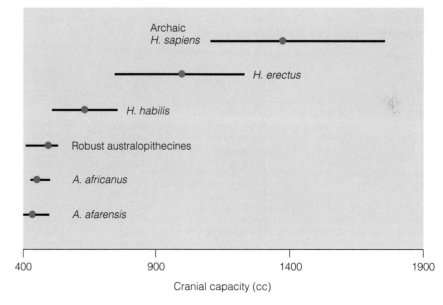

Particular emphasis in the past was placed on a regional population known as the **Neandertals.** The word *Neandertal* is simply the German for "Neander Valley," the site where one of the first specimens was discovered. The Neandertals lived in the regions surrounding the Mediterranean, including Western Europe, Central and Eastern Europe, and the Middle East.

■ FIGURE 8.14
Plot of cranial capacities of
fossil specimens over time for
*Australopithecus, Homo
habilis, Homo erectus,* and
archaic *Homo sapiens.*
(*Source of data:* Aiello and Dunbar
1993)

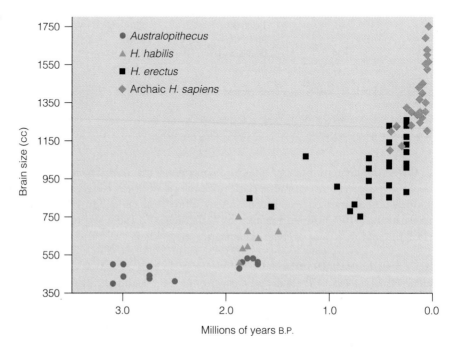

■ **FIGURE 8.15**
The Petralona skull, Greece.
An example of an early archaic
Homo sapiens from Europe.
(From Clark Spencer Larsen,
Robert M. Matter, and Daniel L.
Gebo, *Human Origins: The Fossil
Record,* Second Edition, p. 112.
Copyright © 1991, 1985 by
Waveland Press, Inc., Prospect
Heights, Illinois. Reprinted with
permission from the publisher)

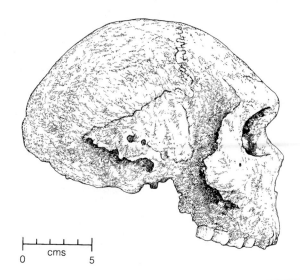

```
 |--+--+--+--+--|
 0       cms      5
```

Neandertal remains have been found dating between roughly 125,000 to 35,000 years B.P. Earlier literature often used the term *Neandertal* to refer to *all* archaic *H. sapiens* populations, but now we confine the term to a specific region and time period.

Physical Characteristics

Archaic brain size is compared to that of other fossil hominids in Figure 8.13. Figure 8.14 shows the brain size of archaic *H. sapiens* compared to other hominids when plotted over time. Both archaic and modern *H. sapiens* have large brains of roughly equal size. The average cranial capacity of modern humans is roughly 1,350 cc (Beals et al. 1984); the average archaic brain size was 1,370 cc (Aiello and Dunbar 1993). The archaic sample masks some important variation. The earliest archaics generally have smaller cranial capacities, showing that an increase in brain size has taken place during the past 200,000 years.

Because both archaic and anatomically modern *H. sapiens* have large brains, brain size cannot be used to distinguish between the two groups. The morphology of the skulls of these two groups, however, is on average different. Archaic *H. sapiens* has a low skull with a sloping forehead, whereas anatomically modern *H. sapiens* has a high skull and a vertical forehead. Also, the face and teeth of archaic *H. sapiens* are larger than those in modern *H. sapiens*. Specimens of archaic *H. sapiens* rarely have a chin, something found in modern *H. sapiens*. The postcranial skeleton of many (not all) archaic *H. sapiens* specimens is very similar to modern forms. In general, the bones of archaic *H. sapiens* are thicker and show greater musculature.

REGIONAL VARIATION   An example of an early archaic *H. sapiens* is shown in Figure 8.15. This skull, from Petralona, Greece, dates to between 200,000 and

▲▲▲▲▲▲▲▲▲▲▲▲▲▲▲▲▲▲▲▲▲▲▲▲▲▲▲▲▲▲

Neandertals A regional population of archaic *Homo sapiens* found in Europe and the Middle East, dating between roughly 125,000 to 35,000 years B.P.

■ FIGURE 8.16
The Broken Hill skull, Kabwe, Zambia. An example of early archaic *Homo sapiens* from Africa. (Neg. no. 410816. Courtesy Department of Library Services, American Museum of Natural History)

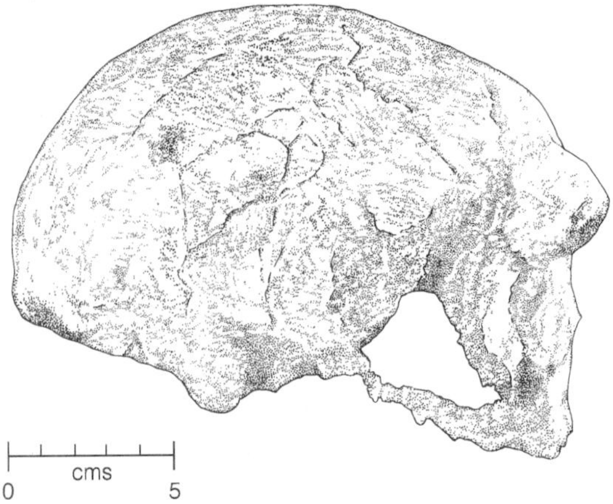

■ FIGURE 8.17
The Dali skull, Dali County, People's Republic of China. An example of archaic *Homo sapiens* from Asia. (From Clark Spencer Larsen, Robert M. Matter, and Daniel L. Gebo, *Human Origins: The Fossil Record*, Second Edition, p. 119. Copyright © 1991, 1985 by Waveland Press, Inc., Prospect Heights, Illinois. Reprinted with permission from the publisher)

cms

0   5

100,000 years B.P. Its cranial capacity (1,230 cc) places it at the upper range of later *H. erectus* or the lower range of archaic *H. sapiens*. Another example of an archaic specimen is the skull shown in Figure 8.16, which was discovered in Zambia, Africa, and dates to roughly 150,000 to 125,000 years B.P. The large brain size (1,285 cc) is readily apparent. The face is rather large and so are the brow ridges. The shape of the skull shows typical archaic features: a sloping forehead and a low skull.

Another example of an archaic *H. sapiens* skull (Figure 8.17) is from the site at Dali, China, and dates to between 200,000 and 150,000 years B.P. The cranial capacity is on the low end of the range for *H. sapiens* (1,120 cc) and the brow ridges are large. The skull is also low and has a sloping forehead, both typical archaic features. The Dali skull also illustrates regional variation. As in many archaic North Asian specimens, the face is smaller and flatter than in other regions of the world. These traits, among others, are also

Neandertals: Names and Images

The name *Neandertal* comes from the site in the Neander Valley in Germany where Neandertals were first found. In German, *tal* means "valley." Hence, *Neandertal* means "Neander Valley." You may be more familiar with an alternative spelling ("Neanderthal") and an alternative pronunciation (emphasizing the "THAL" sound). However, the *h* is silent in German, so that *thal* is actually pronounced "tal." Because of this characteristic of German pronunciation, many (although not all) anthropologists simply drop the *h* in the spelling as well.

The very mention of Neandertals usually invokes a number of images and preconceptions. You may, for example, conjure up one of many images of the Neandertals as crude and simple subhumans with limited intelligence that walk bent over. These images have become such a part of our popular culture that a typical dictionary definition includes "Neandertal" as an adjective meaning "suggesting primitive man in appearance or behavior (*Neandertal* ferocity)" and "extremely old-fashioned or out-of-date," as well as a noun meaning "a rugged or uncouth person" (*Webster's Third International Dictionary*).

Why do Neandertals have such a bad reputation? As discussed in this chapter, Neandertals are viewed by most anthropologists as a regional population of archaic *Homo sapiens*. The distinctive appearance of Neandertals is often acknowledged by scientists who refer to them as a different subspecies of humans—

that is, *Homo sapiens neanderthalensis*, as opposed to modern humans, who are classified in the subspecies *Homo sapiens sapiens*. Some anthropologists argue that Neandertals are sufficiently different to be placed in a different species altogether—*Homo neanderthalensis* (note that the *h* remains in the species and subspecies names, as per international agreement). Regardless of classification, however, we know that Neandertals had large brains, walked upright, and possessed a sophisticated culture including stone tools, hunting, use of fire, and cave burial.

Part of the image problem comes from an inaccurate reconstruction of a Neandertal skeleton in the early 1900s. Because of certain physical features, such as curved thigh bones, scientists of the time believed that Neandertals did not walk completely upright, moving about bent over instead. It was discovered later that the curved bones and other features were simply a reflection of the poor health, including severe arthritis, of that particular Neandertal. Other features once taken to indicate mental inferiority, such as large brow ridges, are now recognized as biomechanical in nature. Even though the scientific interpretation has changed, the popular images of Neandertals remain to this day. More information on the history of Neandertals, including further discussion of their image, can be found in Trinkaus and Shipman (1992) and Stringer and Gamble (1993).

found in earlier and later North Asian specimens (Thorne and Wolpoff 1992).

THE NEANDERTALS Of all the regional populations of archaic *H. sapiens*, the best known is the Neandertals. Many of the Neandertals lived during the time of the **Würm glaciation.** The Pleistocene epoch witnessed alternating periods of glaciation and interglacials as the earth's climate changed. In the Northern Hemisphere large sections of land were covered with advancing ice sheets during glaciations, which receded during interglacial periods. Earlier views on glaciation held that four major glaciations, or "ice ages," took place during the Pleistocene. It is now recognized that the climate changed much more frequently, perhaps as many as 17 times, in this period. Even during times typically characterized as "ice ages," the temperature and southern advancement of ice varied considerably. In any case, the Neander-

▲▲▲▲▲▲▲▲▲▲▲▲▲▲▲▲▲▲▲▲▲▲▲▲▲▲▲▲
Würm glaciation One of the times of intense climatic cooling ("ice ages") during the Pleistocene epoch.

■ FIGURE 8.18
Frontal and side view of La
Ferrassie skull, a Neandertal
from France. (Courtesy of
Milford Wolpoff, University of
Michigan)

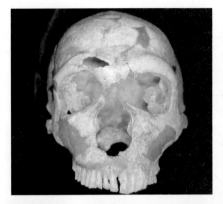

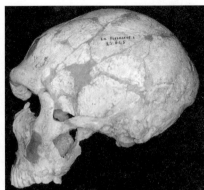

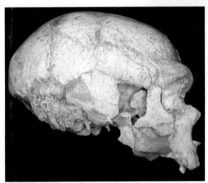

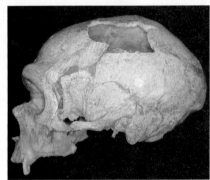

■ FIGURE 8.19
Two side views of La Chapelle
skull, a Neandertal from
France. (Courtesy of Milford
Wolpoff, University of Michigan)

tals lived during times when the climate was cooler in their habitat. They did not live right on the ice, but the reduction in average temperature surely had an effect on their environments, especially in Western Europe. The ability of the Neandertals to survive in these conditions is proof of their cultural adaptations, which included hunting, shelter, and use of fire.

Neandertals had the typical archaic features of sloping forehead, low skull, lack of chin, and large brow ridges. They also possessed several unique characteristics that tend not to be found in other regions (or to be found at a much lower frequency).

The Neandertals had very large brains, averaging 1,465 cc (Aiello and Dunbar 1993). The males had larger average cranial capacities because of their larger body size. In fact, relative to body size, the Neandertals may have had slightly larger brain sizes than many modern human populations. According to a review by Holloway (1985), the structural organization of Neandertal brains, as assessed from endocasts, is no different from that of modern humans.

Neandertals differ from other archaic *H. sapiens* populations in several features. Figures 8.18 and 8.19 show two skulls of Western European Neandertals, both from sites in France between 50,000 and 40,000 years B.P.

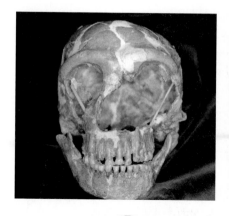
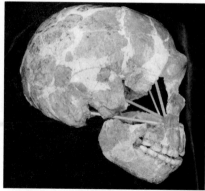

■ FIGURE 8.20
Frontal and side view of
Neandertal skull from Tabun,
Israel. (Courtesy of Milford
Wolpoff, University of Michigan)

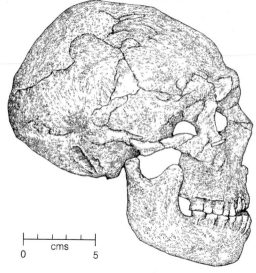

■ FIGURE 8.21
Shanidar I skull, Iraq.
(From Clark Spencer Larsen,
Robert M. Matter, and Daniel L.
Gebo, *Human Origins: The Fossil
Record,* Second Edition, p. 128.
Copyright © 1991, 1985 by
Waveland Press, Inc., Prospect
Heights, Illinois. Reprinted with
permission from the publisher)

cms
0   5

Neandertal faces are generally long and protrude more than in other archaic populations. The nasal region is large, suggesting large noses, and the sinus cavities to the side of the nose expand outward. The large nasal and midfacial areas on Neandertal skulls have often been interpreted as some type of adaptation to a cold climate. However, Rak (1986) suggests that the Neandertal face acted to withstand stresses brought about by the use of relatively large front teeth. The front teeth of Neandertals are large in relation to their back teeth and often show considerable wear, suggesting their use as tools.

There is also variation within Neandertals. Figures 8.20 and 8.21 show the skulls of two Middle Eastern Neandertals. Though they possess the general characteristics of Neandertals, they are not as morphologically extreme. The skulls are a bit more well rounded than most Western European Neandertal skulls. The differences between the two skulls may reflect some aspect of local adaptation to their environments.

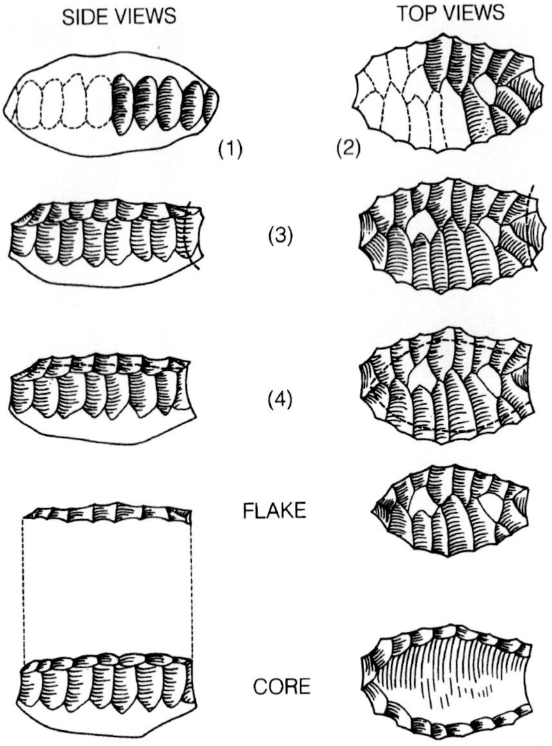

SIDE VIEWS   TOP VIEWS

■ FIGURE 8.22
Manufacture of a Mousterian tool, using the prepared-core method. First, the core is shaped by removing small flakes from the sides and top (a–d). Then the finished tool is removed from the core (e). (From *Archaeology: Discovering Our Past*, 2d ed., by Robert Sharer and Wendy Ashmore, Fig. 10.3. Copyright © 1993 by Mayfield Publishing Company)

(1)   (2)

(3)

(4)

FLAKE

CORE

Neandertal postcranial remains show essentially modern bipedalism, but also a few differences compared with other *H. sapiens* populations. Neandertals were relatively short and stocky. The limb bone segments farthest from the body (lower arm and lower leg) are relatively short, most likely reflecting cold adaptation (Trinkaus 1981). The limb and shoulder bones are more rugged than those of modern humans. The areas of muscle attachment show that the Neandertals were very strong. It has been suggested that Neandertal hands were not as capable of fine manipulation as modern human hands are, or had at least different patterns of manipulation (Stoner and Trinkaus 1981).

Cultural Behavior

Archaic *H. sapiens* were hunters and gatherers, exploiting a wide variety of natural resources. Remains of animal bones at their sites show that they hunted both small game and large, including bears, mammoths, and rhinoceroses. In some areas it appears that archaic *H. sapiens* hunted year round; in others they apparently migrated along with animal herds.

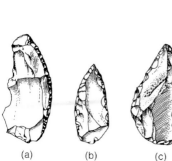

(a)   (b)   (c)   (d)   (e)

■ **FIGURE 8.23**
Examples of Mousterian tools: (a) scraper, (b) point, (c) scraper, (d) point, (e) hand axe. (From *The Old Stone Age* by F. Bordes, 1968. Reprinted with permission of the publisher, Weidenfeld and Nicolson, Ltd.)

STONE TOOL TECHNOLOGY   The stone tools of archaic *H. sapiens* represent an advancement over the Acheulian and chopping tool traditions of *H. erectus*. Much of the evidence for stone tool manufacture comes from Neandertal sites, where the stone tool tradition is known as the **Mousterian.** Similar tools found in other regions where archaic *H. sapiens* lived are sometimes referred to as Mousterian or Mousterianlike, as well as by other names (for example, in Africa, the term *Middle Stone Age* is frequently used). In this chapter, the term *Mousterian* is used in a general sense to refer to the basic patterns of tool manufacture among archaic *H. sapiens*. However, as with *H. erectus*, there is often considerable variation from region to region, reflecting availability of local resources and cultural differences in toolmaking.

The key feature of the Mousterian tradition is the use of a prepared-core technique in tool manufacture. As Figure 8.22 shows, a flint nodule is first chipped around the edges. Small flakes are then removed from the top surface of the core. In the final step, the core is struck precisely at one end.

The use of the prepared-core technique, which produces sharp and symmetric tools (Figure 8.23), tells us two important things about archaic *H. sapiens*. First, they were capable of precise toolmaking, which implies an excellent knowledge of flaking methods and the structural characteristics of stone. Second, they were able to visualize the final tool early in production. Not until the last step does the shape of the finished tool become apparent. Such manufacture is a process quite different from simply chipping away at a stone until a tool is finished.

SYMBOLIC BEHAVIOR   Archaeological evidence suggests that archaic *H. sapiens* may have been capable of symbolic thought, perhaps even holding beliefs in the supernatural. Archaic *H. sapiens* (specifically, some Neandertals) were the first hominids to bury their dead deliberately. Evidence of burial comes from a number of European and Middle Eastern sites, where dead persons' bones have been arranged carefully in graves, often in association with tools, food, and flowers.

▲▲▲▲▲▲▲▲▲▲▲▲▲▲▲▲▲▲▲▲▲▲▲▲▲▲▲▲

Mousterian tradition
The stone tool technology of the Neandertals.

The intentional burial of the dead has suggested a ritualistic purpose to some researchers. At the Shanidar Cave site in Iraq, flowers had been placed all over the bodies, an event that was reconstructed based on the presence of fossil pollen in the graves. Although the Shanidar burial is still considered one of the best examples of symbolic behavior, it is possible the pollen was introduced by rodents burrowing into the grave *after* burial.

The physical condition of fossil remains offers another window on the behavior of archaic H. *sapiens*. By looking at bone fractures, condition of teeth, and other features, we can get a good idea of the age and health status of early humans. Many archaic H. *sapiens* remains are of elderly individuals with numerous medical problems. By looking for signs of healing or infection, we can tell that many of these elderly individuals did not die from these afflictions. How, then, did they survive? Survival of many of the elderly and impaired archaic H. *sapiens* suggests that others cared for them. This implies not only compassion as a social value but also the existence of a social system that allowed for the sharing of food and of resources.

This perspective may be based more on our interpretive biases, however, than on reality. Dettwyler (1991) questions the traditional view of the elderly and disabled as nonproductive members of a group who must be cared for. Drawing on cross-cultural studies, she notes that physically disabled individuals in many societies still frequently make important contributions.

LANGUAGE CAPABILITY   Did archaic H. *sapiens* have language? Lieberman and Crelin (1971), who reconstructed the vocal anatomy of Neandertals, concluded they were incapable of vocalizing certain vowel sounds. The implication was that archaic H. *sapiens* did not possess as wide a range of sounds as modern humans and perhaps had limited language abilities. This hypothesis was criticized, however, because of differences of opinion on vocal anatomy reconstruction. The lack of direct fossil evidence at the heart of the debate was ultimately furnished with the discovery of the first hyoid bone for archaic H. *sapiens*, a bone lying in the neck that can be used to provide information on the structure of the respiratory tract. That this specimen is almost identical in size and shape to the hyoid bone of modern humans indicates that there were no differences in vocal ability between archaics and moderns (Arensberg et al. 1990). Indeed, no evidence exists from brain anatomy to show that archaic H. *sapiens* lacked speech centers (Holloway 1985).

SUMMARY

Following the initial appearance of the genus *Homo* (H. *habilis*), the record of human biological and cultural evolution shows an increase in brain size and complexity, reduction in the size of the face and teeth, and an increasing reliance on cultural adaptations.

The species *Homo erectus* appears to have evolved rapidly from some populations of *H. habilis* in East Africa by 1.8 million years B.P. *H. erectus* had an increased cranial capacity and exhibited a variety of new cultural adaptations, including greater sophistication in stone tool technology, hunting and gathering, and the use of fire. These adaptations allowed *H. erectus* to expand out of Africa into Asia, and possibly into parts of Europe as well. Although it has long been thought that *H. erectus* reached southeast Asia by one million years ago, new evidence suggests that this movement may have happened as early as 1.7 million years B.P. *H. erectus* continued in parts of Africa and Asia until roughly 200,000 years ago.

Fossils showing an increased brain size begin to appear in the fossil record dating roughly 400,000 years B.P. By 200,000 years B.P., the average brain size of this group of hominids is roughly the same as that in modern humans. Although debate continues over whether these hominids should be assigned to a separate species, current usage is to refer to them as "archaic" *H. sapiens*, as compared to ourselves (modern *H. sapiens*). These terms are an attempt to acknowledge differences between earlier forms and ourselves (primarily larger faces and brow ridges, a sloping forehead, a less well-rounded skull, and no chin), but at the same time to recognize the similarity (large brains). One of the best known populations of archaic *H. sapiens* are the Neandertals, found in Europe and the Middle East from 125,000 to 35,000 years B.P. Neandertals are distinctive in having large noses and mid-facial structures, perhaps reflecting climatic adaptation. Contrary to popular thought, the Neandertals had a sophisticated stone tool technology, buried their dead, and adapted to harsh climates.

SUPPLEMENTAL READINGS

Klein, R. G. 1989. *The Human Career: Human Biological and Cultural Origins.* Chicago: University of Chicago Press. An excellent summary of human evolution, with particular attention to the biology and culture of *H. erectus* and *H. sapiens.*

Stringer, C., and Gamble, C. 1993. *In Search of the Neanderthals: Solving the Puzzle of Human Origins.* New York: Thames and Hudson. An excellent and up-to-date review of Neandertal (and other archaics') biology and culture, as well as the history of debates over modern human origins.

Trinkaus, E., and Shipman, P. 1992. *The Neandertals: Changing the Image of Mankind.* New York: Knopf. An excellent historical review of the history of Neandertal discoveries and interpretations.

CHAPTER **9**

The Origin of Modern Humans

Starting over 100,000 years ago, populations of archaic *Homo sapiens* evolved into what we refer to as anatomically modern *Homo sapiens*. This is the name by which we refer to ourselves today, as well as the name by which we classify our early ancestors, who possessed certain physical characteristics unlike those of archaic *H. sapiens*: a more well-rounded skull and a noticeable chin. The overall brain size of these ancestors had changed little from that of later archaic *H. sapiens*. The evolution of archaic to modern *H. sapiens* is a subject of considerable debate today among anthropologists.

At the heart of this debate is a series of basic questions. What is the nature of this change? When and where did it occur? Did the change occur in only one place, or was it widespread? Why did it occur? What cultural changes took place, and how are they related to the biological changes? In short, our questions concern the recent (100,000+ years) history of the human species.

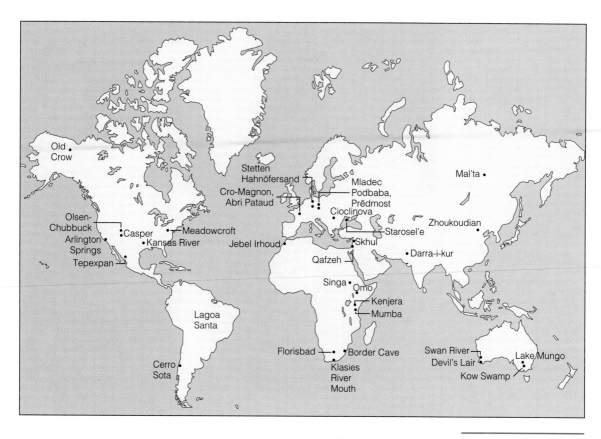

■ FIGURE 9.1
Location of some anatomically modern *H. sapiens* sites.

ANATOMICALLY MODERN *HOMO SAPIENS*

Human evolution did not end with archaic *H. sapiens*. By 35,000 years B.P., all fossil humans are anatomically modern in form. Though it is clear that archaic *H. sapiens* evolved into anatomically modern *H. sapiens*, the exact nature of this evolution is less certain.

Distribution in Time and Space

Anatomically modern *H. sapiens* are found in many sites across both the Old World and the New World (Figure 9.1). Although only modern *H. sapiens* has been found dating within the past 35,000 years, we now have growing evidence that this form is actually much older than once thought. Cranial remains from the Border Cave site in southeast Africa are fragmentary but show typical anatomically modern features (Figure 9.2). The dating for this

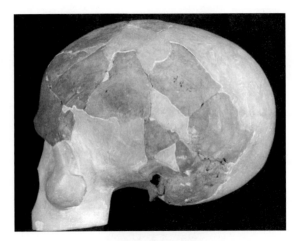

■ FIGURE 9.2
The Border Cave skull, South
Africa. The fragmentary
remains are clearly those of
anatomically modern *Homo
sapiens* (note the vertical
forehead). Dating is not
precise, but current estimates
suggest an age of more than
100,000 years B.P. (Photo by
Peter Faugust by permission of
Phillip V. Tobias)

■ FIGURE 9.3
Side and frontal view of Cro-
Magnon skull, France.
This specimen is one of the
best-known examples of
anatomically modern *Homo
sapiens.* (Neg. no. 109226,
109227. Courtesy Department
of Library Services, American
Museum of Natural History)

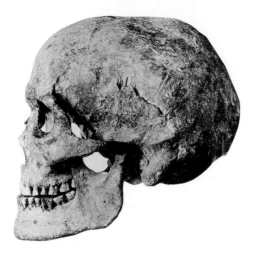

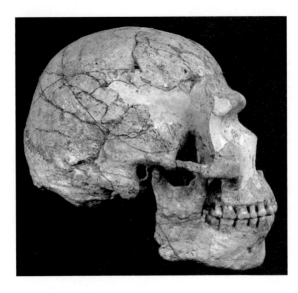

■ FIGURE 9.4
An early anatomically modern
Homo sapiens skull from
Skhul, Israel. (Peabody
Museum, Harvard University,
Photographed by Hillel Burger)

site is not definite but could range between 115,000 and 90,000 years B.P. Modern humans may have occupied the Klasies River Mouth, South Africa, at least as early as 90,000 years B.P. (Grün et al. 1990). Other African sites also provide evidence of an early appearance of anatomically modern *H. sapiens*: Omo, Ethiopia (roughly 130,000 years B.P.) and Laetoli (perhaps 120,000 years B.P.). There is also evidence of an early occurrence of anatomically modern *H. sapiens* in the Middle East, with both the Qafzeh and Skhul sites in Israel dating to 92,000 years B.P. (Grün et al. 1991). Although some argument about these dates continues, it is becoming increasingly certain that modern *H. sapiens* existed *before* the youngest known archaic forms.

Physical Characteristics

Figure 9.3 shows a skull from one of the more famous anatomically modern sites—Cro-Magnon, France, dating between 27,000 and 23,000 years B.P. This skull shows many of the characteristics of anatomically modern *H. sapiens*. It is high and well rounded. There is no occipital bun; the back of the skull is rounded instead. The forehead rises vertically above the eye orbits and does not slope, as in archaic *H. sapiens*. The brow ridges are small, the face does not protrude very much, and a strong chin is evident.

Another example of anatomically modern *H. sapiens* is shown in Figure 9.4, a skull from the Skhul site at Mt. Carmel, Israel. This skull also has a high, well-rounded shape without an occipital bun and with a small chin. Compared to the Cro-Magnon skull, the brow ridges are larger and the face protrudes slightly. The differences between the Skhul and Cro-Magnon skulls are typical of variation within a species, particularly when we consider that they existed at different times in separate places. Other specimens also show similarities and differences when compared to one another. There is clearly variation within both archaic and anatomically modern forms of *H. sapiens*. This variation makes evolutionary relationships difficult to assess.

Cultural Behavior

Discussing the cultural adaptations of anatomically modern *H. sapiens* is difficult because they include prehistoric technologies as well as more recent developments, such as agriculture, generation of electricity, the internal combustion engine, and nuclear energy. So that we may provide a comparison with the culture of the archaic forms, this section is limited to prehistory before the development of agriculture (roughly 12,000 years B.P.).

TOOL TECHNOLOGIES   There is so much variation in the stone tool technologies of anatomically modern *H. sapiens* that it is impossible to define a single tradition. For the sake of discussion, the types of stone tool industries are

■ **FIGURE 9.5**
Examples of Upper Paleolithic
stone tools: (a) knife,
(b) scraper, (c) point,
(d) scraper, (e) point. Tools
a, b, and *c* are from the Peri-
gordian culture; tool *d* is from
the Aurignacian culture; tool *e*
is from the Solutrean culture.
(From *The Old Stone Age* by
F. Bordes, 1968. Reprinted with
permission of the publisher,
Weidenfield and Nicolson, Ltd.)

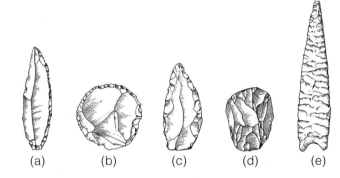

(a)   (b)   (c)   (d)   (e)

■ **FIGURE 9.6**
Example of a flint blade
tool. (From *Human Antiquity:
An Introduction to Physical
Anthropology and Archaeology,*
2nd ed., by Kenneth Feder and
Michael Park, Fig. 12.14.
Copyright © 1993 by Mayfield
Publishing Company.

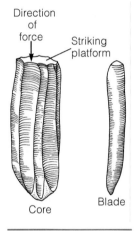

■ **FIGURE 9.7**
Method of blade tool
manufacture. A striking
platform is formed and a
blade tool can then be made
by flaking off a long vertical
piece from the side. (From
Discovering Anthropology by
Daniel R. Gross, Fig. 7.10.
Copyright © 1993 by Mayfield
Publishing Company)

often lumped together under the term **Upper Paleolithic** (which means
"Upper Old Stone Age"). **Lower Paleolithic** consists of the stone tool traditions of *H. habilis* and *H. erectus,* and **Middle Paleolithic** includes the
stone tool traditions of archaic *H. sapiens.* Even though we use a single label
to describe common features of Upper Paleolithic tool industries, do not be
misled into thinking all traditions were the same. Variation, both within and

among sites, is even greater in the Upper Paleolithic than in earlier cultures. This variation demonstrates the increasing sophistication and specialization of stone tools.

Figure 9.5 shows some examples of Upper Paleolithic stone tools. These tools are much more precisely made than the stone tools of earlier hominids, and are also quite a bit more diverse in function and styles. One notable characteristic of the Upper Paleolithic is the development of **blades,** stone tools defined as being at least twice as long as wide (Figure 9.6). Blade tools are made by removing long, narrow flakes off a prepared core. The core is struck by a piece of antler or bone, which in turn is struck by a stone. That is, the core is not hit directly by the hammerstone; rather, the force of the blow is applied through the antler. This method allows very thin and sharp blade tools to be made (Figure 9.7).

Upper Paleolithic tools were also used to make tools out of other resources, such as bone. A small stone tool called a **burin** has an extremely sharp edge that is used to cut, whittle, and engrave bone. Bone was used to make needles, awls, points, knives, and harpoons, as well as art objects. Bone tools and art objects first appear with modern *H. sapiens*; they are not found in the culture of earlier hominids. For years, it appeared that bone tools were fairly recent, dating back roughly 40,000 years. Recent work in Zaire, however, has produced a much earlier age of 90,000 years (Brooks et al. 1995; Yellen et al. 1995).

SHELTER   As with archaic *H. sapiens*, modern *H. sapiens* lived in caves and rock shelters where available. The archaeological evidence also shows definite evidence of manufactured shelter—huts made of wood, animal bone, and animal hides. Although much of this material decomposes, we can still find evidence of support structures. One example of hut building comes from the 18,000-year-old site of Mal'ta in south-central Russia (Figure 9.8). This hut is particularly interesting because people used mammoth ribs and leg bones for structural support. Other sites, such as the 15,000-year-old site of Mezhirich in the Ukraine, contain evidence of shelters built almost entirely from mammoth bones.

▲▲▲

Upper Paleolithic The Upper Old Stone Age; also refers to the stone tool technologies of anatomically modern *Homo sapiens*.

Lower Paleolithic The Lower Old Stone Age; also refers to the stone tool technologies of *Homo habilis* and *Homo erectus*.

Middle Paleolithic The Middle Old Stone Age; also refers to the stone tool technologies of archaic *Homo sapiens*.

blade A stone tool characteristic of the Upper Paleolithic, defined as being at least twice as long as it is wide.

burin A stone tool with a sharp edge that is used to cut and engrave bone.

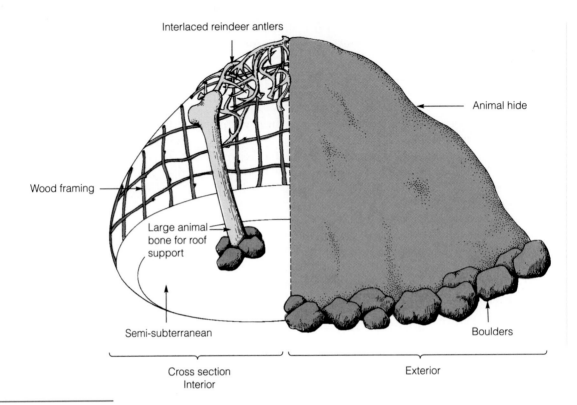

Interlaced reindeer antlers

Animal hide

Wood framing

Large animal
bone for roof
support

Semi-subterranean

Boulders

Cross section
Interior

Exterior

■ FIGURE 9.8
Reconstruction of a hut at the
Mal'ta site in Russia. This site
dates to 18,000 years B.P.
(From *Human Antiquity: An
Introduction to Physical
Anthropology and Archaeology*,
2nd ed. by Kenneth Feder and
Michael Park, Fig. 12.16.
Copyright © 1993 by Mayfield
Publishing Company)

CAVE ART   Another form of symbolic behavior appears with modern *H. sapi-ens*—cave art. Cave art dates back over 30,000 years, (although most is not this old) and has been found in Europe, Africa, and Australia. Some of the best-known cave art, primarily paintings of large game animals and hunting, comes from sites in Europe (Figure 9.9). These paintings are anatomically correct and are well executed. Painting is a human activity that is spiritually rewarding but has no apparent function in day-to-day existence. Why, then, did early humans paint images on the walls of caves? Several interpretations have been offered, including sympathetic magic (capturing the image of an animal may have been felt to improve hunters' chances of actually killing it). Other interpretations focus on cultural symbolism (e.g., male–female images) or a means of communicating ideas and images. We will never know exactly *why* early humans made these paintings. What is clear, however, is that they did something that serves a symbolic purpose. Although we cannot know the reason for these behaviors, the art shows us that humans by this time had developed a need to express themselves symbolically. To these early moderns, life was not just eating and surviving—something else was important to them as well.

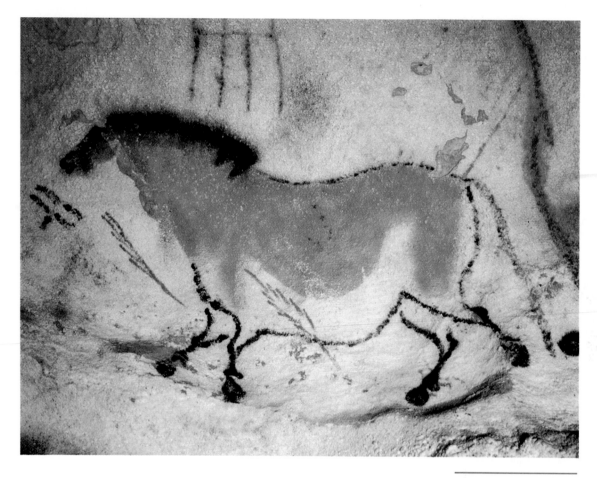

■ FIGURE 9.9
Cave painting of a running
horse from Lascaux Cave,
France. (Museum of Man, Paris;
photographer F. Windels)

OTHER EVIDENCE OF ART Cave paintings are not the only form of art associated
with early modern *H. sapiens*. We also find evidence of engravings, beads
and pendants, and ceramic sculpture. One of the best-known examples is the
"Venus" figurines found throughout parts of Europe. These figures are pregnant females with exaggerated breasts and buttocks (Figure 9.10). Although
these figurines are often interpreted as fertility symbols (fertility would have
been a critical factor to survival), we are not sure of their exact meaning or
function. However, as with cave paintings, the Venus figurines show us that
symbolism was fully a part of the life of early modern *H. sapiens*.

GEOGRAPHIC EXPANSION The archaeological evidence shows that humans became more and more successful in adapting to their environments, and consequently populations grew and expanded.

By 50,000 years B.P., populations of anatomically modern *H. sapiens* had
reached Australia (Roberts et al. 1990). During times of glaciation, the sea
levels drop, extending the land mass of the continents. The drop in sea level

■ FIGURE 9.11
The Bering Land Bridge.
Today the former Soviet Union
and Alaska are separated by
water. During the "Ice Ages,"
water was trapped in glaciers,
producing a drop in the sea
level that exposed the land
area known as the Bering
Land Bridge. This "bridge"
connecting North America and
Asia was actually 2,100 km
wide!

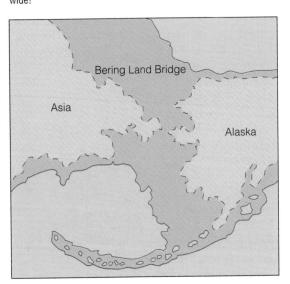

■ TABLE 9.1
Oldest Known Dates for Selected Cultural Traits

	DATE (THOUSANDS OF YEARS B.P.)
Art	40
Bone tools	90
Blade tools	100+?
Ceramics	25
Body Ornamentation	40
Built hearths	50
Storage pits	40
Cave burials	80
Open site burials	40
Huts	50–40
Long-distance exchange of raw materials	60–40
Sea voyaging	55

Source: Stringer and Gamble (1993); Yellen et al. (1995)

A first step in answering our question is to examine the spatial and temporal distribution of the fossils. This may seem relatively simple, but in practice it is not. Differing interpretations of fossil morphology, disagreement about whether physical features are primitive or derived, and debates over the dating of sites all complicate the process. In addition, we must always deal with the fact that the fossil record is incomplete, and our range of dates for any given region may be an underestimate. Figure 9.14 presents the distribution of *H. erectus*, archaic *H. sapiens*, and modern *H. sapiens* according to one interpretation of the evidence (Stringer and Gamble 1993). The oldest known evidence for modern *H. sapiens* (at present) is from Africa (although the Middle East is very close in time). Modern *H. sapiens* appears later in other geographic regions, and latest in Europe.

Does the earlier appearance of modern *H. sapiens* in Africa support the recent African origin model? Yes, but it does not reject the multiregional model, which can incorporate an initial evolution of modern morphology in one region, followed by a spread through gene flow to other regions. The earlier appearance of modern *H. sapiens* in Africa is consistent with some versions of the multiregional model (Wolpoff et al 1994b).

What about regional continuity? The evidence for this is strongest in Australasia (Kramer 1991), and has been suggested for parts of Europe as well (Smith et al. 1989b; Thorne and Wolpoff 1992). In some cases, there is a tendency for moderns to resemble archaics within the same region, although this continuity is still strongly debated. Many researchers feel the case for regional continuity is weak for western Europe and the Middle East. Overall, the fossil evidence can be used to support both models to various extents. Perhaps what we are seeing is something combining aspects of both models: an initial African influence combined with mixture outside of Africa.

The Middle East is particularly interesting, because our current dates show a pattern of occupation by archaics followed by moderns, followed again by archaics (Figure 9.15). To some, the existence of both archaics and moderns in the Middle East is a result of how we "label" fossils; by pigeonholing the fossils into different categories, are we obscuring variation and creating a false impression? Most anthropologists acknowledge the crude nature of the labels "archaic" and "modern," but also point to distinct physical differences. If we are dealing with distinct populations (some claim different species), then what explains their coexistence? One solution has been offered by archaeologist Ofer Bar-Yosef (1994), who suggests that the Middle East has repeatedly served as a refuge for different populations during times of environmental change. During warmer times, the Neandertals may have moved north and west into Europe, and African moderns may have moved into the Middle East. When the climate cooled, the Neandertals could have moved south into the Middle East, and the moderns in the Middle East could have moved back into Africa. If this model is correct, then we

▲▲▲▲▲▲▲▲▲▲▲▲▲▲▲▲▲▲▲▲▲▲▲▲▲▲▲▲▲▲

regional continuity
The appearance of similar traits within a geographic region over time.

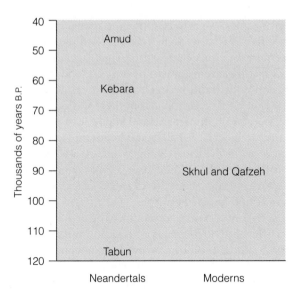

■ FIGURE 9.15
Middle Eastern sites
containing Neandertal and
modern humans based on the
most recent dates. If these
dates are confirmed, it
appears that different
populations occupied the
Middle East at different times.

would get the pattern that we see: occupation of the Middle East at different times by archaics (Neandertals) and moderns. The two populations may have never existed at the same time in the Middle East. More work is needed to confirm this hypothesis, but if nothing else it demonstrates how complicated the picture is of modern human origins.

The Genetic Evidence

In addition to fossil evidence, we can also examine the questions of modern human origins using information on the genetics of living people. We can observe patterns of genetic variation in the present day, and ask what evolutionary model could have given rise to these observed patterns. Whereas with fossils we work from the past to the present, this approach starts with the present in an effort to reconstruct the past. We view the patterns of contemporary genetic variation as reflections of the past.

PATTERNS OF GENETIC VARIATION   We can examine differences within and between living human populations using a variety of data, including blood groups and other genetic markers, DNA sequences, measures of the face and skull, and other measures of variation (see Chapter 13). Another source of information that has been widely used is a form of DNA known as **mitochondrial DNA.** Almost all of our DNA is contained in the chromosomes within the nucleus of our cells (see Chapter 2). Mitochondrial DNA (mtDNA) is an exception—it consists of a small amount of DNA that is contained in the mitochondria, a part of the cell outside the nucleus that is involved in energy production.

For most traits, *both* parents contribute genetically to the child. For mtDNA, however, *only* the female contributes genetically, because female sex cells contain mitochondria, whereas male sex cells consist only of the nucleus. In other words, mtDNA is inherited only through the mother. Your mtDNA came only from your mother, who obtained it from her mother, and so on. You inherit the rest of your DNA from both parents, who inherited from two parents, and so on. For most traits, the number of ancestors doubles every generation you go back: two parents, four grandparents, eight great-grandparents, and so on. For mtDNA, you only have one ancestor in any given generation. This property allows patterns of genetic relationship to be reconstructed without the complication of the gene shuffling that occurs every generation for the rest of your DNA.

Based on genetic evidence to date, several conclusions have been reached regarding the nature of our species' current biological variation. Compared to many other species, we are not that diverse. Genetic studies show, for example, that we are fairly limited in our total genetic diversity when compared to that of the great apes (e.g., Ruvolo et al. 1994). This finding can be explained in two ways. First, our species has been more mobile than many other organisms, such that differences between geographic regions are less than they would be if we were more isolated. Second, our limited diversity may reflect a relatively recent common origin, which supports the recent African origin model.

Another finding used to support the recent African origin model is the greater diversity, for certain data, shown by African populations than by populations in other regions (Cann et al. 1987; Relethford and Harpending 1994). This greater diversity has been used to argue for a recent African origin under the assumption that the oldest population will accumulate the most mutations over a long period of time, and therefore be more genetically diverse (Figure 9.16).

A third finding of genetic studies focuses on the degree of genetic relationship between different geographic regions. Analysis of individual mitochondrial DNA shows an interesting pattern—the human species today forms two clusters reflecting similarity of mtDNA. One cluster consists only of people with African ancestry and the other cluster consists of people of different ancestries, African and non-African. This finding has been interpreted as reflecting population history: an initial origin of modern humans in Africa followed by a subsequent split of non-African populations. These findings were initially viewed as strong evidence for the recent African origin model (Cann et al. 1987; Vigilant et al. 1991). Subsequent work, however, showed flaws in the analysis: some data supported an African origin, others did not (Hedges et al. 1992; Templeton 1992).

Despite these flawed mtDNA analyses, a similar pattern emerges when we look at genetic similarity among populations based on a variety of other genetic data (Cavalli-Sforza et al. 1994). These analyses consistently show the greatest genetic similarity among non-African populations (Figure 9.17).

▲▲▲▲▲▲▲▲▲▲▲▲▲▲▲▲▲▲▲▲▲▲▲▲▲▲▲▲▲

mitochondrial DNA
The DNA inside the mitochondria of cells, inherited only through the mother.

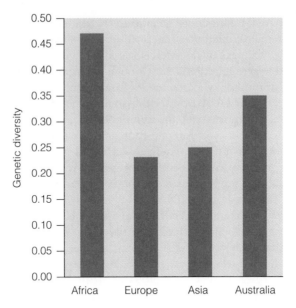

■ **FIGURE 9.16**
Diversity of mitochondrial DNA in several populations. Africa shows the greatest diversity, a finding that could indicate that modern humans arose first in Africa and/or that the average population size in Africa in the past was greater than that in other regions. (*Source of data:* Cann et al. 1987)

■ **FIGURE 9.17**
Genetic distances between major geographic regions. The diagrams are based on the analysis of genetic markers (e.g., blood groups, serum proteins), craniometric measures, and a "pooled" sample that combines genetic markers and craniometrics. These distances have been adjusted for the finding of a larger population size in Africa. All three diagrams show that the greatest genetic distances among humans today are between sub-Saharan Africans and other regions. Such patterns have been taken to support the recent African origin model, but might also reflect differences in population size and migration. (*Source:* Relethford and Harpending 1995).

That is, populations outside of Africa are closer genetically than any are to populations within Africa. Again, this pattern has most often been interpreted as support for the recent African origin model.

POPULATION SIZE AND MODERN HUMAN ORIGINS   Although genetic analyses generally provide results that are consistent with the recent African origin model, the analyses can be interpreted in other ways. Looking at patterns of variation, Relethford and Harpending (1994) found that the average population size of Africa was probably larger than that in other regions over the past 100,000

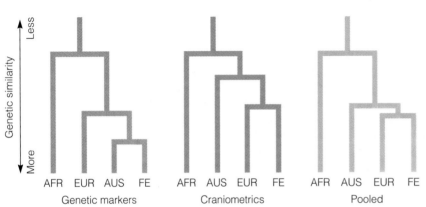

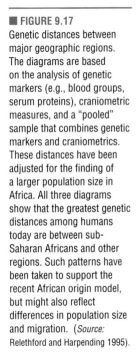

AFR = sub-Saharan Africa
AUS = Australia
EUR = Europe
FE = Far East

years or so. This larger African population can explain many of the patterns of genetic variation. Larger populations, for example, are expected to show greater genetic diversity because there is less effect of genetic drift. Differences in population size can also explain the genetic distinctiveness of African populations. The genetic data may therefore be telling us nothing about origins, but instead be simply reflecting a larger African population in the past (Relethford 1995b).

Population size is also important when considering mitochondrial DNA variation. Initially, the mtDNA evidence was used to support the view that *all* mtDNA in our species today comes from a single woman who lived in Africa some 200,000 years B.P. (often referred to as "Eve"). Of course, a single female ancestor for mtDNA does *not* mean that *all* of our genetic ancestry comes from only one woman in the distant past. Remember that mtDNA is inherited only through the mother. Some females could have produced only sons, in which case their mtDNA would not be passed on, although they still contributed the rest of their DNA to the next generation (this is analogous to inheriting a last name—you generally get the last name from only one parent, although you obviously inherit genetically from both).

Henry Harpending and colleagues (1993) note that variation in mitochondrial DNA shows us that the human species at the time of "Eve" was very small in number. Their work, and that of others, provides estimates that the *entire* human species some 200,000 to 100,000 years B.P. consisted of perhaps only 10,000 adults or fewer (Rogers and Jorde 1995). This finding provides some indirect support for the recent African origin model. That such a small number of people could have been spread out over three continents as required by the multiregional model seems unlikely. The small species size suggests that most humans at that time were in one area—Africa. This finding does not rule out the possibility of some mixture outside of Africa.

A PREHISTORIC POPULATION EXPLOSION? The pattern of human mitochondrial DNA variation tells us even more about ancient population size. Rogers and Harpending (1992) found that mtDNA variation showed evidence that the human species was initially very small in number, but then grew rapidly at some point in the past, perhaps increasing by several hundredfold or more. Mitochondrial DNA data from around the world suggest that this population explosion took place roughly 60,000 to 40,000 years B.P. (Sherry et al. 1994). This date is particularly interesting since it corresponds to the timing of the "creative explosion" claimed by some archaeologists (refer back to Table 9.1). These rapid cultural changes may be related to a rapid growth in the human population at this time. Preliminary analysis also suggests that populations in Africa may have expanded in size before other Old World populations. Of course, much of this work is still somewhat tentative, and needs to be investigated further.

Consensus?

What is the bottom line? Although the fossil data, and particularly the genetic data, lend more support to some version of the recent African origin model, the issue is not yet decided, and, in the tradition of science, we can expect continued analysis and debate. At present, there is some consensus that modern humans arose fairly recently in Africa, but the issue of the genetic involvement in other regions is still not settled. More extensive mixture may have occurred in some regions (such as Australasia) but less in others (Europe). In this sense, the origin of modern humans may have involved several, but not all, regions.

Why Did Modern Humans Evolve?

The alternative models for the origin of modern humans are fascinating to debate, but we don't want to lose track of a basic fact that all agree on: only modern human fossils have been found within the past 35,000 years or so. In addition to explaining the timing and nature of the transition from archaics to moderns, we must also ask ourselves why this transition occurred in the first place. The available evidence suggests that anatomically modern *H. sapiens* had some evolutionary advantage over archaic *H. sapiens*. But what was this advantage?

LANGUAGE AND MODERN HUMAN ORIGINS   It has often been suggested that the development of human language capabilities marks the origin of modern *H. sapiens*. Cranial changes are seen to relate to changes in language ability, with a claim that modern *H. sapiens* was linguistically superior to the archaics. This view is tempting when evidence for the increased symbolic and technological achievements of modern *H. sapiens* is also considered. Can cranial changes and these cultural achievements be related? It is possible—but the basic problem remains that these cultural changes took place well after the initial *biological* changes associated with modern *H. sapiens*. Of course, cave art, bone tools, and other achievements may actually be older than we think, an idea supported to some extent by the new dating of bone tools in Africa. However, basing a model on what has *not* been found is not a good idea. We must always deal with the known fossil and archaeological records and be willing to make appropriate revisions when we make new discoveries.

How can we date the origin of language? This question is central to any discussion of differences in language ability between archaics and moderns. One approach is to examine the fossil evidence of vocal anatomy. Striking differences exist between the vocal tract of a modern human and an ape. The **larynx** is part of the respiratory system that contains the vocal chords for speech. Apes, like other mammals, have their larynx high in the throat. Humans, however, have the larynx further down in the throat, a position

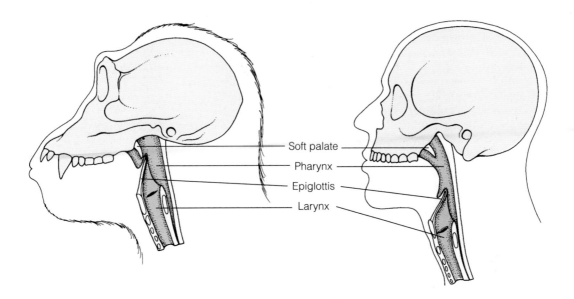

Soft palate
Pharynx
Epiglottis
Larynx

that allows the throat to serve as a resonating chamber capable of a greater number of sounds (Figure 9.18). Humans can make a wider number of sounds, and do it faster, than apes. We pay a price for this adaptation, though—unlike apes, we cannot breathe and eat at the same time, and we are in far greater danger of choking to death. Human infants still have the larynx high in the throat and *can* breathe and swallow at the same time. By early childhood, however, the larynx has descended into the throat and they are no longer capable of this.

The position of the larynx represents a clear-cut anatomical difference between humans and apes, and, as such, larynx position can help in assessing the language abilities of any fossil hominid. Unfortunately, the throat, like all soft tissue, decomposes and we cannot recover it. We can get clues about the positioning of the larynx, however, by looking at the base of a cranium. Note that in Figure 9.18 the lower profile of the ape skull is fairly straight, whereas in the modern human it is flexed. The degree of this flexion is directly related to the position of the larynx. Given this relationship, what do the fossils tell us? Laitman and colleagues (1979) investigated the crania of a number of fossil hominids and concluded that, whereas *Australopithecus* had the ape pattern, the crania of many archaic *H. sapiens* are more similar to modern-day humans. The Neandertals had a pattern that was between those of a modern child and modern adult human, suggesting that their language abilities may have been somewhat different. Other reconstructions and interpretations are possible (Houghton 1993; Schepartz 1993); some suggest there was little difference in language ability between any of the archaics and modern humans. Schepartz (1993) argues instead that complex language began with the initial origin of the genus *Homo*.

■ FIGURE 9.18
The vocal anatomy of a chimpanzee (*left*) and a modern human (*right*). In apes, the larynx is higher in the throat. In humans, it is lower, allowing a greater number of sounds, but increasing the possibility of choking on food. (Redrawn and reprinted by permission of the Smithsonian Institution Press from Roger Lewin: *In the Age of Mankind: A Smithsonian Book of Human Evolution*, 1989: 181, Smithsonian Institution Press)

▲▲▲▲▲▲▲▲▲▲▲▲▲▲▲▲▲▲▲▲▲▲▲▲▲▲▲▲▲

larynx Part of the vocal anatomy in the throat.

The Iceman

Our understanding of ancient times comes from reconstructions based on the fossil and archaeological records, supplemented by evidence from past environments. Although new methods and techniques for analysis have aided our ability to reconstruct the past, we are nevertheless dealing only with bits and pieces of what actually once existed.

Occasionally, though, we come across more detailed evidence. On September 19, 1991, hikers in the glacial mountains between Austria and Italy stumbled upon the body of a man. This is not unusual—bodies are often found in this region, the result of accidents while climbing or hiking in the mountains. Initial investigation, however, showed that this was a naturally occurring mummy (mummification occurs when a corpse is cut off from oxygen). How did the corpse remain so well preserved? The man died in a shallow depression in the ground, and the advancing glacier moved over him, preserving him in a mummified state without carrying his body downhill. In 1991, the ice had receded, and the body was exposed. Because of his discovery in the glacier, he is known today as "The Iceman."

The body became of greater interest because of several items found with it, including a flint knife and an axe. The axe consisted of a wooden shaft attached to what appeared to be a bronze axe head. The bronze implied that the axe and the body dated to the European Bronze Age, roughly 4,000 years B.P. Closer analysis of the axe head showed, however, that it was not bronze (which is a mixture of copper and tin), but almost entirely pure copper. Use of copper is known to be even older than 4,000 B.P. The greater age was confirmed by carbon-14 dating of the body, which placed it at 5,250 B.P.

Research continues on the Iceman, but preliminary study has revealed much about his life and death. Marks have been found on the body that might possibly be tattoos. In addition to the knife and the axe, he had a bow, arrows, and a leather quiver. Remains of his clothes show that they were made of fur, and boots have also been found. He also had two lumps of fungus connected by a leather strap. At first, it was thought that the fungus might have been used as tinder for starting fires. The fungus has now been identified as a species that is know to have antibiotic properties, so we might be seeing some evidence of ancient medicine.

How did the Iceman die? We are not sure although there are several clues. Based on some berries found with the body (which grow only during one season), he appears to have died in late summer or autumn. Climatic reconstruction shows that the nights would have been quite cold. Combined with the high altitude of the find, current thinking is that the Iceman died from exhaustion and dehydration.

For further information, see Sjøvold (1992).

TECHNOLOGY AND BIOLOGICAL CHANGE If changes in language abilities are not the reason for the origin of modern *H. sapiens*, what else might have been involved? Technological changes have also been suggested as mechanisms for the change from archaic to modern forms. This view holds that many of the structural characteristics of archaic *H. sapiens* were the result of stresses generated by the use of their front teeth as tools. The large size and wear patterns of the incisor teeth of archaics (especially Neandertals) support the notion that these teeth were used for a variety of purposes. The stresses generated by heavy use of the front teeth can also be used to explain the large face, large neck muscles, and other features of archaic skulls. Once technological adaptations had developed sufficiently, these physical adaptations were no longer necessary and would not be selected for. Smaller teeth and faces might then be advantageous, because smaller structures require correspondingly less energy for growth and maintenance (Smith et al. 1989a). Similar arguments can be made to explain the reduction in body size and musculature (e.g., Frayer 1984). Once cultural behaviors took the place of larger teeth, faces, and bones, then smaller structures actually became more adaptive.

Calcagno and Gibson (1988) present evidence that larger teeth can be nonadaptive. They cite clinical evidence from contemporary human populations that show that large teeth can have many disadvantages. Larger teeth are more susceptible to dental decay, due to crowding of teeth, and periodontal disease. In earlier prehistoric times, the advantages of larger teeth as tools may have outweighed the disadvantages. When cultural change led to more efficient tools, however, these advantages diminished, and selection would then have been *against* large teeth.

Once again, evolution is best seen in terms of the overall balance between costs and benefits. Human evolution is particularly interesting because human behaviors frequently affect this balance. In the past, as new technologies and behaviors arose, they changed the balance between cost and benefit. At some point in the past, for example, the less rugged and less muscular modern morphology may have shifted from being a disadvantage to being an advantage. The origin of modern *H. sapiens* may itself reflect this type of process. If so, we would expect the kind of "lag" between cultural and biological change that we see in the fossil record. Biological changes allow further cultural changes, which in turn allow further biological changes. Each change shifts the balance.

RECENT BIOLOGICAL AND CULTURAL EVOLUTION IN *HOMO SAPIENS*

Human evolution did not end with the origin of modern *H. sapiens*. Biologically, we have continued to change in subtle ways even over the past 10,000 to 20,000 years or so. Cranial capacity has declined somewhat (Henneberg 1988), probably a reflection of a general decrease in size and ruggedness as discussed in the last section. Teeth have also become somewhat smaller (Brace et al. 1987), most likely reflecting the changing costs and benefits of larger teeth.

Within the very recent past (10,000–15,000 years), the major changes in human evolution have been cultural. One major change in human existence—the invention of agriculture—began roughly 12,000 years ago. Up to this point, humans had been exclusively hunters and gatherers. Agriculture changed the entire ecological equation for human beings. Humans began manipulating the environment to increase the availability of food through the domestication of plants and animals. Many explanations are offered as to why agriculture developed, including that it was a solution to the increased population size that had resulted from more efficient hunting and

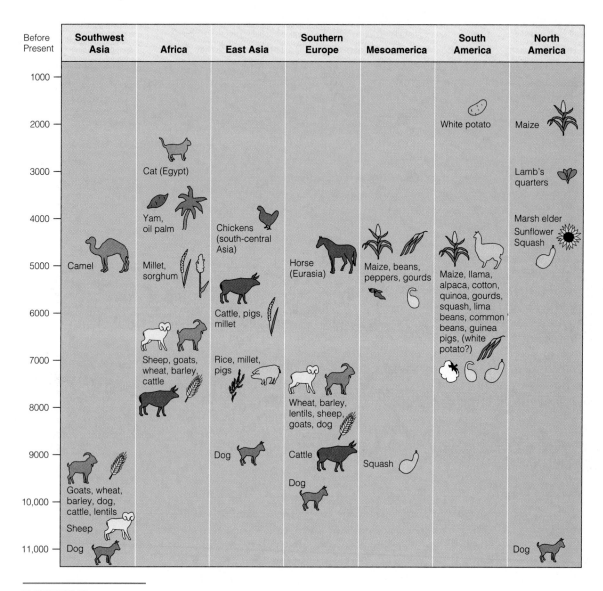

■ FIGURE 9.19

Chronological outline of the origins of domestication and agriculture. (From *Human Antiquity: An Introduction to Physical Anthropology and Archaeology,* 2nd ed., by Kenneth Feder and Michael Park, Fig. 14.1. Copyright © 1993 by Mayfield Publishing Company)

gathering. In any case, the effects of agriculture were and continue to be quite dramatic—the human population grew and continues to do so today (see Chapter 17).

Agriculture did not have a single origin but rather developed independently in many parts of both the Old World and the New World. Over the next several thousand years, the use of agriculture became increasingly dominant around the world (Figure 9.19). Today, there are very few hunters and

■ FIGURE 9.20
The space shuttle is one feature of our species' continuing exploration and utilization of new environments. (Courtesy of NASA)

gatherers left. Our current focus on agriculture often blinds us to the reality that we have changed so much culturally in so short a time. Biologically, we are still hunters and gatherers.

Cultural change continued at an even faster rate following the origin of agriculture and rapid population growth. Cities and state-level societies developed. Exploration brought the inhabitants of the Old World and New World back into contact, and industrialization spread rapidly. Today, only 12,000 years after the time our ancestors survived by hunting and gathering, we are able to explore and live in every environment on earth, and beyond (Figure 9.20). However one feels about the rapid cultural changes of *H. sapiens*, these changes can be viewed as a continuation of the basic adaptations of culture and learning that have been apparent for at least the past 2.5 million years of human evolution.

SUMMARY

Among other features, anatomically modern *Homo sapiens* is characterized by a higher, more well-rounded skull and a smaller face than most archaics, and by the presence of a noticeable chin. Modern *H. sapiens* is best known from fossil records dating over the past 35,000 years. There is growing evidence, however, that these humans appeared first over 100,000 years B.P. in Africa and by 100,000 to 90,000 years B.P. in the Middle East. By 50,000 years B.P., the culture of *H. sapiens* had begun to change rapidly; the use of more sophisticated stone tools (especially blade tools) and bone tools spread, burials of the dead became more elaborate, and art appeared. Modern humans colonized Australia by 50,000 years B.P., and the New World by at least 15,000 years B.P.

There is continuing controversy regarding the origin of anatomically modern humans. The multiregional model hypothesizes that the transition from *H. erectus* to archaic *H. sapiens* to modern *H. sapiens* occurred throughout the Old World. According to this model, the evolution of modern humans took place within a widespread species across several continents. Gene flow is considered here to be sufficient to have maintained a single species of human after the initial dispersal of *H. erectus* from Africa. Conversely, the recent African origin model hypothesizes that the evolution of modern humans occurred in one place—Africa, between 200,000 and 100,000 years B.P.—and that modern humans then spread outward across the world, replacing preexisting archaic populations. There are variants of each model, including the possibility of a primary African origin combined with mixture of modern and archaic populations. Fossil and genetic data have been used to examine these hypotheses. There is still considerable debate about *why* modern humans first evolved.

Human evolution did not end after the initial appearance of modern humans. Although there have been some biological changes during our recent past, most of our species' evolution during the past 10,000 years has been cultural. Perhaps the single most important event was the development of agriculture, which changed our entire way of life. Predicting the specifics of future human evolution is problematic, but it does appear clear that our future will involve more and more cultural change, which occurs at a far greater rate than biological evolution. This does not mean that biological evolution has stopped, but rather that our fate is becoming increasingly affected by cultural change.

SUPPLEMENTAL READINGS

Klein, R. G. 1989. *The Human Career: Human Biological and Cultural Origins*. Chicago: University of Chicago Press. Although somewhat dated in spots, this remains one of the single best summaries of the fossil and archaeological record of human evolution, with considerable attention to the evolution of modern humans.

Stringer, C., and C. Gamble. 1993. *In Search of the Neanderthals: Solving the Puzzle of Human Origins.* New York: Thames and Hudson. This book provides an excellent review of the fossil, archeological, and genetic evidence supporting a recent African origin.

Thorn, A. G., and M. H. Wolpoff. April 1992. The multiregional evolution of humans. *Scientific American* 266(4): 76–83. A nontechnical review of the multiregional model and its supporting evidence.

Wilson, A. C., and R. L. Cann. April 1992. The recent African genesis of humans. *Scientific American* 266(4): 68–73. Appearing in the same issue as the Thorne and Wolpoff article, this paper provides a nontechnical review of some of the genetic evidence supporting a recent African origin model although recent work has questioned their interpretations.

PART FOUR

Human Variation

The Study of
Human Variation

Every day we encounter human biological diversity (Figure 10.1), but we seldom speak of what we see in evolutionary terms. On a day-to-day basis, most people think about variation in terms of the widely used, but imprecise, word *race*. People are often surprised to learn that anthropologists today look at variation in terms of evolutionary forces, and are not concerned (except in an historical sense) with race or racial classifications. Race is a descriptive concept and not an analytic tool. At best, it provides a crude and often misleading label for variation, and explains nothing.

However, because the concept of race is so ingrained in society and structures many of our ideas on variation, it is important to review exactly what race is and is not. Therefore, throughout much of this chapter we review the concept of race and then examine the evolutionary alternative. As we shall see, the evolutionary forces discussed in Chapter 3 form the basis for our understanding of the patterns and causes of human biological variation.

■ FIGURE 10.1

Human biological diversity in external physical traits. (Top left, © Bachman/The Image Works; Moss/Photo Researchers, Inc.; center right, © Renee Lynn/ Photo Researchers, Inc.; bottom left, © Bachman/Photo Researchers, Inc.; bottom right, © David Young-Wolff/ PhotoEdit)

This approach is also used by most people today in their daily exposure to human variation. A problem here is that we use words like *race* without defining them. What do phrases like the "white race," the "Japanese race," and the "Jewish race" mean to you? They are extremely confusing because the term *race* is used to stand for a variety of factors such as skin color, national origin, and religion. Sometimes we use the term in a biological sense, sometimes in a social sense.

The definition of race is no mere academic issue. Race is discussed daily in the newspapers and other media. Race has been used to justify discrimination and persecution of people as well as to grant favored status. Statistics on race are gathered by local, state, federal, and international organizations. Economic and political decisions are often based on race.

Obviously, race is an important concept in our lives. But what exactly is it? How many races are there? What are the differences between races?

The Biological Concept of Race

From a biological standpoint, a **race** is generally defined as "a division of a species that differs from other divisions by the frequency with which certain hereditary traits appear among its members" (Brues 1977:1). Race in this definition has two characteristics. First, it is a group of populations that share some biological characteristics. Second, these populations differ from other groups of populations according to these characteristics. The concept of race seeks to fill the void between the single "human race" and the thousands of local human populations. Race is meant to provide a classification of biologically similar populations.

The race concept works better biologically with some organisms than with others. For organisms that are isolated from one another in different environments, the race concept often provides a usable, though rough, means of summarizing biological variation. For other organisms, such as humans, the concept has less utility. Humans inhabit a wide number of environments and move between them frequently. The high degree of gene flow among human populations, compared to that of many other organisms, means that clear-cut boundaries among groups of populations are difficult to establish.

The race concept presents a number of problems that are outlined in the next section. Given these problems, race and racial classifications provide only a crude tool for description, one with little utility for today's biologist

odontometrics
Measurements of the size of teeth.

dermatoglyphics
Measurements of finger and palm prints.

race A group of populations sharing certain traits that make them distinct from other groups of populations.

The concept of race is difficult to apply to patterns of human variation.

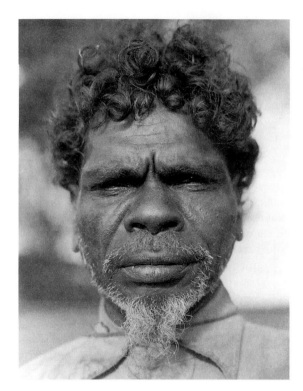

■ FIGURE 10.4
An Australian aborigine with dark skin and curly hair.
(Neg. no. 330831. Photo by A. P. Elkin. Courtesy Department of Library Services, American Museum of Natural History)

or anthropologist, when sophisticated statistical methods and computers allow us to analyze patterns of biological variation more precisely than ever before. Indeed, some authors have suggested that we drop the entire concept for it has little use biologically (Livingstone 1964).

Problems with the Concept of Race

What is wrong with classifying people into races? After all, we can do it accurately. Or can we?

THE NUMBER OF HUMAN RACES   A major problem with the race concept is that scientists have never agreed on the number of human races. How many can you name, or see? Some have suggested that there are three human races: Europeans, Africans, and Asians (often referred to by the archaic terms "Caucasoid," "Negroid," and "Mongoloid," which are almost never used in scientific research today). But many populations do not fit neatly into these three basic categories. What about native Australians (aborigines)? As shown in Figure 10.4, these are dark-skinned people who frequently have curly or wavy hair that is sometimes blond and who have abundant facial hair. On the basis of skin color, we might be tempted to label these people as African, but on the basis of hair and facial shape they might be classified as European. One approach has been to create a fourth category, the "Australoid" race.

As we travel around the world, however, we find more and more populations that do not fit a three- or four-race system. As a result, some authors have added races to their list. There has never been clear consensus on the actual number, though. In 1758, for example, Linnaeus described four major human races in his classification of humans. Since that time, different authors have suggested four, five, and nine major races, among other numbers. There has been little agreement on the number of races or subraces.

Two points emerge from a study of the history of attempts to classify and apply the race concept to human populations. First, the lack of agreement among different researchers indicates that the entire concept of race is arbitrary as it applies to humans. If clearly discernible races existed, their number should have long since been determined without argument. How useful is a classification system when there is so much disagreement about the number of units? Second, something is being described here, although in a crude manner. All racial classifications, for example, note the wide range in skin color among human populations and note further an association with geography. The native peoples of Africa tend to have darker skin than those of northern Europe. The geographic distribution of many traits, such as skin color, is well known. Then why doesn't the race concept work well when describing biological variation?

THE NATURE OF CONTINUOUS VARIATION   Biological variation is real; the order we impose on this variation by using the concept of race is not. Race is a product of human minds, not of nature. One reason race fails to describe variation accurately is that much variation is continuous, whereas race is a discrete unit. In other words, we must reduce variation into a few small categories.

Consider human height as an example. Most of us cannot describe a person's height to the nearest centimeter without actually measuring that person. When we look at someone, we are unlikely to know *exactly* how tall that person is. We would not, however, describe everyone as the same height simply because we do not know the exact values. Instead, we use relative terms such as "short," "medium," and "tall." Often our definitions of these categories do not always agree with other people's (many people call anyone shorter than themselves "short" regardless of their actual height.) Also, some people might add categories, such as "medium tall" or "very short." In any case, these categories have some limited use. When we say that a basketball player is "tall," most people know roughly how tall we mean. But are these categories real? When we forget that these are only convenient crude levels for classification, we can fall into the trap of thinking that they have a reality of their own. Do you actually think all people fall into one of three categories—"short," "medium," or "tall"? Height is a continuous trait that can have an infinite number of values within a certain range.

The same problem applies to races. Many racial classifications in Western societies use skin color as a major distinguishing feature. The races correspond to different measures of skin color—"white," "yellow," "red," "brown," and "black," for example. We know, however, that skin color does not fall into 5, or even 50, different categories. Skin color is a continuous variable. This means that any attempt to divide the continuous range into discrete units (races) is going to be arbitrary.

Figure 10.5 shows the average skin reflectance for three samples of males—one from sub-Saharan Africa (Chopi), one from Asia (Jirels), and one from Europe (the Netherlands). For each sample, the dot represents the average value and the lines represent 1 standard deviation below and above the average. (A standard deviation is a statistical measure of variation. Roughly 68 percent of the cases in each sample lie between the ends of the lines drawn in the figure. Each sample contains some individuals who are lighter or darker.) These three samples are quite distinct from one another. There is no overlap in skin color, and it would be very easy to classify a given person into one of the three groups based on his skin color. Isn't this an accurate reflection of three distinct races?

No. The appearance of three distinct races is a biased reflection because humanity is made up of more than simply these three populations. When we add more populations to the picture, the interpretation changes. Figure 10.6 shows the average skin reflectance and standard deviations for 22 male samples from Africa, Asia, and Europe. Note that there are no longer discrete boundaries that can be used to identify different races. The ranges in skin reflectance overlap one another. In other words, on the basis of skin color, it is not possible to tell where one "race" ends and another starts. We can identify the extremes, but there are no discrete clusters.

Despite these arguments, many people are still convinced that human races are easily identifiable. After all, they say, you can walk down any city street in the United States and point out who is "white" and who is "black" (ignoring for the moment those people who are difficult to classify). Under such circumstances, race is easily identifiable (or is it?). This may be true in a limited area, such as a street in a medium-sized American city, but it does not hold true when we look at the world in general. Races seem distinct in certain situations because disproportionate numbers of peoples from different geographic regions are present. We do not find equal representation of all human populations on most U.S. city streets. For example, we tend to see far fewer Australian aborigines than we see people of predominantly European or African ancestry.

In short, the overall composition of the U.S. population tends to give us a distorted view of the total variation in the world. The majority of early settlers in the United States came from Western Europe, one of the regions in the world whose human populations show the lightest skin color. During the next few centuries, many slaves were brought from West Africa, one of the regions where human skin color is darkest. The result has been a disproportionate representation of the range of skin color. More people in the United States have either very light or very dark skin than any shade in

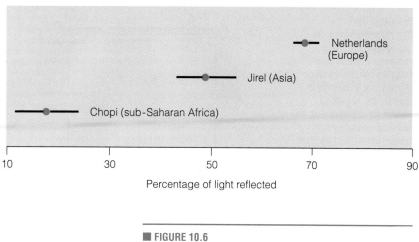

■ FIGURE 10.5
Variation in skin color in three selected human populations (males). Dots indicate the mean skin reflectance measured at a wavelength of 685 nanometers; lines indicate 1 standard deviation on each side of the mean. Compare this with Figure 10.6, which shows more populations. The discontinuity in skin color shown here disappears when more of humanity is sampled. (*All data from published literature*)

■ FIGURE 10.6
Variation in skin color in 22 human populations (males). Dots indicate the mean skin reflectance measured at a wavelength of 685 nanometers; lines indicate 1 standard deviation on each side of the mean.

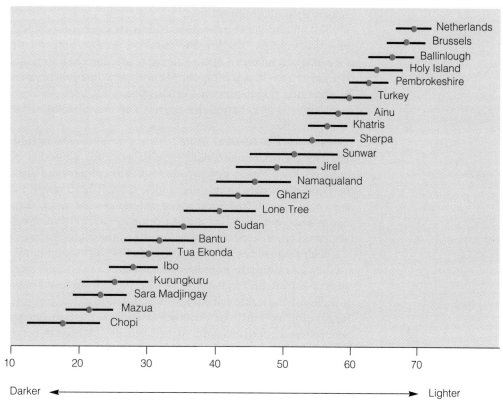

Original settlement of the United States from the perspective of skin color. From the continuous range of skin color in the human species, the majority of earliest settlers were from the two extreme ends—dark-colored West Coast Africans and light-colored Western Europeans. This differential settlement gives rise to the seeming existence of two distinct races in the United States based on skin color.

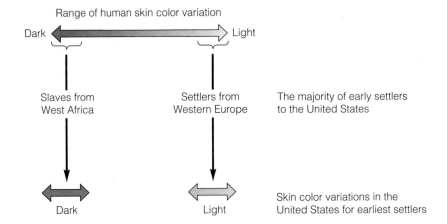

between (Figure 10.7). On the other hand, a tour through other parts of the world will soon give you a different picture. Many of the people in the world are neither so dark nor so light.

Not all biological traits show continuous variation. Blood group phenotypes, for example, are discrete traits. We do not, however, often find situations in which all members of one race have one phenotype and all members of another race have a different phenotype. Some genetic markers are useful in separating populations in certain geographic areas, but many such traits show patterns of variation that are not well described by racial classification.

CORRESPONDENCE OF DIFFERENT TRAITS If race were to be a useful biological concept, the classifications would have to work for a number of independent traits. A classification developed from skin color would also need to show the same racial pattern in other traits, such as head shape, nasal shape, and hair color. If each trait produces a different set of races, then the race concept is not very useful as a description of overall biological similarity. In fact, racial classifications vary according to the biological trait used.

High frequencies of the sickle cell allele (discussed in the next chapter) are found not only in populations belonging to "African races," but also in parts of Europe and India. Any racial classification based on high or low frequencies of the sickle cell allele in a population would not produce the same distribution as skin color. Another example is the frequency of lactase deficiency. Some populations in Africa, because of their dependence on dairy farming, have low frequencies of lactase deficiency, similar to rates found in European populations (lactase deficiency is discussed in the next chapter).

Using different traits often results in different groupings of populations. For examples such as sickle cell and lactase deficiency, we expect this to be the case because the variation in a trait is related to natural selection, which will operate differently in diverse environments. In using racial classifications, however, we often find that as we add more traits the situation becomes even more complex. The fact that traits show different distributions argues against the utility of the race concept for describing human variation.

With the proper choice of variables, however, we can find combinations that are useful in looking at the relationships between populations on a worldwide basis. By examining a number of traits presumed neutral in terms of natural selection, we try to come up with an average pattern that reflects the tendency of gene flow and genetic drift to affect all loci to the same extent. Often we find clusters of populations that agree in a limited sense with geography. That is, we can identify some separation between sub-Saharan African populations, European populations, Middle Eastern populations, and so on. This is expected, given the close relationship of geographic distance and gene flow in human populations. Sub-Saharan African populations should be more similar to each other, on average, than they are to European populations. We can identify large geographic regions that have a *rough* correspondence with the usual definitions of race. But how useful are these labels for describing variation? To answer that, we must look closely at the difference between variation *within* a population and variation *between* populations.

VARIATION BETWEEN AND WITHIN GROUPS   Racial classifications represent a form of **typology,** a set of discrete groupings. Instead of looking at the continuous range of variation, populations are placed into different races. The major problem with the usual application of the race concept and its emphasis on typology is the assumption that most of the variation that exists in the human species is *between* races. Variation *within* races is considered to be less. This is apparent when using group stereotypes (e.g., "they are short," or "they have broad heads"). Such statements provide information about the *average* in a group, but not about its variation. For example, consider the statement that adult males in the United States tend to be taller than adult females in the United States. No one can argue with this statement of averages. However, does it imply that *all* males are taller than *all* females? Of course not. There is variation within both sexes and a great deal of overlap.

The problem with the race concept, then, is that it acknowledges little overlap in genetic characteristics; in other words, the concept sees most variation as being between the races and not within the races. This is interesting because our observations show that the truth is actually completely different—there is much more variation *within* differently identified races than exists *between* them. In general, studies of simple genetic traits show that roughly 10 percent of the total genetic variation of the human species occurs between races. A recent study on cranial and facial characteristics produced the same number (Relethford 1994). The bottom line is that race explains only about 10 percent of human genetic diversity. This low number doesn't say much about race as an accurate description of human variation—it ignores most of the variation.

typology A set of discrete groupings in classification that emphasize average tendencies and ignore variation within groups.

Genetics, Race, and IQ

Perhaps the most controversial topic in the study of human variation is the question of the relationship of genetics, race, and intelligence. What is intelligence? Are IQ tests an accurate measure of intelligence? Are IQ scores due to genetic inheritance or environmental factors, or both? Are there "racial" differences in IQ scores? If so, do they reflect genetics or environment, or both?

Over time, as observations were collected that showed "racial" differences in intelligence test scores, several researchers argued that this difference is at least partially due to genetic differences between the races. A common line of argument goes as follows:

1. IQ scores are a measure of intelligence.
2. Differences in IQ scores are partly due to genetic differences.
3. The races have different average IQ scores.
4. Because races are by definition genetically different, then the racial differences in IQ scores are genetic.

It is worthwhile to examine briefly each of these claims.

What is IQ? It stands for "intelligence quotient" and is a measure derived by dividing a person's "mental age" by her or his chronological age, and is designed so that the average score for a reference population is 100. The IQ test was developed in France by Alfred Binet, who sought a means by which to identify children with learning disabilities. The purpose of the test was not to measure intelligence per se, but rather to identify those children who would most likely require special education. The test was not meant to provide a ranking of intelligence among the rest of the students. That is, someone with an IQ score of 120 was not to be considered inherently "better" or "smarter" than someone with a score of 110.

Is intelligence a single "thing" that can be measured accurately by an IQ test? Although some argue that IQ is a fair measure of intelligence (Herrnstein and Murray 1994), others note that there are many different types of intelligence, some of which may not be assessed as well by conventional IQ tests (Bodmer and Cavalli-Sforza 1976; Hunt 1995). There is an unfortunate tendency to assume that intelligence is a single thing, measurable with a single test (Gould 1981).

These problems change the questions somewhat. Instead of looking at genetic and environmental factors affecting intelligence, what we are really doing is looking at genetic and environmental factors affecting IQ test scores, which might not be the same thing. In terms of IQ, there is evidence for a strong

WHAT USE IS THE RACE CONCEPT? Acknowledging the many problems associated with using race to explain human variation, does the concept have any use? In the scientific study of human variation, the answer is little, if any. It is a descriptive tool, not an analytic one. If we examine the biological characteristics of a population and then assign the population to a given race, all we have accomplished is to label some observed phenomenon. We have not explained the causes of variation, nor why some groups are similar to, or different from, others. The name explains nothing. The race concept does not ask or answer any interesting questions.

Until the 1950s, much of biological anthropology was devoted to racial description and classification. Most sciences go through a descriptive phase, followed later by an explanatory phase in which hypotheses are proposed and tested. Indeed, at least until the work of Charles Darwin, much of biology was basically a descriptive science. Today biological anthropologists rarely treat race as a concept. It has no utility for explanation, and its value for description is limited.

genotypes have a greater probability of surviving or reproducing. If you were interested in looking at the potential effects of natural selection on the MN blood group system, you would want to separate your sample into groups of individuals with the same genotype (MM, MN, or NN). You would then attempt to determine if there were any differences in mortality or fertility among these groups. For instance, do individuals with one genotype live longer than those with other genotypes? Is there any relationship between genotype and the individual's history of disease? Do individuals with certain genotypes have more surviving children than those with other genotypes? Are individuals with one genotype more likely to be sterile than others?

These questions, and others, can be answered in principle by looking at the associations among some measure of health, survival, or fertility and different genotypes. Suppose you were interested in whether or not different MN genotypes have different susceptibilities to diseases. You could select a group, determine its MN genotypes, and monitor its members for the rest of their lives to track their disease histories. Alternatively, you could select a group of individuals having had a given disease and compare their MN genotypes with those of a random sample of people who have not had the disease.

ENVIRONMENTAL CORRESPONDENCE   One way of looking for the effects of natural selection is to analyze patterns of variation over a large geographic region. Given that natural selection is related to environmental variation, differences among locations might reflect changes in environment and in genotype. The goal is to determine the level of correspondence between some aspect or aspects of the physical environment and a genotype. To test the idea that climate is related to body size, you would look at the distribution of body size and see how well it matches the distribution of climatic variables. Again, proper selection of your samples is necessary to ensure that you do not measure some other factor affecting biological variation. This method has other potential problems, such as the fact that migration can affect the level of correspondence. For example, if you were looking at the relationship of skin color and latitude, you would not want to include African Americans or European Americans in your analysis because they are relatively recent migrants to the United States.

DEMOGRAPHIC MEASURES   Natural selection operates on differences in mortality and fertility, both of which may be measured from demographic records. The death rate of a population is a measure of the proportion of deaths occurring within a given period of time. The birth rate measures fertility within a population. These measures can provide an idea of the overall potential for natural selection. They do not tell us what specific effect natural selection will have on a particular set of loci. These measures are also so highly dependent on cultural variation that we cannot always extrapolate to genetic factors. For example, two populations may show different disease rates. Even though it might be tempting to suggest that the difference in disease patterns is due to genetic differences, we must first control for other sources of this variation, cultural and environmental.

Nonetheless, demographic measures do provide us with some information about the potential for natural selection to operate (Crow 1958). With proper controls and research strategies, such measures can even be used to test biological hypotheses in the absence of any direct biological data. A good example of this approach is Meindl and Swedlund's (1977) study of mortality in the populations of Deerfield and Greenfield in historical Massachusetts. Historical data indicated that both populations experienced epidemics of childhood dysentery, a serious disease, between 1802 and 1803. Meindl and Swedlund used death records to determine the effect of these epidemics on the mortality of those who survived the disease. They found that the individuals who survived the disease actually lived longer than those who were not exposed to it. They concluded that the greater longevity of those individuals reflected, in part, genetic differences. One possible interpretation is that those who survived had genetic characteristics that gave them greater resistance to dysentery; this is natural selection in action. Another possibility is that those exposed to the disease developed stronger immune systems as a response. Such augmented resistance is a physiological response, although there is most likely also a genetic component involved. Though such demographic analyses cannot provide any definite answers regarding natural selection, they do provide useful supplements to traditional genetic analysis.

PROBLEMS IN ANALYSIS   Some problems are common to any study of natural selection in human populations, regardless of the specific methods of study. The methods described here can demonstrate a relationship between some measure of fitness and some environmental factor. Correlation does not necessarily imply causation, however. We still need to document the link among genetics, environment, and the action of natural selection.

For example, a high degree of association between a specific blood group genotype and a given disease is suggestive but not conclusive. To complete the analysis, it is necessary to look at the specific biochemical nature of the blood group genotype. What changes in biological structure are related to this genotype, and how do these changes relate to the specific disease? A knowledge of the biochemical nature of the blood groups is required to answer these questions.

Another potential problem is that whatever association we detect may not have been present in the past. It is also possible that natural selection operated on a specific allele in the past but no longer does so. Certain blood group genotypes, for example, are associated with susceptibility to the disease smallpox. Today, smallpox has been eradicated as the result of intensive health care and immunization programs. In the past, however, smallpox was devastating. Thus, smallpox may have been a factor in the natural selection of certain blood types in the past, but it is not at present.

We have an unfortunate tendency to view natural selection in terms of *major* differences between different genotypes. Natural selection is often looked at as an all-or-none phenomenon—one individual survives and another does not. In reality, natural selection often operates on very small differences between different genotypes. One genotype may have only a slight advantage—1 or 2 percent, or even lower—relative to another.

SUMMARY

The study of human variation looks at the patterns and causes of biological diversity among living human beings. Human variation has been studied using a racial approach and an evolutionary approach. The biological concept of race emphasizes differences between groups and deemphasizes variation within groups. In the past, race was used as a crude means by which to describe patterns of human variation. A major problem in using race as a concept is that distinct "races" take on a reality of their own in people's minds. The race concept has limited use in analyses of biological variation, however, particularly for widespread species such as human beings. The race concept uses arbitrary classifications of predominately continuous variation, does not account for patterns of variation among different traits, and does not account for variation within groups. These problems aside, the race concept is further limited because it is purely descriptive and offers no explanation of variation.

The evolutionary approach looks at biological variation in terms of the evolutionary forces of mutation, natural selection, gene flow, and genetic drift. The focus of microevolutionary studies depends on the specific problem being analyzed. If the purpose is to look at average patterns reflecting gene flow and genetic drift, then many traits are analyzed at the same time (multivariate) because these two evolutionary forces affect all loci the same. If the purpose is to look at natural selection, then one trait is analyzed at a time (univariate) in order to find correlations with survival and/or reproduction. The microevolutionary approach is somewhat difficult to use for humans, as compared to laboratory animals, because there are no controls. Nonetheless, various methods have been developed to extract as much information as possible from patterns of human biological diversity.

SUPPLEMENTAL READINGS

Gould, S. J. 1981. *The Mismeasure of Man*. New York: W. W. Norton. An excellent review of the historical controversies regarding intelligence tests, which also addresses problems with the race concept.

Harrison, G. A., J. M. Tanner, D. R. Pilbeam, and P. T. Baker. 1988. *Human Biology: An Introduction to Human Evolution, Variation, Growth, and Adaptability.* 3d ed. Oxford: Oxford University Press.

Molnar, S. 1992. *Human Variation: Races, Types, and Ethnic Groups.* 3d ed. Englewood Cliffs, NJ: Prentice-Hall. This book and the preceding one by Harrison et al. (1988) provide information on patterns of human biological variation and the different approaches to their study.

Shipman, P. 1994. *The Evolution of Racism: Human Differences and the Use and Abuse of Science.* New York: Simon & Schuster. This book (as well as Marks' listed in Chapter 2) look at the race concept historically.

Human Microevolution

In this chapter, we examine several case studies of human microevolution in order to illustrate the different evolutionary approaches discussed in Chapter 10. The first part of this chapter deals with studies that look primarily at the joint effects of gene flow and genetic drift. The remainder of the chapter looks at several studies focusing on natural selection.

CASE STUDIES OF GENE FLOW AND GENETIC DRIFT

Many studies of human microevolution are concerned with population history. How are different populations related? Did they have different histories in terms of settlement or contact with other groups? Do invaders leave traces of their genes behind? Were populations always the same size, or did

The Biological History of the Ancient Egyptians

The ancient Egyptians have long been a source of fascination. Egyptian civilization dates back roughly 5,000 years, and is best known because of its many pyramids. There have been many debates over the origin of the ancient Egyptians. Some argue that this population is distinctly related to Europeans, while others favor a sub-Saharan origin. Still others suggest that the ancient Egyptians did not come from any one specific group but rather represent an in-place evolution in northeastern Africa, with contact with other populations.

The origin of the ancient Egyptians has been argued on the basis of archaeology and other clues. Here, we examine what inferences can be made from patterns of biological variation. One example is given. Genetic distances were computed among 13 samples of ancient skulls—three populations each from sub-Saharan Africa, Europe, the Far East, and Australia, and a sample from the ancient Egyptians (26th–30th dynasties, dating between 2550 and 2150 years B.P.). The data consisted of 57 measurements of the skull and face, provided by Dr. W. W. Howells (Howells 1973, 1989). These data were used to estimate genetic distances (Relethford and Blangero 1990).

Different patterns of genetic distances would result depending on which historical hypothesis was correct. If, for example, the ancient Egyptians came primarily from Europe, then they should be most similar to European populations. If they came from sub-Saharan Africa, then they should be most similar to sub-Saharan African populations. If, however, the ancient Egyptians were not the result of primary movement from one region or another, then their biological relationships would be somewhere intermediate between other geographic regions.

The figure here shows the results very clearly. The ancient Egyptian sample does not cluster with either Europeans or sub-Saharan Africans. More extensive analyses have shown similar results (Brace et al. 1993)—the ancient Egyptians are Egyptian. Their biological affinities reflect their geographic position more than anything else. The fact that Egypt is part of the African continent does not mean that they are closer to other African populations than to non-African groups.

This analysis reveals an important feature of human variation. If we ignore Egypt for the moment, we can see four recognizable clusters—Europe, sub-Saharan Africa, the Far East, and Australia. The clear separation of these clusters seems to argue strongly for four distinct "races." Or does it? By adding Egypt to the analysis, we see the problem of inferring race from widespread geographic samples; other populations fall in between, thus forcing us to add a fifth "race." Of course, if we add still other groups, we have to continually increase our number of races. Our image of distinct races often results from not using a full sampling of humanity.

some grow and expand, while others shrank or became isolated? These are but a few of the types of questions that are dealt with when using biological data to answer questions of human history.

When we look at the biological history of human populations, we are looking at the joint effects of gene flow and genetic drift. Any past migrations, invasions, or contacts between peoples ultimately involves gene flow, so we can analyze gene flow in such a way as to reconstruct these past events. Because the history of human populations also involves changes in population size, we must also consider the effect of genetic drift.

Two case studies are presented here to illustrate how we can analyze past patterns of gene flow and genetic drift. The first focuses on variation on a local level—small tribes in South America. The second looks at patterns of variation on a regional level—Irish counties.

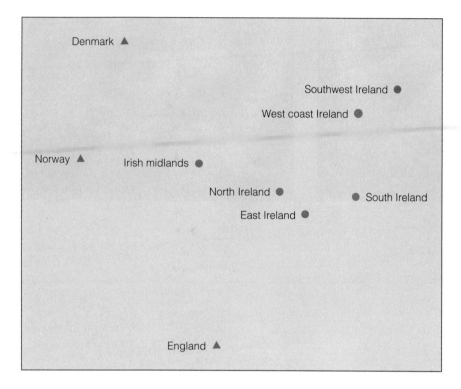

■ FIGURE 11.4
Genetic distance map
comparing six regions of
Ireland with data from
Denmark, Norway, and
England. The genetic
distances were based on head
and facial measurements. The
Irish midlands are closest to
Norway and Denmark, whose
populations represent the
source of Viking invaders
to Ireland. This analysis
supports the hypothesis of
Viking gene flow. (Relethford
and Crawford 1995)

oxygen to body tissues. The normal structure of the beta chain of hemoglobin is coded for by an allele usually called hemoglobin A. In many human
populations, the A allele is the only one present, and as a result everyone has
the *AA*, or normal adult hemoglobin, genotype.

HEMOGLOBIN VARIANTS Many hemoglobin variants are produced by the mutation of an A allele to another form. The most widely studied mutations
include hemoglobin S, C, and E. The S allele is also known as the sickle cell
allele. A person who has two S alleles (genotype SS) has **sickle cell anemia,** a
condition whereby the structure of the red blood cells is altered and oxygen
transport is severely impaired (Figure 11.5). Roughly, only 15 percent of
those with genotype SS survive to adulthood. An estimated 100,000 deaths
per year throughout the world are from sickle cell anemia.

If the S allele is harmful in homozygotes, we expect natural selection to
eliminate S alleles from the population in such a way that the frequency of S
should be relatively low. Mutation introduces the S allele, but natural selection eliminates it. Indeed, in many parts of the world the frequency of S is
extremely low, fitting the model of mutation balanced by selection. In a
number of populations, however, the frequency of S is much higher—often
up to 10 to 20 percent. Such high frequencies seem paradoxical, given the

sickle cell anemia A
genetic disease occurring
in a person homozygous
for the sickle cell allele,
which alters the struc-
ture of red blood cells.

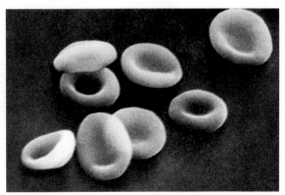

■ FIGURE 11.5
Sickle cell anemia. The blood cells on the left are twisted and deformed compared to the shape of normal red blood cells on the right. (© AP/Wide World Photos)

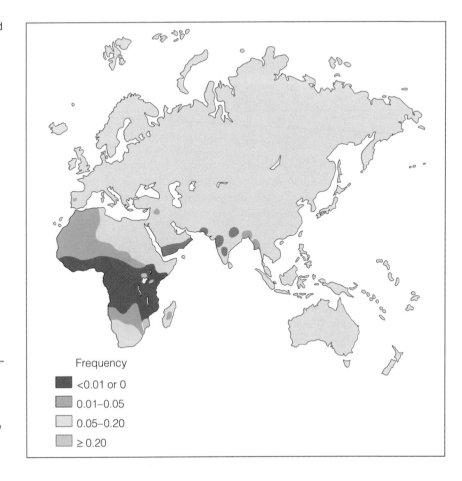

Frequency

■ <0.01 or 0
■ 0.01–0.05
□ 0.05–0.20
□ ≥ 0.20

■ FIGURE 11.6
Distribution of the sickle cell allele in the Old World. Compare high-frequency areas with the high-frequency areas of malaria in Figure 11.7.

harmful effect of the S allele in the homozygous genotype. Why does S reach such high frequencies?

DISTRIBUTION OF THE SICKLE CELL ALLELE AND MALARIA   The distribution of the sickle cell allele is related to the prevalence of a certain form of malaria. Malaria is an **infectious disease**—that is, a disease caused by the introduction into the body of an organic foreign substance, such as a virus or parasite (a disease that is not caused by an organic foreign substance is a **noninfectious disease**). Malaria is caused by a parasite that enters an organism's body, and four different species of the malarial parasite can affect humans. Malaria remains one of the major infectious diseases in the world today. In the late 1970s, as many as 120 million people in the world had some form of malaria (Encyclopaedia Britannica 1988).

The Old World shows a striking correspondence between higher frequencies of the S allele (Figure 11.6) and the prevalence of malaria caused by the parasite *Plasmodium falciparum* (Figure 11.7). This parasite is spread through the bites of certain species of mosquitoes. Except for blood transfusions, humans cannot give malaria to one another directly. Those areas with frequent cases of malaria, such as Central Africa, also have the highest frequencies of the sickle cell allele. The falciparum form of malaria, the most serious of all forms of malaria, is often fatal.

The strong geographic correspondence suggests that sickle cell anemia and malaria are both related to the high frequencies of the S allele. Further experimental work has confirmed this hypothesis. Because the S allele affects the structure of the red blood cells, it makes the blood an inhospitable place for the malaria parasite.

In a malarial environment, people who are heterozygous (genotype AS) actually have an advantage. The presence of one S allele does not give the person sickle cell anemia, but it does change the blood cells sufficiently so that the malaria parasite does not have as serious an effect. Overall, the heterozygote has the greatest fitness in a malarial environment. As discussed in Chapter 3, this is a case of balancing selection, in which selection occurs for the heterozygote (AS) and against both homozygotes (AA from malaria and SS from sickle cell anemia).

If the effects of sickle cell anemia and malaria were equal, then we would expect the frequencies of the normal allele (A) and the sickle cell allele (S) ultimately to reach equal frequencies. The two diseases, however, are not equal in their effects. Sickle cell anemia is much worse. The balance between these two diseases is such that the maximum fitness of an entire

▲▲

infectious disease
A disease caused by the introduction of

an organic foreign substance into the body.

noninfectious disease
A disease caused by factors other than

the introduction of an organic foreign substance into the body.

population occurs when the frequency of S is somewhere between 10 and 20 percent.

An analysis of one African population suggests that for every 100 people with AS who survive to adulthood, 88 people with AA survive and only 14 of those with SS (Bodmer and Cavalli-Sforza 1976). Clearly, the relationship between hemoglobin, sickle cell anemia, and malaria represents a very strong case of natural selection. Instead of a difference in survival between genotypes of only several percent, the differences are quite striking. Such differences can lead to major changes in allele frequencies in a very short period of time. To illustrate the rapidity of such change, Figure 11.8 shows a hypothetical example of changes in the frequency of the sickle cell allele. In this example, the initial frequency of S from mutation was set equal to a reasonable estimate of 0.00001. The fitness values mentioned earlier were used to examine the kind of change in the frequency of S that could take place. Because the initial allele frequency is low, there is little change for the first 40 generations or so. (Of course, if the initial allele frequency were higher, the rate of change would be greater; a higher initial frequency could occur due to genetic drift or the initial occurrence of the mutation in a small popula-

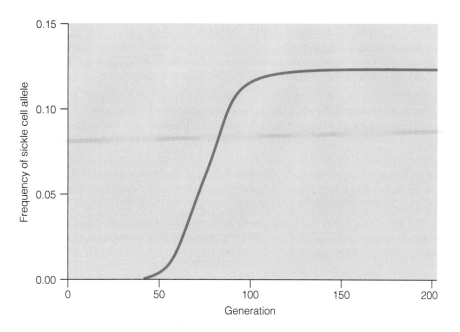

Reconstruction of past changes in sickle cell allele frequency in malarial Africa. This simulation assumes an initial allele frequency of 0.00001 caused by mutation. Relative fitness values are assumed constant over time: AA = 88%, AS = 100%, SS = 14%. The first 40 generations would show little change because the initial allele frequency was so low. After 40 generations, the allele frequency would increase rapidly, reaching an equilibrium after roughly 100 generations.

tion.) As the frequency of S increases, change takes place more rapidly because there are more people with the AS genotype to be selected for. After 100 generations, there is little change in the frequency of the S allele because it has reached an equilibrium based on the balance between the effects of sickle cell anemia and malaria. In this example, the sickle cell allele would reach an equilibrium frequency of 0.122. Of course, this simple illustration does not take other evolutionary forces into account, but it does show how quickly allele frequencies can change under strong natural selection.

The sickle cell example clearly shows the importance of the specific environment on the process of natural selection. In a nonmalarial environment, the AS genotype has no advantage, and the AA genotype has the greatest evolutionary fitness. In such cases, the frequency of the S allele is very low, approaching zero. In a malarial environment, however, the situation is different, and the heterozygote has the advantage. Clearly, we cannot label the S allele as intrinsically "good" or "bad"; it depends on circumstances.

EFFECTS OF CULTURE CHANGE ON SICKLE CELL FREQUENCY Sickle cell anemia also provides an excellent example of the interaction of biology and culture. Livingstone (1958) and others have taken information on the distribution and ecology of the malaria parasite and the mosquito that transmit it, along with information on the prehistory and history of certain regions in Africa, and have presented a hypothesis about changes in the frequency of the sickle cell allele. Several thousand years ago, the African environment was not conducive to the spread of malaria. Large areas of the continent consisted of dense forests. The mosquito that spreads malaria thrives best in ample sunlight and pools of stagnant water. Neither condition then existed in the African forests. The extensive foliage prevented much sunlight from reaching the floor of the forest. In addition, the forest environment was very absorbent, so water did not tend to accumulate in pools. In other words, the environment was not conducive to large populations of mosquitoes. Consequently, the malaria parasite did not have a hospitable environment, either.

This situation changed several thousand years ago when prehistoric African populations brought horticulture into the area. **Horticulture** is a form of farming employing only simple hand tools. As the land was cleared for crops, the entire ecology shifted. Without the many trees, it was easier for sunlight to reach the land surface. Continued use of the land changed the soil chemistry, allowing pools of water to accumulate. Both changes led to an environment ideal for the growth and spread of mosquito populations, and therefore the spread of the malaria parasite. The growth of the human population also provided more hosts for the mosquitoes to feed on, thus increasing the spread of malaria.

Before the development of horticulture in Africa, the frequency of the sickle cell allele was probably low, as it is in nonmalarial environments today. When the incidence of malaria increased, it became evolutionarily advantageous to have the heterozygote AS genotype because those who had it would have greater resistance to malaria without suffering the effects of sickle cell anemia. As shown earlier, this change could have taken place in a short period of time, roughly 100 generations, because of the large differences in fitness among hemoglobin genotypes. The initial introduction of the sickle cell allele, through mutation or gene flow, was followed by a rapid change, reaching an equilibrium point in which the fitness of the entire human population was at a maximum.

This scenario shows that human cultural adaptations (horticulture) can affect the ecology of other organisms (the mosquito and malaria parasite), which can then cause genetic change in the human population (an increase in the frequency of the sickle cell allele). This sequence of events is summarized in Figure 11.9.

Of course, we cannot observe these events directly because they occurred in the past. Nonetheless, all available evidence supports this hypothesis. We know the physiological differences between different hemoglobin types. We also know that low frequencies of S occur in nonmalarial environments and higher frequencies occur where there is malaria. Archaeological evidence shows when and where the spread of horticulture took place in Africa. From studies of modern-day agriculture, we also know that malaria spreads quickly following the clearing of land. Taking all this information together, we find the scenario for changes in the frequency of the sickle cell allele in Africa is most reasonable.

OTHER RELATIONSHIPS WITH MALARIA   A number of other genetic loci appear to have been affected by natural selection from malaria. Two different alleles of

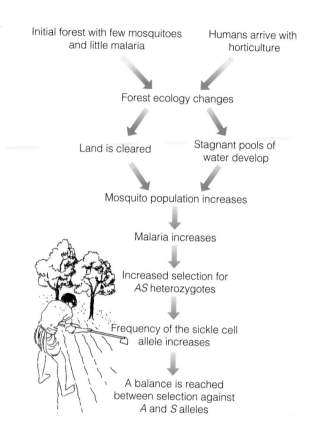

■ **FIGURE 11.9**
Sequence of cultural and environmental changes leading to changes in the frequency of the sickle cell allele in malarial Africa.

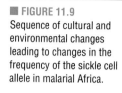

the hemoglobin locus, *C* and *E*, appear in high frequencies in certain malarial environments. Several inherited biochemical disorders, collectively known as thalassemia, are also related to malaria. These disorders do not directly affect the structure of the adult hemoglobin molecule but do interfere with its production. Another genetic trait, G6PD deficiency, leads to a deficiency of a certain enzyme and also appears to confer some resistance to malaria. It is not surprising to find a number of loci related to malaria because it is a severe disease, and any trait that alters the blood sufficiently to confer resistance to the parasite might be selected for over time.

The ABO Blood Group and Natural Selection

The human blood groups have been the subject of many investigations of natural selection. There are many different blood groups, defined on the basis of the type of molecules present on the surface of the red blood cells. Some blood groups are associated with different antibodies that react to various substances invading the blood stream (foreign antigens). Two blood

horticulture A form of farming in which only simple hand tools are used.

groups—MN and ABO—have already been mentioned in previous chapters. Other red blood cell groups include Rhesus, Diego, Duffy, Lutheran, Lewis, and Xg, to name but a few. Some of these blood groups appear to be neutral in terms of natural selection, or perhaps we just have not been able to detect any effects. Also, some may have been selected for or against in the past, but not at present. Others are definitely related to natural selection, but in ways that are difficult to discern.

The ABO blood group is the most widely studied simple genetic trait in human populations. As shown in Chapters 2 and 10, there are three different alleles (A, B, O) in this group: A and B are codominant and O is recessive. There are four possible phenotypes: type A (genotypes AA and AO), type B (genotypes BB and BO), type O (genotype OO, and type AB (genotype AB).

Worldwide, the O allele is the most common, the A allele is next most frequent, and the B allele is the least common. The allele frequencies of all human populations fall within certain limits. The frequency of the O allele ranges from 0.4 to 1.0, the frequency of the A allele ranges from 0 to 0.55, and the frequency of the B allele ranges from 0 to 0.3 (Brues 1977).

If the evolution of the ABO blood group system were totally the result of drift and gene flow, we would expect to see a wider range of allele frequencies. For example, we expect to see populations with frequencies such as A = 0.8, B = 0.1, and O = 0.1. Of the hundreds of human populations studied for the ABO blood group to date, however, none is in this range. The fact that the allele frequencies fall within a certain range suggests that natural selection has been operating to keep the frequencies for the entire species within certain limits.

One possible clue to the effects of natural selection on the ABO blood groups is that certain antibodies are associated with different blood groups. Recall from Chapter 10 that there are two antibodies in the ABO system: anti-A and anti-B, present throughout an individual's life. The anti-A antibody reacts to destroy A-type molecules, and the anti-B antibody reacts to destroy B-type molecules. There is no antibody for O. People with blood type A have the anti-B antibody, people with blood type B have the anti-A antibody, people with blood type O have both, and people with blood type AB have neither (Table 11.1).

The fact that different blood types have different antibodies also has implications for natural selection and susceptibility to different diseases. If you have blood type A, and hence anti-B antibodies, your immune system will tend to fight off any microorganisms that are biochemically similar to type B molecules. For example, the microorganism that causes venereal syphilis is biochemically similar to A molecules. Therefore, people with blood types B and O will have greater resistance to syphilis because they have the anti-A antibodies. People with blood types A and AB will not have this resistance because they lack the anti-A antibodies. It has been suggested that a link exists between various ABO blood types and a number of infectious diseases, such as smallpox, typhoid, influenza, bubonic plague, and

■ TABLE 11.1
ABO Blood Group Phenotypes and Antibodies

GENOTYPES	PHENOTYPE	ANTIGENS	ANTIBODIES
AA AO	A	A	anti-B
BB BO	B	B	anti-A
AB	AB	A, B	none
OO	O	none	anti-A, anti-B

others. Many of these diseases were indeed serious in the past, and differential resistance could be a possible factor in explaining the range of allele frequencies for the ABO system. More work, however, needs to be done to substantiate these claims.

In any case, the action of natural selection is complex because of the wide variety of different disease microorganisms and their relationships to ABO blood types. It has been suggested that each blood type is more susceptible than others to certain diseases. For example, type A seems more susceptible to smallpox, type B seems more susceptible to infantile diarrhea, and type O seems more susceptible to bubonic plague. If these theories are verified, it seems that the frequencies of the ABO alleles are subject to a variety of different types of selection. This makes analysis extremely difficult.

ABO blood types also appear to be related to noninfectious diseases. Some hospital studies have suggested that people with blood type O have a greater chance of getting duodenal and stomach ulcers (this might be related to antibodies because recent work has confirmed that some ulcers are actually infectious in nature, being caused by bacteria). People with blood type A have a greater chance of getting certain forms of cancer. The differences between the phenotypes appear strong, but we do not understand the reasons for these associations. In any case, it is unclear what evolutionary importance these associations have. Most of the noninfectious diseases have severe effects late in life and therefore should not be subject to natural selection because they usually occur after an individual's reproductive life is over. Some people, however, do acquire these diseases early enough in life so that at least the possibility exists that natural selection could be operating through differential survival to noninfectious diseases. We must demonstrate, however, that such selection did (or does) in fact take place, and not merely that it is possible.

Natural selection may also be operating on ABO blood groups as a consequence of incompatibility between mother and fetus. Incompatible matings will often lead to the destruction of red blood cells in the fetus. Most often, ABO incompatibility will lead to spontaneous abortion early in pre-

■ TABLE 11.2
ABO Blood Group Maternal-Fetal Incompatibilities

MOTHER'S GENOTYPE	INCOMPATIBLE FETAL GENOTYPES
AA	AB
AO	AB, BO
BB	AB
BO	AB, AO
AB	None
OO	AO, BO

natal life. Incompatibility occurs when the mother's blood has an antibody corresponding to the type of molecule present in the fetus's blood. An example of incompatibility is a woman with blood type A whose fetus is blood type AB. The woman's blood contains anti-B antibody, which reacts with the B molecules present in the fetus's blood. All possible types of incompatibility between mother and fetus are listed in Table 11.2. Note that in each case the genotype of the fetus is heterozygous. This suggests selection against some heterozygotes.

There seems to be little doubt that natural selection has affected allele frequencies for the ABO blood group system. Studies have shown the relationship among blood type and incompatibility, infectious disease, and noninfectious disease. It does not appear likely that any one of these factors is solely responsible for the observed allele frequency range in human beings. It is also possible that there are other factors of which we are unaware.

Lactase Deficiency

As shown in the sickle cell example, cultural variation can affect genetic variation. **Lactase deficiency** is another example of a genetic trait that is influenced by cultural factors. As mammals, human infants receive nourishment from mother's milk. Infants have an enzyme, lactase, that allows milk sugar, lactose, to be digested. In most human populations, the manufacture of the lactase enzyme is "turned off" by four years of age as it is in most mammals after infancy. A person who has a deficiency of this enzyme as a child or adult will not be able to digest milk efficiently and can develop severe cramps, diarrhea, and other intestinal problems if he or she consumes it.

Most human populations have high frequencies of lactase deficiency, but some populations do not. The enzyme continues to be produced throughout life, and these people can continue to digest milk sugar. Interestingly, a clear relationship exists between the frequency of lactase deficiency in a population and whether or not the population is involved in dairy farming. Table 11.3 lists the frequency of lactase deficiency in a number of populations of African, Asian, and European ancestry. In general, the lowest frequency is found in populations of European ancestry with a known history of dairy farming. The highest frequency of lactase deficiency occurs in populations of African and Asian ancestry that did not practice dairy farming.

The correspondence of low frequencies of lactase deficiency and dairy farming suggests that the ability to digest milk later in life is selected for in environments where milk is a major source of nutrition. This circumstance suggests that humans originally had very high frequencies of lactase deficiency and that as populations grew to rely more and more on milk in their diet after infancy, natural selection acted to decrease the proportion of those with lactase deficiency. After all, we would expect higher survival and reproduction in those individuals best able to utilize available nutrition. An exam-

■ TABLE 11.3
Frequencies of Lactase Deficiency in Some Human Populations

POPULATION		PERCENTAGE OF LACTASE DEFICIENCY
African ancestry	African Americans	70–77
	Ibos	99
	Bantus	90
	Fulani	22
	Yoruba	99
	Baganda	94
Asian ancestry	Asian Americans	95–100
	Thailand	97–100
	Eskimos	72–88
	Native Americans	58–67
European ancestry	European Americans	2–19
	Finland	18
	Switzerland	12
	Sweden	4

Sources: Lerner and Libby (1976:327); Molnar (1992:124)

ination of some discrepancies in the usual pattern of frequencies in Table 11.3 supports this hypothesis. Many African populations, such as the Ibos and Bantus, are known horticultural populations that do not practice dairy farming. The Fulani, however, are a group of African nomadic cattle herders who rely extensively on milk in their diet. The percentage of lactase deficiency among the Fulani is low (22 percent) and similar to the percentage found in European populations.

Skin Color

Human skin color is a complex trait. Several studies have shown that skin color is a polygenic trait although it is not clear how many loci might be involved (Byard 1981). Skin color has a strong genetic component (Williams-Blangero and Blangero 1992) and is affected by the environment, such as the amount of direct sunlight.

THE DISTRIBUTION OF SKIN COLOR The worldwide distribution of human skin color among native populations shows a striking correspondence with latitude. Figure 11.10 shows the relationship between skin color and distance from the equator for 93 male samples from the Old World. Native populations closer to the equator tend to be the darkest, while those farther from the equator tend to be the lightest. The distribution of skin color and

▲▲▲▲▲▲▲▲▲▲▲▲▲▲▲▲▲▲▲▲▲▲▲▲▲▲▲▲▲▲▲

lactase deficiency A condition in which an older child or adult lacks the ability to produce the lactase enzyme needed to digest milk sugar.

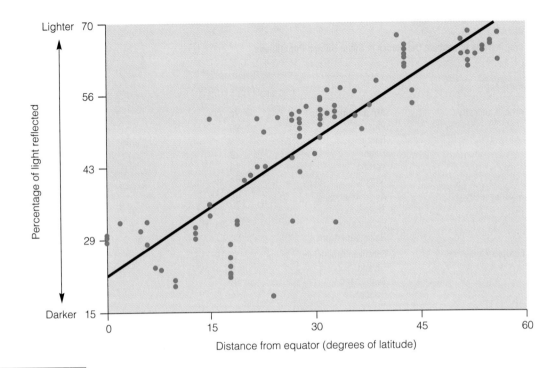

FIGURE 11.10
Geographic distribution of human skin color for 93 human Old World populations (males). Circles indicate the mean skin reflectance measured at a wavelength of 685 nanometers plotted against the distance, in degrees of latitude, from the equator. The solid line indicates the best-fitting linear curve relating skin reflectance and latitude. (*All data from published literature*)

latitude corresponds to the amount of ultraviolet radiation received at the earth's surface. Because of the way sunlight strikes the earth, ultraviolet radiation is strongest at the equator and diminishes in strength as we move away from the equator. It is even more diminished where cloud cover is extensive.

SKIN CANCER, SUNBURN, AND ULTRAVIOLET RADIATION   What are the biological effects of ultraviolet radiation? This radiation causes the skin to tan—that is, to produce more melanin. Too much exposure burns the skin, leading to infection. In sufficient amounts, ultraviolet radiation can lead to skin cancer. The greater the intensity of ultraviolet radiation, the greater the risk for skin cancer at any given level of pigmentation. Among the European-American population of the United States, skin cancer rates are much higher in Texas than in Massachusetts (Damon 1977). Dark-skinned individuals have lower rates of skin cancer because the heavy concentration of melanin near the surface of the skin blocks some of the ultraviolet radiation. Accordingly, the correspondence of latitude and skin color may reflect, in part, the differential effects of skin cancer. Ultraviolet radiation is strongest near the equator, and dark skin is advantageous in such an environment to protect against skin cancer.

Researchers have argued against skin cancer as a selective factor, suggesting that skin cancer, like many cancers, affects mostly older individuals past their reproductive years. If someone dies from skin cancer after reproducing, their death does not affect the process of natural selection. According to this line of reasoning, some researchers have suggested that skin cancer has had a minimal effect, at best, on the evolution of human skin color (e.g., Blum 1961).

The problem with this argument is that the evidence does not support it. Robins (1991) points out that all albinos studied in Nigeria and Tanzania either had skin cancer or precancerous skin lesions by 20 years of age. People are normally dark skinned in these countries, and the albinos, because of a rare genetic condition, would be particularly susceptible to the harmful effects of ultraviolet radiation. From an evolutionary standpoint, the important finding is that skin cancers and precancerous conditions occur *early* in life, contrary to the opinion that they are generally found among the elderly.

Sunburn could also have been an important factor in natural selection. Severe sunburn can lead to infection and can interfere with the body's ability to sweat efficiently. Dark skin could protect from these effects, and thus be selected for.

Natural selection related to skin cancer and sunburn may be part of the answer to the question of worldwide skin color variation, but it is not the entire answer. Even though there is less ultraviolet radiation farther away from the equator and light-skinned people would have less risk for skin cancer and sunburn, this does not explain *why* light skin evolved in such regions. The model only shows that light skin *could* evolve. Skin cancer and sunburn help explain dark skin near the equator but do not explain light skin farther away from the equator.

THE VITAMIN D HYPOTHESIS   A more subtle effect of ultraviolet radiation is the synthesis of vitamin D, a nutrient needed by humans for proper bone growth. Today we may receive vitamin D either through vitamin supplements or through the injection of vitamin D into our milk. Both of these dietary modifications are relatively recent human inventions, however. Formerly, humans had to obtain their vitamin D through diet or from stimulation of the synthesis of certain chemical compounds by ultraviolet radiation. Some foods, such as fish oils, are high in vitamin D but are not found in all environments. For most human populations in the past the major source of vitamin D was the sun.

Because vitamin D synthesis depends on ultraviolet radiation, it seems reasonable to assume that more of it will be produced near the equator, where ultraviolet radiation is strongest. It has been suggested that too much or too little of the vitamin is harmful to the human body. An excess of vitamin D can lead to vitamin poisoning, cause calcification of soft tissues, and interfere with proper kidney functioning, while a lack of it can lead to poor bone development and maintenance, including diseases, such as rickets, that lead to deformed bones.

The idea that vitamin D intake must lie in a certain range, without excess or deficit, is at the core of the vitamin D hypothesis of skin color evolution

(Loomis 1967). According to this hypothesis, in regions close to the equator, where ultraviolet radiation is the greatest, darker skin serves to block the harmful effects of excessive vitamin D production. In areas farther away, dark skin blocks too much of the sun's rays, which leads to insufficiency of vitamin D. Natural selection thus produced a change toward lighter skin color, that would be adaptive in such environments.

The vitamin D hypothesis thus explains the entire distribution of human skin color, showing the adaptive significance of both dark skin and light skin in different environments. Although logical, some investigations have suggested that this model is *not* correct. Holick and colleagues (1981) have shown that vitamin D synthesis reaches a maximum level during continued exposure to ultraviolet radiation. A light-skinned person's prolonged exposure to ultraviolet radiation will *not* lead to toxic vitamin D levels.

Though the vitamin D hypothesis does not hold up as an explanation for dark skin near the equator, can it still be used to explain the occurrence of light skin farther away from the equator? Robins (1991) listed a number of reasons why the vitamin D hypothesis fails here as well. First, rickets is a disease associated with recent urbanization. It is essentially absent in rural areas, and there is little evidence of rickets in the fossil record of our ancestors (who lived in rural, not urban, conditions). Second, although dark skin is not as effective as light skin in synthesizing vitamin D, it is still effective enough for production and maintenance of proper vitamin D levels. Laboratory studies have shown that African Americans can produce their maximum quota of vitamin D in three hours. Though this is not as fast as for European Americans (30 minutes), it is still effective enough for proper health except under conditions of modern urbanization, such as smog and tall buildings that cut down on exposure. Studies have also determined that dark-skinned peoples could produce and maintain sufficient vitamin D in northern climates even with only their heads, necks, and hands exposed to ultraviolet radiation. This is an important point because in cold climates less of the body would be exposed. In sum, the relationship between rickets and limited vitamin D appears confined to recent urban areas and is also associated with lower social class (the poor have less money for milk). For conditions typical of our ancestors, dark skin would *not* be at a disadvantage in terms of limited vitamin D production.

SKIN COLOR AND COLD INJURY   The vitamin D hypothesis, as just noted, does not hold true when explaining the distribution of human skin color, and we must look for other answers. One possibility for the occurrence of light skin at distances away from the equator is cold injury. Reviewing a wide range of data, Post and colleagues (1975) noted that, in cold climates, dark-skinned individuals are at greater risk for frostbite than light-skinned individuals. Data reporting this difference are available on soldiers in World Wars I and II, the Korean War, and those stationed in Alaska during the late 1950s. For example, during the Korean War, African-American soldiers were over four times more likely to get frostbite than European-American soldiers.

These observations suggest that in the colder northern climates darker skin is more prone to cold injury than lighter skin, a hypothesis supported by laboratory experiments on piebald guinea pigs (having both light and dark skin). Cold injury could be induced more frequently and more severely in the darker-skinned animals.

At present, the evidence supports skin cancer and sunburn as selective factors for dark skin in equatorial regions. Farther away from the equator, there is less of an advantage for dark skin, and more of an advantage for light skin, the former being more vulnerable to severe cold injury. Further study will be needed to strengthen support for both of these ideas and to explore the possibility that other factors affect skin color variation. Recent observations that ultraviolet radiation affects functioning of the immune system (Robins 1991) are also worth investigating.

Natural Selection or Developmental Acclimatization?

The finding of environmental correspondence, discussed in Chapter 10, offers clues to the action of natural selection. The case studies of sickle cell and skin color are two excellent examples of how natural selection can tie particular variations to specific environmental conditions. In some cases, the association between human variation and the environment is not as clear. Environmental correlations may instead reflect physiologic adaptation during an individual's life, a phenomenon known as **developmental acclimatization**. Here, changes occur to an individual during its physical growth in a specific environment.

HIGH-ALTITUDE ADAPTATION   Certain characteristics found in high-altitude populations illustrate this effect. Some human populations have lived for long periods of time at elevations over 2,500 meters (roughly 8,200 feet). Because barometric pressure decreases with altitude, oxygen content is less concentrated and less oxygen is available in the blood. Many studies have found an interesting feature of physical growth in high-altitude populations—at all ages, chest dimensions and lung volume are greater than found in low-altitude populations (Figure 11.11) (Frisancho and Baker 1970). These increased dimensions are associated with greater aerobic capacity, which is adaptive at high altitude.

The association of increased chest and lung size in high-altitude populations would seem to suggest past natural selection. In this case, however, closer analysis shows that changes in physical growth are a direct effect of growing up at high altitude (Greska 1990). In addition, studies have found an effect of how long children have lived at high altitude. Among migrants, the

developmental acclimatization
Changes in organ or body structure that occur during the physical growth of any organism.

■ **FIGURE 11.11**
Growth curves for chest
circumference for high-
altitude and low-altitude
Peruvian Indian populations.
At all ages, the high-altitude
population has the greatest
chest circumference.
(Courtesy A. F. Frisancho)

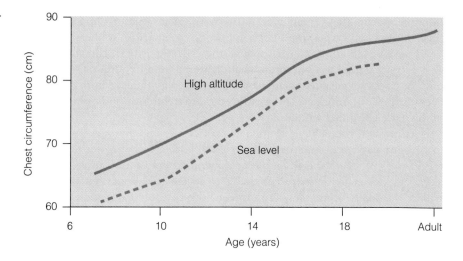

■ **FIGURE 11.11**
Growth curves for chest
circumference for high-
altitude and low-altitude
Peruvian Indian populations.
At all ages, the high-altitude
population has the greatest
chest circumference.
(Courtesy A. F. Frisancho)

younger children were when they moved to a high altitude, the greater the response in their growth patterns. The larger chests and lungs of high-altitude peoples reflect their growing up in that environment—in other words, developmental acclimatization rather than natural selection.

BODY SIZE, BODY SHAPE, AND CLIMATE   Another, more complex, example is the relationship between body size and shape and climate. Among mammals there is a tendency for smaller body size and more linear body shape to be found in hot climates, and a tendency for larger body size and less linear body shape to be found in cold climates (Figure 11.12). In addition, mammals in hot climates tend to have more slender limbs. The relationship between body size, body shape, and limb shape and climate are summarized by **Bergmann's rule** and **Allen's rule,** which relate physical variation to heat loss. In hot climates, for example, individuals with small body mass, linear body shape, and slender limbs tend to lose heat more quickly than other individuals.

Are these relationships the product of natural selection operating over many generations or development acclimatization? The evidence to date suggests that *both* are responsible. When children grow up in a climate different from their ancestors, they tend to grow in ways the indigenous children do (Malina 1975; Roberts 1978). This finding supports the idea that environment directly influences the growth process. The relationship between growth and climate in such children, however, is not as strong as it is among indigenous children. Therefore, long-term natural selection is also responsible for the association of size, shape, and climate observed in adults. Natural selection leads to changes in growth potential that are further modified by environmental factors. It appears that climate can alter the growth patterns of all children, although those with certain genetic predispositions may show greater response.

Bergmann's rule
(1) Among mammals of similar shape, the larger mammal loses heat less rapidly than the smaller mammal, and (2) among mammals of similar size, the mammal with a linear shape will lose heat more rapidly than the mammal with a nonlinear shape.

Allen's rule Mammals in cold climates tend to have short, bulky limbs, allowing less loss of body heat; mammals in hot climates tend to have long, slender limbs, allowing greater loss of body heat.

SUMMARY

Case studies of human microevolution presented in this chapter illustrate some of the methods and results of studies dealing with an evolutionary approach to contemporary human biological variation. The case studies of gene flow and genetic drift emphasize how factors such as social structure, population size, migration patterns, cultural barriers, and history all affect the genetic relationships among human populations.

Several examples of natural selection in human populations are reviewed. Perhaps the best-documented example is the relationship between hemoglobin alleles and two selective forces: sickle cell anemia and malaria. In environments where malaria is common, selection has led to an increase in the sickle cell allele because the heterozygotes are the most fit—they show greater resistance to malaria but do not suffer from the adverse effects of sickle cell anemia. Studies of blood groups and other genetic markers also suggest a role for natural selection in human variation. Skin color is another example of a trait that shows a strong environmental correlation, in this case with latitude. This distribution, combined with other evidence, suggests that dark skin is selected for near the equator primarily to protect against the harmful effects of excess ultraviolet radiation (skin cancer and sunburn). The reason why light skin evolved farther from the equator is not known, although there is strong evidence for some relationship between skin color, temperature, and the likelihood of frostbite.

Physical features found in high-altitude populations, such as increased lung volume, reflect environmental effects on growth rather than natural selection. The relationship between body size and shape and climate, on the other hand, seems to reflect both natural selection and the effect of the environment on growth.

SUPPLEMENTAL READINGS

In addition to the readings suggested for Chapter 10, other sources are:

Cavalli-Sforza, L. L., P. Menozzi, and A. Piazza. 1994. *The History and Geography of Human Genes*. Princeton: Princeton University Press.

Crawford, M. H., and J. H. Mielke, eds. 1982. *Current Developments in Anthropological Genetics*. Vol. 2. *Ecology and Population Structure*. New York: Plenum Press. This book and the preceding one by Cavalli-Sforza et al. (1994) are somewhat detailed, but provide many examples of the use of genetic distance analysis to unravel the effects of gene flow and genetic drift on human biological variation.

Robins, A. H. 1991. *Biological Perspectives on Human Pigmentation*. Cambridge: Cambridge University Press. An excellent review of the biology, variation, and evolution of human skin color. The final chapter on the evolution of human skin color is the best to date.

Human Biology and Culture Change

The past 12,000 years have seen human societies change at an extremely rapid pace. In this short time (by evolutionary standards) our species has gone from hunting and gathering to agriculture as our primary way to feed ourselves. This time has also seen rapid population growth, the development of cities, and an increasingly interconnected world. The rate of culture change has been particularly rapid in the past century, and many of us live in a world quite different from that of our great-grandparents.

Cultural change occurs much more rapidly than evolutionary change. While there have been some average minor changes in human biological evolution during the past 12,000 years (such as some reduction in teeth size), they have been exceptionally minor compared to the cultural changes during this time. Our genetic evolution has not kept up with our cultural evolution. How have these changes affected aspects of our biology? This chapter examines some of these changes, focusing specifically on changing patterns of health and disease, physical growth, and demography.

■ TABLE 12.1
**Cholera: An Example of
a Current Pandemic**

YEAR	OCCURRENCE OF EPIDEMIC
1961	Indonesia (first outbreak)
1963	Bangladesh
1964	India
1965	Former Soviet Union
1970	Africa
1990	Parts of Europe
1991	South America

Source: Dixon and McBride (1992)

THE EVOLUTION OF HUMAN DISEASE

A unique contribution of anthropology has been its investigation into the evolution of human diseases. A shift began roughly 12,000 years ago from hunting and gathering to agriculture. During the past several centuries, further changes have led to the development and spread of large industrial societies. What effects have these rapid shifts, and related environmental and cultural changes, produced on patterns of human health and disease? Part of this question can be answered by looking at contemporary populations at different levels of subsistence. We can also examine the fossil and archaeological record to infer changes in the patterns of disease. This section focuses on general trends in disease across three different levels of subsistence: hunting-gathering, agriculture, and industrialization.

Before considering the evolution of human health and disease, it is necessary to define several terms that refer to the types of disease and rates of disease in populations. As discussed in Chapter 11, an infectious disease is one caused by the introduction of organic matter into the body, such as a virus, bacteria, or a parasite. Noninfectious diseases are those *not* caused by the introduction of organic matter (for example, cancer and diabetes). Infectious diseases can also be classified as *communicable* or *noncommunicable*, depending on whether the disease can be transmitted directly from one person to another. Malaria, for example, is an infectious disease caused by a parasite. It is not, however, a communicable disease because it cannot be passed directly from one human to another (except by means of a blood transfusion). Measles, another infectious disease, is communicable because it *can* be transmitted directly from one human to another.

In terms of *rates* of disease, an **epidemic** pattern is one in which new cases of a disease spread quickly. An **endemic** pattern is a low but constant rate; a few cases are always present, but no major spread occurs. A **pandemic** pattern is an epidemic that takes place over large geographic ranges, such as the bubonic plague pandemics during the Middle Ages that spread throughout Europe. Another example is the 1918 influenza pandemic. Pandemics are not just something that happened in the past; pandemics occur today as well. Currently, the world is experiencing a cholera pandemic that began in 1961, and epidemic spread of the disease has now reached four continents (Table 12.1).

Disease in Hunting-Gathering Societies

Given that humans relied exclusively on hunting and gathering until the relatively recent development of agriculture, a large part of our genetic makeup resulted from adaptations to a hunting-gathering way of life. This fact has powerful implications for the analysis of disease. How do these adaptations affect our response to disease under very different environmental circumstances?

INFECTIOUS DISEASE   The two most common types of infectious diseases in hunting-gathering populations are caused by parasites and **zoonoses** (diseases transmitted from other animals to humans). Parasitic diseases may reflect the long-term evolutionary adaptation of different parasites to human beings. Among hunting-gathering societies, these parasites include lice and pinworms. The zoonoses are introduced through insect bites, animal wounds, and ingestion of contaminated meat. The diseases include sleeping sickness, tetanus, and schistosomiasis (Armelagos and Dewey 1970). The prevalence of various parasitic and zoonotic diseases varies among different hunting-gathering environments. The disease microorganisms found in arctic or temperate environments are generally not found in tropical environments.

In general, hunting-gathering populations do not experience epidemics of infectious disease. This is because of two ecological factors associated with a hunting-gathering way of life: small population size and nomadism (Figure 12.1). Hunters and gatherers live in small groups of roughly 25 to 50 people that interact occasionally with other small groups in their region. Under such conditions, infectious diseases do not spread. There are not enough people to become infected to keep the disease going at high rates. Without more people to infect, the disease microorganisms die. This does not apply to chronic infectious diseases, whose microorganisms can stay alive long enough to infect people coming into the group. Certain diseases caused by parasitic worms fall into this category. In such cases, the prevalence rate of infectious diseases is low. Most infectious diseases in hunting-gathering societies are endemic rather than epidemic (McElroy and Townsend 1989).

The nomadic lifestyle of hunting-gathering groups also reduces risk to certain infectious diseases. The microorganisms infecting humans may not survive in new environments. Other aspects of the hunting-gathering way of life also reduce the chance of epidemics. Given a small, mobile population, there are few problems with sanitation or contamination of the water supply.

NONINFECTIOUS DISEASE   The noninfectious diseases common in industrial societies, such as heart disease, cancer, diabetes, and hypertension, are rare in hunting-gathering societies. Part of the reason for low rates of such noninfectious "Western diseases" may be the diet and lifestyle of hunters and gatherers, but the primary reason may be simply the fact that fewer individu-

epidemic A pattern of disease rate when new cases of a disease spread rapidly through a population.

endemic A pattern of disease rate when new cases of a disease occur at a relatively constant but low rate over time.

pandemic An epidemic that occurs over a large geographic range.

zoonose A disease transmitted directly from animals to humans.

■ FIGURE 12.1
!Kung women gathering
vegetables. The small size and
nomadic nature of hunting-
gathering populations mean
that infectious disease is
endemic, not epidemic.
(M. Shostak/Anthro-Photo)

als among hunters and gatherers are likely to live long enough to develop these diseases.

The nutrition of hunting-gathering populations is varied and provides a well-balanced diet. Perhaps this diet, along with greater levels of exercise, accounts for the lack of cardiovascular problems in such societies. The major nutritional problem in hunting-gathering societies is the scarcity of food during hard times, such as drought. To some extent, hunting-gathering populations have adapted to occasional fluctuations in food supply through reduced rates of growth and smaller body sizes. In any case, the rate of malnutrition and starvation in most hunting-gathering groups is usually very low (Dunn 1968).

The reduced rate of noninfectious diseases in hunting-gathering populations, particularly those diseases that occur in old age, reflects the low life expectancy at birth in these groups (**life expectancy at birth** is a measure of the average length of life). Many noninfectious diseases require long periods of time for full development. Life expectancy at birth is low in hunting-gathering populations—roughly 20 to 40 years (Cohen 1989). These low life expectancies at birth reflect high infant mortality. If many people die early in life, the median age at death will be lowered. Keep in mind that life expectancy at birth is an average length of life. A value of 20 to 40 reflects a large number of infant and child deaths that brings the average down, and does *not* mean that people only lived 20 to 40 years total. Some live much longer; it is the *average* that is 20 to 40 years.

OTHER CAUSES OF DEATH   Apart from endemic infectious disease, what else accounts for the major causes of death in hunting-gathering societies? Injury deaths are one factor. In most environments, death could result from burns and hunting injuries. In arctic hunting-gathering populations, death could also result from drowning and exposure to cold. In some hunting-gathering populations, injuries are the major cause of death (Dunn 1968). For females, an additional factor in low life expectancy is death during childbirth.

Dunn (1968) has also listed a number of types of what he calls "social mortality" in hunting-gathering populations. These are deaths related to cultural behaviors such as infanticide (the killing of newborn children), geronticide (the killing of old people), sacrifice, and warfare. Infanticide and geronticide have been recorded for a number of hunting-gathering populations in past times and have often been interpreted as mechanisms of population size regulation.

Agriculture and Disease

The pattern of human disease is quite different in agricultural societies (both slash-and-burn and intensive agriculture) than that of hunting-gathering societies. Agriculture allows larger population size and requires a

▲▲▲▲▲▲▲▲▲▲▲▲▲▲▲▲▲▲▲▲▲▲▲▲▲▲▲▲▲
life expectancy at birth
A measure of the average length of life for a newborn child.

nonnomadic life. The increased population size and lack of mobility has certain implications for the spread of disease.

INFECTIOUS DISEASE   Large populations of susceptible individuals allow the spread of short-lived microorganisms. Such conditions exist in agricultural populations because of increased population size and the increased probability of coming into contact with someone with the disease. As a result, agricultural populations have often shown epidemics of diseases such as smallpox, measles, mumps, and chicken pox (note that smallpox is no longer a factor; it has been eliminated worldwide, although it was quite a problem in the past). The size of a population needed for an epidemic varies according to disease. Some infectious diseases require larger population sizes for rapid spread.

Sedentary life increases the spread of infectious disease in other ways. Large populations living continuously in the same area can accumulate sewage. Poor sanitation and contamination of the water supply increases the chance for disease epidemics.

Agricultural practices also cause ecological changes, making certain infectious diseases more likely. The introduction of domesticated animals adds to waste accumulation and provides the opportunity for further exposure to diseases carried by animals. Cultivation of the land can also increase the probability of contact with insects carrying disease microorganisms.

The use of feces for fertilization can also have an impact on rates of infectious disease. In addition to contamination from handling these waste products, the food grown in these fertilizers can become contaminated. This problem was so acute in South Korea that steps had to be taken to reduce the use of feces as fertilizer (Cockburn 1971). Also, irrigation can lead to an increase in the spread of infectious disease. One of the major problems in tropical agricultural societies is the increased snail population that lives in irrigation canals and carries schistosomiasis. Irrigation can pass infectious microorganisms from one population to the next (Figure 12.2).

NUTRITIONAL DISEASE   Although agriculture provides populations with the ability to feed more people, this way of life does not guarantee an improvement in nutrition. Extensive investment in a single food crop, such as rice or corn, may provide too limited a diet for many people, and certain nutritional deficiency diseases can result. For example, populations relying extensively on corn as a major food source may show an increase in pellagra (a disease caused by a deficiency in the vitamin niacin) as well as protein deficiency. Dependency on rice is often associated with protein and vitamin deficiencies (McElroy and Townsend 1989). Perhaps the greatest problem of reliance on a single crop is that if that crop fails, starvation can result. The population becomes so dependent on a major crop for all of its food that if a drought or plague wipes it out, not enough food is left for all the people.

■ FIGURE 12.2
Chinese farmers planting rice.
The larger size and sedentary
nature of agricultural
populations contribute to
epidemics of infectious
disease. (Courtesy Kenneth
Feder and Michael Park, Central
Connecticut State University)

An agricultural diet can also lead to dental problems. The increased amount of starches in an agriculturalist's diet, combined with an increase in dirt and grit in the food, can lead to an increase in dental wear and cavities. Such changes are readily apparent in many paleopathological studies (Cohen 1989), showing once more that the advent of agriculture did not mean improved health. On the contrary, such studies have demonstrated that the transition to agriculture was often associated with increases in infectious disease, nutritional deficiencies, and nutritional stress. As with biological evolution, cultural changes have both benefits and costs. Nothing is free.

Urbanization and Disease

Following the origin and spread of agriculture, a number of human populations became urbanized. An urban area is defined in terms of large population size and density as well as a population with occupational specialization that produces a variety of economic goods and services provided to sur-

■ FIGURE 12.3
The skull of a prehistoric
Eskimo who suffered from
syphilis. The marks on the top
of the skull are typical of a
long-term syphilitic infection.
(© Hrdlicka Paleopathology
Collection, Courtesy San Diego
Museum of Man)

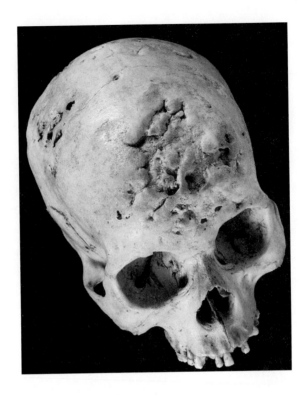

■ FIGURE 12.3
The skull of a prehistoric
Eskimo who suffered from
syphilis. The marks on the top
of the skull are typical of a
long-term syphilitic infection.
(© Hrdlicka Paleopathology
Collection, Courtesy San Diego
Museum of Man)

rounding areas. We can subdivide cities into preindustrial and industrial. Each type of city has its own associated health problems.

DISEASE IN PREINDUSTRIAL CITIES   Preindustrial cities date back to several thousand years B.P. Such cities often developed as market or administrative centers for a region, and their increased population size and density provided ample opportunity for epidemics of infectious disease. In addition, a number of early cities had inadequate sewage disposal and contaminated water, both major factors increasing the spread of epidemics. To feed large numbers of people, food had to be brought in from the surrounding countryside and stored inside the city. In Europe during the Middle Ages, grain was often stored inside the house. Rats and other vermin had easy access to these foods, and their populations increased, furthering the spread of disease. In preindustrial cities located in dry parts of the world, grain was stored in ceramic containers, which limited the access of vermin.

Perhaps the best-known example of an epidemic disease in preindustrial cities is the Black Death in Europe during the fourteenth century. The Black Death is another name for the infectious disease bubonic plague. Caused by a bacterium, the disease affects field rodents, among whom it is spread by fleas. With the development of large urban areas and the corresponding large indoor rat populations, the disease spread to rats in the cities. The rats' fleas then infected humans. The spread of bubonic plague during this time was pandemic, affecting populations throughout Europe. It is estimated that up to 20 million Europeans died from bubonic plague between 1346 and 1352 (McEvedy 1988). The ecological changes accompanying the development of urbanization in Europe provided an opportunity for the rapid spread of fleas, rats, and the disease. Bubonic plague is still around today, including in the American southwest, although treatment by antibiotics has kept the incidence rate low.

DISEASE IN INDUSTRIAL CITIES   Industrialization, which began several centuries ago, accelerated population growth in urban areas. Technological changes allowed more efficient methods of agriculture and provided the means to support more people than in previous eras. The increased growth of urban areas was accompanied initially by further spread of infectious diseases. As industrialization continued, however, the rate of infectious disease declined and the rate of noninfectious disease increased. This shift in disease patterns was accompanied by a reduction in mortality, especially infant mortality, and an increase in life expectancy. In evolutionary terms, all of these changes are very recent.

Culture Contact

With the rise of European exploration in the 1500s, previously separate human populations came into contact with one another. In addition to the vast cultural, economic, and political problems resulting from such contact, infectious diseases could now spread into populations that had no prior immune experience. The results were generally devastating.

The epidemiologic effects of culture contact have been documented for a number of populations, particularly Native Americans and Pacific islanders. Many infectious diseases, such as smallpox, measles, and mumps, were introduced into the New World at this time, leading to massive loss of life in many populations (McNeill 1977; Cohen 1989). A recent review suggests that the actual impact of infectious disease varied across populations— some were hit much harder than others at different times (Larsen 1994). The flow of disease seems to have been primarily in one direction, from the Old World to the New World. One possible exception are treponemal diseases, including venereal syphilis. Venereal syphilis (spread by sexual contact) increased rapidly in Europe after 1500, a date that coincides with the contact between New World and Old World populations. Following European settlement in the Americas, it was also noted that many Native Americans had syphilis. Did the disease evolve in Europe and then spread to the Americas? Or, did it first appear in the New World and then spread to Europe? Evidence from skeletal remains (Figure 12.3) shows that cases of venereal syphilis occurred in the New World *before* European contact. This evidence

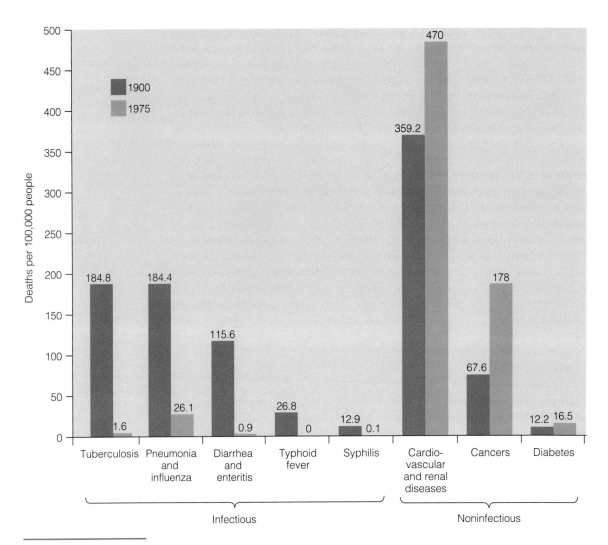

■ **FIGURE 12.4**
Death rates for selected diseases in the United States in 1900 and 1975. Note the decrease in infectious disease deaths and the increase in noninfectious disease deaths.
(*Source of data:* Molnar [1983:219])

rules out the hypothesis that venereal syphilis came from Europe; it appears to have evolved in the New World prior to European contact (Baker and Armelagos 1988).

The Epidemiologic Transition

The shift from infectious diseases to noninfectious diseases as the primary cause of death is a feature of the **epidemiologic transition** model, developed by Omran (1977).

THE NATURE OF THE EPIDEMIOLOGIC TRANSITION   According to Omran's model, a pre-transition population has high death rates, particularly because of epidemics of childhood infectious diseases. As a culture's medical technologies, public health, and sanitation improve, epidemics become less frequent and less intense. Following the transition, the primary cause of death is not infectious diseases but degenerative noninfectious diseases. This shift in disease patterns is also accompanied by an increase in life expectancy at birth.

Figure 12.4 presents death rates per 100,000 people in the United States in 1900 and 1975 for several selected diseases. Note the tremendous decline in the death rates for infectious diseases such as tuberculosis and pneumonia but the increase in death rates from cardiovascular diseases, cancers, and diabetes. In addition, the total number of deaths per year per 100,000 of the population has decreased from 1622 in 1900 to 890 in 1975. A large proportion of this decrease has been a consequence of the reduction of infant mortality (death during the first year of life). In 1900, the infant mortality rate was 162 deaths per 1,000 live births. By 1975, the infant mortality rate had dropped to 14 deaths per 1,000 live births (Molnar 1983).

Thus, there has been a decrease in infectious disease and an increase in noninfectious disease in those societies that have undergone the epidemiologic transition. For the United States, this has resulted in our current pattern of the leading causes of death, shown for 1994 in Figure 12.5. The two major causes of death are heart disease and cancer, followed by stroke, chronic obstructive pulmonary disease, and injuries. Only 2 of the top 12 causes of death in the United States, pneumonia/influenza and AIDS, are infectious diseases.

The epidemiologic transition has also affected life expectancy in developed societies. In the United States in 1900, life expectancy at birth was 49 years. In the United States in 1994, life expectancy had risen to 75.7 years (Haub 1995). Although high, it is not the highest in the world; in 1990, the United States had the sixteenth highest life expectancy at birth in the world (Haub 1992). Not everyone has the same life expectancy at birth. In the United States, females have a higher life expectancy at birth (79 years) than males (72 years), and that for European Americans is higher than that for African Americans (Haub 1995).

The increase in life expectancy is not confined to developed societies. Other groups undergoing modernization and the epidemiologic transition have also shown an increase, such as the residents of the modernizing population of American Samoa. From 1950 to 1980, life expectancy at birth increased 10 years for males and 18 years for females (Crews 1989).

A controversial topic today is the extent to which life expectancy can be expected to increase in developed societies. Based on statistical analysis of death rates, Olshansky and colleagues (1990) argue that even with major reductions in chronic disease, life expectancy at birth will not increase past 85 years of age.

▲▲▲▲▲▲▲▲▲▲▲▲▲▲▲▲▲▲▲▲▲▲▲▲▲▲▲▲▲▲

epidemiologic transition The change in disease patterns in which there is a decline in infectious diseases and an increase in noninfectious diseases.

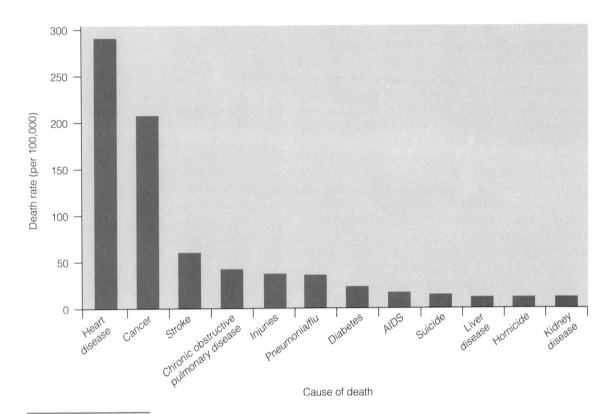

■ FIGURE 12.5
The 12 leading causes of
death in the United States in
1994. The death rate is the
number of deaths per year per
100,000 people. (*Source of
data:* Haub [1995])

In the United States, the last century has seen a reduction in infant mortality, a reduction in infectious diseases as the cause of death, an increase in noninfectious diseases as the cause of death, and an overall increase in life expectancy at birth. There appears to have been no overall change in the total life span of humans, however. **Life span** is the measure of maximum longevity. Discounting Biblical accounts of Methuselah and other unsubstantiated claims, there have been no verified claims of humans living past 120 years. Changes in medicine and health care have increased life expectancy, but they have not, as yet, increased the human life span. This means that more and more people are likely to reach the limit of life, a phenomenon with far-reaching implications that will be discussed in the next chapter.

What has caused these rapid changes in disease rates and life expectancy? Cultural changes in industrial societies have often resulted in average improvements in health care, public sanitation, and water quality. These factors aid in reducing the spread and effect of infectious diseases, particularly in infancy. As a result, more people are likely to live to older ages—long enough, therefore, to develop the long-term noninfectious diseases, such as cancer. These diseases often require lengthy periods of time to reach a debil-

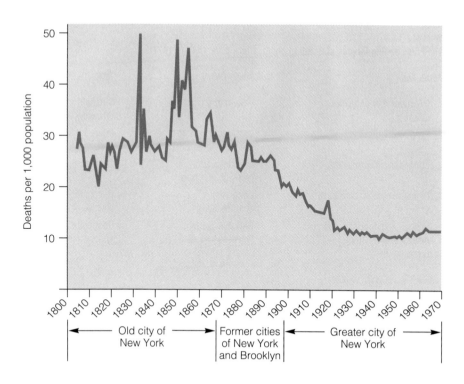

■ FIGURE 12.6
Changes in the death rate in
New York City during the
nineteenth and twentieth
centuries. (*Source:* Omran
[1977:12]. Courtesy of the
Population Reference Bureau, Inc.,
Washington, D.C.)

itating stage. A person who dies in early life from an infectious disease will obviously not have had sufficient time to develop noninfectious disorders.

Other contributing factors are changes in the physical environment brought about by urbanization and industrialization. Industrial pollution of the air and water can lead to increased levels of cancer and other non-infectious diseases. Technological and social changes have also led to the increased abundance of drugs such as alcohol and tobacco, which increase disease. Widespread use of infant formula, rather than breast feeding, in poor countries contributes greatly to infant and childhood health problems. Factors such as stress, lifestyle, crowding, and noise levels also appear to play a role in the disease process.

STUDIES OF THE EPIDEMIOLOGIC TRANSITION The relationship between cultural change and disease rates emerges clearly in specific case studies of the epidemiologic transition. Omran (1977) looked at overall death rates in his study of the epidemiologic transition in New York City. Figure 12.6 shows the changing overall death rate in New York City over time. Before the 1860s, the overall death rate was high and had frequent spikes, primarily because of epidemics of cholera. Following the mid-1860s, both the overall death rate and the intensity of epidemics declined. This decrease corresponds with the establishment of the Health Department. After the 1920s,

life span A measure of the maximum length of life recorded for a species.

■ TABLE 12.2
The Five Leading Causes of Death in Manti, Utah, from 1849 to 1977

1849–1889	1890–1929	1930–1977
1. Infectious and parasitic diseases	Respiratory diseases	Circulatory system diseases
2. Respiratory diseases	Circulatory system diseases	Injuries
3. Congenital abnormalities	Infectious and parasitic diseases	Cancers
4. Digestive system diseases	Congenital abnormalities	Respiratory diseases
5. Injuries, genitourinary system diseases, and nervous system diseases (tied)	Digestive system diseases	Congenital abnormalities

Source: Levison et al. (1981:90)

the spread of better sanitation and water supplies along with an improvement in drugs and health care and the introduction of pasteurized milk caused the death rates to decline even more.

Another study of the epidemiologic transition has been carried out on a smaller scale. Levison and colleagues (1981) analyzed census and burial data from the town of Manti, Utah, from 1849 to 1977. Their study focused on changes in disease patterns as the town changed from a frontier population (1849–1889) to a transitional rural agricultural population (1890–1929) to a modern agricultural community (1930–1977). Census data showed that the life expectancy at birth increased over time, and the major causes of death changed. Table 12.2 lists the five leading causes of death for the three periods. Infectious and parasitic diseases dropped from the primary cause of death in the initial frontier stage to the third cause of death during the transitional stage; it was not among the top five causes of death in the modern stage. Another major shift took place in circulatory diseases, which were not among the top five causes of death in the frontier stage but rose to the second place in the transitional stage and the primary cause of death in the modern stage. By the modern stage, cancers had also risen to become the third cause of death. The changes in disease patterns were associated with improved sanitation, elimination of dependence on contaminated water supplies, and the adoption of newer medical techniques. The type of pattern shown in the Manti study parallels those found in other studies of the epidemiologic transition.

Not all human populations today have experienced the epidemiologic transition. In many Third World nations death rates, especially among

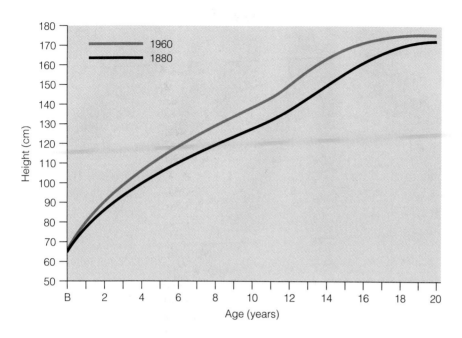

■ FIGURE 12.7
Secular change in European-
American males in North
America. At all ages the males
living in 1960 have greater
height than those who lived
in 1880. (From *Growth and
Development* by Robert M. Malina
© 1975, publisher Burgess
Publishing Company,
Minneapolis, MN)

infants and children, remain high. Inadequate health care, poor sanitation, contaminated water, poor nutrition, and warfare continue to produce high levels of mortality. These populational differences show up most clearly in rates of infant mortality. Worldwide, 8 percent of all children die in the first year of life. In a few nations, such as Japan, this rate is as low as 1 percent, whereas in some Asian and African nations it is as high as 20 percent (Teitelbaum 1988).

Secular Changes in Human Growth

The epidemiologic transition affects more than disease and death rates; its effects have also been observed in studies of child growth. During the past century, many industrialized nations have shown several secular changes in child growth. A **secular change** is simply a change in the pattern of growth across generations.

TYPES OF SECULAR CHANGES   Three basic secular changes have been observed over the past century: (1) an increase in height, (2) an increase in weight, and (3) a decrease in the age of sexual maturation. Children in many Westernized nations are today taller and heavier than children the same age a century or so ago. Figure 12.7 shows the average distance curve for height of North American males of European ancestry in 1880 and 1960. There is no notice-able difference in body length at birth. Note, however, that at all postnatal

secular change A
change in the average
pattern of growth in
a population over
different generations.

■ FIGURE 12.8
Secular change in age at
menarche (the age of the
female's first menstrual
period) in the United States
and several European
countries. (From *Growth and
Development* by Robert M. Malina
© 1975, publisher Burgess
Publishing Company,
Minneapolis, MN)

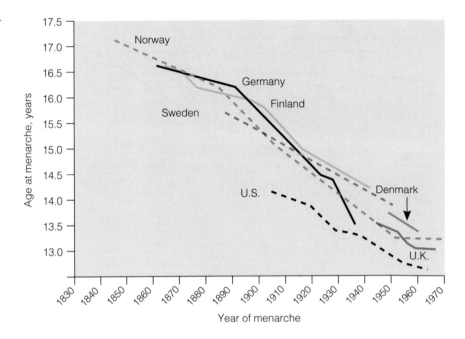

ages the 1960 males are consistently taller than the 1880 males. This difference is most noticeable during adolescence. Comparison of distance curves for weight show the same pattern.

Another secular change is a decrease in the age of maturation. This is most apparent in a specific measure of human development—the **age at menarche,** the age at which a female experiences her first menstrual period. Figure 12.8 plots the average age at menarche for the United States and several European industrial nations over time. The general trend is one of earlier biological maturation.

CAUSES OF SECULAR CHANGE   The basic secular changes observed in industrialized nations during the past century reflect environmental change. There is no evidence that genetic potential has changed in such a short period of time; rather, environmental changes have allowed more people to reach their genetic potential for growth. These trends, however, should not be projected indefinitely into the future! Some data suggest that the secular changes in height, weight, and age at menarche have slowed down or stopped in some countries (Eveleth and Tanner 1990). Future environmental improvements could allow more and more children to reach their genetic potential for growth, but we should not expect average heights of 8 feet or more in another 100 years!

Many environmental factors have been suggested as responsible for these secular changes, including improved nutrition, reduction of childhood infectious disease, improved availability of health care, improved standard of living, and reduction of family size. Many of these factors are inter-related, making precise identification of causes difficult.

Malina (1979) notes that improved nutrition has often been cited as a primary cause of the observed secular changes. Though availability of nutritional intake has improved for many people, especially during infancy, Malina does not think it is solely responsible for secular changes. Many factors have operated together to produce the secular changes. Malina does suggest that one of the most important factors was an improvement in health conditions, resulting in the reduction in childhood infectious disease. Thus, the epidemiologic transition appears to be related to secular changes in human growth as well.

Some Contemporary Issues

The evolution of human health and disease did not end with the epidemiologic transition—it continues today. Cultural influences on disease continue to change, as does the environment and even the organisms responsible for infectious disease. Although even a review of all contemporary health problems is beyond the scope of an introductory text, several brief examples are given to illustrate *some* of our species' current health issues.

THE "NEW WORLD SYNDROME"   Kenneth Weiss and colleagues (1984) have applied the label **New World syndrome** to a set of noninfectious diseases that appear in elevated frequencies among Native Americans and groups with substantial Native-American admixture. These diseases include noninsulin-dependent diabetes (Figure 12.9), gallstones, gall bladder cancer, and increased obesity. Rates for these diseases tend to be highest in Native-American populations. Among admixed populations, such as Mexicans and Mexican Americans, the disease rates vary with the amount of Native-American admixture. In other words, the more Native-American ancestry a person has, the greater the risk of developing these diseases, other factors being equal. In addition, all these diseases tend to run in families.

These three characteristics point to genetic susceptibility to the diseases among Native-American peoples. Noninfectious diseases, however, are affected not only by genetic predispositions but also by environmental factors. In the case of the New World syndrome, rates of these diseases have increased dramatically since World War II. To understand this increase, we

▲▲

age at menarche The age at which a female experiences her first menstrual period.

New World syndrome A set of noninfectious diseases that appears in elevated frequencies in

persons of Native-American ancestry.

■ FIGURE 12.9
Prevalence rates (percent) for noninsulin-dependent diabetes in selected samples from the United States, and grouped by ethnicity: European Americans, Mexican Americans, and Native Americans. Native Americans have the highest prevalence rates, followed by Mexican Americans (who have considerable Native-American ancestry). (*Source of data:* Weiss et al. [1984], using samples that consist of adults 25 years or older)

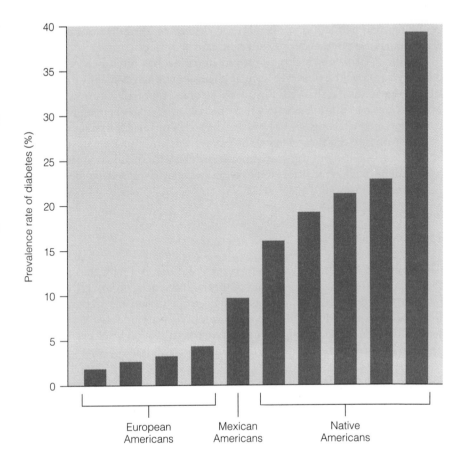

need to look not only at genetic factors but also at changing environmental conditions.

Weiss and colleagues argue there is strong evidence that genetic susceptibilities to the New World syndrome diseases existed in the earliest inhabitants of the Americas. If such genetic predispositions are unique among New World populations, then there must have been rapid genetic change since the initial occupation of the Americas by migrants from Asia. Weiss and colleagues think that the genes that currently predispose individuals to the New World syndrome were originally advantageous. Today, however, these same genetic factors are generally disadvantageous. Weiss and colleagues therefore ask the question: "What kind of gene has disadvantage now but advantage among northern hunter-gatherers?" (1984:171). They suggest that the relationship of all diseases in the syndrome to nutrient utilization provides a possible answer: these genes conferred changes in metabolism, allowing more efficient use of food resources and fat storage. Given the importance of fat resources in hunting-gathering populations, particularly during pregnancy and nursing, such genes would be advantageous in an environment characterized by frequent food shortages.

Today, however, these same genetic factors are proving disadvantageous to individuals with Native-American ancestry. The reason may lie in the continued "westernization" of these populations and the associated changes in diet. An increase in carbohydrates and fats in the diet will result in greater fat storage, leading to obesity and increased risk for other noninfectious disorders. Populations without Native-American ancestry have also shown increases in certain noninfectious diseases because of changes in culture and lifestyle. Native Americans and related populations, however, show even greater increases because of their additional genetic susceptibility.

AIDS At present, **acquired immune deficiency syndrome (AIDS)** is a growing medical problem in many parts of the world. This disease results in the breakdown of the body's immune defense system, ultimately leading to death. Research has linked AIDS to infection from HIV (human immunodeficiency virus). The origin of HIV is unclear, but it may have started as a zoonosis. The virus is transmitted through sexual intercourse, particularly anal intercourse. AIDS is also transmitted by transfusions of contaminated blood and by sharing of contaminated needles among drug users. The disease can also be transmitted from an infected pregnant woman to her fetus.

From 1981 through the end of 1994, over 440,000 cases of AIDS have been reported in the United States, based on the revised diagnostic criteria of 1993. Of these cases, over 270,000 had died by the end of 1994. Analysis of new cases diagnosed in 1994 shows that the vast majority of adult or adolescent cases were male (82 percent). Analysis of risk factors among male and female adults and adolescents (Figure 12.10) shows the primary risk group is men who have had sex with another man (44 percent), followed by male intravenous drug users (20 percent). The next largest category is women who are IV drug users (7 percent), followed by women who obtained AIDS through heterosexual contact (slightly less than 7 percent) and finally, men who obtained AIDS through heterosexual contact (slightly less than 4 percent) (Centers for Disease Control and Prevention 1995).

In other parts of the world the epidemiologic pattern of AIDS risk is different. In much of Africa, for example, the primary spread of AIDS is through heterosexual contact (McGrath 1990). Although some feel that the AIDS epidemic is slowing down in the United States, the epidemic in Africa is still increasing, with indication of an increase in Asia as well. As of 1993, an estimated 12 million people worldwide had the HIV virus (Cowley 1993).

Even though AIDS is a recent disease, it has already had major effects on American culture. The threat of such a deadly disease has led to proposed quarantines, increased discrimination against homosexuals, and the burning of houses of AIDS-infected children. Perhaps the greatest change, however, has been a reduction in sexual activity with multiple partners or with partners whose backgrounds are not known.

▲▲▲▲▲▲▲▲▲▲▲▲▲▲▲▲▲▲▲▲▲▲▲▲▲▲▲▲▲▲

acquired immune deficiency syndrome (AIDS) A fatal viral disease that results in the breakdown of the body's immune defense system.

■ FIGURE 12.10
Risk factors of new cases
of AIDS in the United States
in 1994. (*Source of data:*
Centers for Disease Control and
Prevention, 1995)

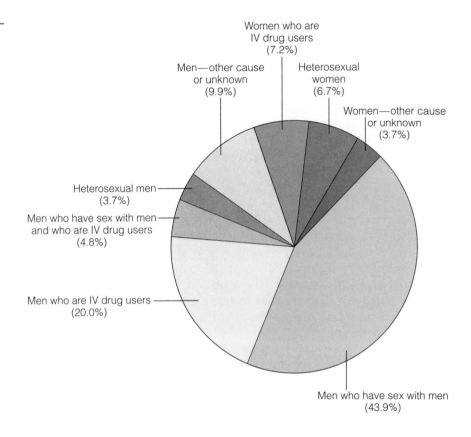

In sum, the current spread of AIDS shows us a clear example of how a disease can affect society both biologically and culturally. This is not a new phenomenon. During the Middle Ages, the Black Death continued to have a profound effect on culture long after the epidemics were over. Images of death and despair endured in the arts and in literature.

By studying diseases such as AIDS and the Black Death, medical anthropologists not only contribute to an understanding of the spread of diseases but also show us the relationships between disease and society. We cannot view health and disease as an isolated segment of our total lives. They affect all aspects of living.

PROTEIN-CALORIE MALNUTRITION Low quantity and quality of nutrition is a major problem in the world today, affecting millions of infants and children. Undernutrition, particularly during infancy, can have severe effects. Not only is the physical growth stunted, but mental retardation may also result. Without an adequate diet, infants and children are more susceptible to infectious disease. Severe undernutrition is highly prevalent in Third World nations, where poor nutrition is often associated with overpopulation, poverty, inad-

The Coming Plague?

In May 1995, the world focused much of its attention on Zaire, in Africa, where there was an outbreak of a frequently fatal disease: Ebola. Although the Ebola virus was only discovered in 1976, previous epidemics had killed hundreds of people in Zaire and Uganda. The Ebola virus is very mysterious; its origin is still unknown and it is not clear what factors precipitate epidemics (Cowley et al. 1995).

What makes this recent outbreak alarming is that it is not the only case of a recent epidemic of an infectious disease. There have been a number of newly identified infectious diseases within the past few decades, including the HIV virus that causes AIDS. Other examples include Lyme disease, the Kyasanur Forest virus, the O'nyong-nyong virus, hepatitis C and E viruses, Legionnaire's disease, toxic-shock syndrome, and cat-scratch fever, among others. There have also been new variants of old diseases, such as a new type of cholera bacterium and strains of tuberculosis that are antibiotic-resistant (Levins et al. 1994; Karlen 1995).

The continued outbreak of new infectious diseases, and the reemergence of old ones, has caused scientists to reevaluate the historic nature of the epidemiologic transition. In 1975, it was written that virtually all infectious diseases had been eliminated in the Western world (Levins et al. 1994). Smallpox was eliminated worldwide in 1977, and tuberculosis and polio were close behind. It was perhaps natural for many to feel optimistic regarding these changes, and to project the epidemiologic transition into the future, where all infectious diseases had been conquered.

The situation now looks much more complex. It is unlikely that infectious diseases will be eliminated. The microorganisms responsible for such diseases continue to evolve, often resulting in new and devastating epidemics. In addition, we have to keep in mind that human culture continually modifies the environment, such that old diseases often get a new opportunity for growth, or evolve themselves to adapt to the new environment. Rates of tuberculosis, for example, have risen in past years in some locations after a long period of steady decline. It seems that the tuberculosis bacterium has evolved a resistance to the traditional antibiotics used to control it. What this means is that we must now seek new antibiotics, which in turn will likely lead to new antibiotic-resistant strains of tuberculosis. Because microorganisms evolve faster than humans, we might find ourselves in an eternal struggle to catch up.

Any time the environment changes, there is an opportunity for the emergence of new infectious diseases. New technologies often lend themselves to the development of infectious disease by creating microenvironments conducive to bacterial spread. Air-conditioning, for example, is implicated in the origin and spread of Legionnaire's disease. New environments are also created by rapid deforestation and conversion of land for agriculture and industrialization. In addition, this continued conversion of remote and isolated habitats allows previously rare microorganisms to come into contact with the human species. Another problem is that continued pollution increases the mutation rate of microorganisms in addition to interfering with ecosystems (Levins et al. 1994). Also, we live in a world where it is easier than ever for an infectious disease to spread across nations and continents. New forms of travel (such as the airplane) and international commerce allow quick contact between human groups, including those that have no prior immune experience (Levins et al. 1994; Karlen 1995).

The continued emergence of infectious diseases, particularly those that are antibiotic-resistant and often fatal, has led many to suggest that our problems with infectious disease are far from over, and indeed may soon rise again. One current example is a book entitled *The Coming Plague* (1994) by Laurie Garrett, who warns of these problems and others. Will we soon see the emergence of worldwide pandemics equivalent in mortality to the Black Death of the Middle Ages or the 1918 influenza pandemic, both of which killed millions of people? Will we someday look back on the latter half of the twentieth century as a "golden age," where epidemic infectious diseases were *temporarily* controlled by drugs before the microorganisms evolved beyond them? Although the future is unknown, it is now clear to all that predictions about the elimination of infectious disease were premature. We will always have to deal with infectious disease, and the nature of the threat will change over time as the microorganisms continue to evolve and as we continue to change our environment. We win many battles, but we cannot give up even for a moment in the fight against infectious disease.

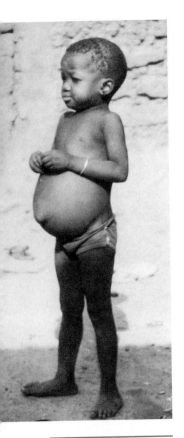

■ FIGURE 12.11
Child with kwashiorkor in
Mali, West Africa. (Courtesy
Katherine Dettwyler)

equate sewage disposal, contaminated water, high rates of infectious disease, and economic and political conflicts.

A number of nutritional problems, collectively known as **protein-calorie malnutrition,** results from an inadequate amount of proteins and/or calories in the diet. Protein-calorie malnutrition is the most serious nutritional problem on the planet. Its various forms have different physical symptoms, but all stem from the basic problems of an inadequate diet and have the same ultimate effects, ranging from growth retardation to death.

The most severe types of protein-calorie malnutrition are **kwashiorkor** (a severe deficiency in proteins but not calories) and **marasmus** (severe deficiencies in both proteins and calories). Kwashiorkor occurs most often in infants and young children who are weaned from their mother's breast onto a diet lacking in proteins. The infant suffers growth retardation, muscle wasting, and lowered resistance to disease. One of the symptoms of kwashiorkor is the swelling of the body (Figure 12.11). Marasmus is also most prevalent during infancy and similarly leads to growth retardation, muscle wasting, and death. A child suffering from marasmus typically looks emaciated (Figure 12.12). The devastating effects of protein-calorie malnutrition should not be underestimated; between 5 and 45 percent of children in some developing nations suffer from one of these nutritional diseases.

Although the physical appearance of children with kwashiorkor and marasmus differs, both suffer from an inadequate diet. Population pressure and poverty certainly play a major role in much of protein-calorie malnutrition, but they are not the only factors that come into play. Some researchers, such as anthropologist Katherine Dettwyler, have argued that cultural beliefs regarding nutrition are at least as important. Such beliefs include stressing quantity over quality, postponing the age at which children eat solid foods, and other practices that compromise proper nutrition. Thus, the elimination of protein-calorie malnutrition will require more than an attack on population growth and the reduction of disease; it will also require nutritional education (Dettwyler 1994).

THE DEMOGRAPHIC EVOLUTION OF HUMAN POPULATIONS

The interrelationship of biology and culture in human populations is perhaps most clearly visible in demographic patterns. **Demography** is the study of the size, composition, and distribution of human populations. Like epidemiology, demography is an interdisciplinary subject. Demography is studied by anthropologists, biologists, geographers, historians, economists, sociologists, and others.

As with the study of human health and disease, anthropology brings to demography comparative, evolutionary, and holistic perspectives. Anthropologists do not focus only on demographic processes within a single society, such as the United States. We examine all types of societies, from

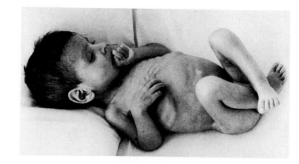

■ FIGURE 12.12
A child with marasmus, a severe protein and calorie deficiency. (World Health Organization photo by A. Isaza)

hunter-gatherers, to agricultural, to industrialized nations. We also look at demographic processes in an evolutionary context, seeking to understand demographic shifts in the evolution of our species. Using a holistic perspective, we link demographic processes with patterns of biological and cultural variation.

The Study of Demography

Demographic studies focus on the measurement of three characteristics: fertility, mortality, and migration.

DEMOGRAPHIC MEASURES   In literate human populations the demographic measures of fertility, mortality, and migration are often revealed in census records and similar data. Birth records, for example, provide data for computing different measures of fertility. Death records provide information for determining the rate of deaths, the age at death, and the cause of death. In societies where written records are not kept, anthropologists gather demographic data from interviews. The measure of fertility provides us with information on the rate of actual births in a population. When we count birth records or interview people to find out how many children they have had, we are measuring the **fertility** of a population. On the other hand, we are also sometimes interested in measurements of **fecundity,** or the number of individuals capable of having children. Measurements of fertility and fecundity are not always the same; people that are capable of having children do not necessarily have them.

protein-calorie malnutrition A group of nutritional diseases resulting from inadequate amounts of protein and/or calories.

kwashiorkor An extreme form of protein-calorie malnutrition resulting from a severe deficiency in proteins but not calories.

marasmus An extreme form of protein-calorie malnutrition resulting from severe deficiencies in both proteins and calories.

demography The study of the size, composition, and distribution of human populations.

fertility Actual reproduction: the number of births per individual.

fecundity Potential reproduction: the number of people capable of having children.

■ FIGURE 12.13
Mortality rates in the United States in 1970 as a function of age. This figure shows the typical mortality curve for human populations. Death rates decrease rapidly after the first year of life and increase again among the elderly. (*Source of data:* Fries and Crapo [1981:146])

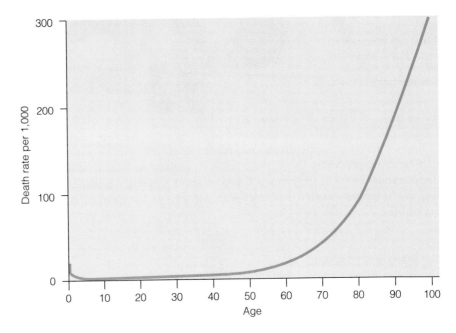

The measure of **mortality** is the measurement of death. Like fertility, mortality can be influenced by biological and cultural factors. The age at death and the cause of death may relate to biological factors, such as susceptibility to certain diseases. Culture can also affect the timing and cause of death. Differences in social class may affect quality of health care. Warfare may increase the probability of early death, as will hazardous employment. A long history of drug use or poor nutrition also affects the probability of death.

Mortality rates are strongly related to age. Plotting death rates against age gives a characteristic curve, as shown in Figure 12.13 for the United States in 1970. Death rates drop quickly after the first year of life, remaining relatively low and constant through midadulthood. Death rates increase rapidly with age among the elderly. The *exact* shape of the curve will vary from one population to the another. In underdeveloped nations, for example, infant mortality will be higher. The overall shape of the curve is basically the same in all human populations (Gage 1989).

Migration is the movement of people, normally for long periods of time, from one location (village, city, state, country) to another. As with fertility and mortality, migration is affected by biological and cultural factors and in turn has an effect on biology and culture.

POPULATION GROWTH   The overall size of a population results from the net effects of fertility, mortality, and migration. Births increase the population size and deaths decrease the population size. Migration can either increase or decrease the population size, depending on whether more people move into

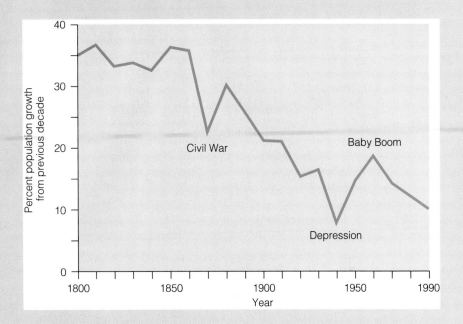

Changes in the rate of population growth in the United States from 1790 to 1990. The percentage of increase in population size from the previous decade is plotted against year. Note the reversal of the downward trend during the Baby Boom years.

the mid-1980s, the average number of children per couple was less than replacement (that is, less than two children on average per couple). Of course, the United States continues to grow because so many women were born during the Baby Boom. Even if the average number of children per women is less than two, the sheer number of women will continue to lead to increased population growth for a short time. In fact, the total number of births in the United States rose starting in 1977 and peaked in 1990 (Gabriel 1995). This short burst of births is often referred to as the "Baby Boomlet," brought about by the fact that so many of the original Baby Boomers were now in their child-bearing years. Thus, the Baby Boom continues to affect fertility levels and population growth a generation later.

(*Source of data:* U.S. Department of Commerce 1991)

The demographic transition model has several problems. Mortality and fertility rates represent a continuous range and cannot easily be separated into "low" and "high" phases. Situations unique to certain populations, such as the Baby Boom in the United States, may result in fluctuating rates of fertility (see the Special Topic box). Also, it is not clear to what extent stage 1 has been characteristic of most human history (Swedlund and Armelagos 1976). In spite of these problems and others, the model does provide a rough summary of the types of average changes found accompanying economic and industrial development.

WORLD POPULATION GROWTH The total human population of the world has increased throughout human evolution, especially during the past several centuries. Estimates of prehistoric population size are crude, but they do provide us with an idea of the extent of population growth. For example,

■ FIGURE 12.16
World population growth
since the origin of agriculture.
(From *Population: An Introduction
to Concepts and Issues*, Second
Edition, by John R. Weeks © 1978
by Wadsworth Publishing
Company)

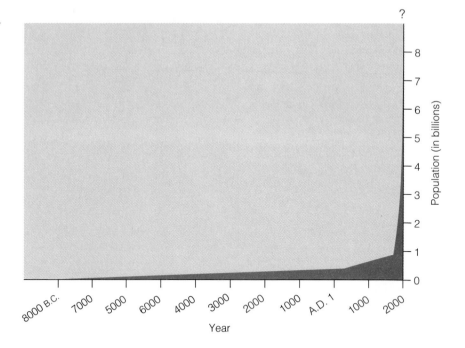

the total world population 50,000 years B.P. was most likely to be in the neighborhood of 1.3 million people. By 10,000 years B.P., the estimated population was 6 million people (Weiss 1984). These low numbers are consistent with what we know about hunting-and-gathering cultures and their carrying capacities.

Following the development and spread of agriculture, the population of the world increased more and more rapidly. The major acceleration came following the Industrial Revolution (roughly 1750). Since this time, the world's population has increased at an exponential rate to the present size (Figure 12.16). Between 1750 and 1950, the world's population tripled in size. Between 1950 and 1990, the world's population increased from 2.5 billion to 5.3 billion—an increase of 112 percent (Horiuchi 1992). The world population was estimated to be 5,607,000,000 people in mid-1994. The current rate of growth is an increase of roughly 245,000 people per day, reflecting an estimated 386,000 births and 141,000 deaths each day (Haub 1995).

The projected world population in the year 2000 is over 6 billion, and over 8 billion by the year 2050 (Haub 1992). Such projections are difficult to compute, relying on extrapolation of current trends. It is possible to be overly optimistic or pessimistic when evaluating trends. Bouvier (1984) believes that by the year 2034 the actual rate of world population growth will begin to diminish. This estimate is based on the continued transition to developed nations, an increase in the efforts to control fertility in developing nations, and a continued increase in life expectancy throughout the world.

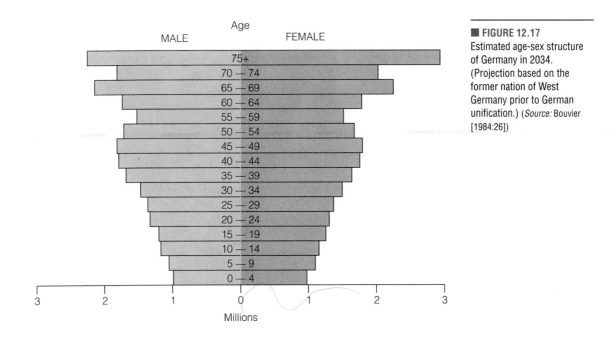

Age

MALE   FEMALE

75+
70 — 74
65 — 69
60 — 64
55 — 59
50 — 54
45 — 49
40 — 44
35 — 39
30 — 34
25 — 29
20 — 24
15 — 19
10 — 14
5 — 9
0 — 4

3   2   1   0   1   2   3

Millions

■ FIGURE 12.17
Estimated age-sex structure of Germany in 2034. (Projection based on the former nation of West Germany prior to German unification.) (*Source:* Bouvier [1984:26])

Regardless of the specific estimate, the current trend is toward continued population growth. Many people are concerned with a probable lack of resources, such as food and energy. Others feel less concerned and believe new technologies will help bridge the gap between population size and resources. Many developing nations today are making efforts to control fertility, such as providing increased awareness of birth control. The effectiveness of such measures varies depending on the political, economic, social, and religious nature of specific nations.

Implications of Changing Age Structure

The transition to developed nations with low rates of fertility and mortality will lead to many changes in culture. The age-sex structure of such nations continues to show a shrinking base and a widening apex. As fewer people are born and as people live longer, the age-sex structure of developed nations will continue to resemble a rectangle. Figure 12.17 shows the estimated population pyramid of western Germany in the year 2034, based on current trends and expected economic changes. Bouvier (1984) presented this figure as typical of a Western European developed nation that is expected to become more of a service and information-based economy and less a manufacturing-based economy. Figure 12.17 shows that the elderly will make up the majority of such a population.

We can expect many cultural changes to accompany such a shift to an older population. Many of these shifts are apparent today in North America. For example, if we assume current average ages for retirement, it is clear that there will be fewer people of working age in the future. Such a shift might be seen as having both advantages and disadvantages. A smaller labor pool might mean better economic opportunities for working-age people. On the other hand, we may also expect greater taxation to help provide for the well-being of the retired portion of the population.

Many questions are being asked by those concerned with social and economic shifts. For example, how well will our Social Security system function when more people are drawing from it? What changes need to be made in the insurance industries? How can we provide adequate health and other care to an aging population?

Economic shifts can also be examined. Perhaps one of the best examples of the effects of changing age structure is in our system of higher education. During the 1960s and early 1970s, as more and more Baby Boom children reached college age, the demand for colleges and universities increased. This demand was accompanied by an increased desire for a college education, in part because of a changing economy and the value of a college degree in earning potential. As college enrollments increased, more schools were built, and more faculty and staff were hired. By the mid-1970s, the effects of the Baby Boom were over, and enrollments began to diminish at many institutions. How, then, can we afford to maintain our colleges? Increases in tuition and taxes are remedies, but they are generally not very popular. Should schools be closed? If so, what happens to the local economies, which are often highly dependent on these schools? What about the future? If we cut back on programs now, will we need to start them up again in a few years?

Business provides another example of these far-reaching changes. Sound business practice dictates the gearing of products to specific age groups. As the numbers in different age groups change, so does demand for specific products. In the entertainment industry, for example, teenagers have been, and still are, major consumers of tapes and compact discs. As our population ages, however, there will be more demand for tapes and CDs from the growing middle-aged population. Today this is apparent in the Baby Boomers' demands for "oldies," music from the time they were teenagers. What type of changes will occur in this industry and others in the future as a consequence of the changing age structure?

These questions have no easy answers. Awareness of the problems and their connection to a variety of economic, social, and political factors is a start in the right direction. Today's world is marked by an unusually high level of change. A society's successful integration of demographic change requires analysis of current trends and, above all, a basic acknowledgment that, for good or ill, these changes are indeed taking place.

SUMMARY

The rapid cultural changes in our species over the past 12,000 years have led to many alterations in human biological variation, including changes in patterns of health and disease and in the demographic structure of our species. Anthropogy's comparative approach allows us to look at the relationships of health and disease to cultural as well as to biological evolution. Hunting-gathering populations have different patterns of disease than do agricultural or industrialized populations. Ecological differences account for much of this difference. In hunting-gathering populations, the group size is too small to sustain large epidemics; the major causes of death are from injuries and infections from animals. In agricultural societies, population size is larger, the group is sedentary, and there are often problems in sewage disposal and water supply; all of these factors result in increased epidemics of infectious disease.

Industrialized nations have gone through an "epidemiologic transition": the primary causes of death have shifted again, from infectious to noninfectious diseases. The epidemiologic transition was brought about by a variety of factors, perhaps the most significant of which was the development of clean water and the proper disposal of sewage. This change in disease patterns has had other effects as well. Life expectancy at birth has increased, primarily because of the elimination or reduction of childhood infectious diseases. There have also been several secular changes in human growth, with children being taller and heavier at any given age, and reaching sexual maturity more quickly. These changes also relate to the reduction of infectious diseases. This reduction in the amount of infectious diseases means that more of us live to older ages, and as a consequence we are more likely to develop chronic noninfectious diseases.

The demographic structure of human populations has also been affected strongly by rapid cultural change. Populations with high fertility and mortality rates have more infants and young children than any other age group. As populations undergo economic development, the mortality rate drops, leading to both population growth and an increase in the proportion of older people. The demographic implications of changing economic development are often summarized in terms of a "demographic transition," where mortality rates drop first and then later a drop in fertility rates follows.

Patterns of fertility and mortality are affected extensively by cultural change. In today's world, the total population continues to increase, particularly among Third World nations. In the United States, population growth continues but at a slower rate than in the recent past. Changes in demographic structure will lead in the near future to strikingly different distributions of the world's population, both by nation and age group.

SUPPLEMENTAL READINGS

Cohen, M. N. 1989. *Health and the Rise of Civilization*. New Haven: Yale University Press. An excellent review of epidemiologic changes in the human species prior to industrialization, with particular attention to the transition from hunting and gathering to agriculture.

Karlen, A. 1995. *Man and Microbes: Diseases and Plagues in History and Modern Times*. New York: G. P. Putnam. A review of the history of infectious disease in the human species, including some discussion of the future.

Scientific American, ed. 1974. *The Human Population*. San Francisco: W. H. Freeman. Although out of date, this collection of papers from *Scientific American* is still a good introduction to the field of demography.

Epilogue:
The Future of
Our Species

This book has focused on human biological variation and evolution, past and present. What about the future? Can biological anthropology, or indeed any science, make predictions about the future of our species? What possible directions will our biological and cultural evolution take?

One thing is for certain—we continue to evolve both biologically and culturally and will do so in the future. Human evolution is increasingly complex because of our biocultural nature. Much of our adaptive nature is culturally based. We can adapt to a situation more quickly through cultural evolution than through biological evolution. Theoretically, we can also direct our cultural evolution. We can focus our efforts on solutions to specific problems, such as finding a vaccine for AIDS or developing ways to further reduce dental decay. Biological evolution, however, has no inherent direction. Natural selection works on existing variation, not on what we might desire or need.

Our success with cultural adaptations should not lead us to conclude that we do not continue to evolve biologically. Regardless of our triumphs in the field of medicine, many incurable diseases still carry on the process of natural selection. Biological variation still takes place in potential and realized fertility. Perhaps as many as a third to half of all human conceptions fail to produce live births. We still live in a world in which up to 50 percent of the children have an inadequate diet. Even if all inhabitants of the world were raised to an adequate standard of living tomorrow, we would still be subject to natural selection and biological evolution. The fact that we are cultural organisms does not detract from the fact that we are also biological organisms. Scholars in various fields throughout history have argued about whether humans and human behavior should be studied biologically, as products of nature, or culturally, as products of nurture. Both sides were wrong. Humans must be studied as *both* biological and cultural organisms.

Given that we will continue to evolve, *how* will we evolve? This question cannot be answered. Evolution has many random elements that cannot be predicted. Also, the biocultural nature of humans makes prediction even harder. The incredible rate of cultural and technological change in the past century was not predicted. What kinds of cultural evolution are possible in the next hundred years? We may be able to forecast some short-term changes, but we know nothing about the cultural capabilities of our species hundreds or thousands of years in the future.

Another problem is that our own viewpoint can influence our predictions. An optimistic view might focus on the success of past cultural adaptations and the rate of acquisition of knowledge and then develop a scenario including increased standard of living for all, cheap energy sources, and an elevated life expectancy. A pessimistic view might consider all the horrors of the past and present, and project a grim future. A pessimist might envisage widespread famine, overcrowding, pollution, disease, and warfare. Most likely, any possible future will be neither pie-in-the-sky nor doom, but a combination of positive and negative changes. If the study of evolution tells us one thing, it is that every change has potential costs and benefits. We need to temper our optimism and pessimism with a sense of balance.

In any consideration of the future, we must acknowledge change as basic to life. Many people find it tempting to suggest we would be better off living a "simpler" life. Others argue that we should stop trying to deal with our problems and let nature take its course or that we should trust in the acts of God. This is unacceptable—indeed our understanding of human evolution argues for the reverse. Our adaptive pattern has been one of learning and problem solving. More than that, this is our primate heritage. Our biology has allowed us to develop the basic mammalian patterns of learned behavior to a high degree. We have the capability for rational thought, for reason, and for learning. Even if many of our cultural inventions have led to suffering and pain, our *potential* for good is immense. In any case, we must continue along the path of learning and intelligence; it is our very nature. Good or bad, the capabilities of the human mind and spirit may be infinite.

Taxonomy of Living Primates

The chart that begins on the next page lists representatives of all living primate groups. As discussed in Chapter 4, there are alternative classifications, especially the strepsirhine-haplorhine subdivision and the different schemes for classifying hominoids. The taxonomy listed here is a "traditional" one, used more widely than any other.

Each primate suborder is broken down to the level of the genus, and the number of species within each genus is also given. The overall taxonomy is from Fleagle (1988), excepting the breakdown within the hylobatids, which is from Bramblett (1994). The number of species within each genus and the common names are from Bramblett (1994).

| | | | | ORDER: PRIMATES | | |
| | | | | SUBORDER: PROSIMII | | |

INFRAORDER	SUPERFAMILY	FAMILY	SUBFAMILY	GENUS	NUMBER OF SPECIES	COMMON NAME
Lemuriformes	Lemuroidea	Indriidae		*Indris*	1	Indrid
				Propithecus	2	Sifaka
				Avahi	1	Woolly lemur
		Daubentoniidae		*Daubentonia*	1	Aye-aye
		Lepilemuridae		*Lepilemur*	1	Lepilemur
		Lemuridae		*Hapalemur*	3	Gentle lemur
				Lemur	6	Lemur
				Varecia	1	Ruffed lemur
	Lorisoidea	Cheirogaleidae		*Microcebus*	2	Mouse lemur
				Mirza	1	Coquerel's mouse lemur
				Cheirogaleus	2	Dwarf lemur
				Allocebus	1	Hairy-eared dwarf lemur
				Phaner	1	Fork-marked lemur
		Galagidae		*Galagoides*	4	Bush baby
				Euoticus	2	Needle-clawed bush baby
				Galago	3	Bush baby
				Otolemur	2	Greater bush baby
		Lorisidae		*Periodicticus*	1	Potto
				Arctocebus	1	Angwantibo
				Nycticebus	2	Slow loris
				Loris	1	Slender loris
Tarsiiformes		Tarsiidae		*Tarsius*	3	Tarsier

				ORDER: PRIMATES SUBORDER: ANTHROPOIDEA		
INFRAORDER	*SUPERFAMILY*	*FAMILY*	*SUBFAMILY*	*GENUS*	*NUMBER OF SPECIES*	*COMMON NAME*
Platyrrhini	Ceboidea	Callitricidae	Callitrichinae	*Cebuella*	1	Pygmy marmoset
				Callithrix	3	Marmoset
				Saguinus	11	Tamarin
				Leontopithecus	1	Lion tamarin
				Callimico	1	Goeldi's marmoset
		Cebidae	Cebinae	*Saimiri*	2	Squirrel monkey
				Cebus	4	Capuchin
			Aotinae	*Aotus*	1	Owl monkey
				Callicebus	3	Titi
		Atelidae	Pitheciinae	*Pithecia*	3	Saki
				Chiropotes	2	Bearded saki
				Cacajao	3	Uakari
			Atelinae	*Alouatta*	6	Howler monkey
				Lagothrix	2	Woolly monkey
				Brachyteles	1	Woolly spider monkey
				Ateles	4	Spider monkey

ORDER: PRIMATES
SUBORDER: ANTHROPOIDEA

INFRAORDER	SUPERFAMILY	FAMILY	SUBFAMILY	GENUS	NUMBER OF SPECIES	COMMON NAME
Catarrhini	Cercopithecoidea	Cercopithecidae	Cercopithecinae	*Allenopithecus*	1	Swamp guenon
				Erythrocebus	1	Patas
				Miopithecus	1	Talapoin guenon
				Cercopithecus	17	Guenon
				Macaca	19	Macaque
				Cercocebus	4	Mangabey
				Papio	5	Baboon
				Mandrillus	2	Mandrill
				Theropithecus	1	Gelada baboon
			Colobinae	*Procolobus*	1	Olive colobus
				Piliocolobus	2	Red colobus
				Colobus	4	Colobus
				Presbytis	16	Langur
				Simias	1	Pig-tailed langur
				Nasalis	1	Proboscis monkey
				Pygathrix	1	Douc langur
				Rhinopithecus	2	Snub-nosed monkey

| | | | | ORDER: PRIMATES | | |
| | | | | SUBORDER: ANTHROPOIDEA | | |

INFRAORDER	SUPERFAMILY	FAMILY	SUBFAMILY	GENUS	NUMBER OF SPECIES	COMMON NAME
	Hominoidea	Hylobatidae		*Hylobates*	6	Gibbon
				Symphalangus	1	Siamang
		Pongidae		*Pongo*	1	Orangutan
				Gorilla	1	Gorilla
				Pan	2	Chimpanzee
						Bonobo
		Hominidae		*Homo*	1	Human

APPENDIX 2

Conversion Factors

Conversion Factors for Common Measures Used in the Text

TO CONVERT	INTO	MULTIPLY BY
Centimeters	Inches	0.3937
Cubic centimeters	Cubic inches	0.06102
Cubic inches	Cubic centimeters	16.39
Feet	Meters	0.3048
Grams	Ounces	0.03527
Inches	Centimeters	2.54
Inches	Millimeters	25.4
Kilograms	Pounds	2.205
Kilometers	Miles	0.6214
Kilometers	Yards	1,094
Meters	Feet	3.281
Meters	Yards	1.094
Miles	Kilometers	1.609
Millimeters	Inches	0.03937
Ounces	Grams	28.349527
Pounds	Kilograms	0.4536
Yards	Kilometers	9.144×10^{-4}
Yards	Meters	0.9144

Source: Frisancho (1993)

Temperature conversion:

From Celsius to Fahrenheit: $(C° \times 1.8) + 32$

From Fahrenheit to Celsius: $(F° - 32) / 1.8$

Comparative Primate Skeletal Anatomy

This appendix provides a general background in comparative primate anatomy by showing the skeletons of three primates—a modern human, an ape (gorilla), and an Old World monkey (baboon). In addition to noting the differences between these species, you should also note the similarities, particularly in terms of the homology of the skeletons (see Chapter 4 for a review of the principle of homology).

■ **FIGURE 1**

The human skeleton is made up of 206 bones on average (not all of which are shown here). Of these, 29 bones are found in the crania, 27 are found in *each* hand, and 26 are found in *each* foot. Note the homology between the human skeleton and the skeleton of the gorilla (Figure 2) and the baboon (Figure 3). Also note differences in certain anatomical structures, such as the pelvis, that reflect human bipedalism (discussed in Chapter 5).

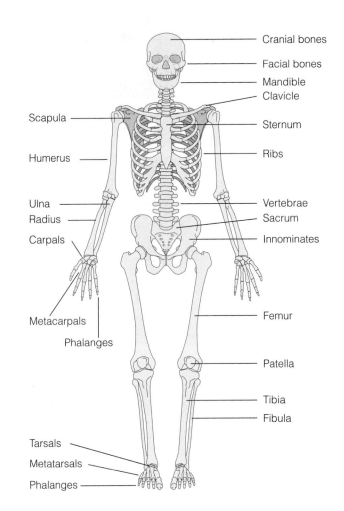

Cranial bones
Facial bones
Mandible
Clavicle
Scapula
Sternum
Humerus
Ribs
Ulna
Vertebrae
Radius
Sacrum
Carpals
Innominates
Metacarpals
Phalanges
Femur
Patella
Tibia
Fibula
Tarsals
Metatarsals
Phalanges

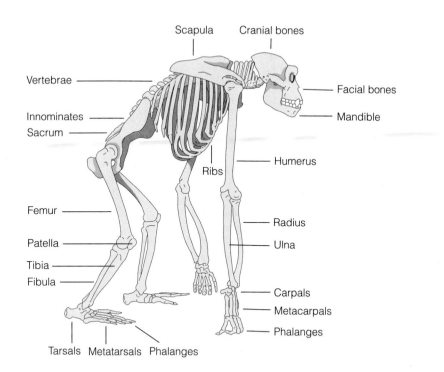

Scapula

Cranial bones

Vertebrae

Facial bones

Mandible

Innominates

Sacrum

Humerus

Ribs

Femur

Radius

Patella

Ulna

Tibia

Fibula

Carpals

Metacarpals

Phalanges

Tarsals   Metatarsals   Phalanges

■ FIGURE 2
Skeleton of a gorilla, one of the African apes (discussed in Chapter 4) shown in the typical knuckle-walking mode of locomotion. Note the longer arms and shorter legs when compared with the human (Figure 1) and the baboon (Figure 3).

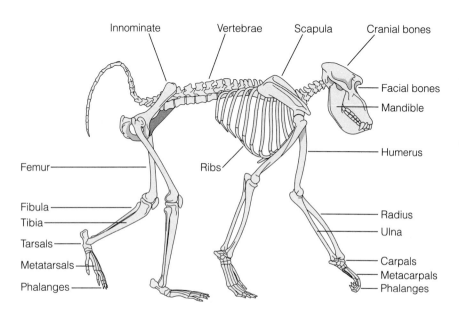

Innominate

Vertebrae

Scapula

Cranial bones

Facial bones

Mandible

Humerus

Femur

Ribs

Fibula

Tibia

Radius

Ulna

Tarsals

Metatarsals

Carpals

Metacarpals

Phalanges

Phalanges

■ FIGURE 3
Skeleton of a baboon, an Old World monkey, shown in the typical quadrupedal mode of locomotion. Note the similar length of the arms and legs, particularly when compared with the human (Figure 1) and the gorilla (Figure 3).

Glossary

Acheulian tradition. The stone tool technology associated with some populations of *Homo erectus*. Many of these tools were constructed using a biface method.

acquired characteristics. Lamarck's hypothesis that traits change in response to environmental demands and are passed on to offspring.

acquired immune deficiency syndrome (AIDS). A fatal disease that results in the breakdown of the body's immune defense system.

adaptation. The process of successful interaction between a population and an environment. Cultural or biological traits that offer an advantage in a given environment are adaptations.

adaptive radiation. The formation of many new species following the availability of new environments or the development of a new adaptation.

age at menarche. The age at which a human female experiences her first menstrual period.

age-sex structure. A measure of the composition of a population in terms of the numbers of males and females at different ages.

allele. The alternative forms of a gene that occur at a given locus. Some genes have only one allele, some have two, and some have many alternative forms. Alleles occur in pairs, one on each chromosome.

Allen's rule. States that mammals in cold climates tend to have shorter and bulkier limbs, allowing less loss of body heat, whereas mammals in hot climates tend to have long, slender limbs, allowing greater loss of body heat.

allometry. The study of the change in proportion of various body parts as a consequence of their growth at different rates.

anagenesis. The transformation of a single species over time.

analogous trait. Physical trait that has a similar function in two species but a different structure. The wings of a bird and those of a flying insect are an example of an analogous trait; both perform the same function but have different structures.

anatomically modern *Homo sapiens*. The modern form of the human species, which dates back 100,000 years or more.

Anthropoidea (anthropoids). The suborder of primates consisting of monkeys, apes, and humans.

anthropological archaeology. The subfield of anthropology that focuses on cultural variation in prehistoric (and some historic) populations through an analysis of the culture's remains.

anthropology. The science that investigates human biological and cultural variation and evolution.

anthropometrics. Measurements of the human body, skull, and face.

antibody. A substance that reacts to other substances invading the body (antigens).

antigen. A substance invading the body that stimulates the production of antibodies.

arboreal. Living in trees.

archaic *Homo sapiens*. An earlier variant of *Homo sapiens*, found at dates ranging from over 400,000 to 35,000 years B.P. Archaic forms had roughly the same brain size as modern humans but a different-shaped skull, including a sloping forehead and lower cranial height.

***Ardipithecus ramidus*.** The oldest known hominid, dating to 4.4 million years B.P. in Africa, and very primitive. This species may represent a side branch in early human evolution, and not be a direct ancestor of later hominids.

argon-argon dating. A chronometric dating method based on the half-life of radioactive argon that can be used with very small samples.

assortative mating. Mating between phenotypically similar individuals: for example, between two people with the same hair color.

australopithecine. A general term used to refer to any species in the genus *Australopithecus*.

***Australopithecus*.** A genus of fossil hominid that lived in Africa between 4.2 and 1 million years B.P., characterized by bipedal locomotion, small brain size, large face, and large teeth.

***Australopithecus aethiopicus*.** The oldest known robust australopithecine, dating to 2.5 million years B.P. in East Africa. Some view this species as an early example of *A. boisei*. It combines derived features seen in other robust australopithecines (e.g., large cheek bones, sagittal crest) with primitive features seen in *A. afarensis* (e.g., protruding face, apelike features of the base of the cranium).

Australopithecus afarensis. A primitive australopithecine, dating between 4 and 3 million years B.P. and found in East Africa. The teeth and postcranial skeleton show a number of primitive and apelike features.

Australopithecus africanus. A species of australopithecine dating between 3 and 2 million years B.P. and found in South Africa. The teeth and skull of this species are not as large as those of the robust australopithecines.

Australopithecus anamensis. The oldest known australopithecine, dating to 4.2 to 3.9 million years B.P. in East Africa. It was a biped but had many primitive apelike features of the skull and teeth. It may represent the ancestor of all later hominids.

Australopithecus boisei. The most robust of the australopithecines, dating between 2 and 1 million years B.P. and found in East Africa. This species has extremely large back teeth and a large supporting facial and cranial structure, indicating large chewing muscles.

Australopithecus robustus. A robust species of australopithecine, dating between 2 and 1 million years B.P. and found in South Africa. This species has large back teeth, although not as large on average as *Australopithecus boisei*.

balancing selection. Selection for the heterozygote and against the homozygotes (the heterozygote is most fit). Allele frequencies move toward an equilibrium defined by the fitness values of the two homozygotes.

bases. Chemical units that make up part of the DNA molecule. There are four bases (adenine, thymine, guanine, cytosine). The sequence of bases in the DNA molecule specifies genetic instructions.

Bergmann's rule. States that (1) among mammals of similar shape, the larger mammal loses heat less rapidly than the smaller mammal, and (2) among mammals of similar size, the mammal with a linear shape will lose heat more rapidly than the mammal with a nonlinear shape.

biface. Stone tool with both sides worked. The result is a more symmetric and efficient tool.

bilateral symmetry. Symmetry in which the right and left sides of the body are approximately mirror images, a characteristic of vertebrates.

binocular stereoscopic vision. Overlapping fields of vision (binocular), with both sides of the brain receiving images from both eyes (stereoscopic). Binocular stereoscopic vision provides depth perception.

biocultural approach. A method of studying humans that looks at the interaction between biology and culture in evolutionary adaptation.

biological anthropology. The subfield of anthropology formerly referred to as physical anthropology that focuses on the biological evolution of humans and human ancestors, the relationship of humans to other organisms, and patterns of biological variation within and among human populations.

bipedalism. Moving about on two legs. Unlike the movement of other bipedal animals such as kangaroos, human bipedalism is further characterized by a striding motion.

blade. A stone tool characteristic of the Upper Paleolithic, defined as being at least twice as long as it is wide. Blade tools were made using an efficient and precise method.

B.P. Abbreviation for "Before Present," the internationally accepted form of designating past dates. The "Present" has been set arbitrarily at the year 1950. A date of 75,000 years B.P. thus means 75,000 years before the year 1950.

brachiation. A method of movement that uses the arms to swing from branch to branch. Gibbons and siamangs are true brachiators.

breeding population. A group of organisms that tend to choose mates from within the group.

brow ridge. The large ridge of bone above the eye orbit. Brow ridges are most noticeable in *Homo erectus* and archaic *Homo sapiens*.

burin. A stone tool with a sharp edge that is used to cut and engrave bone.

canine. One of four types of teeth found in mammals. The canine teeth are located in the front of the jaw behind the incisors. Mammals normally use these teeth for puncturing and defense. Unlike most mammals, humans have small canine teeth that function like incisors.

carbon-14 dating. A chronometric dating method based on the half-life of carbon-14. This method can be applied to organic remains such as charcoal dating back over the past 50,000 years or so.

carrying capacity. The maximum population size capable of being supported in a given environment.

catastrophism. The hypothesis that patterns of evolutionary change observed in the fossil records can be explained by repeated catastrophes followed by repopulation from other areas by different organisms.

Cenozoic era. The third and most recent geologic era of the Phanerozoic eon, dating roughly to the past 65 million years, also known as the "Age of Mammals." The first primates appeared during the Cenozoic era.

cerebrum. The area of the forebrain that consists of the outermost layer of brain cells. The cerebrum is associated with memory, learning, and intelligence.

Chordata. A vertebrate phylum consisting of organisms that possess a notochord at some period during their life.

chromosomes. Long strands of DNA sequences.

chronometric dating. Method of dating fossils or sites that provides an estimate of the specific date (subject to probabilistic limits).

cladogenesis. The formation of one or more new species from another over time.

codominant. Pertaining to two alleles, when both alleles affect the phenotype of a heterozygous genotype and neither is dominant over the other.

comparative approach. A method used by anthropologists that compares populations to determine common and unique behaviors or biological traits.

continental drift. The movement of continental land masses on top of a partially molten layer of the earth's mantle. Because of continental drift, the relative location of the continents has changed over time.

cranial capacity. A measurement of the interior volume of the brain case, used as an approximate estimate of brain size.

crossing over. The result of segments of DNA switching between pairs of chromosomes. Crossing over is an exception to linkage.

cultural anthropology. The subfield of anthropology that focuses on variations in cultural behaviors among human populations.

culture. Behavior that is learned and socially transmitted rather than instinctual and genetically transmitted.

demographic transition theory. A model of demographic change that states that as a population

becomes economically developed, there will first be a reduction in death rates (leading to population growth), followed by a reduction in birth rates.

demography. The study of the size, composition, and distribution of populations.

dendrochronology. A chronometric dating method based on the fact that trees in dry climates tend to accumulate one growth ring per year. The width of the rings varies according to climate, and a sample can be compared with a master chart of tree rings over the past 10,000 years.

derived trait. A trait that has changed from an ancestral state. For example, the large human brain is a derived trait relative to the common ancestor of humans and apes.

dermatoglyphics. Measurements of finger and palm prints, including classification of type and counts of ridges.

developmental acclimatization. Changes in organ or body structure that occur during the physical growth of any organism.

diastema. A gap next to the canine teeth that allows space for the canine on the opposing jaw.

distance curve. A measure of size over time—as, for example, a person's height at different ages.

diurnal. Active during the day.

DNA. Deoxyribonucleic acid. The molecule that provides the genetic code for biological structures and the means to translate this code.

dominance hierarchy. The ranking system within a society that indicates those individuals who are dominant in social behaviors.

dominant allele. An allele that masks the effect of the other allele (which is recessive) in a heterozygous genotype.

electron spin resonance. A chronometric dating method that estimates dates from observation of radioactive atoms trapped in the calcite crystals present in a number of materials, such as bones and shells. This method is useful for dating sites back to roughly one million years.

electrophoresis. A laboratory method that uses electric current to separate proteins, allowing genotypes to be determined.

embryo. The stage of prenatal life lasting from roughly two to eight weeks following conception, characterized by structural development.

endemic. Pertaining to disease, when new cases occur at a relatively constant but low rate over time.

endocast. A cast of the interior of the brain case, used in the analysis of brain size and structure.

Eocene epoch. The second epoch of the Cenozoic era, dating roughly between 55 and 38 million years B.P. The first true primates, early prosimians, appeared during this epoch.

eon. The major subdivision of geologic time.

epidemic. Pertaining to disease, when new cases spread rapidly through a population.

epidemiologic transition. The change in disease patterns, seen in many developed regions of the world, in which there is a decline in infectious diseases and an increase in noninfectious diseases.

era. Subdivision of a geological eon.

Eurasia. The combined land masses of Europe and Asia.

evolution. The transformation of species of organic life over long periods of time. Anthropologists study both the cultural and biological evolution of the human species.

evolutionary forces. The mechanisms that can cause changes in allele frequencies from one generation to the next. The four evolutionary forces are: mutation, natural selection, genetic drift, and gene flow.

exogamy. The tendency to choose mates from outside the local population.

faunal correlation. A relative dating method in which sites can be assigned an approximate age based on the similarity of animal remains with other dated sites.

fecundity. Potential reproduction, often defined as the number of people capable of having children.

fertility. Actual reproduction—the number of births per individual.

fetus. The stage of prenatal growth from roughly eight weeks following conception until birth, characterized by further development and rapid growth.

fission-fusion. A form of population structure in which a group breaks into smaller populations (fission) and may then later combine with other populations to form a larger group (fusion).

fission-track dating. A chronometric dating method based on the number of tracks made across volcanic rock as uranium decays into lead.

fitness. The probability of survival and reproduction of an organism. Fitness is generally measured in terms of the different genotypes for a given locus.

foramen magnum. The large opening at the base of the skull where the spinal cord enters.

gene. A section of DNA that has an identifiable structure or function.

gene flow. A mechanism for evolutionary change resulting from the movement of genes from one population to another. Gene flow introduces new genes into a population and also acts to make populations more similar genetically to one another.

generalized structure. A biological structure adapted to a wide range of conditions and used in very general ways. For example, the grasping hands of humans are generalized structures allowing climbing, food gathering, toolmaking, and a variety of other functions.

genetic distance. An average measure of relatedness between populations based on a number of traits. Genetic distances are used for understanding effects of genetic drift and gene flow, which should affect all loci to the same extent.

genetic distance map. A picture that shows the genetic relationships between populations, based on genetic distance measures.

genetic drift. A mechanism for evolutionary change resulting from the random fluctuations of gene frequencies from one generation to the next, or from any form of random sampling of a larger gene pool.

genotype. For a given locus, the genetic endowment of an individual from the two alleles present.

genus. A taxonomic category designating groups of species with similar adaptations.

gradualism. A model of macroevolutionary change whereby evolutionary changes occur at a slow, steady rate over time.

half-life. The average length of time it takes for half of a radioactive substance to decay into another form.

Hardy-Weinberg equilibrium. A mathematical model demonstrating that, in the absence of evolutionary forces, allele frequencies remain constant from one generation to the next.

hemoglobin. The molecule in blood cells that transports oxygen.

heritability. The proportion of total variance in a trait attributable to genetic variation. This measure is not always the same; the actual value depends on the degree of environmental variation in any population.

heterozygous. Pertaining to the two alleles at a given locus being different.

holistic. Refers to the viewpoint that all aspects of existence are interrelated and important in understanding human variation and evolution.

home base. Campsite where hunters brought back food for sharing with other members of their group.

hominid. Humans and humanlike ancestors. Hominids are defined by a number of unique derived traits, particularly bipedalism.

hominoid. A group of anthropoids consisting of apes and humans. Hominoids have a shoulder structure adapted for climbing and hanging, lack a tail, are generally larger than monkeys, and have the largest brain size: body size ratio among primates.

Homo. A genus of hominid with three recognized species (*Homo erectus*, *Homo habilis*, and *Homo sapiens*), dating from 2.5 million years B.P. The major characteristic of *Homo* is a large brain size and dependence on culture as a means of adaptation.

Homo erectus. A species of the genus *Homo* that lived between 1.8 and 0.2 million years B.P. *Homo erectus* first appeared in Africa and later spread to Asia (and possibly Europe). *Homo erectus* had a larger brain size than *Homo habilis* but not as large as *Homo sapiens*.

Homo habilis. The oldest known species in the genus *Homo*, dating between 2.5 and 1.5 million years B.P. and found in Africa. In overall appearance, this species is similar to the australopithecines but has a larger cranial capacity (an average of roughly 630 cc, with a range of 509 to 752 cc).

homoiotherm. Organism capable of maintaining a constant body temperature under most circumstances. Mammals are homoiotherms.

homologous trait. Physical trait in two species that has a similar structure but may or may not show a similar function. The arm bones in humans and whales are an example of homologous structure; the bones are the same, but they are used for different functions.

homozygous. Pertaining to both alleles at a given locus being identical.

horticulture. A form of farming in which only simple hand tools are used.

hypothesis. An explanation of observed facts. To be scientific, a hypothesis must be testable.

inbreeding. Mating between biologically related individuals.

incisor. One of four types of teeth found in mammals. The incisors are the flat front teeth used for cutting, slicing, and gnawing food.

infectious disease. A disease caused by the introduction of an organic foreign substance into the body. Such substances include viruses and parasites.

insectivore. An order of mammals adapted to insect eating.

knuckle walking. A form of movement used by chimpanzees and gorillas that is characterized by all four limbs touching the ground, with the weight of the arms resting on the knuckles of the hands.

kwashiorkor. An extreme form of protein-calorie malnutrition, resulting from a severe deficiency in proteins but not calories.

lactase deficiency. A condition in which an older child or adult lacks the ability to produce the lactase enzyme needed to digest milk sugar.

larynx. Part of the vocal anatomy in the throat.

lemur. A prosimian found today on the island of Madagascar. Lemurs include both nocturnal and diurnal species.

life expectancy at birth. A measure of the average length of life for a newborn child.

life span. A measure of the maximum length of life recorded for a species. In humans, this measure is currently 120 years.

linguistic anthropology. The subfield of anthropology that focuses on the nature of human language, the relationship of language to culture, and the languages of nonliterate peoples.

linkage. The situation in which alleles on the same chromosome are inherited together.

locus. The specific location of a gene on a chromosome. (Plural *loci*.)

loris. Nocturnal prosimian found today in Asia and Africa.

Lower Paleolithic. The Lower Old Stone Age. A general term used to refer collectively to the stone tool technologies of *Homo habilis* and *Homo erectus*.

macroevolution. Long-term evolutionary change. The study of macroevolution focuses on biological evolution over many generations and on the origin of higher taxonomic categories, such as species.

major genes. Genes that have the primary effect on the phenotypic distribution of a complex trait. Additional variation can be due to smaller effects from other loci and/or environmental influences.

marasmus. An extreme form of protein-calorie malnutrition resulting from severe deficiencies in both proteins and calories.

mass extinction. Many species becoming extinct at roughly the same time.

meiosis. The creation of sex cells by replication of chromosomes followed by cell division. Each sex cell than contains 50 percent of an individual's chromosomes (one from each pair).

Mendelian genetics. The branch of genetics concerned with patterns and processes of inheritance. This field was named after Gregor Mendel, the first scientist to work out many of these principles.

Mendel's Law of Independent Assortment. The segregation of any pair of chromosomes does not affect the probability of segregation for other pairs of chromosomes.

Mendel's Law of Segregation. Sex cells contain one of each pair of alleles.

Mesozoic era. The second geologic era of the Phanerozoic eon, dating roughly between 245 and 65 million years B.P., also known as the "Age of Reptiles." The first mammals and birds also appeared during the Mesozoic era.

messenger RNA. The form of RNA that transports the genetic instructions from the DNA molecule to the site of protein synthesis.

microevolution. Short-term evolutionary change. The study of microevolution focuses on changes in allele frequencies from one generation to the next.

Middle Paleolithic. The Middle Old Stone Age. A general term used to refer collectively to the stone tool technologies of archaic *Homo sapiens*.

migration. The movement of individuals from one population to another. Migration may be short-term or long-term, and may or may not have genetic effects.

Miocene epoch. The fourth epoch of the Cenozoic era, dating roughly between 22 and 5 million years B.P. The first apes evolved during the Miocene.

mitochondrial DNA. A small amount of DNA that is located in the mitochondria of cells. Mitochondrial DNA is inherited only through the mother.

mitosis. The process of replication of chromosomes in body cells. Each cell produces two identical copies.

molar. One of four types of teeth found in mammals. The molars are back teeth used for crushing and grinding food.

molecular dating. The application of methods of genetic analysis to estimate the sequence and timing of divergent evolutionary lines.

monogamous family group. Social structure in which the primary social group consists of an adult male, an adult female, and their immature offspring.

monogamy. An exclusive sexual bond between an adult male and an adult female for a long period of time.

monosymy. A condition in which only one chromosome rather than a pair is present in body cells.

mortality. Death. Mortality, fertility, and migration are the three prime measures of population size.

mosaic evolution. The concept that major evolutionary changes tend to take place in stages, not all at once. Human evolution shows a mosaic pattern in the fact that small canine teeth, large brains, and tool use did not all evolve at the same time.

Mousterian tradition. The stone tool technology of the Neandertals, characterized by the careful preparation of a stone core from which finished flakes can be removed.

multimale/multifemale group. A type of social structure in which the primary social group is made up of several adult males, several adult females, and their offspring.

multiregional model. The hypothesis that modern humans evolved throughout the Old World as a single species after the first dispersion of *Homo erectus* out of Africa. According to this view, the transition from *Homo erectus* to archaic *Homo sapiens* to modern *Homo sapiens* occurred within a single evolutionary line throughout the Old World.

multivariate analysis. The analysis of human biological variation that takes into consideration the interrelationship of several traits at a time.

mutation. A mechanism for evolutionary change resulting from a random change in the genetic code. Mutation is the ultimate source of all genetic variation. Mutations must occur in sex cells to cause evolutionary change.

natural increase. The change in population size expected because of fertility and mortality but not migration. Natural increase is the number of births minus the number of deaths.

natural selection. A mechanism for evolutionary change resulting from the differential survival and reproduction organisms because of their biological characteristics.

Neandertal. Member of a regional population of archaic *Homo sapiens* found in Europe and the Middle East, dating between roughly 125,000 to 35,000 years B.P. The relationship between Neandertals and later *Homo sapiens* populations in these regions is still being debated.

neoteny. The retention of juvenile characteristics into adulthood. The rounded skull and large brain of humans are examples of neoteny.

New World syndrome. A set of noninfectious diseases that appear in elevated frequencies in individuals with Native-American ancestry.

nocturnal. Active during the night.

noninfectious disease. A disease caused by factors other than the introduction of an organic foreign substance into the body (e.g., age, nutrition).

nonrandom mating. Patterns of mate choice, other than total random mating, that influence the distributions of genotype and phenotype frequencies. Nonrandom mating does not lead to changes in allele frequencies.

occipital bun. A slight protrusion of the rear region of the skull, a feature often found in Neandertals.

odontometrics. Measurements of the size of teeth.

Oldowan tradition. The stone tool culture of *Homo habilis*. Oldowan tools are often simple tools made by removing several flakes from a stone. The flakes removed could also be used as cutting tools.

Oligocene epoch. The third epoch of the Cenozoic era, dating roughly between 38 and 22 million years B.P.., when there was an adaptive radiation of anthropoids.

orthogenesis. A discredited idea that evolution would continue in a given direction because of some vaguely defined nonphysical "force."

Paleocene epoch. The first epoch of the Cenozoic era, dating roughly between 65 and 55 million years B.P. The primatelike mammals lived during the Paleocene.

paleoecology. The study of ancient environments.

paleomagnetic reversal. A method of dating sites based on the fact that the earth's magnetic pole has shifted back and forth from the north to the south in the past at irregular intervals.

Paleozoic era. The first geologic era of the Phanerozoic eon, dating roughly between 545 and 245 million years B.P. The first vertebrates appeared during this era, including the reptiles and mammallike reptiles.

palynology. The study of fossil pollen. Palynology allows prehistoric plant species to be identified.

pandemic. An epidemic that occurs over a large geographic range.

period. Subdivision of a geologic era.

Phanerozoic eon. The past 545 million years.

phenotype. The observable appearance of a given genotype in the organism. The phenotype is determined by the relationship of the two alleles at a given locus, the number of loci, and often environmental influences as well.

placenta. An organ that develops inside a pregnant placental mammal. It provides the fetus with oxygen and food and helps filter out harmful substances.

pleiotropy. A single allele having multiple effects on an organism.

polyandrous group. A rare type of primate social structure, consisting of a small number of adult males, one reproductively active adult female, and their offspring. Other adult females may belong to the group but are not reproductively active.

polyandry. In humans, a form of marriage in which a wife has several husbands. In more general terms, it refers to an adult female having several mates.

polygamy. In general terms, it refers to having more than one mate.

polygenic. Refers to a trait that is affected by two or more loci. Complex traits, such as skin color and height, are polygenic.

polygyny. In humans, a form of marriage in which a husband has several wives. In more general terms, it refers to an adult male having several mates.

population pyramid. A graphic illustration of the age-sex structure of a population.

postcranial. Referring to that part of the skeleton below the skull.

postnatal. Referring to the period of life from birth until death.

postorbital bar. The bony ring that separates the eye orbit from the back of the skull. The postorbital bar is a primate characteristic.

postorbital constriction. The narrowness of the skull behind the eye orbits. Early hominids,

Larsen, C. S. 1994. In the wake of Columbus: Native population biology in the postcontact Americas. *Yearbook of Physical Anthropology* 37:109–54.

Larsen, C. S., R. M. Matter, and D. L. Gebo. 1991. *Human Origins: The Fossil Record.* 2d edition. Prospect Heights, Ill.: Waveland.

Leakey, L. S. B., P. V. Tobias, and J. R. Napier. 1964. A new species of the genus *Homo* from Olduvai Gorge. *Nature* 202:7–10.

Leakey, M. G., C. S. Feibel, I. McDougall, and A. Walker. 1995. New four-million-year-old hominid species from Kanapoi and Allia Bay, Kenya. *Nature* 376:565–71.

Leigh, S. R. 1992. Cranial capacity evolution in *Homo erectus* and early *Homo sapiens. American Journal of Physical Anthropology* 87:1–13.

Leonard, W. H., T. L. Leatherman, J. W. Carey, and R. B. Thomas. 1990. Contributions of nutrition versus hypoxia to growth in rural Andean populations. *American Journal of Human Biology* 2:613–26.

Leutenegger, W. 1982. Sexual dimorphism in nonhuman primates. In *Sexual Dimorphism in Homo sapiens: A Question of Size,* ed. R. L. Hall, pp. 11–36. New York: Praeger.

Levins, R., T. Awerbuch, U. Brinkman, I. Eckardt, P. Epstein, N. Makhoul, C. A. de Possas, C. Puccia, A. Spielman, and M. E. Wilson. 1994. The emergence of new diseases. *American Scientist* 82:52–60.

Levison, C. H., D. W. Hastings, and J. N. Harrison. 1981. Epidemiologic transition in a frontier town—Manti, Utah: 1849-1977. *American Journal of Physical Anthropology* 56:83–93.

Lewis, D. E., Jr. 1990. Stress, migration, and blood pressure in Kiribati. *American Journal of Human Biology* 2:139–51.

Lewontin, R. C. 1972. The apportionment of human diversity. In *Evolutionary Biology.* Vol. 6, ed. T. Dobzhansky, pp. 381–98. New York: Plenum Press.

Lieberman, P., and E. S. Crelin. 1971. On the speech of Neanderthal. *Linguistic Inquiry* 2:203–22.

Linden, E. 1981. *Apes, Men, and Language.* Rev. ed. Middlesex, England: Penguin Books.

Livingstone, F. B. 1958. Anthropological implications of sickle cell gene distribution in West Africa. *American Anthropologist* 60:533–62.

———. 1964. On the nonexistence of human races. In *The Concept of Race,* ed. A. Montagu, pp. 46–60. New York: Collier.

Loehlin, J. C., G. Lindzey, and J. N. Spuhler. 1975. *Race Differences in Intelligence.* San Francisco: W. H. Freeman.

Loomis, W. F. 1967. Skin-pigment regulation of vitamin-D biosynthesis in man. *Science* 157:501–6.

Lovejoy, C. O. 1981. The origin of man. *Science* 211: 341–50.

———. 1982. Models of human evolution. *Science* 217:304–6.

McEvedy, C. 1988. The bubonic plague. *Scientific American* 258(2): 118–23.

McGrath, J. W. 1990. AIDS in Africa: A bioanthropological perspective. *American Journal of Human Biology* 2:381–96.

McGrew, W. C. 1992. *Chimpanzee Material Culture.* Cambridge: Cambridge University Press.

McHenry, H. M. 1992. How big were the early hominids? *Evolutionary Anthropology* 1:15–20.

McNeill, W. H. 1977. *Plagues and Peoples.* New York: Doubleday.

Malina, R. M. 1975. *Growth and Development: The First Twenty Years in Man.* Minneapolis, Minn.: Burgess.

———. 1979. Secular changes in size and maturity: Causes and effects. *Monograph for the Society of Research in Child Development* 44:59–102.

Markham, R., and C. P. Groves. 1990. Brief communication: Weights of wild orangutans. *American Journal of Physical Anthropology* 81:1–3.

Marks, J. 1995. *Human Biodiversity: Genes, Races, and History.* New York: Aldine de Gruyter.

Marks, J., and R. B. Lyles. 1994. Rethinking genes. *Evolutionary Anthropology* 3:139–46.

Martin, R. D. 1981. Relative brain size and basal metabolic rate in terrestrial vertebrates. *Nature* 293:57–60.

Mascia-Lees, F. E., J. H. Relethford, and T. Sorger. 1986. Evolutionary perspectives on permanent breast enlargement in human females. *American Anthropologist* 88:423–28.

Mayr, E. 1982. *The Growth of Biological Thought.* Cambridge: Harvard University Press.

Meindl, R. S., and A. C. Swedlund. 1977. Secular trends in mortality in the Connecticut River Valley, 1700–1850. *Human Biology* 49:389–414.

Miller, J. A. 1991. Does brain size variability provide evidence of multiple species in *Homo habilis? American Journal of Physical Anthropology* 84: 385–98.

Mittermeier, R. A., and E. J. Sterling. 1992. Conservation of primates. In *The Cambridge Encyclopedia of Human Evolution,* ed. S. Jones, R. Martin, and D. Pilbeam, pp. 33–36. Cambridge: Cambridge University Press.

Molnar, S. 1983. *Human Variation: Races, Types and Ethnic Groups.* 2d ed. Englewood Cliffs, N.J.: Prentice-Hall.

———. 1992. *Human Variation: Races, Types, and Ethnic Groups.* 3d ed. Englewood Cliffs, N.J.: Prentice-Hall.

Montagu, A., ed. 1984. *Science and Creationism.* Oxford: Oxford University Press.

Moran, E. F. 1982. *Human Adaptability: An Introduction to Ecological Anthropology*. Boulder, Colo.: Westview Press.

Oates, J. F. 1987. Food distribution and foraging behavior. In *Primate Societies*, ed. B. B. Smuts, D. L. Cheney, R. M. Seyfarth, R. W. Wrangham, and T. T. Struhsaker, pp. 197–209. Chicago: University of Chicago Press.

Olshansky, S. J., B. A. Carnes, and C. Cassel. 1990. In search of Methuselah: Estimating the upper limit to human longevity. *Science* 250:634–40.

Omran, A. R. 1977. Epidemiologic transition in the United States: The health factor in population change. *Population Bulletin* 32:3–42.

Parés, J. M., and A. Pérez-González. 1995. Paleomagnetic age for fossil hominids at Atapuerca archaeological site, Spain. *Science* 269:830–32.

Pasachoff, J. M. 1979. *Astronomy: From the Earth to the Universe*. Philadelphia: W. B. Saunders.

Pfeiffer, J. E. 1985. *The Emergence of Humankind*. 4th ed. New York: Harper & Row.

Pianka, E. R. 1983. *Evolutionary Ecology*. 3d ed. New York: Harper & Row.

Pilbeam, D. 1982. New hominoid skull material from the Miocene of Pakistan. *Nature* 295:232–34.

———. 1984. The descent of hominoids and hominids. *Scientific American* 250(3): 84–96.

Pilbeam, D., G. E. Meyer, C. Badgley, M. D. Rose, M. H. L. Pickford, A. K. Behrensmeyer, and S. M. Ibrahim Shah. 1977. New hominoid primates from the Siwaliks of Pakistan and their bearing on hominoid evolution. *Nature* 270: 689–95.

Pope, G. G. 1989. Bamboo and human evolution. *Natural History*, October: 49–56.

Post, P. W., F. Daniels, Jr., and R. T. Binford, Jr. 1975. Cold injury and the evolution of "white" skin. *Human Biology* 47:65–80.

Potts, M. 1988. Birth control. In *The New Encyclopaedia Britannica*. Vol. 15, pp. 113–20. Chicago: Encyclopaedia Britannica.

Rak, Y. 1986. The Neanderthal: A new look at an old face. *Journal of Human Evolution* 15:151–64.

Rak, Y., and B. Arensburg. 1987. Kebara 2 Neanderthal pelvis: First look at a complete inlet. *American Journal of Physical Anthropology* 73:227–31.

Reid, R. M. 1973. Inbreeding in human populations. In *Methods and Theories of Anthropological Genetics*, ed. M. H. Crawford and P. L. Workman, pp. 83–116. Albuquerque: University of New Mexico Press.

Relethford, J. H. 1994. Craniometric variation among human populations. *American Journal of Physical Anthropology* 95:53–62.

———. 1995. Genetics and modern human origins. *Evolutionary Anthropology* 4: 53–63.

———. 1996. Genetic drift obscures population history: Problem and solution. *Human Biology* 68: 29–44.

Relethford, J. H., and J. Blangero. 1990. Detection of differential gene flow from patterns of quantitative variation. *Human Biology* 62:5–25.

Relethford, J. H., and M. H. Crawford. 1995. Anthropometric variation and the population history of Ireland. *American Journal of Physical Anthropology* 96:25–38.

Relethford, J. H., and H. C. Harpending. 1994. Craniometric variation, genetic theory, and modern human origins. *American Journal of Physical Anthropology* 95:249–70.

———. 1995. Ancient differences in population size can mimic a recent African origin of modern humans. In *Current Anthropology* 36: 667–74.

Richards, A. F. 1985. *Primates in Nature*. New York: W. H. Freeman.

Rightmire, G. P. 1992. *Homo erectus*: Ancestor or evolutionary side branch? *Evolutionary Anthropology* 1:43–49.

Roberts, D. F. 1968. Genetic effects of population size reduction. *Nature* 220:1084–88.

———. 1978. *Climate and Human Variability*. 2d ed. Menlo Park, Calif.: Benjamin Cummings.

Roberts, R. G., R. Jones, and M. A. Smith. 1990. Thermoluminescence dating of a 50,000-year-old human occupation site in northern Australia. *Nature* 345:153–56.

Robins, A. H. 1991. *Biological Perspectives on Human Pigmentation*. Cambridge: Cambridge University Press.

Rodman, P. S., and H. M. McHenry. 1980. Bioenergetics and the origin of human bipedalism. *American Journal of Physical Anthropology* 52:103–6.

Roebroeks, W. 1994. Updating the earliest occupation of Europe. *Current Anthropology* 35:301–5.

Rogers, A. R., and H. C. Harpending. 1992. Population growth makes waves in the distribution of pairwise genetic differences. *Molecular and Evolutionary Biology* 9:552–69.

Rogers, A. R., and L. B. Jorde. 1995. Genetic evidence on modern human origins. *Human Biology* 67:1–36.

Rogers, R. A., L. A. Rogers, and L. D. Martin. 1992. How the door opened: The peopling of the New World. *Human Biology* 64:281–302.

Rose, M. D. 1986. Further hominoid postcranial specimens from the Late Miocene Nagri formations of Pakistan. *Journal of Human Evolution* 15:333–67.

Rowell, T. E. 1966. Forest-living baboons in Uganda. *Journal of Zoology, London* 149:344–64.

Roychoudhury, A. K., and M. Nei. 1988. *Human Polymorphic Genes: World Distribution*. Oxford: Oxford University Press.

Ruff, C. B. 1993. Climatic adaptation and hominid evolution: The thermoregulatory imperative. *Evolutionary Anthropology* 2:53–60.

Ruvolo, M., D. Pan, S. Zehr, T. Goldberg, T. R. Disotell, and M. von Dornum. 1994. Gene trees and hominoid phylogeny. *Proceedings of the National Academy of Science, USA* 91:8900–4.

Sagan, C. 1977. *The Dragons of Eden: Speculations on the Evolution of Human Intelligence*. New York: Ballantine Books.

Sarich, V. M., and A. C. Wilson. 1967. Immunological time scale for hominoid evolution. *Science* 158: 1200–3.

Savage-Rumbaugh, S., and R. Lewin. 1994. *Kanzi: The Ape at the Brink of the Human Mind*. New York: John Wiley & Sons.

Scammon, R. E. 1930. The measurement of the body in childhood. In *The Measurement of Man*, ed. J. A. Harris, C. M. Jackson, D. G. Paterson, and R. E. Scammon, pp. 171–215. Minneapolis: University of Minnesota Press.

Scarr, S., and A. Weinberg. 1978. Attitudes, interests, and IQ. *Human Nature* 1(4): 29–36.

Schepartz, L. A. 1993. Language and modern human origins. *Yearbook of Physical Anthropology* 36: 91–126.

Schopf, J. W., ed. 1992. *Major Events in the History of Life*. Boston: Jones and Bartlett.

Schopf, J. W. 1993. Microfossils of the early Archean Apex chert: New evidence of the antiquity of life. *Science* 260:640–46.

Schow, D. J., and J. Frentzen. 1986. *The Outer Limits: The Official Companion*. New York: Ace.

Schwartz, J. H. 1987. *The Red Ape: Orang-utans and Human Origins*. Boston: Houghton Mifflin.

Shea, B. T., and A. M. Gomez. 1988. Tooth scaling and evolutionary dwarfism: An investigation of allometry in human pygmies. *American Journal of Physical Anthropology* 77:117–32.

Sheehan, P. M., D. E. Fastovsky, R. G. Hoffman, C. B. Berghaus, and D. L. Gabriel. 1991. Sudden extinction of the dinosaurs: Latest Cretaceous, Upper Great Plains, U.S.A. *Science* 254:835–39.

Sherry, S. T., A. R. Rogers, H. Harpending, H. Soodyall, T. Jenkins, and M. Stoneking. 1994. Mismatch distributions of mtDNA reveal recent human populations expansions. *Human Biology* 66:761–75.

Simons, E. L., and T. Rasmussen. 1994. A whole new world of ancestors: Eocene anthropoids from Africa. *Evolutionary Anthropology* 3:128–39.

Sjøvold, T. 1992. The Stone Age Iceman from the Alps: The find and the current status of investigation. *Evolutionary Anthropology* 1:117–24.

Smith, F. H., A. B. Falsetti, and S. M. Donnelly. 1989a. Modern human origins. *Yearbook of Physical Anthropology* 32:35–68.

Smith, F. H., J. F. Simek, and M. S. Harrill. 1989b. Geographic variation in supraorbital torus reduction during the later Pleistocene (c. 80,000–15,000 B.P.). In *The Human Revolution*, ed. P. Mellars and C. Stringer, pp. 172–93. Princeton: Princeton University Press.

Smouse, P. E. 1982. Genetic architecture of swidden agricultural tribes from the lowland rain forests of South America. In *Current Developments in Anthropological Genetics. Vol. 2, Ecology and Population Structure*, ed. M. H. Crawford and J. H. Mielke, pp. 139–78. New York: Plenum Press.

Snowden, C. T. 1990. Language capacities of nonhuman animals. *Yearbook of Physical Anthropology* 33:215–43.

Spencer, M. A., and B. Demes. 1993. Biomechanical analysis of masticatory system configuration in Neandertals and Inuits. *American Journal of Physical Anthropology* 91:1–20.

Spiess, E. B. 1977. *Genes in Populations*. New York: John Wiley.

Stanley, S. M. 1979. *Macroevolution: Pattern and Process*. San Francisco: W. H. Freeman.

———. 1981. *The New Evolutionary Timetable: Fossils, Genes, and the Origin of Species*. New York: Basic Books.

Stebbins, G. L. 1982. *Darwin to DNA, Molecules to Humanity*. San Francisco: W. H. Freeman.

Stern, J. T., Jr., and R. L. Susman. 1983. The locomotor anatomy of *Australopithecus afarensis*. *American Journal of Physical Anthropology* 60:279–317.

Stone, A. C., and M. Stoneking. 1993. Ancient DNA from a Pre-Columbian Amerindian population. *American Journal of Physical Anthropology* 92:463–71.

Stoner, B. P., and E. Trinkaus. 1981. Getting a grip on the Neandertals: Were they all thumbs? *American Journal of Physical Anthropology* 54:281–82.

Stringer, C. B. 1986. The credibility of *Homo habilis*. In *Major Topics in Primate and Human Evolution*, ed. B. Wood, L. Martin and P. Andrews, pp. 266–94. Cambridge: Cambridge University Press.

———. 1994. Out of Africa—A personal history. In *Origins of Anatomically Modern Humans*, ed. M. H. Nitecki and D. V. Nitecki, pp. 149–72. New York: Plenum Press.

Stringer, C. B., and P. Andrews. 1988. Genetic and fossil evidence for the origin of modern humans. *Science* 239:1263–68.

Stringer, C., and C. Gamble. 1993. *In Search of the Neanderthals: Solving the Puzzle of Human Origins*. New York: Thames and Hudson.

Strum, S. C., and W. Mitchell. 1987. Baboon models and muddles. In *The Evolution of Human Behavior: Primate Models*, ed. W. G. Kinzey, pp. 87–104. Albany, N.Y.: State University of New York Press.

Sussman, R. W., J. M. Cheverud, and T. Q. Bartlett. 1995. Infant killing as an evolutionary strategy: Reality or myth? *Evolutionary Anthropology* 3:149–51.

Sutton, H. E., and R. P. Wagner. 1985. *Genetics: A Human Concern*. New York: Macmillan.

Swisher, C. C., G. H. Curtis, T. Jacob, A. G. Getty, A. Suprijo, and Widiasmoro. 1994. Age of the earliest known hominids in Java, Indonesia. *Science* 263:1118–21.

Szabo, G. 1967. The regional anatomy of the human integument with special reference to the distribution of hair follicles, sweat glands and melanocytes. *Philosophical Transactions of the Royal Society of London.* 252B: 447–85.

Tague, R. G. 1992. Sexual dimorphism in the human bony pelvis, with a consideration of the Neandertal pelvis from Kebara Cave, Israel. *American Journal of Physical Anthropology* 88:1–21.

Tattersall, I. 1995. *The Fossil Trail: How We Know What We Think We Know About Human Evolution.* New York: Oxford University Press.

Teitelbaum, M. S. 1988. Population. In *The New Encyclopaedia Britannica.* Vol. 25, pp. 1038–47. Chicago: Encyclopaedia Britannica.

Templeton, A. R. 1992. Human origins and analysis of mitochondrial DNA sequences. *Science* 255:737.

Terrace, H. S. 1979. *Nim: A Chimpanzee Who Learned Sign Language.* New York: Knopf.

Thomas, D. H. 1986. *Refiguring Anthropology: First Principles of Probability and Statistics.* Prospect Heights, Ill.: Waveland Press.

Thorne, A. G., and M. H. Wolpoff. 1992. The multiregional evolution of humans. *Scientific American* 266(4): 76–83.

Tobias, P. V. 1971. *The Brain in Hominid Evolution.* New York: Columbia University Press.

Trinkaus, E. 1981. Neanderthal limb proportions and cold adaptation. In *Aspects of Human Evolution*, ed. C. B. Stringer, pp. 187–224. London: Taylor and Francis.

Trinkaus, E., and M. LeMay. 1982. Occipital bunning among later Pleistocene hominids. *American Journal of Physical Anthropology* 57:27–35.

Trinkaus, E., and P. Shipman. 1992. *The Neandertals: Changing the Image of Mankind.* New York: Knopf.

United States Department of Commerce. 1991. *1990 Census Profile, March 1991.* Washington: U.S. Department of Commerce, Economics and Statistics Administration, Bureau of the Census.

Vigilant, L., M. Stoneking, H. Harpending, K. Hawkes, and A. C. Wilson. 1991. African populations and the evolution of human mitochondrial DNA. *Science* 253:1503–7.

Vrba, E. S. 1985. Ecological and adaptive changes associated with early hominid evolution. In *Ancestors: The Hard Evidence*, ed. E. Delson, pp. 63–71. New York: Alan R. Liss.

Walker, A., and M. Teaford. 1989. The hunt for *Proconsul. Scientific American* 260(1): 76–82.

Ward, C. V., A. Walker, and M. F. Teaford. 1991. *Proconsul* did not have a tail. *Journal of Human Evolution* 21:215–20.

Washburn, S. L. 1960. Tools and human evolution. *Scientific American* 203:62–75.

Watts, E. S. 1986. Evolution of the human growth curve. In *Human Growth: A Comprehensive Treatise.* Vol. 1, *Developmental Biology, Prenatal Growth*, ed. F. Falkner and J. M. Tanner, pp. 153–66. New York: Plenum Press.

Weiss, K. M. 1984. On the number of members of the genus *Homo* who have ever lived, and some evolutionary implications. *Human Biology* 56:637–49.

Weiss, K. M., R. E. Ferrell, and C. L. Hanis. 1984. A New World syndrome of metabolic diseases with a genetic and evolutionary basis. *Yearbook of Physical Anthropology* 27:153–78.

Wheeler, P. E. 1991a. The influence of bipedalism on the energy and water budgets of early hominids. *Journal of Human Evolution* 21:117–36.

———. 1991b. The thermoregulatory advantage of hominid bipedalism in open equatorial environments: The contribution of increased convective heat loss and cutaneous evaporative cooling. *Journal of Human Evolution* 21:107–15.

White, R., and J. M. Lalouel. 1988. Chromosome mapping with DNA markers. *Scientific American* 258:40–48.

White, T. D., G. Suwa, and B. Asfaw. 1994. *Australopithecus ramidus*, a new species of early hominid from Aramis, Ethiopia. *Nature* 371:306–12.

White, T. D., G. Suwa, and B. Asfaw. 1995. Corrigendum: *Australopithecus ramidus*, a new species of early hominid from Aramis, Ethiopia. *Nature* 375:88.

Wilford, J. N. 1985. *The Riddle of the Dinosaur.* New York: Knopf.

Willerman, L., R. Schultz, J. N. Rutledge, and E. D. Bigler. 1991. In vivo brain size and intelligence. *Intelligence* 15:223–28.

Williams-Blangero, S., and J. Blangero. 1992. Quantitative genetic analysis of skin reflectance: A multivariate approach. *Human Biology* 64:35–49.

Wilson, E. O. 1980. *Sociobiology: The Abridged Edition.* Cambridge: Harvard University Press.

WoldeGabriel, G., P. Renne, T. D. White, G. Suwa, J. de Heinzelin, W. K. Hart, and G. Heiken. 1995. Age of early hominids. *Nature* 376:559.

WoldeGabriel, G., T. D. White, G. Suwa, P. Renne, J. de Heinzelin, W. K. Hart, and G. Heiken. 1994. Ecological and temporal placement of early Pliocene hominids at Aramis, Ethiopia. *Nature* 371:330–33.

Wolfe, L. D. 1995. Current research in field primatology. In *Biological Anthropology: The State of the Science*, ed. N. T. Boaz and L. D. Wolfe, pp. 149–68. Bend, Ore.: International Institute for Human Evolutionary Research.

Wolpoff, M. H. 1980. *Paleoanthropology*. New York: Knopf.

Wolpoff, M. H., A. G. Thorne, F. H. Smith, D. W. Frayer, and G. G. Pope. 1994. Multiregional evolution: A world-wide source for modern human populations. In *Origins of Anatomically Modern Humans*, ed. M. H. Nitecki and D. V. Nitecki, pp. 175–200. New York: Plenum Press.

Wood, B. 1992. Origin and evolution of the genus *Homo*. *Nature* 355:783–90.

Wood, C. S. 1979. *Human Sickness and Health: A Biocultural View*. Mountain View, Calif.: Mayfield.

Wood, J. W. 1994. *Dynamics of Human Reproduction: Biology, Biometry, Demography*. New York: Aldine de Gruyter.

Woodham-Smith, C. 1962. *The Great Hunger: Ireland 1845–1849*. New York: Harper & Row.

Woodward, V. 1992. *Human Heredity and Society*. St. Paul, Minn.: West.

Wrangham, R. W. 1987. Evolution of social structure. In *Primate Societies*, ed. B. B. Smuts, D. L. Cheney, R. M. Seyfarth, R. W. Wrangham, and T. T. Struhsaker, pp. 282–96. Chicago: University of Chicago Press.

Wright, P. C. 1992. Primate ecology, rainforest conservation, and economic development: Building a national park in Madagascar. *Evolutionary Anthropology* 1:25–33.

Yellen, J. E., A. S. Brooks, E. Cornelissen, M. J. Mahlman, and K. Stewart. 1995. A Middle Stone Age worked bone industry from Katanda, Upper Semliki Valley, Zaire. *Science* 268:553–56.

Zimmer, C. 1995. Coming onto the land. *Discover*, June 1995:119–27.

Index